ISABEL MANCINELLI

D0169344

ISABEL MANCINELLI

Basic Elements
of Landscape
Architectural Design

Basic Elements of Landscape Architectural Design

Norman K. Booth
Department of Landscape Architecture
Ohio State University

WAVELAND
PRESS, INC.
Prospect Heights, Illinois

For information about this book, write or call:
   Waveland Press, Inc.
   P.O. Box 400
   Prospect Heights, Illinois 60070
   (708) 634-0081

Copyright © 1983 by Norman K. Booth
1990 reissued by Waveland Press, Inc.

ISBN 0-88133-478-2

*All rights reserved. No part of this book may be reproduced,
stored in a retrieval system, or transmitted in any form or
by any means without permission in writing from the
publisher.*

Printed in the United States of America

7   6   5   4

This book is dedicated to the memory of my mother,
whose artistic talents and love of the outdoors
showed me the beauty and value of our natural environment.

Contents

Preface

Landscape architecture is a professional design discipline that, in the broadest sense, deals with integrating people and the outdoor environment in a manner beneficial to both. The American Society of Landscape Architects defines landscape architecture as "the art of design, planning, or management of the land, arrangement of natural and man-made elements thereon through application of cultural and scientific knowledge, with concern for resource conservation and stewardship, to the end that the resultant environment serves useful and enjoyable purpose."[1] Over the years, landscape architects have been involved in projects associated with all aspects of the outdoor environment from the design of intimate gardens to the planning and management of land areas hundreds of square miles in size. From the most comprehensive viewpoint, the landscape architect has the ability to study, analyze, and solve a myriad of design problems that relate to the outdoor environment.

To be able to address the vast and complex range of potential design and environmental issues, the landscape architect must possess knowledge and skills in a variety of related disciplines including art, civil engineering, ecology, geography, sociology, psychology, horticulture, and business. In the future, the professional landscape architect will also have to be knowledgeable about computer science and be able to contend with shrinking resources combined with increasing numbers of people with leisure time to spend. The landscape architect of the future, as in the past, must be a well-educated, highly skilled, and versatile individual who can adapt to the unique conditions of each new project.

Within this broad context, the profession of landscape architecture has been and will continue to be a design discipline, combining art and science, whose primary focus is the sensitive joining of people and their outdoor activities with the land.[2] Even though the professional boundaries will expand in the future into new areas of knowledge and skills, landscape architects will also maintain their traditional expertise in the imaginative creation of outdoor environments that sensitively deal with the ecological, social, economic, and aesthetic issues of the site and client while also being visually and emotionally appealing. Ultimately, it is the task of the landscape architect to give birth to outdoor experiences that are profitable, stimulating, and enjoyable from day to day, month to month, and year to year.

For every art and design discipline, including landscape architecture, certain media are characteristic and inherent to that discipline. These media are used by artists and designers of that discipline to transfer their objectives, ideas, concepts, and emotions into a "sensible form" for others to appreciate and use. The sculptor, for example, typically gives reality to ideas through the use of clay, stone, wood, or steel. The illustrator may use paint, ink, pencil, or pastel. Similarly, the landscape architect utilizes two general sets of media to transfer ideas into a comprehensible form: (1) pencil, ink, magic marker, paper, cardboard, computer, and the like used to portray a design intent in a graphic or model form, and (2) landform, plant materials, buildings, pavement, site structures (steps, ramps, walls, etc.), and

---

[1] Constitution, *ASLA Members' Handbook 81* (Washington, D.C.: The American Society of Landscape Architects, 1981), p. 346.

[2] See also Norman T. Newton, "Landscape Architecture: A Profession in Confusion?," *Landscape Architecture* 64 (4):256 (July 1974).

water used to create the actual three-dimensional reality of the design. The first set of media are used to depict the idea of the design in a representative manner, while the second set of media are, in fact, the elements of the design itself. This second set of media are the basic physical elements of landscape architectural design.

The intent of this book is to introduce the reader to those physical design media of landscape architecture that result in the "sensible form." More specifically, the objective is to present the vocabulary, significance, characteristics, potential uses, and design guidelines for landform, plant materials, buildings, pavement, site structures, and water in landscape architectural design. A separate chapter is devoted to each of the physical design elements. The first chapter concerns itself with landform—the floor and beginning point of most designs. The next two chapters deal with plant material and buildings, which, along with landform, are the major structural and spatial components of most landscape architectural designs. Pavement and site structures, often used to furnish and enhance outdoor rooms while complementing landform, plant material, and buildings, are discussed in the following chapters. Water, in many instances used as an embellishing and enriching element, is the last element discussed. Finally, the last chapter outlines a design process as a framework for integrating all the physical design elements into one encompassing landscape architectural design.

This book was originally conceived as a helpful resource for individuals beginning their design careers in landscape architecture as well as for those who simply wished to gain a basic understanding of the significance and use of the major physical components of the outdoor environment. While the focus of the book is on landscape architectural design, the ideas presented here are not intended to be limited to only this design discipline. Students in other professional disciplines including architecture, planning, and civil engineering whose expertise also re-

lates to the outdoor environment along with landscape design and construction should find the content of this book educational as well.

This book began a number of years ago as a set of notes and handouts given to second- and third-quarter landscape architectural design students. I found a need then and now to present key design theories and concepts in simple words and illustrations. Of particular challenge was the desire to present ideas in basic terms that could be easily understood by novice designers without the sometimes oblique and esoteric expressions used by experienced professionals.

The thoughts and theories presented here are fundamental to landscape architecture. Most are common knowledge among professionals and have been learned through education, experience, observation, and reading. Other ideas have evolved in my own practice, from travel, and through my experience of teaching students and observing and criticizing their work in design studio. Some of these thoughts have been formulated in attempting to help students overcome common mistakes and misconceptions typical in the early phases of their design career.

And, this book is envisioned as a beginning. It should not be read as the complete or final word on any of the subjects presented. The reader is encouraged to seek out additional sources and knowledge on all the subject areas to supplement the thoughts and theories offered here. I assume the reader will complement knowledge gained here with a personal ethic and philosophy of design that will weigh and appropriately apply the suggested guidelines to each new design situation.

Landscape architecture is an exciting and challenging profession. I hope you, the reader, will gain a better understanding and awareness of the physical design elements of landscape architecture from this book so that you may receive the same thrill and personal satisfaction that I have in studying and designing the outdoor environment.

A number of people's encouragement and support have made this book possible. I would like to thank Janet Jordon and Kathleen MacLean for their long hours of typing and valuable editorial suggestions. Thanks also go to Jot D. Carpenter for his continued support over the years. Stephen Drown, James Hiss, and Lawrence Walquist, Jr., are given a special, warm thank you for their moral support as both personal friends and partners. Most helpful of all have been the students I have taught and from whom I have learned so much. To all of you, I am deeply indebted.

1

Landform

Significance

Landscape architects utilize a variety of physical design elements to meet their objectives in creating and managing outdoor spaces for human use and enjoyment. Among these elements, landform is one of the most important and ever present. Landform serves as the base for all outdoor activity and may be thought of as both an artistic and utilitarian element in its design applications. This chapter outlines the significance, means of expression, types of landforms, and their potential functions as physical elements at both the regional and the site scale in landscape architectural design.

"Landform" is synonymous with "topography" and refers to the three-dimensional relief of the earth's surface. In simple terms, landform is the "lay of the land." At the regional scale, landform may include such diverse types as valleys, mountains, rolling hills, prairies, and plains. These landform types are typically referred to as "macrolandforms." At the site scale, landform may encompass mounds, berms, slopes, level areas, or elevation changes via steps and ramps, all of which may be generally categorized as "microlandforms." At the smallest scale, "minilandforms" might include the subtle undulations or ripples of a sand dune or the textural variation of stones and rocks in a walk. In all situations, landform is the surficial ground element of the exterior environment.

Landform has great significance in the landscape because of its direct association with so many other elements and aspects of the outdoor environment. Topography affects, among other things, the aesthetic character of an area, the definition and perception of space, views, drainage, microclimate, land use, and the organization of functions on a par-

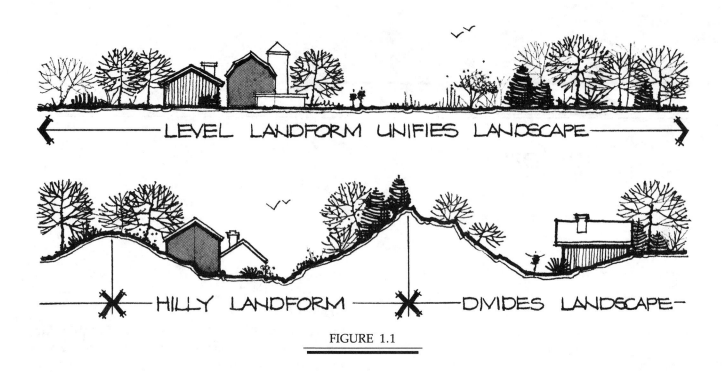

FIGURE 1.1

ticular site. Landform also has an impact on the role and prominence of other physical design elements in the landscape including plant material, pavement, water, and buildings. All these other physical design elements plus additional components utilized in the landscape must at some point come to rest on, and relate to, the ground's surface. Few items seen or manipulated as design elements in the outdoors float in space. Consequently, an alteration in the landform at a particular point also means a change in the spatial delineation, appearance, and sometimes the function of the other physical elements also located at this point. The shape, slope, and orientation of the ground's surface influences everything on it and above it. While landform has a rather direct impact on all the other physical design elements, it is not necessarily the most important of all. This of course varies greatly with the particular situation and scope of consideration.

Because all other design elements must at some point relate to the ground plane, landform is the one common component in exterior environment. It can be considered a thread that ties all the elements and spaces of the landscape together into a continuum that ends along the horizon or at water's edge. In regions and sites of level topography, this commonality can function as a unifying factor, visually and functionally connecting other components in the landscape (see Figure 1.1). Conversely, this unifying capability is lost in hilly and mountainous areas where ridges and high points tend to segment the land into separate spaces and use areas.

Landform has other noteworthy influences on the outdoor environment as well. Landform can be thought of as establishing the underlying structure of any given portion of the landscape. It acts like the framework of a building or the bones of an animal; it formulates the overall order and form of the environment. Other elements are then seen as being a covering or facade on top of this frame. Thus in evaluating a given site during the site analysis phase of the design process, it is often wise to study the topography early, particularly if it is not flat or uniform. The site's landform can suggest to the designer the overall organization and orientation that various uses, spaces, and other elements should take to be compatible with the inherent composition of the site, as shown in Figures 1.2 and 1.3. In both figures, the size and shape of the site is the same. Yet the landform configuration in Figure 1.2 suggests a linear layout of elements to follow the ridge line while in Figure 1.3 the landform permits a more sprawling and multidirectional arrangement. An experienced designer is able to skillfully "read" the topography of a site or region and interpret its implications for design or management of that area.

3

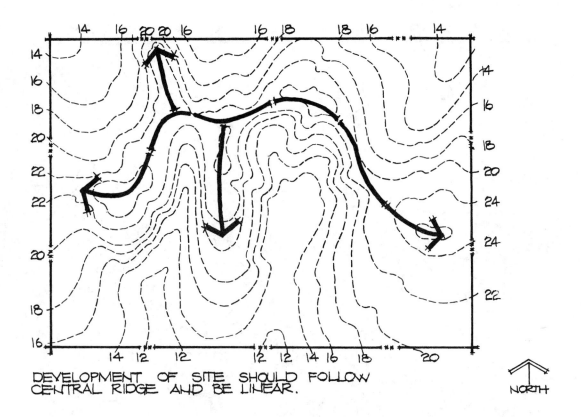

DEVELOPMENT OF SITE SHOULD FOLLOW
CENTRAL RIDGE AND BE LINEAR.

NORTH

FIGURE 1.2

FIGURE 1.3

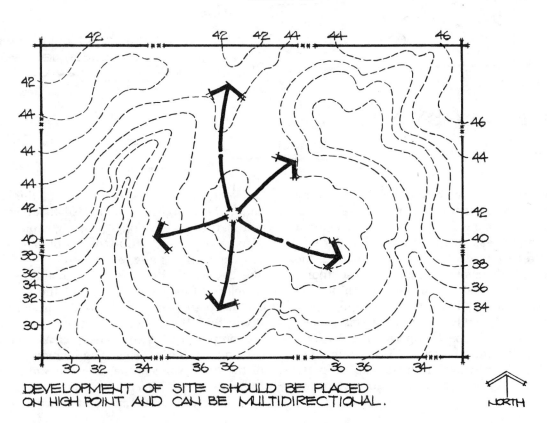

DEVELOPMENT OF SITE SHOULD BE PLACED
ON HIGH POINT AND CAN BE MULTIDIRECTIONAL.

NORTH

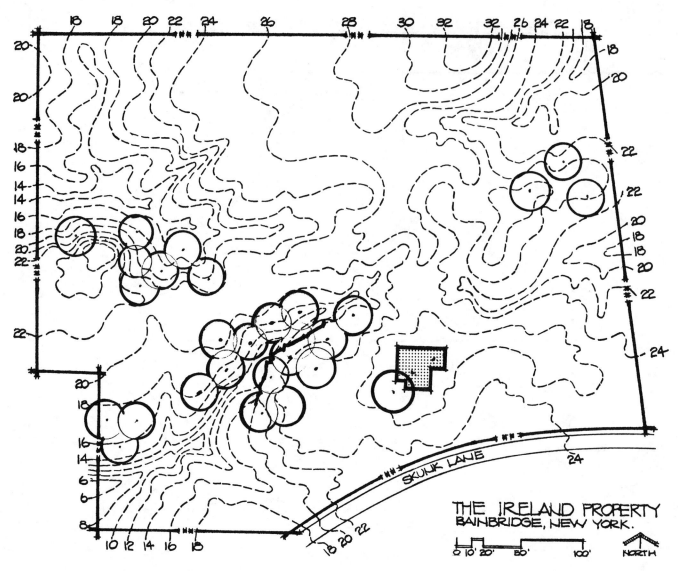

EXAMPLE OF A BASE PLAN.

FIGURE 1.4

Similarly, landform can be considered as a setting or stage for the placement of other design elements and functions. It is the foundation for all exterior spaces and land uses. This is why the ground surface is often referred to as the "base plane" (i.e., the starting point for the evolution of a design solution). As such, one of the first tasks in the design process is typically to obtain a "base sheet" or topographic plan of the site. As in Figure 1.4, this base sheet usually shows contour lines, property lines, existing structures, roads, and sometimes vegetation. The base sheet can be obtained from on-site property and topographic surveys or by aerial surveys of the site.

Having obtained a base sheet of the site's landform, the designer is then able to utilize it as the foundation for developing a design solution. All design concepts and proposals are prepared and studied as tracing paper overlays on top of the base sheet. One of the early steps in this process is to develop a functional diagram of the proposed uses on the base plane as illustrated in Figure 1.5. In doing this, the designer studies the relationship of the proposed uses to each other as well as to the existing landform. This diagrammatic organization of the base plane or stage of the site is critical because its layout affects the order, scale and proportion, character or theme, and functional quality of

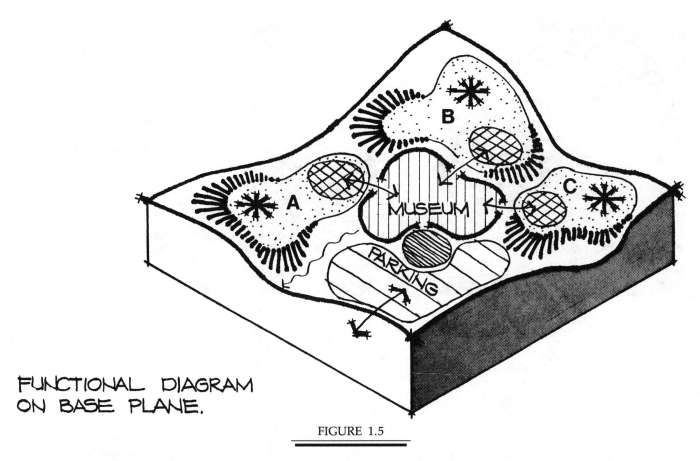

FUNCTIONAL DIAGRAM
ON BASE PLANE.

FIGURE 1.5

the outdoor environment. A well-established arrangement of the base plane provides a sound footing for the integration of other design elements including vertical and overhead planes. On the other hand, a poorly organized base plane contributes to problems throughout an environment that usually cannot be easily compensated for by skillful design during subsequent phases. It must be pointed out here, however, that the landscape architect's attention should not be limited only to the base plane even though its arrangement is crucial. Ultimately, the designer must be concerned with the three-dimensional experience of a design and how it will feel to be in it.

The significance of landform to the landscape architectural profession is further emphasized by the name itself: *land*scape architecture. *Webster's New Collegiate Dictionary* describes "landscape," among other definitions, as "a picture representing a view of natural inland scenery."[1] It further defines "landscape" as "the landforms of a region in the aggregate."[2] The word "land" by itself is defined by Webster's as "the surface of the earth and all its natural resources."[3] It can be clearly seen from these particular definitions that earth and soil along with their three-dimensional form are inherent in the concept of landscape. "Landform" and "landscape" are mutually supportive in terms of definition. If "architecture" is then defined as "the art or science of building,"[4] it is possible to interpret "landscape architecture" as the art or science of building on and with the earth's surface.

One of the landscape architect's unique and distinguishing characteristics is the ability to work sensitively with and manipulate landform. While several other professions also deal with various aspects of landform, none of them does so with the same depth of knowledge and skill as the landscape architect. The trademark of the landscape architectural profession includes the modification and stewardship of the earth's surface for our use and enjoyment.

As stated previously, landform influences a number of other factors dealt with in the location and

[1]*Webster's New Collegiate Dictionary*, 1977 ed. (Springfield, Mass: G. & C. Merriam Company, 1977), p. 646.
[2]Ibid.

[3]Ibid., p. 645.
[4]Ibid., p. 59.

FIGURE 1.6

FIGURE 1.7

FIGURE 1.8

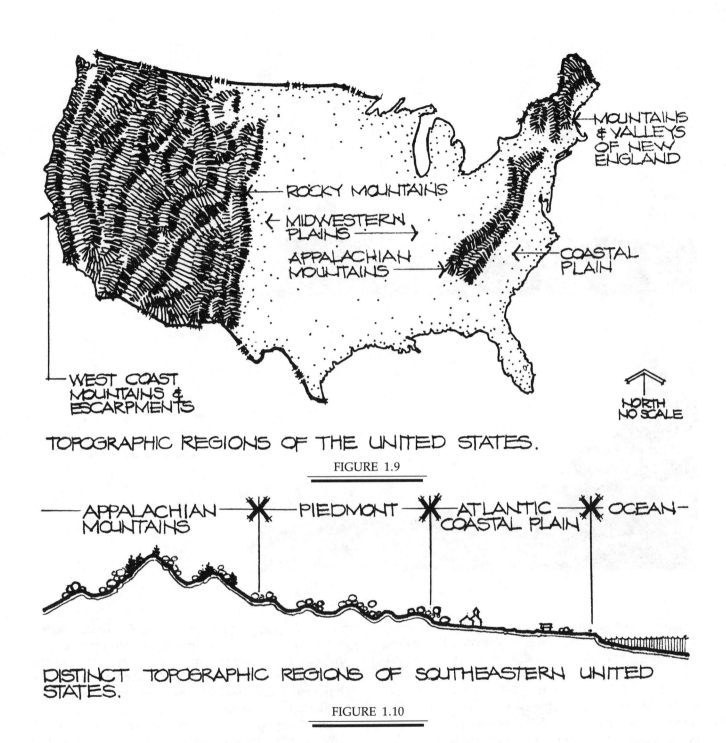

TOPOGRAPHIC REGIONS OF THE UNITED STATES.

FIGURE 1.9

DISTINCT TOPOGRAPHIC REGIONS OF SOUTHEASTERN UNITED STATES.

FIGURE 1.10

design of exterior spaces. Some of these are discussed in greater detail in the following paragraphs.

Aesthetic Character. Landform has a direct bearing upon the aesthetic character and rhythm of the landscape at any scale. Mountains, hills, valleys, plains, and prairies are each different regional landform types that have their own unique, identifiable character. Figures 1.6, 1.7, and 1.8 show the different

landscape characters provided by variations in landform. Many regions of a country are distinguished primarily by the landform predominant in the area. For example, the major regions of the United States are often identified by their topography (Figure 1.9): The East Coast (coastal plains, hills, and valleys), the Appalachians (mountains), the Midwest (plains and prairies), the Rockies (mountains), and the West Coast (mountains, valleys, and coastal escarpments).

FIGURE 1.11

FIGURE 1.12

While each of these regions can also be additionally differentiated by such factors as climate, vegetation, and culture, landform remains one of the most visually distinguishing features.

Each of these larger geographic regions of the United States can be further subdivided into smaller topographic areas of well-defined character, again based upon their predominant landform type. For instance, the Southeastern United States is often described as consisting of three distinct topographic regions: plain, piedmont, and mountains (Figure 1.10). The plain, or more correctly, the Atlantic coastal plain, is distinguished by broad expanses of low, flat land covered by rich truck farms and coastal villages. The piedmont is characterized by gently rolling uplands where hay and grains are the major agricultural crop. Finally, the Appalachian Mountains form

the third region of rugged, sharp mountain ranges and tight valleys where farming, small communities, and mining industries are found essentially on the lower slopes and valley floors. Again, the visual character of each one of these regions is directly derived from its topography.

The comparison between visually level areas and hilly or mountainous areas serves as an additional illustration of the influence of landform on landscape character. Relatively level sites and regions, like the ocean or large lakes, tend to appear quite open and expansive, as shown in Figure 1.11. One can often see great distances (if other elements do not interfere) to the horizon or other enclosing higher points of ground. Consequently, level areas often have a strong internal sense of visual continuity and unity. Different parts of the landscape can be

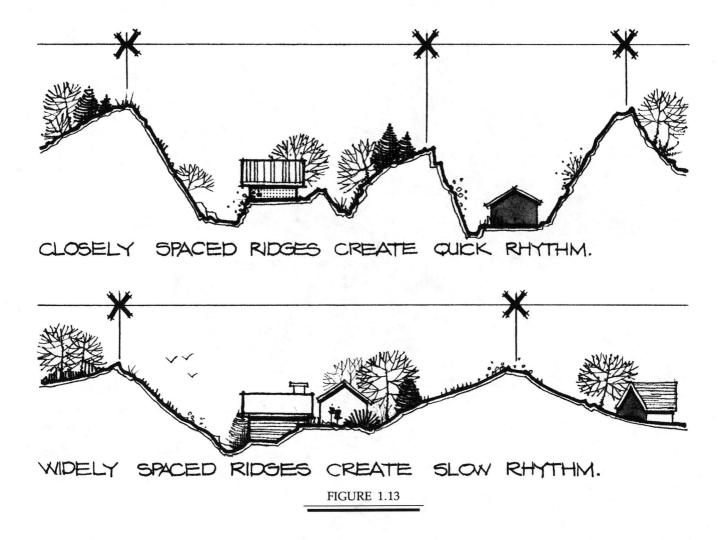

CLOSELY SPACED RIDGES CREATE QUICK RHYTHM.

WIDELY SPACED RIDGES CREATE SLOW RHYTHM.

FIGURE 1.13

seen and appreciated as smaller parts of the whole. Furthermore, the sky is frequently a dominant element of prairielike regions where clouds and the sun form a strong ceiling and light source. In comparison with visually level landforms, hilly and mountainous areas are apt to provide a sensation of separation and isolation from one valley to another (Figure 1.12). When a person is in the valley between higher points of ground, the mountain slopes take on visual importance and the sky is reduced to a smaller area directly overhead.

The size and spacing of the valleys (low points) and ridges (high points) within a hilly or mountainous region can also have a direct effect on the perceptual rhythm of the landscape, as illustrated in Figure 1.13. The proportional relationship perceived between solid (ridge or high point) and void (valley or low point) as one moves through the landscape establishes a rhythmic cadence not unlike that found in music. The rhythm of the West Virginia landscape

is, for example, different from that of New England and different still from that in western Colorado.

In addition to influencing regional landscape character and rhythm, the various landform types can also have a direct impact on the aesthetic character of patterns and forms that are visually compatible with them. One example of this is found in the comparison of the designs of different European gardens in relation to the type of landform on which they were placed. For example, Italian Renaissance gardens such as Villa Lante and Villa d'Este have responded to the hilly Italian landform by being terraced in a series of well-defined levels that tend to be outward-oriented to take advantage of views into and across a valley (Figure 1.14). Clearly delineated vistas from a high point to a lower point on the sites further create dramatic views while the use of falling water acknowledges the gravitational movement down the slopes.

French Renaissance gardens such as Vaux-le-Vi-

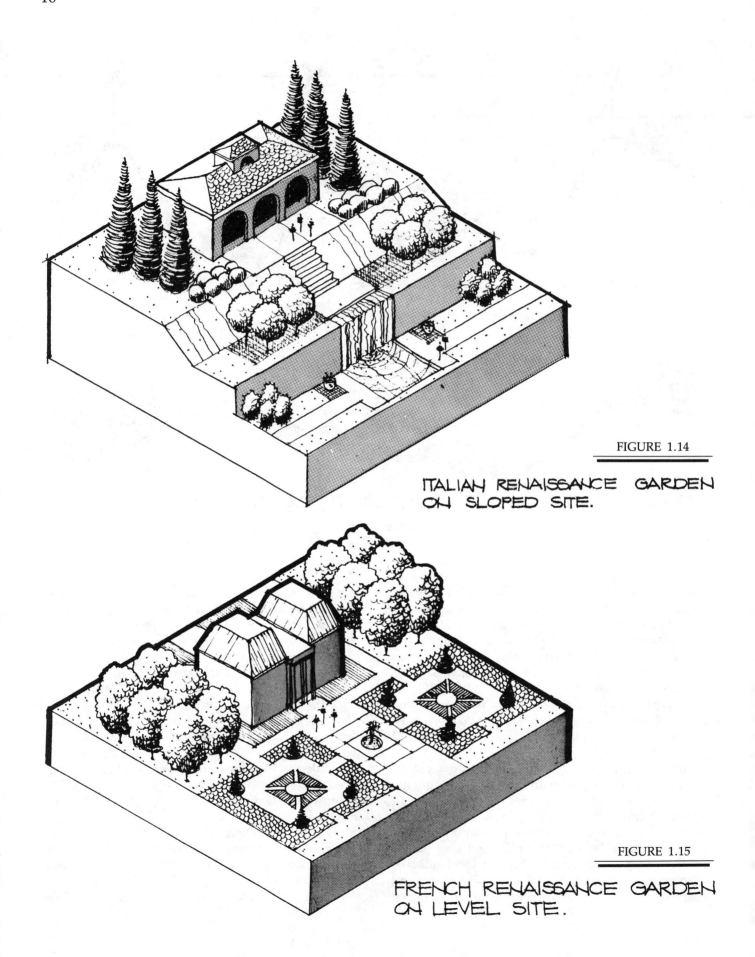

FIGURE 1.14

ITALIAN RENAISSANCE GARDEN
ON SLOPED SITE.

FIGURE 1.15

FRENCH RENAISSANCE GARDEN
ON LEVEL SITE.

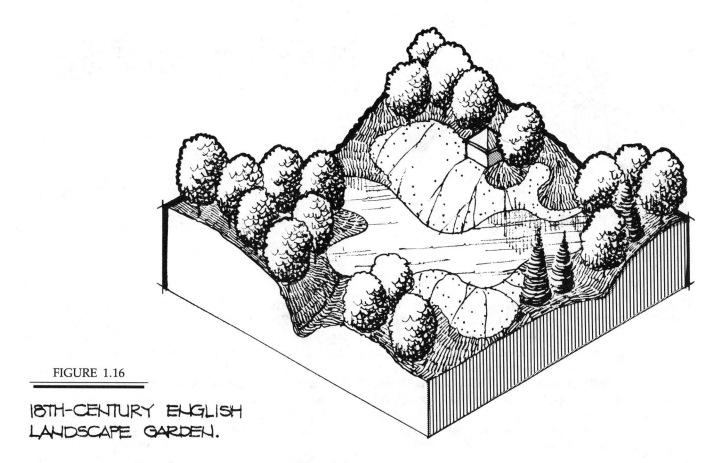

FIGURE 1.16

18TH-CENTURY ENGLISH
LANDSCAPE GARDEN.

comte and Versailles have likewise responded directly to their topographic context. The generally level, gently rolling landform on which these gardens have evolved easily lends itself to the hard, stiff, geometry characteristic of the French Renaissance style. Long, straight axes and vistas, large bodies of still water, and intricate patterns of parterre all are elements and patterns expressive of level landform's character (Figure 1.15).

In England, still another character of garden and design style is found in association with the landform present there. The eighteenth-century ''landscape gardening school'' that evolved in response to the cultural and economic changes of the time is typified by soft, undulating landforms, naturalistic masses of trees, and curvilinear bodies of water (Figure 1.16). These characteristics of the landscape gardening school exemplify the hilly and gently rolling topography typical of much of the English countryside.

The character and layout of the Italian Renaissance, French Renaissance, and English landscape gardening school styles is directly related to the personality of the landform in the region where each style evolved. If any one of these three styles were

relocated on the landform inherent in either of the other two, it would appear out of place.

Spatial Sensation. A person's perception about the limits and feeling of outdoor space is also affected by landform. Sites or regions that are visually level lack spatial definition based on landform alone. Level topography is only a ground plane element lacking vertical definition. Slopes and higher points of ground, on the other hand, occupy a portion of the vertical plane and have the ability to define and enclose space, as illustrated in Figure 1.17. The steeper and/or higher the slope, the greater the sensation of outdoor space created. In addition to the definition of space, landform affects the feeling of a space. Smooth, flowing landforms produce a sensuous and relaxed sensation while bold, rugged landforms are apt to nurture a feeling of excitement and aggressiveness in a space (Figure 1.18).

Likewise, the slope of a surface on which one stands affects the spatial feeling. A person is more apt to feel secure and at ease when standing on a level portion of ground than on a sloped one. Sloped ground surfaces are often uncomfortable to stand on and frequently induce a person to move. The sloped

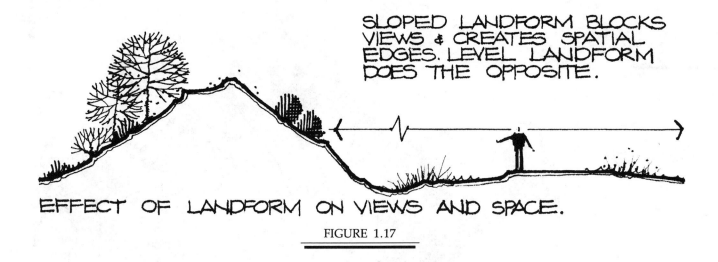

SLOPED LANDFORM BLOCKS VIEWS & CREATES SPATIAL EDGES. LEVEL LANDFORM DOES THE OPPOSITE.

EFFECT OF LANDFORM ON VIEWS AND SPACE.

FIGURE 1.17

floor surfaces of the Guggenheim Museum in New York City designed by Frank Lloyd Wright are a classic architectural example of the power of sloped ground planes. Here, the sloped walking areas from which visitors view the pictures hanging on the walls subtly push people along and prevent them from conveniently stopping too long to observe any one display. It has been reported Wright created these inclined ground planes on purpose to express the power of architecture over art.

Views. Closely linked to the concept of spatial definition is that of views. Again in the vertical plane, landform can affect what and how much is seen at any one point, establish dramatic vistas, create sequential viewing or "progressive realization" of an

object, or completely hide undesirable elements (see Figures 1.76 and 1.79). In terms of the ground plane, landform has the ability to impact the height and distance relationship between the viewer (or vantage point) and the object or space being looked at. The viewer may be placed lower than, on the same elevation as, or higher than the object being viewed. Each relationship is apt to produce a slightly different perception of the object being viewed.

Drainage. Most precipitation that falls eventually reaches the earth's surface and that which does not percolate into the ground or evaporate becomes surface runoff. The amount of runoff, its direction of flow, and its rate of flow are all related to the landform. Generally speaking (without reference to spe-

FIGURE 1.18

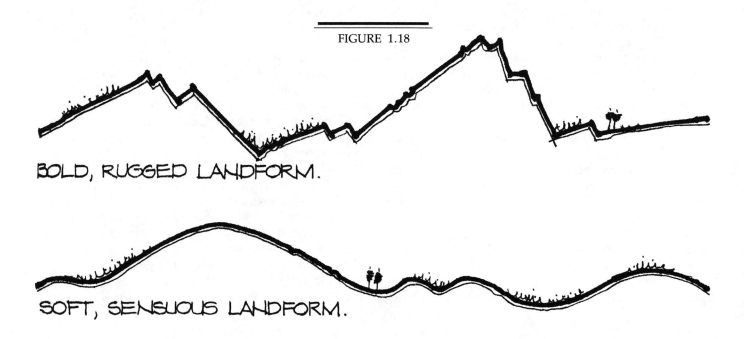

BOLD, RUGGED LANDFORM.

SOFT, SENSUOUS LANDFORM.

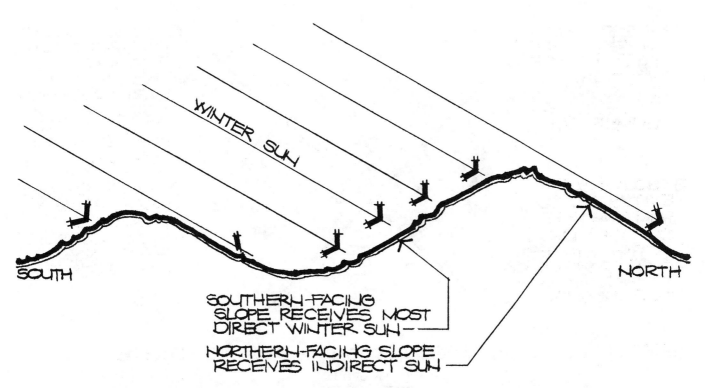

EFFECT OF SLOPE ORIENTATION ON RECEPTION OF WINTER SUN.

FIGURE 1.19

cific soil type), the steeper the ground, the more the quantity and the faster the rate of runoff. Ground that is too steep is susceptible to erosion due to excessive velocity, while ground with too little slope is likely to be wet from insufficient drainage. In considering drainage, it is suggested, for example, that slopes with only shrub material be held to a maximum slope of 10 percent to prevent erosion while lawn areas be graded to slopes of not less than 1 percent to avoid the occurrence of wet areas.[5] (See p. 31 for definition of slope percentage.) Modifying surface drainage and directing it to appropriate points in a site is an important and integral part of site design. A design that has poor drainage is in most instances unacceptable despite its appearance and quality of spaces. One exception to this is a marsh or wetland preserved as a wildlife habitat.

Microclimate. Landform affects sun exposure, wind exposure, and precipitation accumulation. In the continental temperate zone, slopes facing south receive more direct sun during the winter months than

any other slope orientation. North-facing slopes receive very little if any direct sun during the winter, as shown in Figure 1.19. In summer all slope orientations receive some sun with the western slopes being the hottest owing to direct exposure to the afternoon sun. Figure 1.20 shows the overall characteristics and desirability of the major slope orientations in terms of sun in the continental temperate zone.

In analyzing wind direction in the continental temperate zone, the northwest-facing slopes are exposed to the cold winds while the southeast slopes are the most protected during the winter, as shown in Figure 1.21. During the summer months, slopes facing southwest receive the most benefit from the cooling effect of the southwest summer breezes. In summary, southeast-facing slopes in the continental temperate zone are the most desirable for development in the context of both sun and wind owing to protection from the winter wind, exposure to the summer breezes, exposure to the winter sun, and indirect exposure to the hot afternoon summer sun.

The influence of slope orientation on microclimate is further substantiated by observance of both natural and artificial elements. In the prologue to his

---

[5]Harlow C. Landphair and Fred Klatt, Jr., *Landscape Architecture Construction* (New York: Elsevier North Holland, 1979), p. 39.

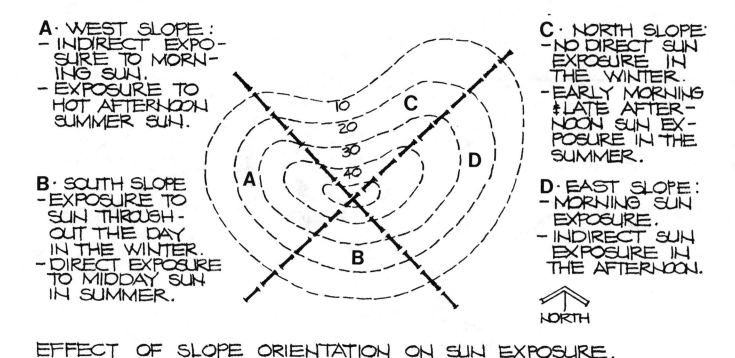

A. WEST SLOPE:
- INDIRECT EXPO-
SURE TO MORN-
ING SUN.
- EXPOSURE TO
HOT AFTERNOON
SUMMER SUN.

B. SOUTH SLOPE
- EXPOSURE TO
SUN THROUGH-
OUT THE DAY
IN THE WINTER.
- DIRECT EXPOSURE
TO MIDDAY SUN
IN SUMMER.

C. NORTH SLOPE:
- NO DIRECT SUN
EXPOSURE IN
THE WINTER.
- EARLY MORNING
& LATE AFTER-
NOON SUN EX-
POSURE IN THE
SUMMER.

D. EAST SLOPE:
- MORNING SUN
EXPOSURE.
- INDIRECT SUN
EXPOSURE IN
THE AFTERNOON.

NORTH

EFFECT OF SLOPE ORIENTATION ON SUN EXPOSURE.

FIGURE 1.20

book *Landscape Architecture*, John O. Simonds tells a story about a hunter who shows a boy that the holes to a gopher community on a North Dakota prairie are on southeast slopes to take advantage of the favorable sun and wind exposure.[6] Paul J. Grillo, author of *Form, Function and Design*, suggests that communities and cities sited on south- and east-facing slopes along rivers and lakes have experienced more noticeable growth and development than those located on west- or north-oriented slopes. He notes Cincinnati, Albany, Providence, and Hartford as cities that have advantageous microclimatic orientation due to slope and shore location.[7]

As noted previously, topographic variation also influences the amount of precipitation that falls at a particular location. The effect of the coastal mountain range and the Sierra Nevadas in California on the regions to their east is a well-documented example of higher areas of ground creating "rain shadows." Another illustration is the Olympic Peninsula in the state of Washington (Figure 1.22). Here, differences in elevation produce a dramatic variation in the amount of precipitation. Along the Pacific coastline on the western side of the Olympic mountain range, an average of 10 in (25.5 cm) of rainfall occurs each year. Further east and higher in elevation in the Hoh Rain Forest, an average of 140 in (355.5 cm)– 150 in (381 cm) of precipitation falls. And higher still in elevation (7,965 ft (2428 m) above sea level) at Mt. Olympus at the upper end of the Hoh River, as many as 200 in (508 cm) of precipitation occurs annually.[8] On the northern and eastern sides of the Olympic range, much less precipitation occurs because of the "rain shadow." Along the Hood Canal, for example, annual precipitation is only 15 in (38 cm)–20 in (51 cm).[9] While horizontal distances between these various points is not great, the difference in precipitation is pronounced as a result of the landforms.

Functional Use of the Land. Slope steepness, configuration of valleys and ridges, and the character of landform all affect the location and organization of different functions and land uses of the landscape.

[6]John O. Simonds, *Landscape Architecture* (New York: McGraw-Hill, 1961), p. 1.
[7]Paul J. Grillo, *Form, Function and Design* (New York: Dover, 1975), pp. 112–113.

[8]May Lou Hanify and Craig Blencowe, *Guide to the Hoh Rain Forest* (Seattle: Superior Publishing Company, 1974).
[9]Bob Spring, Ira Spring, and Harvey Manning, *The Olympic National Park* (Seattle: Superior Publishing Company, n.d.), p. 11.

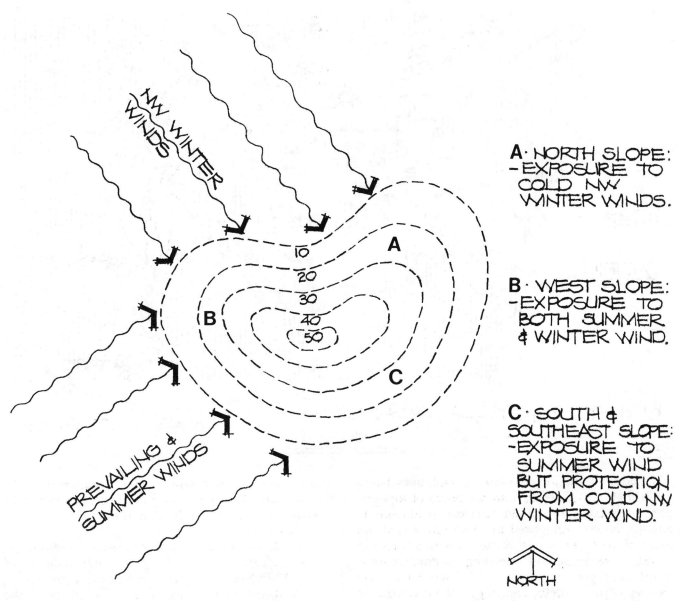

A. NORTH SLOPE:
– EXPOSURE TO COLD NW WINTER WINDS.

B. WEST SLOPE:
– EXPOSURE TO BOTH SUMMER & WINTER WIND.

C. SOUTH & SOUTHEAST SLOPE:
– EXPOSURE TO SUMMER WIND BUT PROTECTION FROM COLD NW WINTER WIND.

NORTH

EFFECT OF SLOPE ORIENTATION ON WIND EXPOSURE IN THE TEMPERATE CLIMATE ZONE.

FIGURE 1.21

Every land use or site function has an optimum slope condition on which it operates best. This desired optimum condition suggests where the function should or should not be placed on a given site. For example, tennis courts should ideally be placed on 1 to 3 percent slopes. It would not be judicious design practice to place a tennis court on a 10 percent slope as this would require extensive alteration of the ground at great monetary and environmental expense. As a rule of thumb, the flatter the slope (though not less than 1 percent), the more flexible and capable it is for development. Relatively gentle slopes require a minimum of grading in siting buildings, permit the use of common and less expensive types of construction, and allow for easy installation of roads and utilities. By comparison, the steeper the slope, the more restrictions on what land uses are feasible and respectful of the site.

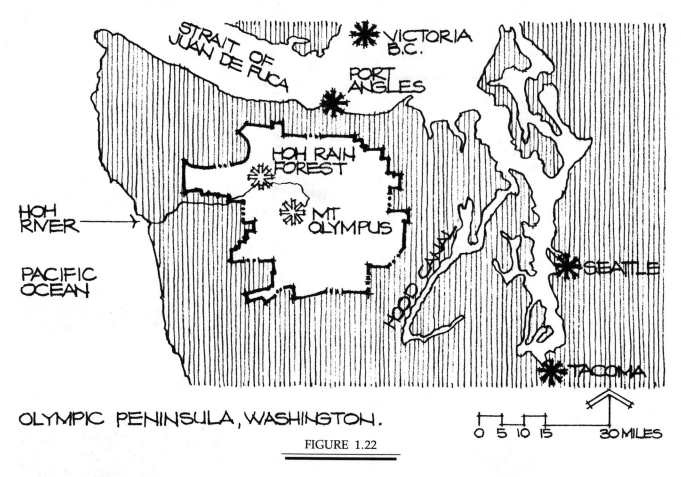

OLYMPIC PENINSULA, WASHINGTON.

FIGURE 1.22

In addition to the location of land uses based upon their compatibility with steepness of topography, the relationship of one land use or function to another is also influenced by landform. On flatter areas of land, the layout of different functions can be rather sprawling and spreading. Alternative functional concepts are many on flat landforms. On steeper slopes, valleys, and ridges, the organization of different land uses is apt to be more condensed and linear. Options and alternatives are fewer on steeper ground in terms of interrelationship of land uses.

Landform also affects regional land use and development patterns. For instance, land use and road patterns tend to be rather straight and rectangular in flatter areas of the country such as the Midwest (Figure 1.23). Here, topography posed few constraints on the public-land survey system that subdivided the landscape into a grid pattern. In regions where prominent valleys and ridges exist, regional development patterns tend to be different. One example of this is eastern Pennsylvania, where valleys and ridges are oriented in a distinct northeast-southwest direction. When looking at a road map of this region (Figure 1.23), one can see that the layout of most

roads and villages reflects the landform by also being strongly oriented in a northeast-southwest direction. Few roads are located in a northwest-southeast direction.

Another instance of the influence of landform on land use patterns is observed when the landscape of New York/New England is compared with that of the Midwest (Figure 1.24). In the eastern states, the valley floors are typically used for cultivated farmland, roads, and communities. The valley sides are used for pasture land while the hilltops are often wooded. In the Midwest, a somewhat opposite land use exists owing to the flatter landform. Here, the flat plateaus between the rivers and streams are used predominately for cultivated farmland while valleys are often wooded (as well as too steep for cultivation) and sometimes used for scenic or recreational purposes. These two different types of regional land use patterns have resulted in response to the landform of each area.

In summary, then, one can see from these discussions and illustrations that landform is indeed a significant and influential physical element in the outdoor environment. It affects how the land is per-

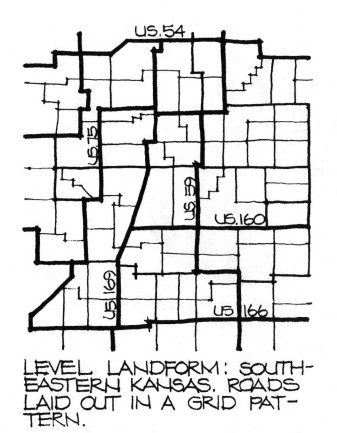

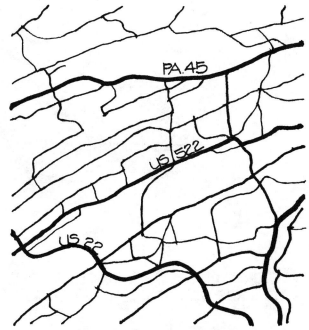

LEVEL LANDFORM: SOUTH-
EASTERN KANSAS. ROADS
LAID OUT IN A GRID PAT-
TERN.

MOUNTAINOUS LANDFORM:
EASTERN PENNSYLVANIA.
ROADS FOLLOW VALLEYS
AND RIDGES.

FIGURE 1.23

FIGURE 1.24

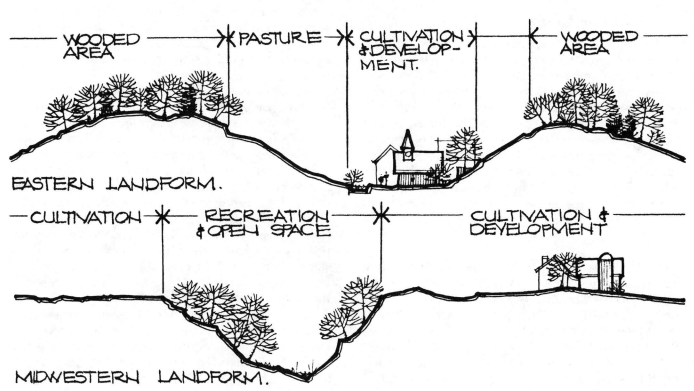

EASTERN LANDFORM.

MIDWESTERN LANDFORM.

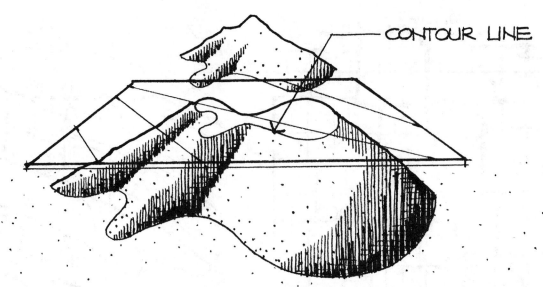

A CONTOUR LINE WOULD BE CREATED IF A PLANE OF GLASS CUT HORIZONTALLY ACROSS A LANDFORM.

FIGURE 1.25

ceived, used, and designed. And as has been previously noted, landform directly interacts with all the other physical design elements placed on the ground plane in a manner affecting their function, character, and appearance.

Expression of Landform

To be able to work effectively with landform in landscape architectural design, it is first necessary to have a clear understanding of the different techniques for expressing it. Some of the more common means for depicting and manipulating topography include contours, value and color, hachures, mathematical expressions, three-dimensional models, and computer graphics. Each of these methods for representing landform has its own particular characteristics and applications where it is most useful. The following sections outline the alternative methods for expressing topography and the use guidelines for each.

Contour Lines. Contour lines are the most commonly used plan graphic expression of landform. Because landscape architects currently deal with site design primarily in plan, contour lines can also be considered the most universal method for expressing landform within the profession. A "contour line" is defined as a line on a plan drawing that connects all the points that are an equal vertical distance

above or below a horizontal reference plane, sometimes referred to as a datum or bench mark. In theory, a contour line would be shown as the outline of a landform if it were cut by a horizontal plane of glass, as illustrated in Figure 1.25. It should be kept in mind that contour lines are only an artificial means for representing landform and do not exist in reality except as traced by the edge of a flat, quiet body of water on its shoreline (this is a helpful means for visualizing what a contour line represents).

A related term that also requires definition is contour interval. A "contour interval" is the vertical distance between any two contour lines on a given plan and is a constant number often noted in the legend, or title block, of the drawing. For example, a 2-ft (or 1 m) contour interval means there is a 2-ft (or 1 m) elevation change between each contour line in the plan. The contour interval remains the same throughout a given drawing unless otherwise noted (unlike the horizontal distance between contour lines, which varies throughout a plan according to slope steepness). However, the contour interval often changes from one plan to another depending on the scale of the plan, the steepness of the site, and the complexity of the landform being represented. At the scale of most site plans (⅛ in = 1 ft−0 in to 1 in = 100 ft), the contour interval is typically 1 ft, 2 ft, or 5 ft (.5 m, 1 m or 2 m). At the regional scale (1 in = 500 ft or 1:24,000), the contour interval of a

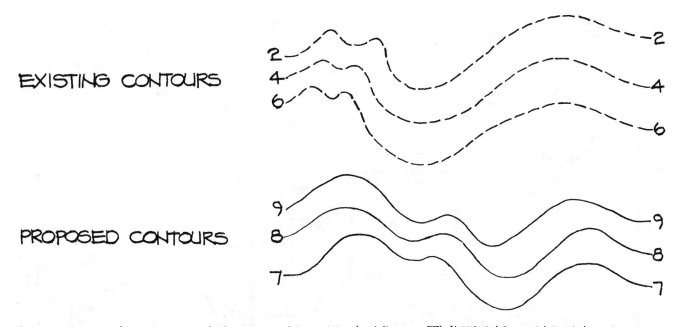

EXISTING CONTOURS

PROPOSED CONTOURS

EXISTING & PROPOSED CONTOUR LINES; EXISTING SHOWN AS DASHED LINES; PROPOSED SHOWN AS SOLID LINES.

FIGURE 1.26

plan may be as much as 20 ft, 25 ft, or 50 ft (5 m, 10 m, and 15 m).

When working with contour lines, a number of basic principles should be kept in mind. First, an existing contour line (one representing the landform of a site before alteration) is drawn freehand and is shown as a dashed line as illustrated in Figure 1.26. Second, a proposed contour line (one representing the ground's surface after alteration) is shown on plan as a solid line. Any change or alteration in the ground's surface is referred to as "grading." Grading or molding the landform is necessary on a site to

FIGURE 1.27

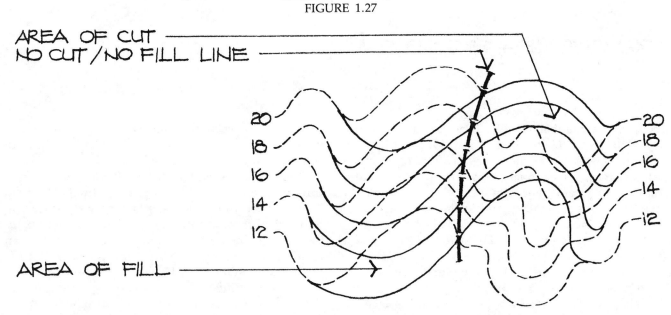

AREA OF CUT
NO CUT/NO FILL LINE

AREA OF FILL

EXISTING & PROPOSED CONTOUR LINES SHOWING CUT & FILL.

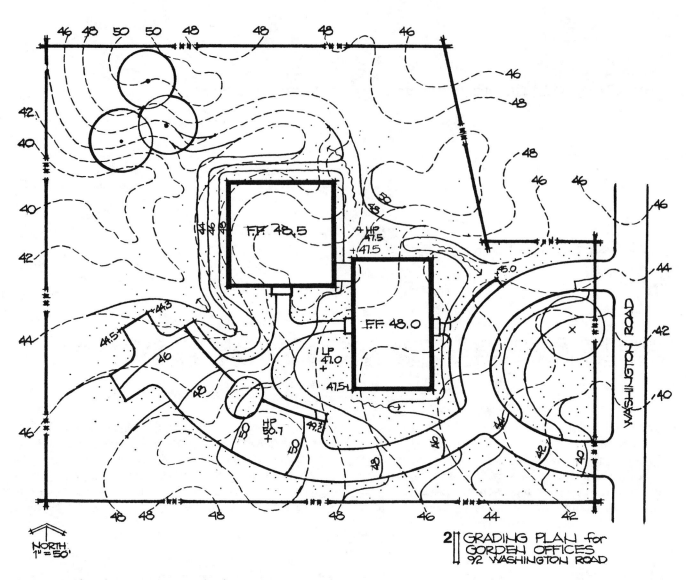

EXAMPLE OF A GRADING PLAN.

FIGURE 1.28

accomplish a number of objectives: (1) to establish proper drainage, (2) to modify the site in order to accommodate such elements as buildings, roads, parking areas, recreational fields, and the like, and (3) to create an aesthetically pleasing ground plane. Other purposes for grading and related uses of landform are outlined later in this chapter. Grading is an integral part of landscape architectural design and should be considered simultaneously with the layout of functions and forms in plan. The tendency of beginning designers to think of grading only after the plan shapes and locations have been fixed is incorrect and only leads to problems later in the design

process. The vertical manipulation of the land is fully as important as the horizontal organization of spaces and functions themselves.

When soil is added to a portion of the site through grading, it is referred to as "fill." The term "cut" is used to describe the taking away or excavation of soil from a portion of the site. Usually grading on a given site requires both cut and fill. Fill can be identified on a plan when a proposed contour is moved downhill (toward lower numbered contours) from the existing contour location, as indicated in Figure 1.27. Cut is identified on plan when the proposed contour line moves uphill (toward higher

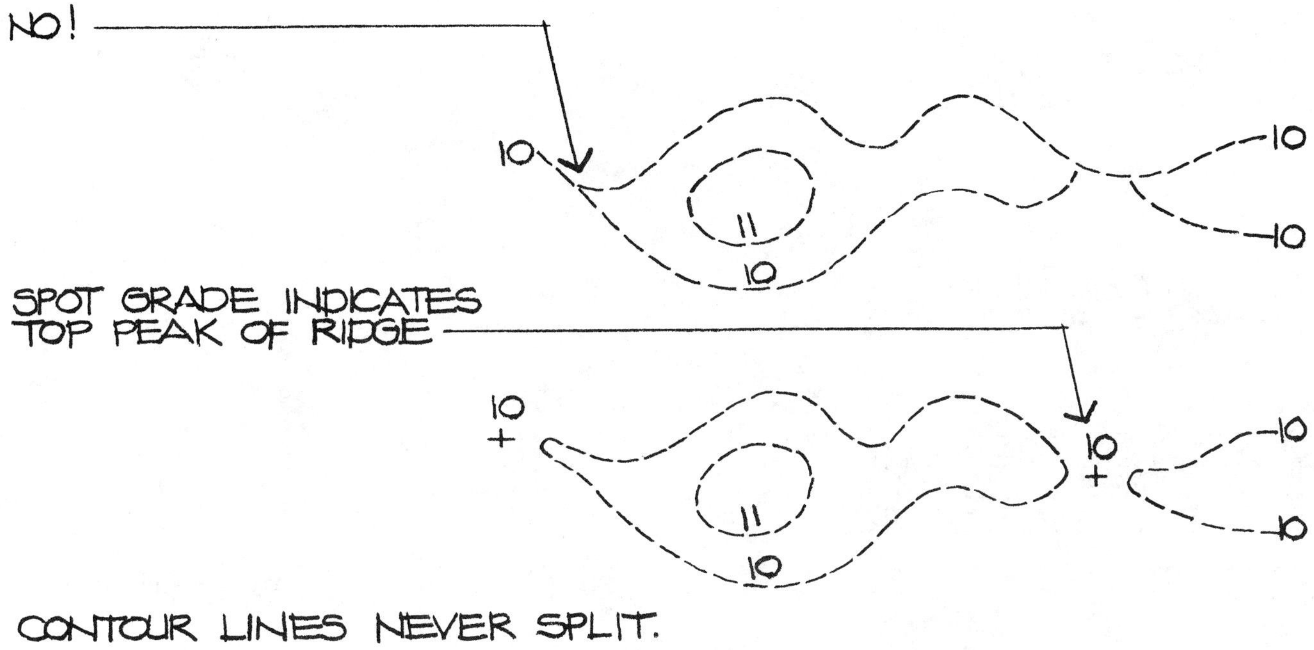

NO!

SPOT GRADE INDICATES
TOP PEAK OF RIDGE

CONTOUR LINES NEVER SPLIT.

FIGURE 1.29

numbered contours) from the existing contour location. A plan drawn specifically to show the proposed grading of a site is termed a "grading plan" (Figure 1.28). A grading plan shows both existing and proposed contour lines as well as the outline of all buildings, roads, walks, walls, and other structural elements of the design. The grading plan, which is one of many construction drawings, also shows the location of drainage structures such as drop inlets and catch basins as well as precise elevation at specific points throughout the site by means of spot grades.

A third principle for using contour lines is that they always close on themselves; they never simply end. A contour line always joins and meets itself even if it is many miles away from a particular site. For example, consider the contour line of one-foot elevation. It travels the entire coastline of a continent and eventually forms a closed loop. Contour lines that close on themselves within the boundaries of a particular site typically signify either a high point or low point, depending on how they are numbered (see later paragraphs of this section).

Fourth, contour lines never split, at least in terms of common practice. In other words, a single contour line never divides itself to form two separate contour lines of the same elevation as indicated in

the top half of Figure 1.29. This principle of contour lines is reinforced by a corollary that states that contour lines must occur in pairs. For the person just beginning to read and draw contour lines, the possibility of a contour line splitting itself might seem like a logical occurrence as a means of representing a point on a plan where the top edge of a peaked ridge widens out or rises in elevation. In fact, this is mathematically and theoretically possible. However, the generally accepted custom of drawing contour lines in pairs near the tops of ridges or bottoms of valleys eliminates the use of single contour lines to show one dimensional edges like the top peak of a ridge. Instead, such edges are normally indicated as a series of spot grades, as illustrated in the bottom half of Figure 1.29. This principle of contour lines might be better understood if it is also kept in mind that every contour line has higher ground on one side of it and lower ground on the other. Lower ground cannot be found on both sides of a contour line.

Fifth, contour lines never cross one another except to represent a natural bridge or overhang. Because soil by itself cannot be made to conform to such configurations, contour lines should not cross at all on a plan of an earthen site that has no walls or overhangs. However, where walls do exist, the

NO (EXCEPT FOR A NATURAL OVERHANG).

14
12
10

14
12
10

"8" CONTOUR LINE "TRAVELS" ALONG WALL.

8
6
4

8
6
4

VERTICAL PLANE; CONTOUR LINES FALL ON TOP OF ONE ANOTHER.

CONTOUR LINES NEVER CROSS EXCEPT TO SHOW AN OVERHANG OR VERTICAL PLANE.

FIGURE 1.30

FIGURE 1.31

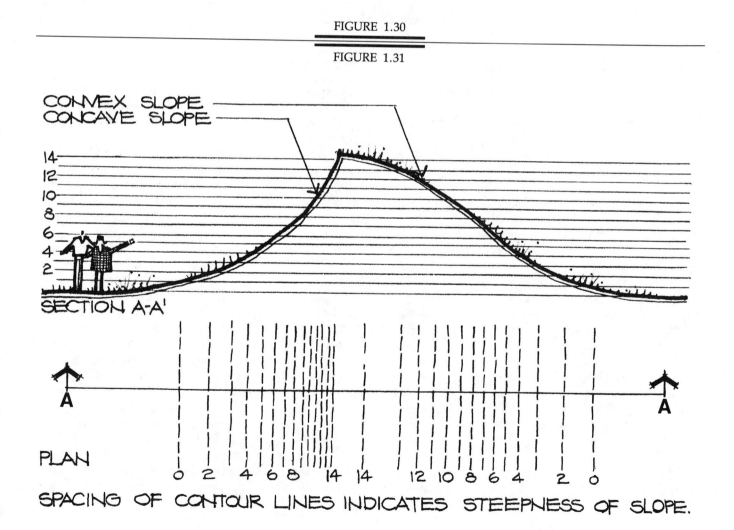

CONVEX SLOPE
CONCAVE SLOPE

14
12
10
8
6
4
2

SECTION A-A'

A

A

PLAN

0 2 4 6 8 14   14   12 10 8 6 4   2   0

SPACING OF CONTOUR LINES INDICATES STEEPNESS OF SLOPE.

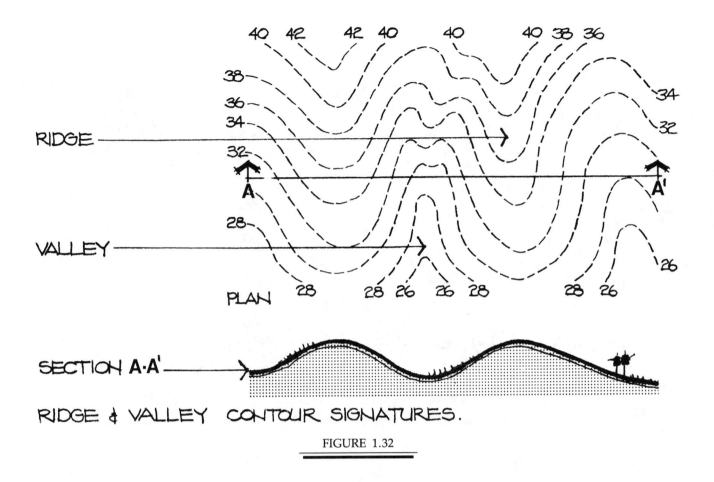

RIDGE & VALLEY CONTOUR SIGNATURES.

FIGURE 1.32

contour lines will fall one on top of the other to form a single line in plan, as shown in Figure 1.30.

The location, arrangement, and character of the contour lines on a plan, in a sense, act as symbolic vocabulary, establishing "signatures" from which we can "read" the landform of a site. For instance, the horizontal distance between contour lines on plan (*not* to be confused with the contour interval) indicates the relative degree of steepness and the uniformity of a slope. The closer the contour lines are to each other, the steeper the slope. Equal spacing between contour lines expresses a uniform slope while varied spacing depicts an irregular slope. Similarly, a slope that has its contour lines spaced farther apart toward the bottom or toe of the slope and closer together near its crest is referred to as a concave slope (Figure 1.31). A convex slope is shown in an opposite fashion: the contour lines are spaced closer together near the bottom and more distant toward the top.

The signature of a valley (or ravine and swale) is depicted on plan by contour lines that point uphill; that is, they point toward higher numbered contour lines (Figure 1.32). Conversely, the signature of a ridge is shown on a plan (Figure 1.32) by contour lines that point downhill; that is, they point toward lower numbered contour lines. Valleys and ridges may also be identified on a plan by locations where two contour lines of the same elevation approximately parallel each other (one must study the plan further to determine if it is a valley or a ridge). A summit or convex landform (not to be confused with a convex slope) is delineated on plan (Figure 1.33) by concentric, closed contour lines with the highest labeled contour line in the center. A depression or concave landform (not to be confused with a concave slope) is shown in an opposite manner by concentric, closed contour lines with the lowest numbered contour line in the center. Furthermore, the lowest contour line of a depression is drawn with short hachures on the inside or lower edge of the contour line itself. In reading a contour plan of a site, it is sometimes difficult to identify each one of these landform types individually because they occur together in a continuum, as indicated in Figures 1.34 and 1.35. For instance, it can be seen that the

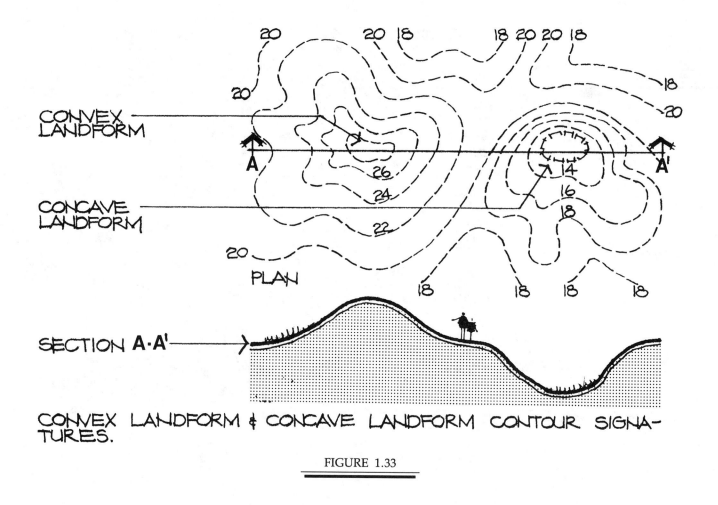

CONVEX LANDFORM & CONCAVE LANDFORM CONTOUR SIGNATURES.

FIGURE 1.33

side of a valley may also be the side of a ridge or similarly a convex landform may occur in close association with a ridge.

Spot Elevations. Spot elevations are another method for expressing elevation on a plan drawing or section. A spot elevation represents the vertical elevation above or below a horizontal reference plane at a single, particular point. It is shown on plan by a cross mark or dot and labeled with the appropriate number (Figure 1.36). As previously suggested, contour lines themselves are labeled with whole numbers because they represent full units of measure above or below a given reference plane. Spot elevations, on the other hand, are labeled by means of whole numbers with decimals because they are most often located between, not on, two contour lines. For example, a spot elevation might be labeled 51.3 or 75.15. Decimals instead of fractions are used because the surveying system of determining topographic elevation has evolved from a scientific base of numbers. Surveying rods used along with levels in the field to identify or set elevations are also cali-

brated in tenths and hundredths of a foot (at least in the United States).

The exact elevation of a spot grade is based on a proportional relationship between the location of the spot grade and the distance to the contour lines on either side. In determining the elevations of a spot grade through a procedure called "interpolation," it is normally assumed that the spot grade is located on a uniform slope that rises or falls at a constant rate between the two contour lines. Thus the proportional relationship of the horizontal distance between the spot grade and the next contour line on both the downhill and uphill side is the same as the proportional relationship in vertical elevation. For instance, a spot grade that lies horizontally halfway between two contour lines has an elevation that is also half the vertical distance (contour interval) between the same two contour lines. Therefore in interpolating the elevation of a spot grade, it is first necessary to determine both the scale of the drawing and the contour interval. The next step is to measure the scale horizontal distance the spot grade is from the next contour line on both the downhill and

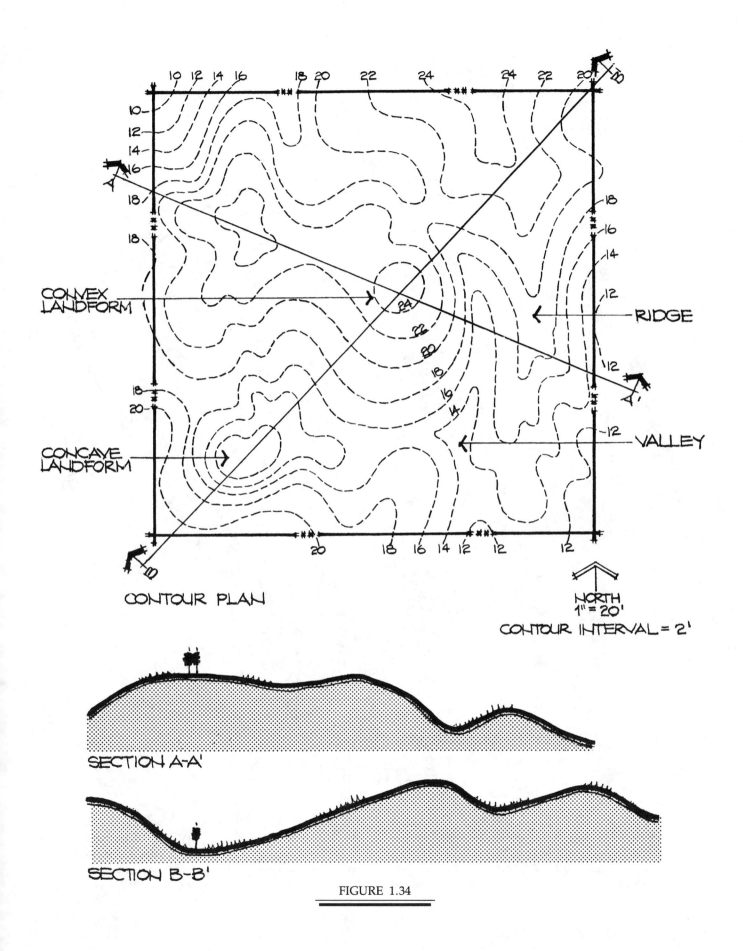

CONTOUR PLAN

CONVEX LANDFORM

CONCAVE LANDFORM

RIDGE

VALLEY

NORTH
1" = 20'

CONTOUR INTERVAL = 2'

SECTION A-A'

SECTION B-B'

FIGURE 1.34

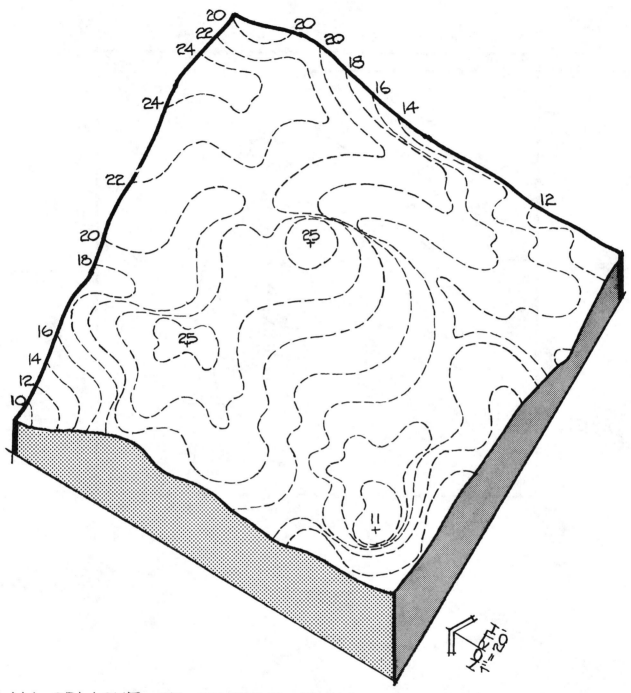

PLAN OBLIQUE OF CONTOUR PLAN.

FIGURE 1.35

uphill side (measured perpendicular to the direction of the lines). Now the proportional relationship between these two distances can be established. For example, if the spot grade is 4 ft from the 16-ft contour and 16 ft from the 17-ft contour, it would be one-fifth of the total distance between the two contour lines. Therefore the elevation of the spot grade would also be one-fifth of the vertical distance (contour interval) between the contour lines or 0.2 ft. The spot grade in this instance would be 16.2. Simi-

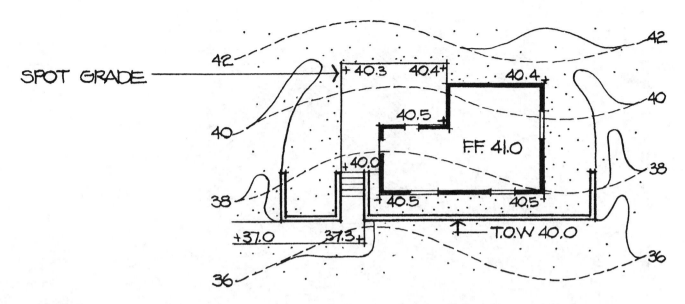

SPOT GRADES IDENTIFY THE ELEVATION AT A SPECIFIC POINT.

FIGURE 1.36

larly, if a point was 20 ft from the 30-ft contour line and 10 ft from the 32-ft contour, the spot elevation would be two-thirds of the contour interval, or 31.33. The same principle of proportion relationships also exists for contours and spot grades measured in meters. Spot elevations are typically rounded to the nearest tenth or hundredth of a foot, depending on the complexity of the ground surface and the degree of accuracy required. Spot elevations are used to depict the elevation at such places as the corners of buildings, high points, low points, tops and bottoms of curbs and steps, and tops of walls (TOW). Spot elevations are most commonly used on grading plans and other construction drawings such as drainage plans and planting plans.

Hachures. Hachures are still another graphic means for representing landform on plan. Hachures by definition are short, disconnected lines drawn perpendicular to the slope and contour lines. With this technique, the contour lines themselves are first lightly drawn in and then the hachures are placed between the contours. An example of hachures is shown in Figure 1.37. Hachures are more abstract and less exact than contour lines but nevertheless are commonly used on illustrative site plans or presentation drawings to show landform graphically. Because of their more general character and because

they obscure most of the detail on the ground plane, hachures should not be used on grading plans or other construction drawings. The thickness and spacing of the hachures is an effective method for visually portraying the steepness of a slope. The closer and thicker the hachures are drawn, the steeper the suggestion of a slope. Hachures may also be drawn on plan to give the effect of light and shadow and thereby a more three-dimensional feeling to the drawing. Accordingly, the hachures are drawn darker and closer together on a shaded slope and lighter and farther apart on a sunlit slope.

Value and Color. Value (tones of gray) and color may be used, like hachures, to represent landform. One typical use of value and color is in a topographic "elevational relief map" that shows different increments of elevation by varied shades or colors (Figure 1.38). Each separate value or color used on a given elevational relief plan shows an area where the height of the ground lies between two assigned elevations. For example, a particular shade of brown might delineate the entire area on a site that lies between the 50- and 60-ft elevation, while another shade of brown covers the area between the 60- and 70-ft elevation. With this approach, the lighter values are used for the higher elevations to give an effective illusion of height. The appearance of an ele-

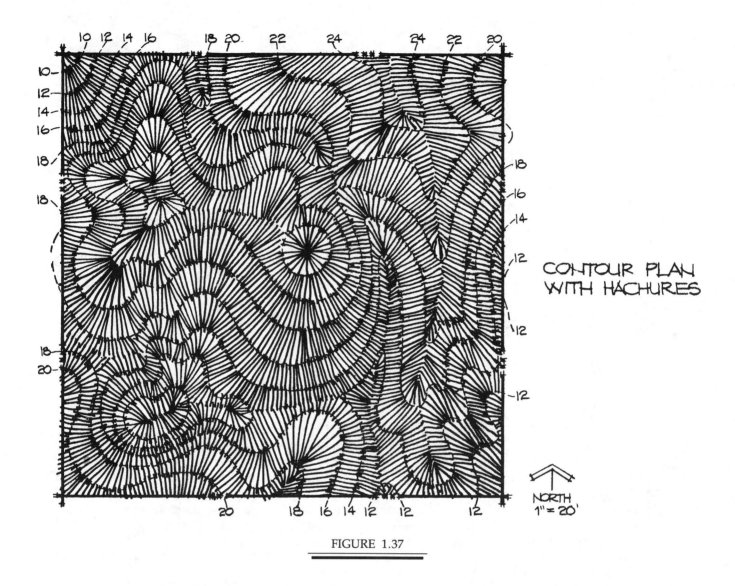

CONTOUR PLAN
WITH HACHURES

NORTH
1" = 20'

FIGURE 1.37

vational relief plan is best when the gradation from dark to light tones is gradual and even. To portray accurately the overall topographic relief on an elevational relief plan, the range of elevational difference should remain a constant from one increment to another. In the example cited previously in this paragraph, the elevational difference of each increment was a constant of 10 feet. An elevational relief plan is a helpful analytical tool to determine the amount of topographic change between the highest and lowest areas of the site and to compare the relative elevations between two different points of the site.

Values and colors are also used on slope analysis maps. Like the elevational relief map, a "slope analysis map" is a device for expressing and understanding the structure of the landform on a particu-

lar site. Slope analysis maps are based on steepness of slope and often represent steeper slopes with darker tones and more gentle slopes with lighter tones, as illustrated in Figure 1.39. A slope analysis map is valuable for determining the capability of different site areas for proposed land uses or elements and is prepared during the site analysis phase of the design process. Its usefulness as an analytical tool is related to the number of slope categories identified and the percentage of slope steepness represented by each. The determination of these variables should be based on the complexity of the existing topography of a site coupled with the proposed land uses. For example, a site to be developed for single-family housing might be analyzed on the following basis: 0–1% slope: too flat for proper drainage; 1–5% slope: ideal topographic conditions requiring minimum cut

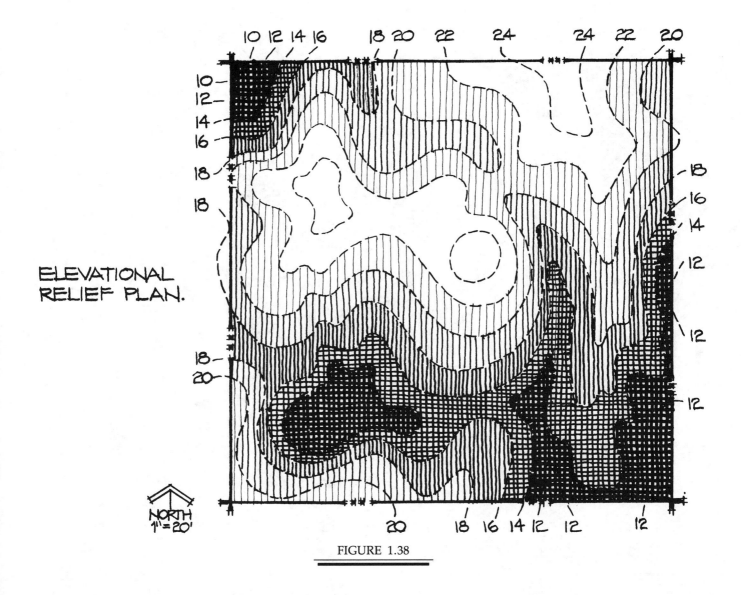

FIGURE 1.38

and fill; 5–10% slope: good building conditions requiring more careful siting at the upper range of steepness; 10–15% slope: housing units should be split-level and sited parallel to the contours to minimize cut and fill, and retaining walls may be required; 15% slope and above: housing units will require special architectural adaptations such as pole construction; road and utility access will be difficult and costly. (For an explanation of percentage of slope, see p. 31.) By comparison, a site to be developed for a shopping center and related parking could be analyzed as follows: 0–1% slope: too flat for proper drainage; 1–5% slope: ideal and preferred condition for development; 5–8% slope: development possible with some cut and fill required; parking aisles should be placed parallel to the contours; 8% slope and above: development should be prohib-

ited to avoid unacceptable environmental damage. It should be pointed out that a slope analysis map is truly an "analysis" only when the designer begins to make evaluations and conclusions about the slope categories identified and graphically mapped. If the designer only goes through the process of calculating and mapping the categories without making judgments about the appropriateness or restrictions of each, then the end product is best labeled slope "inventory" (see section on Site Analysis in Chapter 7 for an explanation of the difference between site "inventory" and site "analysis").

Model. A model is perhaps the most effective method for expressing landform, especially for the layperson or novice designer who often has difficulty in interpreting a two-dimensional contour

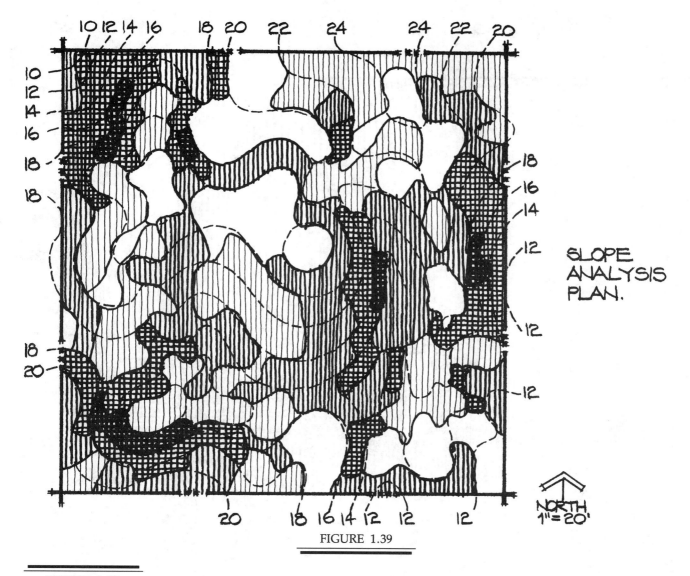

SLOPE
ANALYSIS
PLAN.

NORTH
1" = 20'

FIGURE 1.39

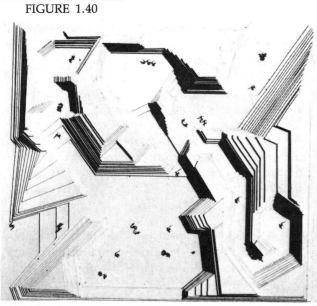

FIGURE 1.40

plan. A model leaves little room for miscommunication and is usually a worthwhile sales and promotional tool. Unfortunately, models are bulky, hard to store and transport, and time-consuming and costly to construct. A topographic model may be built out of clay, chipboard (Figure 1.40), cork, foam-core board, cardboard, or styrofoam. The choice of the material should be based on the model's purpose, budget, and complexity of the landform to be represented. If in-house capabilities are insufficient to construct a topographic model, an individual or firm may want to investigate one of the several commercial companies that build styrofoam topographic models using a router to cut and define the contour levels.

Computer Graphics. A number of computer programs now in existence permit the user to develop both two- and three-dimensional views of a given

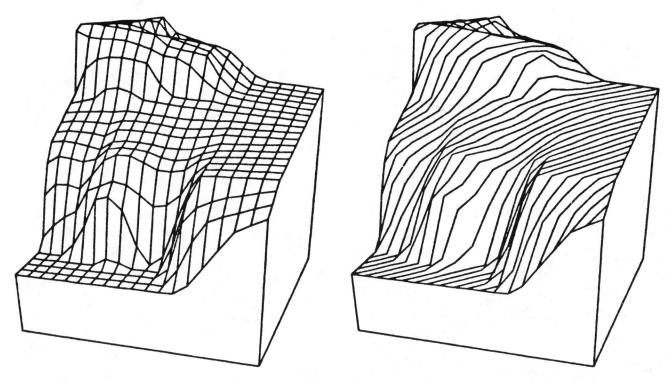

EXAMPLES OF COMPUTER GENERATED LANDFORM MODELS.

FIGURE 1.41

area of topography. Depending upon the program and the capabilities of the system, the output may be displayed on a terminal screen or printed as a "hard copy" on paper like that shown in Figure 1.41. The advantage of some computer graphic systems is that they permit the user to see the area of topography from a number of vantage points. The potential application of this procedure in terms of site grading is particularly exciting because it permits the designer to "see" the results of moving the contours in plan and to be able to evaluate and refine the proposal before it is actually constructed. Some more sophisticated computer graphic systems permit the viewer to "get down into" the design and "walk around." Again, the potential usefulness of such a procedure for the designer is limitless.

Ratio Method. In addition to the several graphic and models methods for representing landform, two mathematical techniques for expressing steepness of slope are also often used when designing exterior spaces. As the name implies, the ratio method defines slope steepness by means of a ratio between the horizontal distance and the vertical elevation change within the slope (4:1, 2:1, etc.). By conven-

tion, the first figure of the ratio represents the horizontal distance of the slope while the second figure (always reduced to a factor of one) represents the vertical elevation change, as illustrated in Figure 1.42. The ratio method is most usually applied to the slopes on a small-scale project site. The ratio method is also used to provide design standards and guidelines, some of which are outlined below.

- 2:1—absolute maximum slope allowed on a site without experiencing erosion. All 2:1 slopes should be covered with ground cover or other plant material to prevent erosion.
- 3:1—preferred maximum slope for most lawn and planting areas.
- 4:1—maximum slope maintainable with a lawn mower.

Percentage Method. The other mathematical means for portraying slope steepness is by percent. The percent of slope is obtained by dividing the vertical elevation change by the horizontal distance covered within the slope (vertical elevation change ÷ horizontal distance = percent of slope). A handy rule of

32

REMEMBER, RE-
DUCE VERTICAL
HEIGHT TO A FAC-
TOR OF 1.

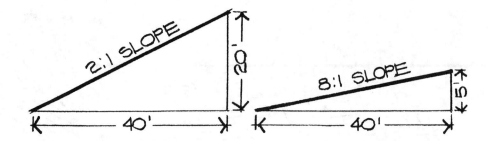

3:1 SLOPE SHOWN
BETWEEN ARROWS
(12' HORIZONTALLY,
4' VERTICALLY)

RATIO METHOD.

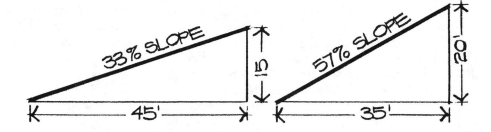

FIGURE 1.42

FIGURE 1.43

$$\frac{RISE}{RUN} = \% \text{ SLOPE}$$

$$\frac{15'}{45'} = .33 = 33\%$$

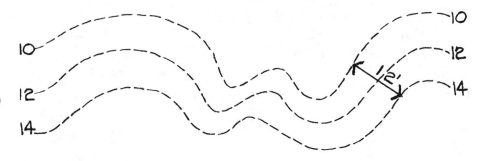

$$\frac{4'}{10'} = .40 = 40\%$$

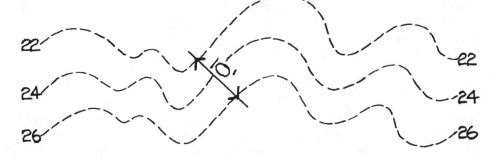

PERCENTAGE METHOD.

thumb for remembering this procedure is as follows: Rise over (divided by) run = percent of slope. For example, a slope that rises 10 vertical feet (3.05m) within 50 horizontal feet (15.25m) would be expressed as a 20% slope (10 ÷ 50 = 0.20, or 20%), as shown by Figure 1.43. Another means for understanding percent of slope is to equate the vertical elevation change to what it would be in 100 horizontal units of distance. For example, a slope that has an 8ft (or 8m) elevation change in 100ft (or 100m) horizontal distance is an 8% slope. The percent of slope should *not* be confused with the angle of the slope related to a horizontal plane.

Of the two mathematical methods for representing steepness of slope, the percentage method is the more widely used. As mentioned earlier, it is the common basis for developing a slope analysis map. Like the ratio method, the percentage method is also used to establish design standards and criteria.

0–1% Too flat This slope condition generally drains too poorly and is therefore considered undesirable for development of most exterior uses and functions except for wetland preserves. A 0–1% slope is typically best left as open space or a conservation area where occasional standing water will not cause any negative effects.

1–5% Flat This slope condition is considered ideal for many exterior spaces and functions. It provides the maximum flexibility for development and can accommodate massive site elements such as major buildings, parking lots, tennis courts, or athletic fields without causing grading problems. One potential drawback of this slope condition is that it may become visually monotonous by itself if it extends over too large an area. In addition, drainage in impervious soils may be a problem with this slope category at the flatter rate of slope. Within this range of slopes, some more specific standards are as follows:

1% slope: the suggested minimum slope for lawns and grass areas.[10]

2% slope: suggested maximum slope for grassed athletic fields.[11] This same slope is also considered the maximum for terrace and patio paving.[12]

3% slope: the point at which a slope in the ground's surface becomes obvious. Below 3%, the ground appears to be level.

5–10% This slope condition is also suitable for most types of land uses and functions though care must be taken in siting elements with respect to the direction and orientation of the slope. This slope condition offers the possibility of providing exciting level changes with walls and steps in more dense and urban developments. Drainage is generally good in this slope condition though uncontrolled drainage can cause erosion. A 10% slope is typically the suggested maximum for walks.[13]

10–15% Rolling This slope condition is considered too steep for many land uses and functions. Grading should be kept to a minimum to prevent problems of erosion. All major constructed elements should be sited parallel to the contours in order to minimize cut and fill and to blend in visually with the topography. This slope does provide a general outward orientation with potential views of the surrounding landscape from higher vantage points.

15%+ Steep Slopes above 15% are too steep for most land uses and functions. Environmental and monetary costs usually prohibit major development. However, sensitive and ingenious adaptation to this slope condition can create stunning architectural solutions and breathtaking views.

---

[10]Harlow C. Landphair and Fred Klatt, Jr., *Landscape Architecture Construction* (New York: Elsevier North Holland, 1979), p. 39.

[11]Ibid.
[12]Albe E. Munson, *Construction Design for Landscape Architects* (New York: McGraw-Hill, 1974), p. 31.
[13]Ibid.

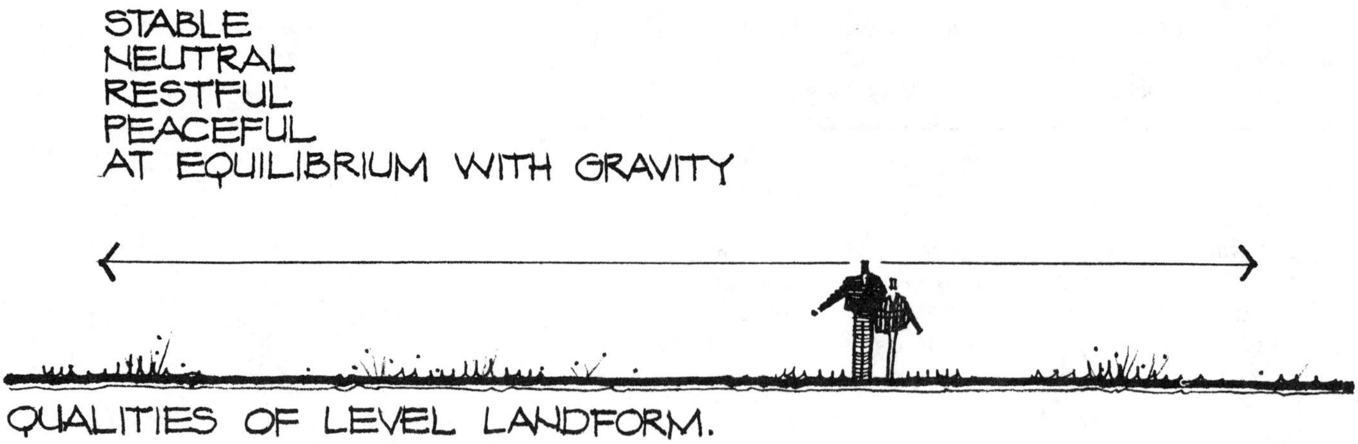

STABLE
NEUTRAL
RESTFUL
PEACEFUL
AT EQUILIBRIUM WITH GRAVITY

QUALITIES OF LEVEL LANDFORM.

FIGURE 1.44

Landform Types by Form

Landform may be categorized and studied in a number of different ways including scale, character, steepness, geological origin, and form. While each of these classifications of landform is a helpful aid in analyzing and understanding topography, form is one of the more important categories for landscape architects concerned with both the visual and functional qualities of the land. In terms of form, the landscape is a continuous composition of solid masses and open voids. The solids are the space defining elements (the landform itself), while the voids are the hollow areas created in between the solids. In the exterior environment, these solids and voids are to a large extent established by the various landform types outlined below: level, convex, ridge, concave, and valley. Although segmented for the purpose of discussion, these landform types are in actuality found side by side, blending into and reinforcing one another as previously shown in Figures 1.34 and 1.35.

Level Landform. Level landform is defined as any land area visually parallel to the plane of the horizon. While theoretically possible, there is no such entity as a perfectly level landform in the exterior environment because all ground has some degree of slope even if imperceptibly small. Consequently, the term "level landform" is used here to mean any landform that generally appears "level," even if it is slightly sloped or gently rolling. It should also be pointed out that some people distinguish "level" landform from "flat," although most lay people and

dictionary definitions use them as synonymous and interchangeable terms. For example, Webster's defines "flat" as "a level surface of land with little or no relief: PLAIN."[14] Yet in the most explicit sense, "level" means horizontal plane and "flat" means even or consistent plane.

Visually level landform may vary in scale from a small area on an individual site to the vast prairies and plains characteristic of such states as Illinois, Iowa, Kansas, and Florida. Despite scale, level landform has some unique visual and functional characteristics in comparison with other landform types. For instance, the level landform is the simplest and most stable of all. Because of its lack of any distinct elevational variation, the level landform is static, nonmoving, and in balance with the earth's gravitational forces (Figure 1.44). This landform has also achieved an equilibrium with geological influences of the earth. Because of this, a person feels comfortable and surefooted when standing on or walking across a level landform. A level area of ground provides an ideal location for people to stand and gather or sit and rest because no extra energy has to be expended to balance their weight against the pull of gravity. A person is not pulled to one side or another or confronted with a feeling of "falling over" when standing or sitting on relatively level ground. For the same reason, level areas are also choice sites for buildings. In fact, we typically attempt to artificially create level areas and terraces in sloping topography for the placement of buildings because of the stability established.

[14]*Webster's New Collegiate Dictionary*, 1977 ed., p. 437.

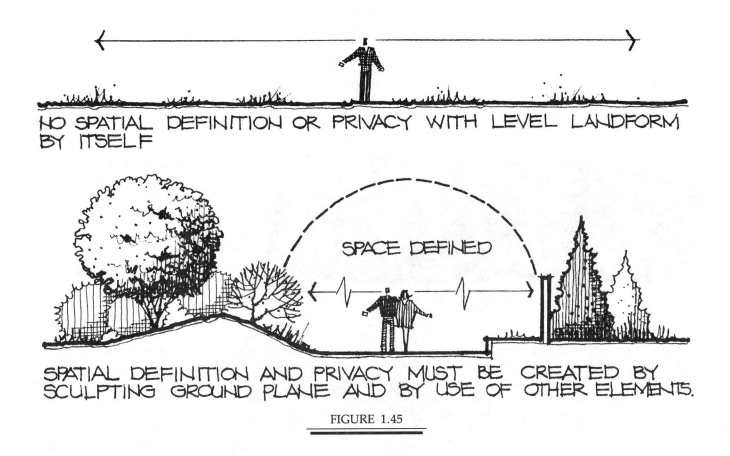

NO SPATIAL DEFINITION OR PRIVACY WITH LEVEL LANDFORM BY ITSELF

SPACE DEFINED

SPATIAL DEFINITION AND PRIVACY MUST BE CREATED BY SCULPTING GROUND PLANE AND BY USE OF OTHER ELEMENTS.

FIGURE 1.45

The lack of the third dimension of a level landform creates an open, spacious, exposed feeling, as suggested in Figure 1.45. There is no definition of enclosed space (though the sky and horizon line do act as implied spatial edges), no sense of privacy, no protection from objectionable sights and sounds, and no defense against sun and wind.[15] The ground plane itself must be altered and/or other design elements such as vegetation and walls must be added to the site to alleviate the problems associated with the lack of spatial definition (Figure 1.45).

Also owing to the openness of the level landform, views may extend uninterrupted for considerable distances (Figure 1.46). The horizon line, often the limit of vision, may take on great significance with its abstract silhouette character seen against the sky. These potentially long views may help establish a sense of unity on the level landform because most elements can be easily seen and visually related to one another. The long *allées* of the French Renaissance garden style, often arranged in the goosefoot pattern, were powerful visual connectors because

they were usually located on relatively level topography.

On a level landform, there is an innate emphasis on the horizontal; horizontal lines and forms are harmonious elements that fit comfortably into the environmental setting, as suggested in Figure 1.47. The "prairie house" architectural style of Frank Lloyd Wright utilized strong horizontal forms and lines in direct response to the level landscape of Illinois, Iowa, and Wisconsin. In addition to the use of horizontal lines, this architectural style often included pronounced roof overhangs to shade building walls in the visually level, open landscape.

In contrast to the horizontal, any vertical element that is introduced to a level landform has the potential of becoming a dominant element and focal point, as shown in Figure 1.48. It does not take much height to attract attention on an otherwise level area of ground. Again, driving through the Midwestern states, one's eye is easily drawn toward storage silos and church steeples of small farm communities. Even the limited height of overpasses and interchanges along the interstates causes them to stand out and be easily seen from far away.

---

[15]John O. Simonds, *Landscape Architecture*, p. 65.

FIGURE 1.46

The visual neutrality of the level landform allows it to be further characterized as peaceful and restful. This quality makes flat topography a very suitable setting for quiet, still, reflective sheets of water. The tranquil character of quiet water in turn enhances and reinforces the restful nature of the landform itself. In an opposite sense, the peaceful aspect of level landform allows it to serve as a setting or backdrop to the eye-catching use of other elements. Bold forms and colors can be placed on a flat site to take advantage of this quality as in the case of a sculpturelike piece of architecture. The tabletop quality of the level landform allows it to act as a stage for the theatrical focal point. The chateaux at Vaux-le-Vicomte and Versailles, for example, took on great visual prominence because they so easily stood out against the surrounding flat setting of the adjoining gardens. This quality was magnified to some extent by slightly elevating the ground floor of both chateaux above the garden levels themselves. Beyond this, the neutral quality of the level landform allows the ground surface to be sculpted into pleasant solids and voids. This is often desirable simply to add interest and relieve the monotony of an existing level landform.

In addition to being a neutral setting, the level landform can be described as multidirectional. As illustrated in Figure 1.49, it allows for equal choice of

FIGURE 1.47

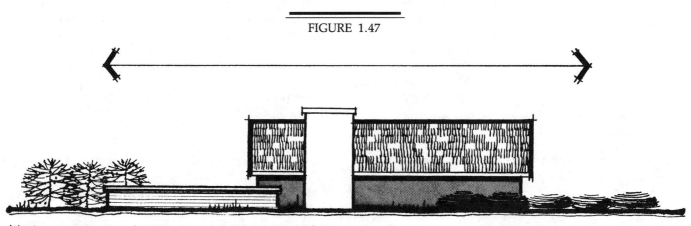

HORIZONTAL FORMS ARE AT HARMONY WITH LEVEL LANDFORM.

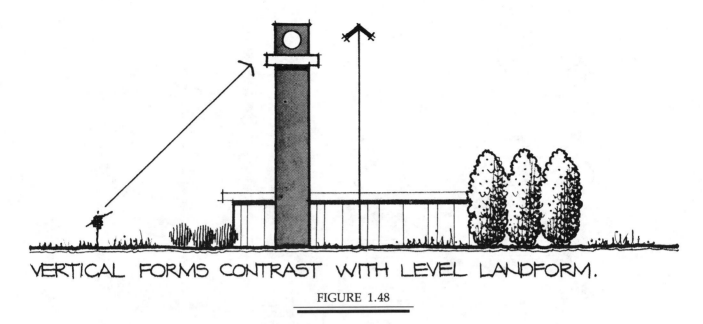

VERTICAL FORMS CONTRAST WITH LEVEL LANDFORM.

FIGURE 1.48

movement in all directions to and from a particular point. The ground plane of a level landform in and of itself offers few clues as to what direction of movement or layout orientation is correct. All possibilities are of equal validity based on the landform. Many landscape architects find it initially more difficult and challenging to design on a level landform than one that has more distinct slopes and elevation changes because the site permits so many design alternatives.

Because of this quality of level landforms, design forms and elements that are added to a level landform may easily and appropriately be spreading and multidirectional. Massive buildings or other sprawling elements such as parking lots or athletic fields can be located on level ground with minimal grading. Figure 1.50 graphically portrays the scale and layout of a multibuilding complex compatible with the level landform.

Similarly, abstract geometric, crystalline, or mod-

FIGURE 1.49

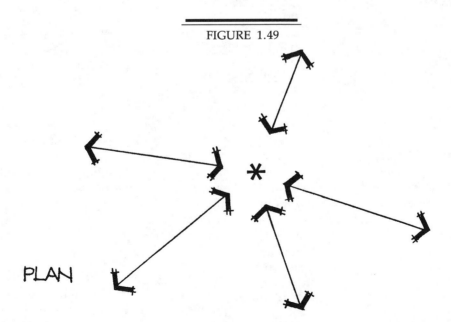

PLAN

LEVEL LANDFORM ALLOWS MULTIDIRECTIONAL DEVELOP-
MENT FROM A GIVEN POINT.

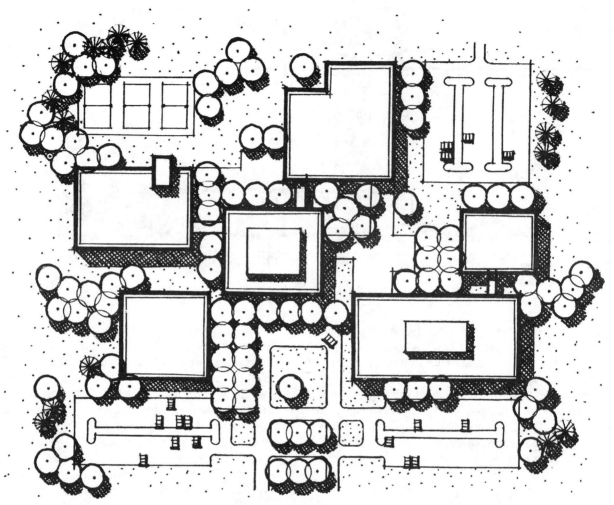

MASSIVE, SPREADING BUILDINGS, PARKING AREAS, AND REC-REATIONAL FACILITIES ARE BEST LOCATED ON LEVEL LANDFORM.

FIGURE 1.50

ular patterns that repeat themselves in a potentially endless fashion (Figure 1.51) are also appropriately located on level ground.[16] Again, the tabletop quality of the level landform permits the extension and repetition of patterns and modules to occur without limitation due to topography. And there exists a much greater sense of unity within a pattern on level land because the various parts can all be related to the whole. One example of strict geometrical patterns applied effectively to level landform is found in the use of parterres and other ground designs in French Renaissance gardens.

Another example is the building plan based on a module of a single unit such as might occur in a dormitory or office building that is then "stamped out" in a recurring manner across the landscape. All in all, level topography is a very flexible and practical type of landform with many potential visual and functional uses.

Convex Landform. The second basic landform type is the convex landform, best described as a high point of ground defined by a generally concentric arrangement of contours. Examples of convex landforms include knolls, knobs, buttes, and mountain or hill summits. A convex landform is a positive

---

[16]Ibid., p. 64.

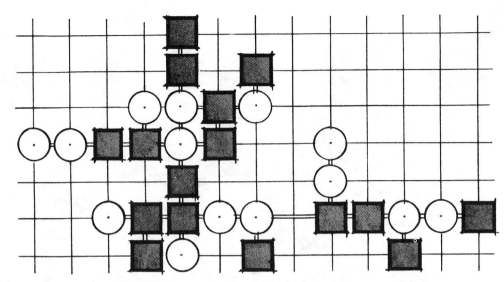

ABSTRACT, CRYSTALLINE, MODULAR PATTERNS ARE EASILY PLACED ON A LEVEL LANDFORM.

FIGURE 1.51

solid (mass) and a negative space (filled space). Compared with the flat landform, the convex landform is a dynamic, aggressive, exciting landform implying power and strength in defiance of gravity (Figure 1.52). Throughout history, the hilltop has held both military and psychological significance. An army that holds a strategic hilltop often controls the surrounding area as well (thus fostering the "king of the mountain" concept). Emotionally, having to "walk up to" something as compared with "down to" seems to create a greater feeling of reverence and respect for the object or person. Churches, government buildings, and other important structures are often placed on top of convex landforms to take advantage of this feeling of being "looked up to." Their symbolic importance is enhanced by this siting. The United States Capitol ("Capitol Hill"), the White House, and the Washington Monument are all sited on higher points of ground in relation to the mall that they adjoin.

FIGURE 1.52

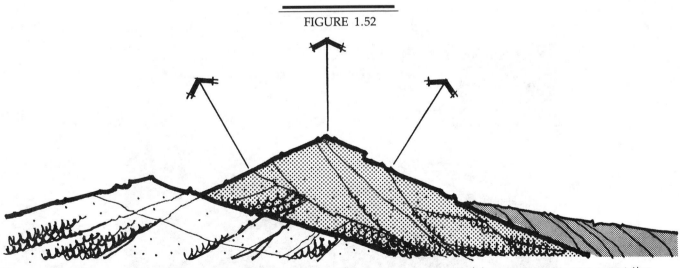

A CONVEX LANDFORM CAN SERVE AS A FOCAL POINT ON THE LANDSCAPE.

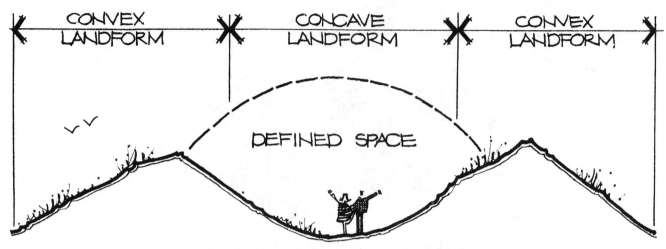

CONVEX LANDFORM   CONCAVE LANDFORM   CONVEX LANDFORM

DEFINED SPACE

TWO ADJOINING CONVEX LANDFORMS CREATE A CONCAVE LANDFORM.

FIGURE 1.53

The convex landform, while a negative space itself, does establish the edges for surrounding spaces by means of its side slopes. The slopes and crest of a convex landform establish the perceived limits of a space and control views into and from it (Figure 1.53). Generally speaking, the higher the summit of a convex landform and the steeper its side slopes, the stronger the definition of space (also see later sections of this chapter on the use of landform to define space).

As a positive point on the landscape, the convex landform has other aesthetic and functional characteristics as well. The convex landform can serve as a focal point or dominant element in the landscape, particularly when surrounded by lower, more neutral forms. Mt. Katahdin in Maine or Mt. Rainier in Washington (Figure 1.54) serve as exclamation points, captivating the viewer's attention. And owing to this property, a convex landform can also serve as a landmark for referencing one's position or

FIGURE 1.54

ELEMENTS LOCATED ON THE SUMMIT OF A CONVEX LANDFORM ACCENTUATE ITS HEIGHT.

FIGURE 1.55

movement in the landscape. A person's location can be determined by periodic glances to the prominent high point of ground.

The focal point quality of convex landforms can be enhanced by placing other elements such as buildings or trees on the summit, as illustrated in Figure 1.55. This adds height to the convex landform, making it more readily seen from the encircling environment and adding to its symbolic importance. A classic example of this is the placement of

Coit Tower on Telegraph Hill in San Francisco (Figure 1.56). Together, the tower and the higher point of ground function as a well-known landmark.

The height of a convex landform may also be accentuated by lines and forms that move straight up its sides to the summit perpendicular to the contours (Figure 1.57). Lines and forms that wrap around a convex landform parallel to the contours diminish the perceived height.

Another characteristic of the convex landform,

FIGURE 1.56

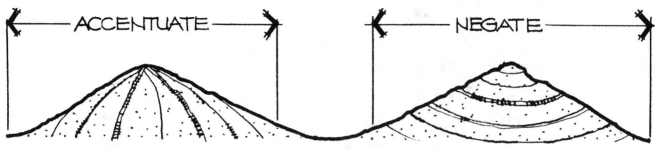

LINES/FORMS PERPENDICULAR TO CONTOURS ACCENTUATE CONVEX LANDFORM WHILE LINES/FORMS PARALLEL TO CONTOURS NEGATE IT.

FIGURE 1.57

shown in Figure 1.58, is that a person located on it will have a general feeling of outward orientation. Depending on relative height and slope steepness, definite and sometimes striking views are created outward and somewhat downward from the higher vantage point. Actually, more attention is often directed away from the vantage point (or site) to another point in the landscape than the point where one is standing. Consequently, convex landforms provide superior viewing areas from which to observe the surrounding environment. For this reason, they make excellent building sites. Higher points of ground in such hilly urban areas as Pittsburgh, Cincinnati, San Francisco, and Seattle have considerable real estate value and in some instances are legally regulated by zoning ordinances in an effort to preserve the views to and from these areas. The scenic overlooks along highways or fire towers in forested country are other examples that take advantage of views away from a higher point of ground. One example of the potential views from a convex landform is shown in Figure 1.59. Another example is the placement of mushroomlike platforms on Mt. Washington overlooking the city of Pittsburgh. These platforms take advantage of the outward orientation to provide breathtaking views of downtown Pittsburgh and the adjoining river valleys.

The convex landform also lends itself to the dynamic and exciting use of falling water. Falling water expresses the gravitational pull and movement down the slopes of a hill or mountain (see Chapter 6 on water). In nature, examples of dramatic falling water are found at such locations as Niagara Falls, Yosemite National Park, Yellowstone National Park,

FIGURE 1.58

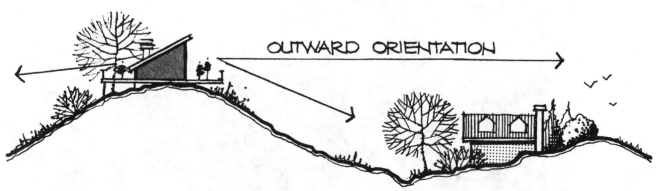

A CONVEX LANDFORM PROVIDES A SENSE OF OUTWARD ORIENTATION.

FIGURE 1.59

and numerous other locations throughout the United States. The use of water at Villa d'Este in Italy exemplifies the gravitational forces (and counterforces) of water falling from a high point of ground in an artificial setting.

Lastly, the convex landform is a topographic element that distinctly modifies microclimate in the exterior environment. As discussed earlier in this chapter, different slopes of a convex landform may have noticeable variations in sun and wind exposure because of their orientation. South- and southeast-facing slopes are favorable locations in the continental temperate climate zone because of their direct exposure to the sun in the winter. Conversely, north-facing slopes are undesirable sites for most development because they receive little if any direct sun in the winter, making them cold. In terms of wind, southeast slopes of a convex landform in the continental temperate zone are windiest in summer, while northwest-facing slopes are exposed to the coldest winter winds. In winter a convex landform blocks wind from the areas to the southeast of the high point, allowing them to be warmer and more energy efficient (Figure 1.60).

In summary, the convex landform is a visually strong element in the landscape with a number of

FIGURE 1.60

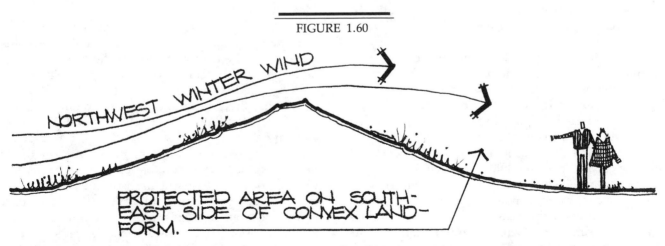

NORTHWEST WINTER WIND

PROTECTED AREA ON SOUTH-EAST SIDE OF CONVEX LAND-FORM.

CONVEX LANDFORMS CAN BE USED ON THE NORTHWEST SIDE OF A SPACE TO BLOCK COLD WINTER WIND.

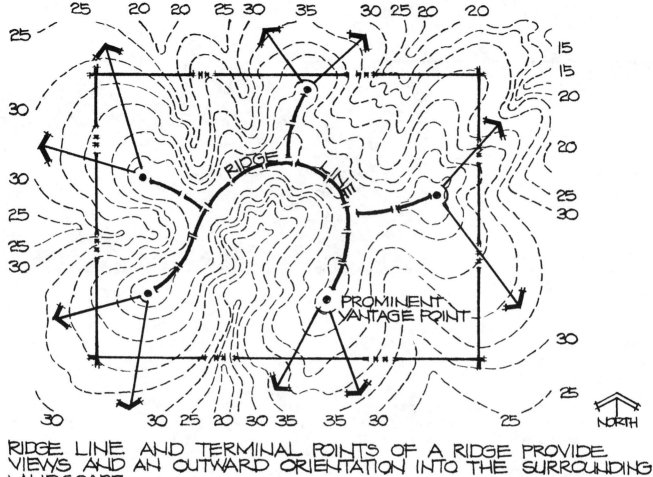

RIDGE LINE AND TERMINAL POINTS OF A RIDGE PROVIDE VIEWS AND AN OUTWARD ORIENTATION INTO THE SURROUNDING LANDSCAPE.

FIGURE 1.61

potentially exciting and dramatic uses. Because of its possible dominance, the convex landform must be used carefully and thoughtfully.

Ridge. A landform type similar to the convex landform is the ridge. A "ridge" is a high point of ground that is linear in its overall mass as compared with a convex landform that tends to be more compact and concentric. A ridge may be thought of as a "stretched out" version of a convex landform. Similar to the convex landform, a ridge defines edges of outdoor space and modifies microclimate on its slopes and in the surrounding environment. A ridge also provides vantage points that have a general feeling of outward orientation into the surrounding landscape. Although there are often many points along a ridge that furnish views, the ends or terminal points of a ridge are apt to give the most panoramic views in a wide angle of vision, as shown in

Figure 1.61. Such views often make these points ideal building sites.

Unique to the ridge is its directional quality and implication of movement. From a visual standpoint, a ridge has the ability to capture the eye and lead it along its length. Therefore ridges in the landscape may be used to move the eye through a series of spaces or direct it to specific focal points. From a functional standpoint, both vehicular and pedestrian circulation work most easily if they are located on top of or at least parallel to the ridge. Movement can be quite difficult if not impossible against or perpendicular to a ridge, particularly if the sides of the ridge are steep. Consequently, the ridge tops make logical locations for roads, paths, and other elements of circulation. And outward views plus positive drainage is provided in such locations as well. This concept, portrayed in Figure 1.62, is often utilized in the site planning of housing projects where the

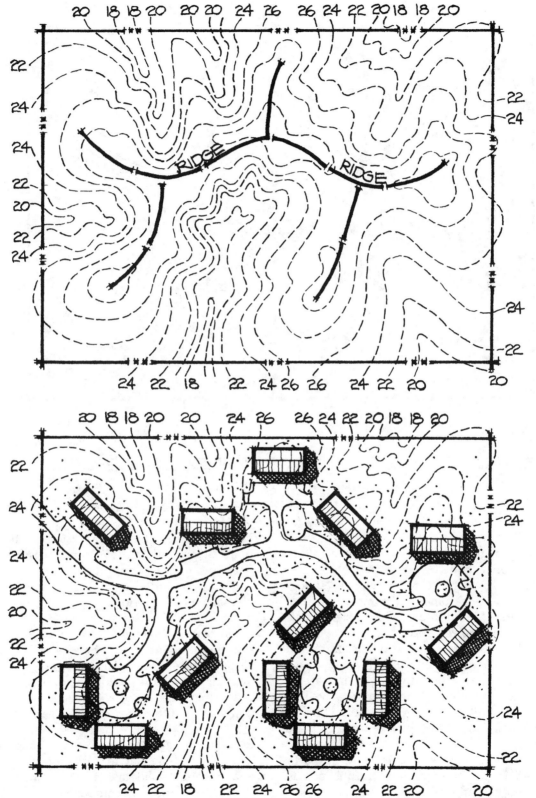

BUILDINGS, ROADS, AND PARKING ARE SITED IN A LINEAR MANNER ON TOP OF RIDGES.

FIGURE 1.62

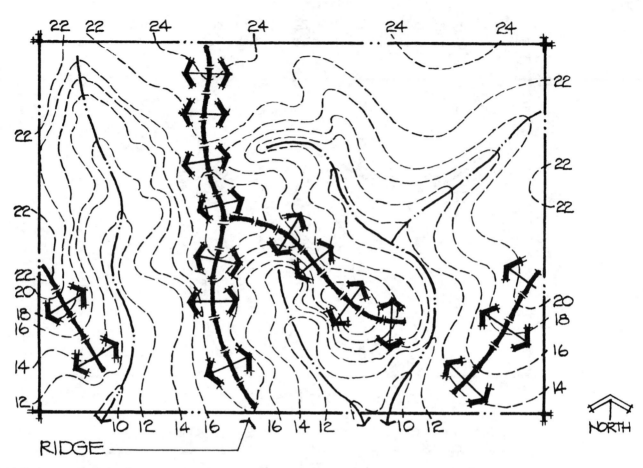

RIDGE

A RIDGE FUNCTIONS AS A WATERSHED DIVIDE.

FIGURE 1.63

roads, parking, and housing units are placed in a linear manner along the ridge tops while the valleys and swales in between are preserved as open space. This concept works very effectively with the topography while respecting some of the more sensitive areas of the site. As indicated here, design forms and structures themselves should also be proportionally long and narrow in layout when located on the top and side slopes of a ridge. Such an approach allows the design forms (buildings, parking areas, etc.) to blend in visually with the ridge as well as minimize the amount of cut and fill. Sprawling or multidirectional layouts are typically inappropriate for the ridge.

One other characteristic and use of the ridge in the exterior environment is that it often functions as a separator. As a spatial edge, the ridge acts as a wall dividing one space or valley from another. Boundaries around one region or site are often visually defined by the presence of a ridge, establish-

ing a feeling of "here" and "there." The linear high point of ground also functionally isolates one area from another. This may be an advantage when the land uses on either side of the ridge are incompatible. Conversely, a ridge may be an inconvenience if it separates two uses that would ideally work best when placed directly side by side. From a drainage standpoint, a ridge functions as a "watershed divide" (Figure 1.63). Water that falls on one side of the ridge top flows into one drainage basin while water that falls on the opposite side of the ridge flows into a different drainage basin.

Concave Landform. The concave landform can be defined as a bowllike depression in the landscape. It is a negative solid and positive space (void) that completes a landform composition when placed next to a convex form. A concave landform can be recognized in plan by contour lines that are concentric in their overall arrangement with the lowest num-

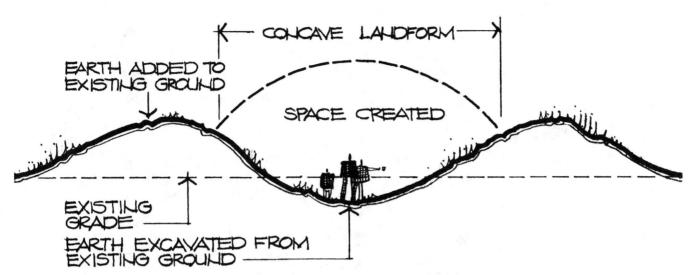

A METHOD FOR CREATING A CONCAVE LANDFORM FROM FLAT TO-POGRAPHY.

FIGURE 1.64

bered lines located near the center. A concave landform can be created when earth is excavated from an area of ground or when two convex landforms are situated next to each other, as shown in Figure 1.64. Concave landforms are the fundamental spaces of the landscape in which most of our activities are located. They are the basic, underlying structure of outdoor rooms. The degree of spatial enclosure in a concave landform depends upon the relative height and steepness of the surrounding slopes in relation to the width of the space.

The concave landform is an inward-oriented and self-centered space. It focuses the attention of anyone in the space toward its center or bottom floor. As portrayed in Figure 1.65, the concave landform produces a feeling of seclusion, isolation, refuge, confinement, privacy, and to some extent protection from the surrounding environment. The sense of security though is rather false because the concave landform is vulnerable from higher ground surrounding it. When in a concave form, one has a weak connection to other nearby spaces and func-

FIGURE 1.65

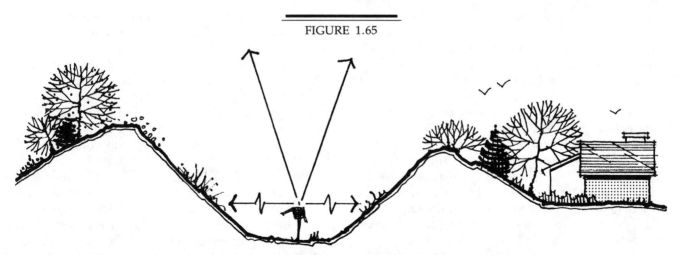

LATERAL VIEWS BLOCKED BY LANDFORM; A FEELING OF ISO-LATION AND PRIVACY RESULTS.

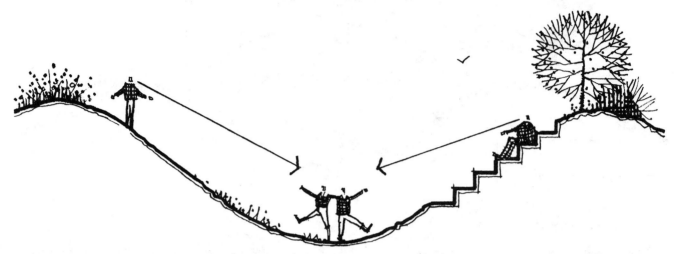

VIEWS DIRECTED INWARD AND DOWNWARD IN A CONCAVE
LANDFORM.

FIGURE 1.66

tions. One may not be able to see out from or beyond the outer rim of the convex landform to other areas of the landscape. Likewise, one may not be able physically to get out of the concave landform. Depending on the steepness of its sides, it may both figuratively and literally hold a person in its space.

The enclosure and inward orientation of a concave landform make it ideal for staging performances on its bottom floor where they can be viewed by observers on the side slopes of the space. The actor-audience relationship is handily adapted to the "fishbowl" quality of the concave landform (illustrated in Figure 1.66). For this reason, amphitheaters or other similar structures involving viewing audiences are logically located on sloped ground or in natural concave landforms. Rockefeller Center in New York City is a classic example of an urban concave landform, where ice skaters perform several levels below the street for the passersby and sightseers attracted to the area.

The concave landform has several other characteristics. It is protected from direct exposure to the wind that blows over the top of the space. And the concave landform is apt to act as a sun pocket where air temperatures are higher because of the direct exposure of the slopes to the sun. All in all, a concave landform is typically warmer and less windy than other sites in the same general region. While possessing a favorable microclimate, the concave land-

form has the disadvantage of being potentially wet, especially near its lower floor area. Precipitation that falls in a concave landform drains toward and collects in its depression unless some means is provided to catch and carry it out of the area. In fact, a concave landform can be thought of as a drainage basin or watershed within its own limits. Thus a concave landform has an additional potential use as a site for a permanent lake, pond, or retention basin that holds water temporarily after a storm.

Valley. The valley is the last landform type we discuss. It combines some of the characteristics of both the concave landform and the ridge previously outlined. Like the concave landform, the valley is a low area in the landscape that functions as positive space or room where many activities occur. But like the ridge, the valley is also linear and directional. It will be remembered from earlier paragraphs that a valley can be recognized in plan by contours that point uphill.

Because of its directional quality, the valley is also a suitable location for movement through the landscape. Many forms of primitive travel occurred along the valley floor or on streams or rivers of the valley owing to the relative ease of movement. Today, local roads and even interstate highways frequently wind through valleys for the same reasons Indian footpaths did. The difference, however, between placing

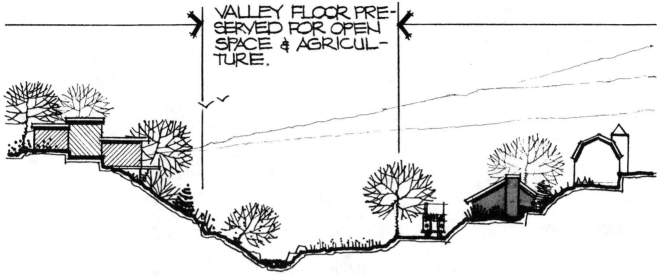

VALLEY FLOOR PRE-
SERVED FOR OPEN
SPACE & AGRICUL-
TURE.

WHEN POSSIBLE, VALLEY FLOOR SHOULD BE PRESERVED AS
OPEN SPACE; DEVELOPMENT SHOULD OCCUR ON VALLEY SIDES.

FIGURE 1.67

circulation in a valley as compared with on a ridge is that a valley is typically a sensitive ecological and hydrological area with the location of streams and rivers and associated floodplains. Likewise, the valley floor is often fertile ground and consequently the location of very productive agricultural land. Therefore more care is required in siting roads and development in a valley to avoid wet areas and the destruction of the sensitive ecology. Given an equal choice between locating roads and development in a valley or on a ridge, it is advisable in most cases to place these uses on the ridge, thus preserving the valley for more compatible land uses like agriculture, recreation, or conservation. If roads and development must be placed in the valley, then they should be located along the edges of the valley floor above the floodplain or on the valley sides as suggested in Figure 1.67. In these locations, structures and other design elements should generally be linear to fit the slope of the ground and reflect the directional quality of the valley.

Functional Uses of Landform

There are a number of functional and aesthetic uses of landform in the outdoor environment. Some are quite common and taken for granted while others are limited to special situations. Some uses of landform have already been alluded to in previous sec-

tions of this chapter. In all cases, the use of landform depends on the designer's skill and imagination. It should never be forgotten that what one does with the landform in a design ultimately affects all the other design elements placed on the ground. The various uses outlined on the next few pages have been separated for ease of description. However, many of these would occur simultaneously in a design.

Spatial Definition. Landform may be used to create and define exterior space by several different means. Space may be created by excavating into the existing base plane, filling (adding) earth and building up from the existing base plane, complementing existing convex landforms with added high points, or changing elevation to establish terraces or level variations. Most of these techniques are effective means for creating concave and valley landforms. When defining exterior spaces with landform, three variables are critical in influencing our perception of space: (1) the floor area of the space, (2) the steepness of the enclosing slopes, and (3) the horizon/silhouette line. These are graphically shown in Figure 1.68.

The floor area of the space is the bottom or base plane of the space and generally represents the "usable" area. It may appear as a distinct flat area or be more subtly defined, blending into and appearing to

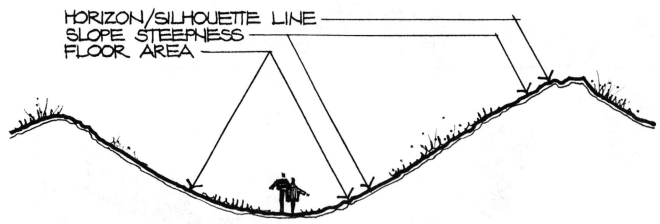

THREE VARIABLES OF LANDFORM AFFECTING SPATIAL PERCEPTION.

FIGURE 1.68

be part of the side slopes. Typically, the larger the floor area of a space, the larger the space is perceived to be.

The second variable affecting our sense of space created by landform is slope. Slope assumes the function of the vertical plane by acting as walls of an exterior space. As stated several times previously, the slope steepness has a bearing upon spatial definition: the steeper the slope, the more pronounced the delineation of space.

The horizon/silhouette line, the third variable influencing spatial perception, represents the edge between the perceived top of the landform and the sky. We read this line as being the upper edge of the slope, or rim of space, regardless of its size. Its position with respect to height and distance from the position of the viewer, as illustrated in Figure 1.69, affects views out of the space and the perceived spatial limits. The area seen within these limits is sometimes referred to as a "view shed." At the regional

FIGURE 1.69

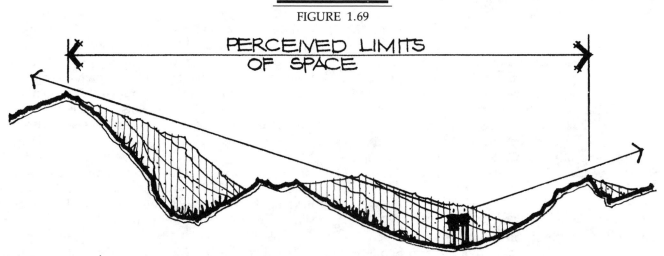

HORIZON/SILHOUETTE LINE DEFINES LIMITS OF SPACE.

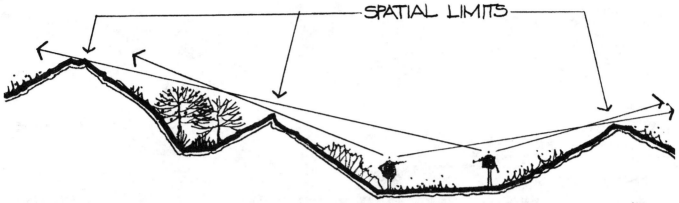

THE PERCEPTION OF SPACE AND ITS LIMITS CHANGES AS ONE MOVES FROM ONE LOCATION TO ANOTHER.

FIGURE 1.70

scale, the horizon/silhouette line may be defined by the ridge of the distant hills or mountains many miles away. This very large space may then be subdivided into smaller spaces in the more immediate foreground. Figure 1.70 shows that the horizon/silhouette line (and the related perception of space) is apt to change as one moves through and about a space. The space may seem to expand or contract depending on one's position in relation to the horizon/silhouette line.

All three variables (floor area, slope steepness, and horizon/silhouette line) interact simultaneously with one another to enclose space. The degree of enclosure perceived in any given space depends on the amount of area within the field of vision (the size of area seen with normal eyesight) filled by the floor

FIGURE 1.71

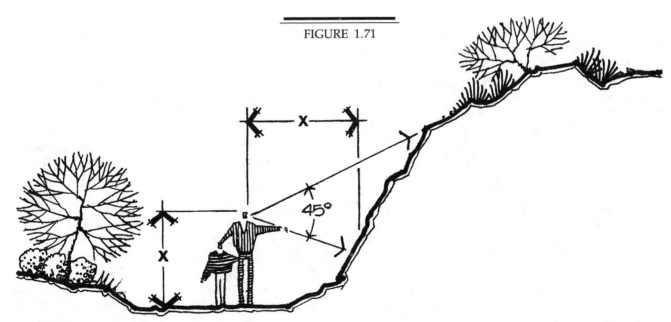

A SENSE OF FULL SPATIAL ENCLOSURE OCCURS WHEN A LANDFORM MASS FILLS A 45° CONE OF VISION.

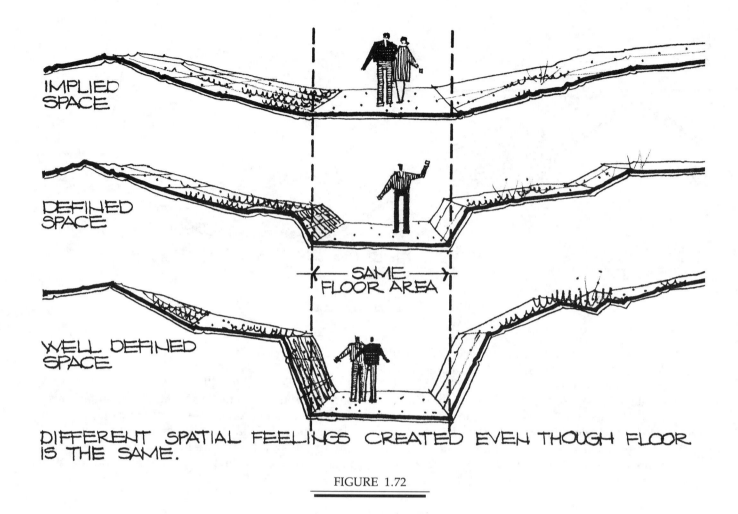

IMPLIED SPACE

DEFINED SPACE

SAME FLOOR AREA

WELL DEFINED SPACE

DIFFERENT SPATIAL FEELINGS CREATED EVEN THOUGH FLOOR IS THE SAME.

FIGURE 1.72

area, horizon/silhouette line, and slope. The normal field of vision spans a vertical angle of about 60 degrees with 40 degrees above the eye-level plane and 20 degrees below the eye-level plane.[17] The feeling of full enclosure illustrated in Figure 1.71 is gained when the combination of the three variables fills and/or extends beyond a 45-degree cone of vision (or creates a 1:1 distance to height ratio).[18] And only a minimum sense of enclosure occurs when the variables occupy an 18-degree field of vision.[19]

Using the variables of floor area, slope steepness, and horizon/silhouette line, the landscape architect can create an almost limitless variety of spatial experiences from an intimate space to a monumental one, or from a twisting linear valley space to a static, contained space. One may even mold different qualities of space by utilizing the variables in different combinations. For example, three vastly different spaces can be created by varying the slope and horizon/silhouette line while keeping the size of the floor area constant, as shown in Figure 1.72. Likewise, the character of the floor area itself may be changed to establish dissimilar qualities of space. As mentioned previously, a relatively level floor area provides a stable space while a sloped floor area creates an unstable space. A person feels uncomfortable having to stand too long in a space that has a tilted ground surface and is therefore encouraged to move on to another space or location. The one factor that cannot be affected by landform is the overhead plane. Unless a cave is formed (which is rare), landform is unable to manipulate what happens on the ceiling of an exterior space (other than influencing the amount of sky seen).

Landform cannot only define the edges of a space

[17]Yoshinobu Ashihara, *Exterior Design in Architecture*, rev. ed. (New York: Van Nostrand Reinhold, 1981), p. 42.
[18]Gary O. Robinette, *Plants, People and Environmental Quality* (Washington D.C.: U.S. Department of the Interior, National Park Service, 1972), p. 18.
[19]Ibid.

LANDFORM USED TO DIRECT VIEWS TO A DESIRED POINT IN THE LANDSCAPE.

FIGURE 1.73

but also its orientation. A space, like a liquid, tends to move toward areas of least resistance. Thus the general orientation of a space is toward open views. Using landform, a mass of high ground on one side and a mass of low ground on another produces a spatial orientation toward the lower, more open side and away from the higher ground. Figure 1.17 illustrated this point. Similarly, spatial orientation also tends to move downhill, like water, to lower ground. As a result, a space with a sloped floor area will orient and focus itself on the area of the lowest floor elevation.

In creating space or fulfilling other functions such as directing surface drainage or influencing movement, the ground's surface should not be graded to a slope steeper than 50 percent, or 2:1. A 2:1 slope is the commonly accepted absolute maximum slope for soil to be graded to. Slopes over 2:1 are highly susceptible to erosion unless stabilized with stone (riprap) or other hard, nonerodible material. Even a 2:1 slope is quite vulnerable to erosion and must be covered with ground cover and other plant material.

Control Views. As outlined earlier, landform, by filling the vertical plane, can direct views to specific points in the landscape, influence what and how much is seen at any given point (view shed), create sequential viewing or progressive realization, and completely block views from objectionable scenes. As with spatial orientation, views are directed along lines of least resistance toward open spaces. To en-

frame views to a particular focal point in the environment, as illustrated in Figure 1.73 landform can be built up on one or both sides of the sight line. The higher ground on either side of the sight line acts as blinders blocking out any distractions while concentrating attention on the focal point itself.

Landform may be used to "show off" or exhibit a particular object or scene as well. Objects placed on a high point of ground or summit are of course easily seen from potentially great distances. Likewise, objects or areas located on the side slopes of a valley or ridge are also readily seen from lower areas in the valley or slopes on the opposite facing side of the valley (Figure 1.74). The steeper the slopes, the more they become like vertical walls and the more they directly stop and capture the line of sight. One example where this concept is sometimes applied is in a zoo where a particular animal exhibit is placed on a side slope so it can be more easily and completely seen. Another similar use of landform is to create a series of vantage points from which to view an object or space. Each vantage point can be so located as to provide a new or different perspective of the object being viewed.

A related use of landform is to establish spatial sequences that alternately reveal and hide views of objects or scenes. This concept is referred to as "sequential viewing" or "progressive realization."[20] As

---

[20]Ibid., p. 30.

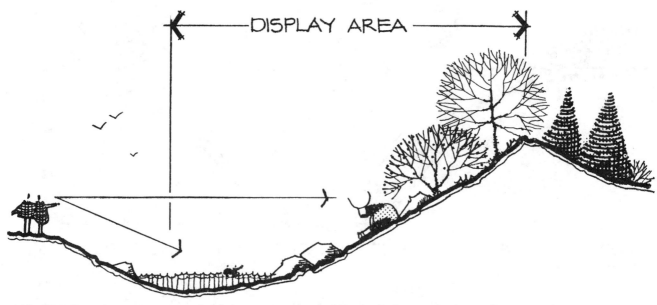

TILTED SLOPE IS ABLE TO EASILY DISPLAY THE ELEMENTS ON IT TO VIEWERS.

FIGURE 1.74

illustrated in Figure 1.75, a sense of anticipation and curiosity can be created when one sees only a portion of an object. The viewer is teased by liking the partial view of the object but nevertheless being unable to observe the whole thing. When this occurs, the viewer is encouraged to move toward the object with the hope of seeing more of it. This concept can be taken one step further by using landform to create a sequence of changing views as one moves toward an object. As one possibility, shown in the top half of Figure 1.76, an attractive object at the top of a hill may at first be seen from the valley floor. Then

as one moves toward the object and up the hill, the object is next hidden, then revealed, then hidden for a second time, and finally revealed in its entirety as one arrives at the top. In other situations the crest of a slope, illustrated in the bottom half of Figure 1.76, can hide an object at the toe of the slope from the more distant vantage points on top of the high point. But the same object can be suddenly exposed as the viewer moves toward the crest. This same concept is also shown in Figures 1.77 and 1.78. In Figure 1.77, the view is focused on the distant terminus of the axis while views to the area just below

FIGURE 1.75

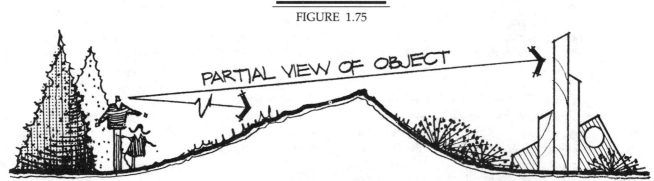

EARTH MOUND PARTIALLY CONCEALS ATTRACTIVE OBJECT AND THEREFORE ESTABLISHES A FEELING OF ANTICIPATION.

LANDFORM CREATES SEQUENCE OF REVEALING & CONCEALING FOCAL POINT AS ONE MOVES TOWARD IT.

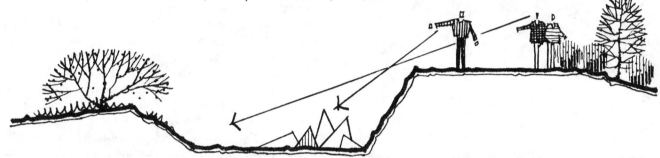

FROM A DISTANCE, CREST HIDES FOCAL POINT; AS ONE MOVES TOWARD EDGE, FOCAL POINT IS REVEALED.

FIGURE 1.76

FIGURE 1.77

FIGURE 1.78

viewer's position with respect to the landform configuration has influenced what is or is not seen.

In an opposite fashion, landform may be built up in the form of earth mounds or berms to screen out displeasing objects or scenes (Figure 1.79). This approach is common along roads, parking areas, and commercial establishments to block undesirable views of cars, service areas, and storage. This use of landform is most applicable where space permits the slope to be graded to the desirable steepness. It will be recalled from earlier sections of this chapter that earth should be graded only to a 4:1 slope if it is to be covered with turf and mowed with a lawn mower. With this criterion, it would be necessary to have an area at least 40 ft (12.2m) wide to accommodate an earth mound 5 ft (1.525m) in height (20 ft (6.1m) needed per side at 4:1). Less space would be required if the slope were steeper. Consequently, if space is limited, some means for screening bad views other than earth mounds should be utilized.

As already indicated, the crest of a slope itself can screen views of objectionable objects located at the toe of the slope for vantage points on top of the hill (Figure 1.80). Such a technique could be used to hide roads, parking lots, or service areas in a park setting while maintaining desirable views to more distant portions of the landscape. A similar method was used in the English landscape garden style to hide walls and fences. In pastoral landscapes, walls referred to as "ha-ha walls" were placed below the slope crests in valleys and depressions so that they could not be seen from certain vantage points, as illustrated in Figure 1.81. The result was a view of the pastureland as a continuous and flowing unit, uninterrupted by walls or fences.

the wall on the opposite side are blocked. As one moves forward toward the wall, a new view previously unseen (Figure 1.78), is revealed showing a small herb garden and brick terrace. Again, the

FIGURE 1.79

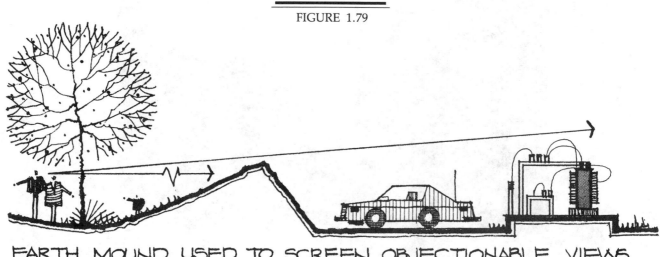

EARTH MOUND USED TO SCREEN OBJECTIONABLE VIEWS.

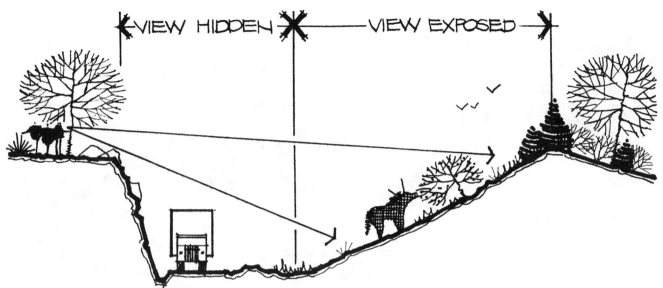

CREST OF SLOPE USED TO SCREEN OBJECTIONABLE VIEW AT ITS BASE.

FIGURE 1.80

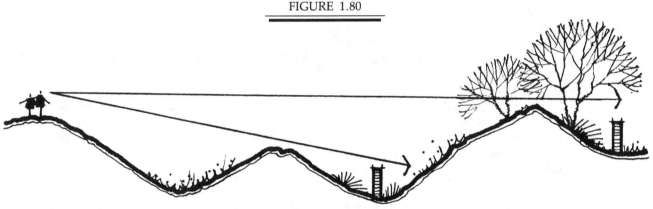

HA-HA WALL CONCEPT : WALLS/FENCES PLACED IN VALLEYS AND DEPRESSIONS TO HIDE THEM FROM VIEW.

FIGURE 1.81

A term that has significance for views and the location of elements in the landscape is the "military crest."[21] The military crest illustrated in Figure 1.82 is the point near the top of a slope or brow from which the entire slope below can be seen. This strategic vantage point has historically been vital for an army's control and defense of the high point and surrounding countryside (hence its name). The military crest is also a desirable building location because of the views it affords. It provides clear views of the immediate slope in the foreground as well as

more distant views to the middle ground and background. Furthermore, the military crest is an important point for locating structures that visually blend in with the landform. When an object is placed on the summit of a convex landform (Figure 1.83), it is easily seen as a silhouette against the sky and is more exposed to the wind. This same object located down slope from the summit near or just below the military crest tends to blend in visually with the landform if the summit remains silhouetted against the sky. The summit and slope above the object then serve as a backdrop to the object, "absorbing" its outline and protecting the object against the wind. This concept is not only the key to siting buildings

[21]Kevin Lynch, *Site Planning*, 2nd ed. (Cambridge: M.I.T. Press, 1971), p. 50.

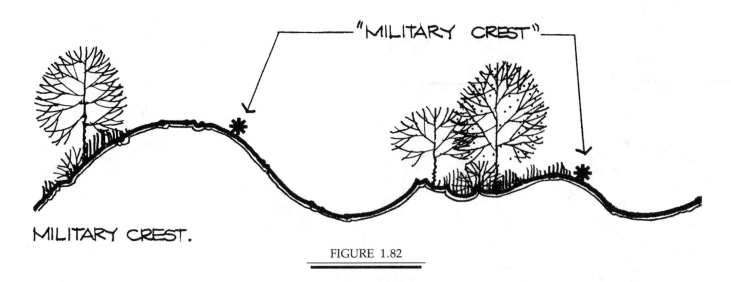

"MILITARY CREST"

MILITARY CREST.

FIGURE 1.82

but should also be considered in the location of other elements such as roads and high-power transmission lines.

Influence Movement. Landform may be used in the exterior environment to influence the direction, speed, and rhythm of both pedestrian and vehicular movement. As suggested previously, the configuration of the ground's surface has a direct bearing on where and how we move through the landscape. Typically, circulation follows paths of least resistance, which in terms of topography are usually relatively level flat areas devoid of any obstacles. Here, minimum energy expenditure is necessary to walk in a surefooted, uninterrupted manner. Thus an ideal

location for roads and paths is on the level landform, along the valley floor, or on top of the ridge, as suggested previously. The level landform of course permits the greatest degree of flexibility in movement.

As slope of the ground surface increases and/or more obstacles occur, movement becomes more difficult. More physical energy must be used to get up and down slopes; consequently more travel time is required and sometimes frequent stops are necessary to rest. For walking, each step needs to be more carefully placed when going up or down a slope, and our sense of balance is disrupted on sloped ground. The result of all this is that circulation across sloped surfaces should be minimized and, when feasible, not allowed to exceed 10 percent in

FIGURE 1.83

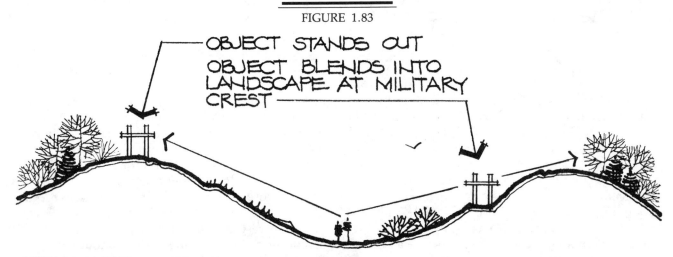

OBJECT STANDS OUT

OBJECT BLENDS INTO LANDSCAPE AT MILITARY CREST

STRUCTURES SHOULD BE PLACED ON MILITARY CREST, NOT SUMMIT IF THEY ARE TO BLEND INTO LANDSCAPE.

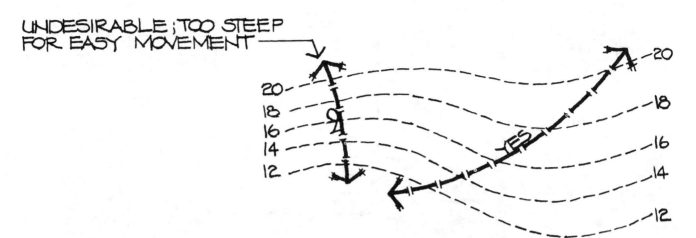

WHEN FEASIBLE, CIRCULATION SHOULD OCCUR PARALLEL OR ASKEW TO CONTOURS, NOT PERPENDICULAR.

FIGURE 1.84

the cases of pedestrian movement. If movement is required up or down a steeper area of ground than this, as in Figure 1.84, it should occur askew to the contours, not perpendicular to them, to minimize path steepness. When there is a need to cross a ridgelike landform, it is easiest to do so by moving through a "gap" or "saddle" if one is present (Figure 1.85).

Another application of these principles is to affect

the rate of movement in a design as illustrated in Figure 1.86. If the intent in a portion of a design is to permit people to move quickly through an area, a level ground area should be used. If, on the other hand, the objective is to make the user walk more slowly through a space, sloped surfaces or changes in elevation between a series of levels should be applied. And where it is intended to have people stop their movement altogether, a level ground area

FIGURE 1.85

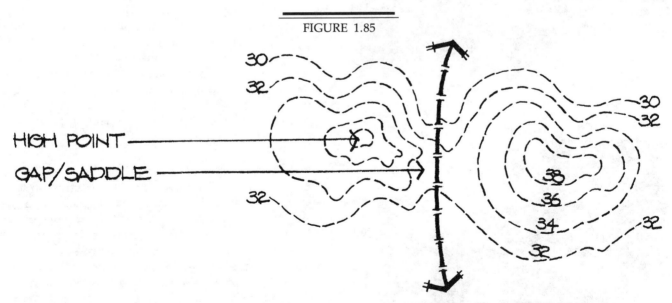

TO CROSS A RIDGE, CIRCULATION IS EASIEST THROUGH A GAP OR SADDLE.

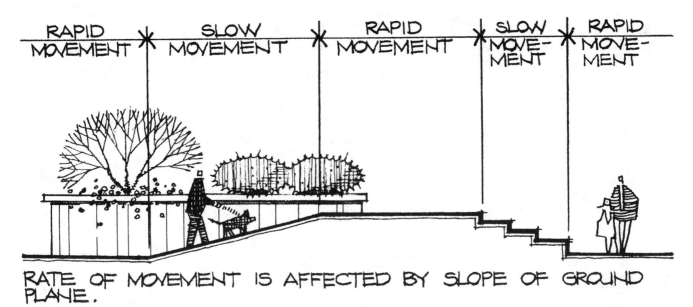

RAPID MOVEMENT | SLOW MOVEMENT | RAPID MOVEMENT | SLOW MOVEMENT | RAPID MOVEMENT

RATE OF MOVEMENT IS AFFECTED BY SLOPE OF GROUND PLANE.

FIGURE 1.86

FIGURE 1.87

FIGURE 1.88

should again be utilized. Athena Tacha, an artist who teaches at Oberlin College, utilizes landform in her environmental sculpture as a means of directly influencing the regularity, speed, and direction of walking in her designs.[22]

Landform in the form of slopes and earth mounds can be used as obstacles or barriers, forcing movement around them and through the valleylike spaces. The degree of control and containment may vary with the situation from subtle to well-defined regulation, depending on the steepness of the defining slopes. Earth mounds and slopes have direct application in large open spaces where there is a large volume of pedestrian traffic moving through them such as in shopping malls or college campuses. Two examples of landform used in this manner are shown in Figures 1.87 and 1.88.

Affect Microclimate. Landform can be used in the landscape to modify microclimate. In terms of sun, south-facing sloped surfaces can be used or artificially created to establish areas that receive direct winter sun with resulting warmer surface and air temperatures (Figure 1.19). Similarly, sun pockets with a southern orientation can be created with landform to provide spaces that are warmer and more enjoyably used for longer periods of the year.

---

[22]Athena Tacha, "Rhythm as Form," *Landscape Architecture* 68 (3):196 (May 1978).

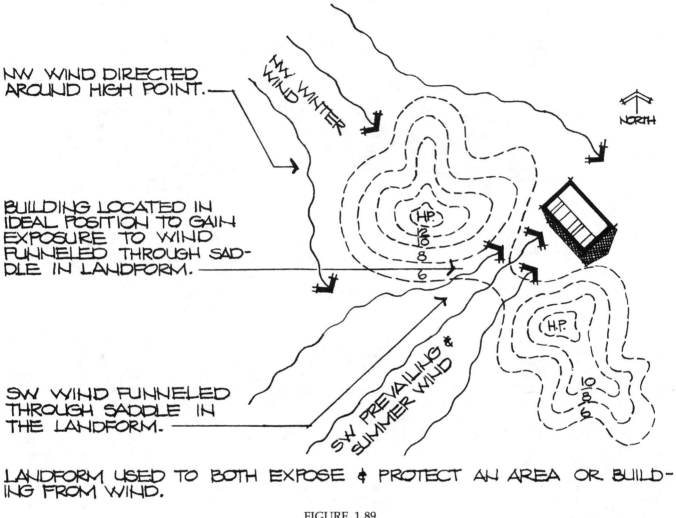

NW WIND DIRECTED AROUND HIGH POINT.

NW WIND WINTER

NORTH

BUILDING LOCATED IN IDEAL POSITION TO GAIN EXPOSURE TO WIND FUNNELED THROUGH SADDLE IN LANDFORM.

H.P. 12 10 8 6

H.P. 10 8 6

SW WIND FUNNELED THROUGH SADDLE IN THE LANDFORM.

SW PREVAILING & SUMMER WIND

LANDFORM USED TO BOTH EXPOSE & PROTECT AN AREA OR BUILDING FROM WIND.

FIGURE 1.89

In terms of wind, landforms such as convex forms, ridges, or earth mounds can be used to block cold winds from a site during the winter season (Figure 1.60). To do this, the earth should be built up on the sides of the site or use area facing the winter winds. In the continental temperate climate zone of the United States, for example, this generally is on the west and north sides of a space. A similar function of landform is to build up earth along the north and west sides of a building wall. The earth here functions as an additional layer of insulation that reduces heat loss and infiltration of cold air. In contrast, landform may be used to capture and channel the wind in the summer months. Wind can be channeled through a valley or low, saddlelike space between two high points (Figure 1.89). If this valley or low point is oriented on a southwest-northeast axis

and is then situated on the southwest side of a space in the temperate climate zone of the United States, then the southwest summer wind can be funneled into the outdoor space. Different orientations of this opening will be required in other climatic regions. The wind that flows through this type of opening is apt to be intensified because of the effects of funneling and consequently causes a greater cooling effect.

Aesthetic Uses. Finally, landform can be used as a compositional and visual element. Earth for the most part is a plastic medium with the capability of being sculpted into aesthetically pleasing solids and voids of almost any character. Earth is quite similar to clay with its pliable qualities, allowing it to be pushed and pulled to create a desired form. In the landscape, anything from a pick and shovel to huge

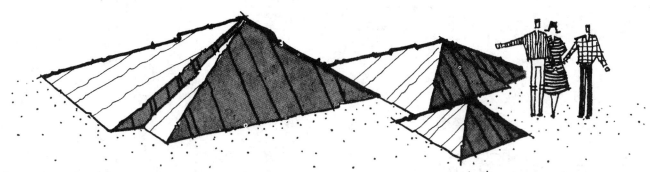

LANDFORM MAY BE USED AS A SCULPTURAL ELEMENT WITH STRIKING PATTERNS OF LIGHT AND SHADE.

FIGURE 1.90

earthmovers and bulldozers can be used to artistically excavate, push, or fill earth in designs varying in scale from a small, enclosed condominium garden to a site thousands of acres in size.

The potential visual qualities of landform are numerous. As soil, landform can be shaped into soft, sensuous forms that can easily capture the eye and move it through the landscape. With rock and concrete, landform can be molded into hard forms with well-defined edges and planes. Each of these uses of landform suggests a design with distinctly different visual qualities and feelings.

Landform not only has the ability to be shaped in a variety of ways but may also produce different visual effects under the influence of light and climate. The way sunlight strikes a particular ground form and the pattern of shade produced are apt to be a delight in themselves (Figure 1.90). And of course these factors change throughout the day as well as from one season to another. The visual effects of rain and snow also modify the appearance of landforms.

The molding of the earth's surface, while always a basis for landscape architectural design and an integral part of the functions previously discussed, can be thought of as a pure art form in its own right as well. Sometimes referred to as "site sculpture," "earth art," or "earth works," this artistic endeavor attempts to create works of art by molding landform in the exterior environment just as a sculptor models a piece of clay. Such artists as Robert Smithson, Robert Morris, and Athena Tacha, and French landscape

architect Jacques Simon have used landform both in its soft, natural state and in its hard, manmade state to create "environmental sculptures" of different scales and characters. Athena Tacha has used landform in her designs as an expression of rhythm and time through twisting and stepping ground forms. Her objective is to involve people in her designs by using landform to directly influence how people use and move through the design.[23]

In 1979, King County (Seattle) in the state of Washington sponsored an International Earthwork Sculpture Symposium to focus on the potential of reclaiming strip mines, gravel pits, mining heaps, barrow pits, and other earth disturbances as works of earth sculpture. As a related effort, a number of artists were commissioned to prepare design solutions for gravel pits in the greater Seattle area. Other examples can also be cited for other artists and areas of the country.

Edward Bye and Lawrence Halprin are two landscape architects among many who have employed landform as an integral sculptural element in their designs. For one Long Island estate project, Bye molded a large open lawn area into subtle, rolling undulations to reflect the rolling English countryside near Salisbury.[24] This landscape is not only appealing in the summer but also during the winter

---

[23]Ibid., pp. 196–198.
[24]A. E. Bye, "Shifting Subsoil by Grader and Bulldozer Recreates the Contours of Salisbury Plain," *Landscape Architecture* 59 (4): 278–280 (July 1969).

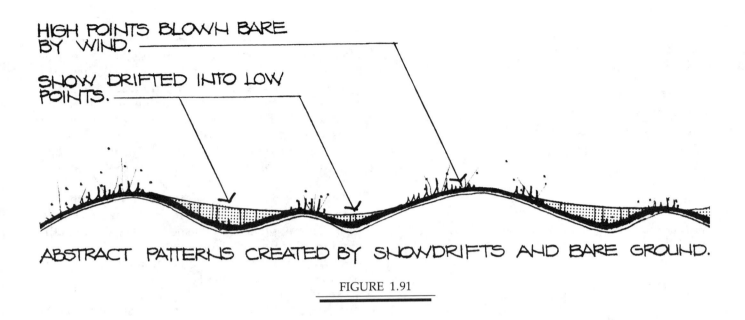

HIGH POINTS BLOWN BARE BY WIND.

SNOW DRIFTED INTO LOW POINTS.

ABSTRACT PATTERNS CREATED BY SNOWDRIFTS AND BARE GROUND.

FIGURE 1.91

months when abstract patterns of exposed summits and snow-filled swales are created in the lawn area by the interaction of sun and wind (Figure 1.91). Lawrence Halprin is noted for the use of water and bold, sculptural fountain forms. Halprin has spent numerous hours observing rock and land formations, especially in the High Sierras, and has been able to abstract these into hard, manmade landforms in some of his designs. The Lovejoy Plaza and the Auditorium Forecourt, both in Portland, Oregon, and the plaza in Manhatten Square Park in Roches-

ter, New York, are examples of Halprin's use of dramatic abstract landforms. In each, the ground plane has been stepped in a manner resembling cut contour lines of a model to establish striking forms and patterns.

When aesthetically shaping landform, a number of principles should be kept in mind. First, the landform should have a harmonious character with the overall appearance of the site and region. A hard-edged landform, for example, would not be compatible in a setting of rolling hills and gentle slopes. The

FIGURE 1.92

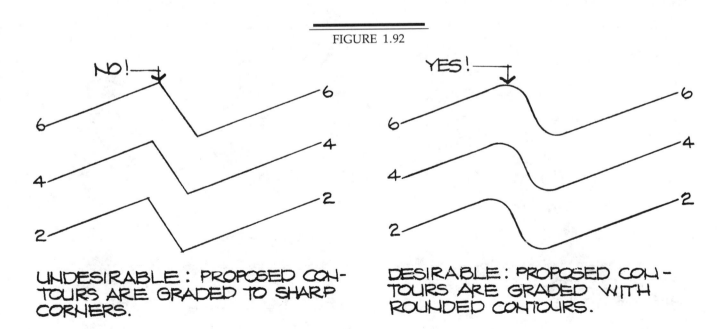

NO!

6

4

2

6

4

2

UNDESIRABLE: PROPOSED CONTOURS ARE GRADED TO SHARP CORNERS.

YES!

6

4

2

6

4

2

DESIRABLE: PROPOSED CONTOURS ARE GRADED WITH ROUNDED CONTOURS.

UNDESIRABLE: TOP OF MOUND
HAS BEEN GRADED TO A
SHARP POINT.

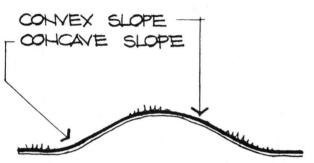

CONVEX SLOPE
CONCAVE SLOPE

DESIRABLE: TOP & SIDES OF
MOUND ARE ROUNDED TO BLEND
INTO EXISTING PLANES.

FIGURE 1.93

new or graded landform should look as if it "belongs." This is especially critical when blending slopes and earth mounds into an existing slope. Unless it is intended, sharp points or edges between planes should be avoided when grading with soil by itself. This is often effectively accomplished in plan by rounding the intersections or corners of contour lines when they change direction, as shown in Figure 1.92. In section, the top or crest of the slope should be shaped into a convex slope (not to be confused with a convex landform), while the toe should be graded into a concave slope (again, not to be confused with a concave landform), as shown in Figure 1.93. This approach establishes a visually smooth, comfortable transition from one plane or slope to another. Likewise, earth mounds should not be graded to a too pointed summit. This looks awkward and is susceptible to erosion. Earth mounds should also not be applied to a site like lumps of clay on a tabletop or snakes twisting through the site. Berms should seem to be an integral part of the site, not some applied afterthought. This can be accomplished by blending the slopes of mounds to the other ground planes as suggested previously and by visually linking the earth mounds and high points with one another so they "flow together."

Another suggestion for shaping the ground plane is to create strong, clean forms. The landform should

FIGURE 1.94

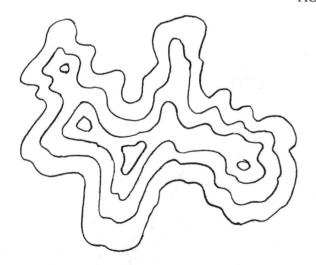

UNDESIRABLE: FORMS CRE-
ATED BY CONTOUR LINES
ARE "BUSY" & WEAK.

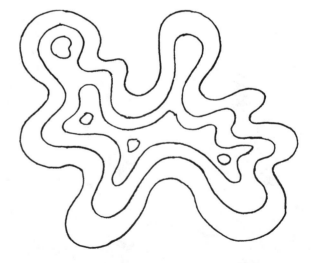

DESIRABLE: FORMS CREAT-
ED BY CONTOUR LINES ARE
STRONG & FULL-CURVED.

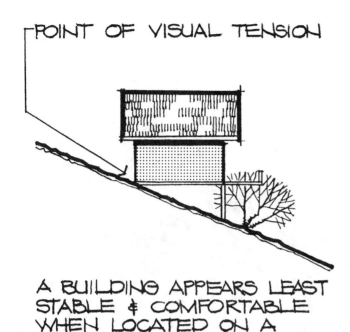

POINT OF VISUAL TENSION

A BUILDING APPEARS LEAST STABLE & COMFORTABLE WHEN LOCATED ON A SLOPED SITE.

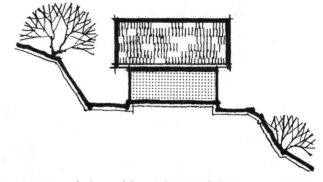

A BUILDING APPEARS MOST STABLE & COMFORTABLE WHEN LOCATED ON A PORTION OF LEVEL GROUND.

FIGURE 1.95

not become too busy or lumpy. For a naturalistic scheme, the contours should be formed into strong curves that echo one another as they move up and down the slope, as illustrated in Figure 1.94. For a scheme with definite planes, the contour lines should be straight and parallel to one another. Any wiggles or bumps should be eliminated. Generally the same basic design principles that apply to other media apply to the grading of landform as well.

Landform has other aesthetic functions beyond its use as the sole compositional element in a design. In some situations landform can serve as an integral element in a piece of architecture by extending planes of the building into the landscape or by serving as a ground element for the building to relate to. As an element of structural support, the ground plane may be flat, rolling, sloped, or mounded to create a pedestal for the building to rest on. Of all these options, the one that makes a building appear most stable and strongly connected to the site is the level terraced site (Figure 1.95). A building looks least comfortable when sited on sloped or rolling topography. Here, points of uneasy tension are created between the building and the site. Likewise, the building may appear about to tip over or fall down if it has a precarious visual connection to the surrounding base plane. This concern for the visual relation between building and supporting landform has changed from one era to another. Capability Brown, best known for his imitation of naturalistic and pastoral landscapes, has been criticized by some authors because of the lack of straight lines or level planes immediately adjacent to the homes and buildings in his designs.[25]

Summary

Landform is a very significant element in the exterior environment. It influences the aesthetic character of outdoor spaces, spatial perception, views, drainage, microclimate, and land use organization. Because of its importance and the fact that all other elements in the landscape rest on the ground plane, it is one of the first considerations in the evolution of a design. How landscape architects shape landform affects the appearance and function of buildings, plant material, pavement, water, and walls.

[25]Norman Newton, *Design on the Land* (Cambridge: Belknap Press of Harvard University Press, 1971), pp. 212–214.

2

Plant Materials

Significance

Plant materials are another extremely important physical element in the design and management of the outdoor environment. Along with landform and buildings, plant materials constitute the major components used by landscape architects in most projects to organize space and solve problems. And beyond serving essentially practical roles as structural elements of a design, plant materials provide a touch of life and beauty in an environment. This chapter focuses upon a number of factors related to the use of plant materials in the landscape including unique characteristics, functional uses, architectural and space-defining functions, visual characteristics, and aesthetic uses along with a suggested process for designing with plants in the evolution of a design solution.

The term "plant material" is used in this chapter to represent native and cultivated woody plants of all types, from ground cover to trees. With only a few exceptions, herbaceous plants and annuals are not included in the discussion, even though they too are important elements in some types of settings. Woody plants themselves are extremely diverse in size, form, color, texture, and overall character. They are potentially one of the most varied elements of all in the landscape with infinite possible functions resulting.

Despite the numerous potential functions of plant material, many lay people and design professionals think exclusively of plant material as decoration. As a result, plants are often placed in the design of an outdoor space as a final step in the completion of a project. Foundation planting around the base of homes and small commercial buildings is one example of this narrow, uneducated approach. Foundation planting is typically added to a building as an afterthought to the building's design in order to "dress it up." Today, foundation planting is nothing more than an outdated practice in cosmetics that was once applied to hide exposed foundations.[1]

Similar attitudes about the use of plant material also have affected the popular image and knowledge about the profession of landscape architecture. Again, many lay persons and uninformed design professionals equate landscape architecture to essentially designing with plant material for ornamentation. A corollary of this attitude is the notion that designing an outdoor space is limited to the process of arranging plants in a visually pleasing manner. Likewise, the landscape architect is mistakenly believed to be an expert on all matters related to plants including their propagation, growth requirements and habits, disease and pest control, as well as their use as beautification elements in the landscape. Commonly, when a person is identified as a landscape architect, the response is to request an opinion on where to locate a favorite tree or to diagnose the reason for the yellowing and falling of leaves from a particular shrub. In similar thought the primary professional duty of the landscape architect is considered to be "landscaping," a term misused both within the profession and without as synonymous with "plant arrangement" or planting design. The term "landscaping" is a narrow one and should not be used as a substitute for the name "landscape architecture."

The misunderstanding of the relative importance of plant material has resulted in a public relations problem for the profession of landscape architecture. In 1972, the "Report on the Profession" by Albert Fein to the American Society of Landscape Architects suggested the profession consider changing its name, partially in an attempt to divorce the profession from the "landscaping" syndrome. The report stated: "Another aspect of public posture has to do with the name of the profession. The Gallup Study indicates rather widespread dissatisfaction with the title 'landscape architecture.' "[2] The report went on to suggest cautiously that a name which implied a broader professional expertise would more truly represent the profession.[3] This thought of a new name has since been dropped.

The illusion of plant material's preeminent role in landscape architectural design stems from a general misunderstanding of the profession's expertise and a confusion about the distinction between landscape architecture and the nursery industry. In addition, some lay people still believe the primary focus of landscape architecture is residential garden design and estate planning in which plant material is actually one of the critical design elements. However, the landscape architectural profession is involved in a much broader spectrum of projects than this with an underlying concern for the stewardship of all land resources regardless of scale. With this wider concern, plant material, while still a significant design element, is considered just one of many potential tools at the landscape architect's disposal to satisfy the objectives of a given situation. And plant material is viewed not just as decorative elements but also as having other equally and sometimes more valuable functions in landscape architectural design.

The landscape architect's expertise with regard to plant material lies in a thorough knowledge of its functions and a sensitive, skilled ability to utilize it in the context of a given design. This includes an understanding of its design characteristics such as size, form, color, and texture and a knowledge of its growth habits and requirements. The landscape architect does not need a thorough acquaintance with the botanical minutiae such as the shape of bud scars, petiole size, or serration of the leaf. Nor does the landscape architect need to be an expert on plant propagation and cultivation. Such knowledge is rightly held by horticulturalists and nurserymen. The landscape architect's wisdom should be an understanding of the overall visual characteristics of a plant, its ecological requirements for proper growth, and its environmental impact when planted in a given situation.

Plant materials have a number of traits that set them apart from other landscape architectural design elements. Perhaps the most significant characteristic is that plant materials are living, growing elements. Few if any of the other materials dealt with in landscape architecture or the other design professions are living, variable elements. A number of other unique qualities result from this. First, plant materials are dynamic; that is, they are constantly changing color, texture, opaqueness, and overall character with seasons and with growth. For example, some deciduous plants in the continental temperate zone have four distinctly different visual characteristics based on the seasons of the year: (1) spring with flowers and lush yellow-green foliage, (2) summer

[1]Fred K. Buscher and Jot D. Carpenter, "A Brief History of Foundation Planting," *Landscape Architecture* 67(5): 413–416 (Sept. 1977).

[2]Albert Fein, "Report on the Profession," *Landscape Architecture* 63(1): 45–46 (Oct. 1972).

[3]Ibid., p. 46.

with dark green foliage, (3) autumn with brightly colored foliage, and (4) winter with bare branches and visible trunk bark. While some plants in other climatic zones may not vary as dramatically as deciduous plants do, they nevertheless alter with seasonal flowers and the development of new foliage in response to warm and cool or wet and dry seasons. Even in the desert, plants modulate in appearance especially during winter and spring bloom. And all plants expand with growth. This growth is often imperceptible on a short-term, day-to-day basis, but it is apt to be very dramatic over a long span of time.

Both these dynamic qualities of plant materials have implications for their use in design. The changing seasonal appearance of some plant materials makes them difficult to select and place within a planting design. The designer must not only be concerned with how a plant or group of plants will appear and function at one particular season but also with how it will fill its role throughout the year and with growth that develops over time. A mistake can easily be made in selecting a plant that is attractive at one season within its setting but quite unattractive the remainder of the time. This problem is simplified somewhat if only some of the elements of a plant composition are allowed to change throughout the year while others remain more visually constant. The problem is most complex, and potentially chaotic, when all the elements vary, some at one pace, others at another.

The growth aspect of plant material has other implications too. Typically, young nursery stock is planted in the installation of a new design because it is less expensive and easier to transplant and has a greater chance for survival than more mature stock. But this also has distinct disadvantages for the designer. It may take many years for this young nursery stock to reach its mature height, width, and overall shape. For larger trees in temperate climates, 15 to 20 years are often needed for a newly planted tree to reach an appearance of maturity and even more may be required for it to reach its full dimensions. The problem is compounded because ground cover and shrubs typically reach maturity before trees do, thus requiring a maintenance program of periodic replacement for ground cover and shrubs that have gone beyond their prime. As a consequence, the landscape architect is not able to adequately judge and evaluate the intended quality of a design for many years (perhaps more than 20 to 25 years). This makes it extremely difficult to conclude what was good or bad about a design so that improvements can be made in the next design.

This time factor difficulty is not present (at least not in the same magnitude) in other design professions, where judgment of the design can take place almost immediately upon completion of the project. True, a building or piece of sculpture may weather with time, but the change cannot be compared with the change in a sapling that grows from 6 ft (2m) in height after installation to more than 50 ft (15m) many years later.

Thus the landscape architect must not only study the short-term effect of the design with plant material but the long-term consequences as well. This poses additional problems in attempting to explain to a client what a design will look and feel like soon after completion. Typically, the landscape architect creates and draws a design based on plants that are approximately 75 to 100 percent of their mature size. A client must be informed of this fact to understand what the immediate result of the design will be and how it will change with time. If this is not made clear, the client is apt to be shocked and disappointed to see a different environment from that displayed in a model or graphic plan where plant materials were shown as nearly or completely mature elements. To avoid the initially spotty appearance that results from installing nursery-stock–sized plants, some designers overplant numerous smaller-sized plants that more quickly fill an area. The problem with this approach, however, is that the plants soon overgrow each other and the space in which they were planted. This requires extra maintenance and cost to selectively thin the planting or to prune the plants to a manageable size.

A second distinguishing characteristic of plant materials based on their being living design elements is that they require a certain set of environmental conditions for survival and proper growth. Such factors as soil chemistry, soil drainage, sun exposure, wind exposure, and temperature ranges all influence the health of a plant. Because each plant species needs a particular set of environmental conditions for optimal growth, one of the first steps in designing with plants is to determine what conditions exist on a given site. Having ascertained this, one may then choose the plants that will grow under those conditions.

All plant materials also require some degree of maintenance for adequate health. Plants are not like some design elements that, having been installed, can be forgotten. Certain plant species require more care than others, but even plant species indigenous to a particular region require attention from time to time. Watering, pruning, fertilizing, and pest control are major maintenance tasks that vary in frequency from one plant to another.

One desirable objective of a design using plant material is to select plants requiring little upkeep. One such approach becoming more accepted is to use native plants in ecological groupings rather than popular, nursery variety cultivars. For example, some landscape architects in the Midwest are using native prairie grasses and flowers in their designs along with native trees and shrubs to create more self-sustaining environments.[4] Such a concept is not only more self-supporting but also requires less time and money to maintain.

Again, because plants are living, we often hold a special reverence for them that goes beyond the more practical concern about whether they receive adequate water or fertilizer. Like animals, plants are a form of life that many people believe should be preserved and protected against harm and death. Looking back in history, we find that certain primitive cultures such as the Mandeling tribe in Indonesia and some American Indian tribes actually refused to cut down living trees out of religious respect for their life.[5] Even today, we often hear about the struggle to save a particular tree or woodland from destruction in the wake of new development. In addition, there is often an emotional attachment for plants resulting from nurturing them and watching them grow. Like people, plants have a way of becoming part of our lives and when something happens to them, we feel personally and emotionally injured. The stories of people talking to and having mental telepathy with their plants as described in the book *The Secret Life of Plants*, by Peter Tompkins and Christopher Bird, tends to further support the potential attachment people have for plant material. All in all, the symbolic quality of plant materials sets them apart from other design elements.

Still another characteristic of plant materials is that they provide a feeling of the natural within an environment, especially in urban settings where plant materials offer visual refreshment to the harshness of the surroundings. Plant materials not only provide relative softness in a controlled, rigid environment but also a quality of irregularity. Plant materials in their natural habit of growth cannot be controlled to the same degree as manmade elements. While the overall habit of growth of an unpruned,

naturally growing plant can be predicted based on its species, a factor of nature still remains to influence the size and the form. Plants of a particular species are like people; they all fit a general mold while the specifics vary from individual to individual. Where will a branch develop? How high and long will it be? What will be the autumn color and will it be the same as last year? To make a plant conform to precise standards requires extra care, time, and money. General maintenance and/or bonsai techniques, for example, can be employed to manage the size and form of a plant. These exceptions aside, most plant materials react to the irregularities of nature to provide little surprises throughout the environment.

Functional Uses of Plant Material

As already indicated, plant material fulfill a number of roles in the landscape other than decoration and ornamentation. Although the visual quality of plant materials is an important one, it is necessary to understand other possible functions as well so that plant materials can be used to their fullest potential in the outdoor environment. Among the numerous uses in the landscape, plant materials may create space or outdoor rooms, block unsightly views, stabilize steep slopes, direct movement through the landscape, visually unify a group of buildings, and modify exposure to sun and wind. An individual plant or group of plants may serve only one of these functions in a particular setting or it may fulfill a number of them simultaneously.

In addition to these plant material functions in any one design, plant materials also solve a number of environmental problems as well. Plant materials cleanse the air, retain moisture in the soil, prevent erosion and loss of soil, modify air temperatures, and provide habitats for birds and animals. A green belt planting 600 ft (183m) wide can reduce airborne particulate matter by as much as 75 percent.[6] A watershed that has been developed and stripped of most of its native vegetation experiences a notable increase in amount and rate of surface runoff with resulting higher erosion, especially during construction when soil is unprotected. In a woodland, the volume of sediment may be in the magnitude of 100

[4]Darrel G. Morrison, "Restoring the Midwestern Landscape," *Landscape Architecture* 65(4): 398–403 (October 1975).

[5]James Underwood Crockett and Editors of Time-Life Books, *Trees* (New York: Time-Life Books, 1972), p. 7.

[6]Gary O. Robinette, *Plants, People and Environmental Quality* (Washington, D.C.: U.S. Department of the Interior, National Park Service, 1972), p. 56.

	STRUCTURAL	ENVIRONMENTAL	VISUAL
ARCHITECTURAL *	✳		
ENGINEERING*		✳	
CLIMATE CONTROL*		✳	
AESTHETIC *			✳

*ROBINETTE'S TERM-
INOLOGY

FIGURE 2.1

tons/sq mi/yr, (350kg/hectare/yr.), while in heavy development the volume of sediment can reach 100,000 tons/sq mi/yr (350270kg/hectare/yr.).[7] The lack of a complete, year-round vegetative cover on agricultural land contributes to an erosion rate of 500 tons/sq mi/yr (1751kg/hectare/yr.), a loss that occurs year after year.[8]

While improving the general quality of the environment, plant materials also contribute to real estate value of buildings and their sites. It has been estimated that a well-designed site, including plant materials around a home, can add 30 percent to the value of the property.[9] If well used, plant materials are a good investment, not a one-time expense with no return.

At this point it would be helpful to categorize the various functional uses of plant material to understand them better. One way to do this is to realize that plant materials can fulfill three major functions in the outdoor environment: structural, environmental, and visual. As structural elements, plant materials act as walls, ceilings, and floors in the landscape by defining and organizing space, affecting views, and influencing direction of movement. The size, form, solidity, and opaqueness of plants are important considerations when dealing with plant materials as structural elements. As environmental elements, plant materials affect air quality, serve as erosion control aids, influence water quality, and modify climate. Finally, as visual elements, plant materials may be used as dominant focal points and visual connectors or linkages or for their characteristics of size, form, color, and texture. In this last category plant materials are utilized for their appearance. Again, a plant or groups of plants can serve more than one of these functions at the same time in a design.

Gary O. Robinette in his book *Plants, People and Environmental Quality* classifies the functional uses of plant materials in a slightly different manner. He identifies the four major categories of plant functions as architectural uses, engineering uses, climate control uses, and aesthetic uses.[10] Architectural uses of plant materials, discussed in greater detail in the following pages, include definition of space, screening of undesirable views, provision of privacy in outdoor spaces, and creation of spatial and view sequences (progressive realization).[11] Engineering uses of plant materials include control and prevention of glare, control of erosion, control and modification of noise, and directing of vehicular and pedestrian traffic.[12] Climate control uses of plant material include shading, buffering and modifying wind movement, modifying air temperatures, and influencing rain and snow accumulation.[13] Aesthetic uses of plant materials, also outlined in greater detail below,

---

[7]Charles Thurlow, William Toner, and Duncan Erley, *Performance Standards for Sensitive Lands; A Practical Guide for Local Administrators* (Chicago: American Society of Planning Officials, 1975), p. 11.

[8]Ibid.

[9]"Study Says Trees Can Provide Cleansing Effect in Environment," *Columbus Dispatch*, June 25, 1978, Sec. I, p. 10.

[10]Gary O. Robinette, *Plants, People and Environmental Quality*, pp. 6–9.

[11]Ibid., p. 6.

[12]Ibid., p. 7.

[13]Ibid., p. 8.

involve providing visual accents, enframing views, complementing other design elements, acknowledging special points in the environment, and serving as a neutral background to focal points.[14]

The following comparisons, illustrated in Figure 2.1, are useful for equating the two systems of classification: (1) structural uses are similar to Robinette's architectural uses, (2) environmental uses are similar to Robinette's engineering and climate control uses, and (3) visual uses are similar to Robinette's aesthetic uses. No matter which classification system or set of terms is used, the most important points to understand are (1) what functions plant materials can serve, and (2) how they can be used in the landscape to fulfill their intended functions most effectively. While all functions are important, this chapter concentrates on the structural/architectural and visual/aesthetic uses because they contribute most to the organization of a landscape architectural design project.

Architectural Uses of Plant Material

Architectural uses of plant material are extremely important in the overall organization of the outdoor environment and the creation of outdoor space. In the development of a design, the architectural uses are usually one of the first studied. The visual characteristics of plant materials are generally selected only after their architectural functions have been resolved. As stated previously, plant materials used architecturally in the landscape function as structural components such as floors, ceilings, walls, windows, and doors. Architecturally, plants are the spatial envelope of a design or outdoor room. However, the term "architectural use" is not meant to imply the use of plants in only rigid, artificial environments. Plant materials in natural settings may also be equally successful in accomplishing "architectural" functions. The following sections discuss several of the more noteworthy architectural uses of plant material.

<u>Creation of Space</u>. A sense of space depends upon actual and implied enclosure created by modifying the ground plane, vertical plane, and overhead plane both individually and collectively. Plant materials may be used in the landscape to influence each of these planes of enclosure. On the ground plane, ground cover or low shrubs may subtly imply spatial

---

[14]Ibid., p. 9.

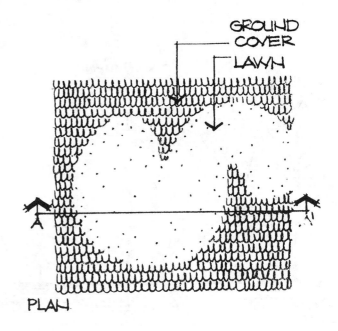

IMPLIED SPATIAL EDGE CREATED BETWEEN GROUND COVER AND LAWN.

FIGURE 2.2

definition through variations in height and material. Here, plants do not physically define space vertically but do suggest a wall at a lower level. As illustrated in Figure 2.2, the edge between a lawn area and a ground cover bed suggests the limits of a space without any physical barrier or alteration of views into and from the implied space. Of all the potential ways plant materials can define space, this is the weakest and least important.

In the vertical plane, plant materials can influence the perception of space in several ways. First, tree trunks act as vertical columns in an exterior setting, again defining space more by implication than in ac-

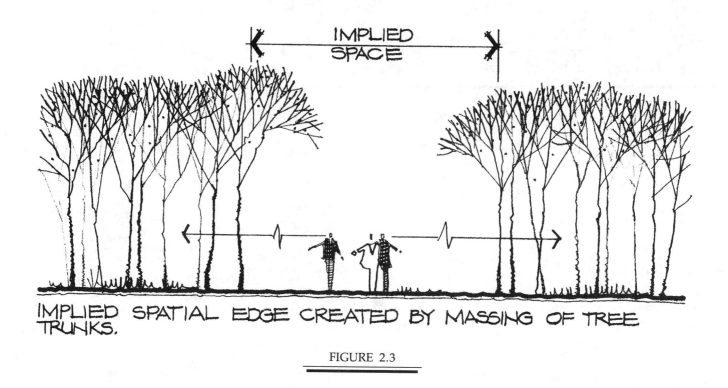

IMPLIED SPATIAL EDGE CREATED BY MASSING OF TREE TRUNKS.

FIGURE 2.3

tuality (Figure 2.3). The degree of enclosure will vary with the size of the trunks, their density of massing, and their pattern of arrangement. The more trunks present, as in a natural wooded condition, the stronger the feeling of enclosure (Figure 2.4). Other examples of tree trunks implying spatial edges can be observed along a street lined with trees or in the country where the massing of trunks in hedgerows or woodlots during the winter suggests limits of space even without foliage.

FIGURE 2.4

The foliage mass of plants is the second means for influencing the vertical plane of spatial enclosure. Here too, the density and height of the foliage mass affects the quality of the space. The taller the plant and the larger and more closely its leaves or needles are spaced, the stronger the feeling of enclosure. One definite change of enclosure is apt to occur with seasonal variation in deciduous foliage. In summer, a space may be completely enveloped with foliage (Figure 2.5), giving the space an inward feeling of isolation. In winter, on the other hand, the same space may by comparison seem larger and more open with views extending some distance beyond the limits of the space itself. Spatial definition in winter is implied by the branches and trunks of the plants. Evergreen plants, of course, provide the strongest year-round definition of space in the vertical plane.

The overhead plane of a space can also be modified by plant material. The foliage mass and branches in the canopy of trees create ceilings over an outdoor space, limiting the view to the sky and affecting the vertical scale of the space (Figure 2.6). Here too, there are many variables including season, foliage/branch density, and the spacing pattern of the trees themselves. The sense of a ceiling is strongest when the trees are placed so their canopies overlap, thus shutting out exposure to the sky. In *Trees in Urban Design*, Henry F. Arnold recommends that trees in urban settings be spaced 10 (3m) to 15 ft

SUMMER SEASON

SPACE IS ENCLOSED AND INWARD ORIENTED.

WINTER SEASON

SPACE IS MORE OPEN WITH VIEWS EXTENDING BEYOND SPACE.

FIGURE 2.5

FIGURE 2.6

OVERHEAD PLANE

OVERHEAD PLANE CREATED BY BOTTOM OF TREE CANOPY.

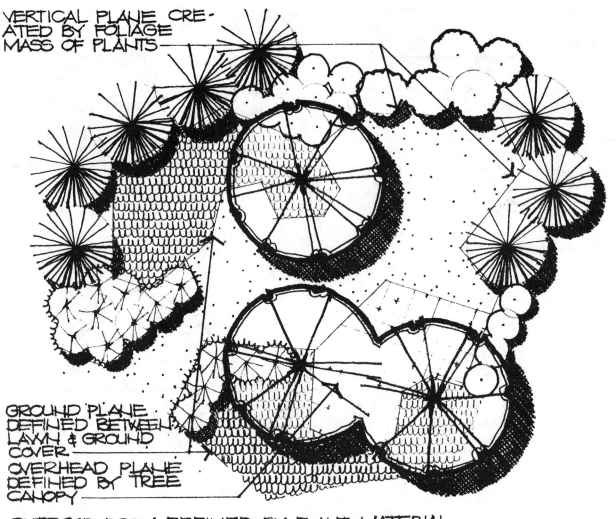

VERTICAL PLANE CRE-
ATED BY FOLIAGE
MASS OF PLANTS

GROUND PLANE
DEFINED BETWEEN
LAWN & GROUND
COVER

OVERHEAD PLANE
DEFINED BY TREE
CANOPY

OUTDOOR ROOM DEFINED BY PLANT MATERIAL.

FIGURE 2.7

(5m) apart. He also observes that trees lose their visual effectiveness when planted more than 30 ft (9m) apart.[15]

As indicated in Figure 2.7, the three enclosing variables of space (ground plane, vertical plane, and overhead plane) operate together in defining rooms in the exterior environment and may be altered or combined in an almost infinite variety of ways. In all situations, the degree of perceived enclosure varies with the relative height of the surrounding vegetation, its spacing, density, and the position of the

viewer relative to the surrounding vegetation, as described in Chapter 1. For example, a space feels very enclosed when the encircling plant materials are tall, dense, tightly spaced, and placed close to the viewer.

In the formation of outdoor space with plant material, as with any other design elements, one should first determine the objectives to be met and the spatial quality desired (open, enclosed, intimate, monumental, etc.). Having done this, the landscape architect can then proceed to select and organize the plants that fulfill these desired criteria. For instance, some basic spatial types created with plants are described in the following paragraphs and shown in the accompanying illustrations.

[15]Henry F. Arnold, *Trees in Urban Design* (New York: Van Nostrand Reinhold, 1980), p. 62.

Open space. Using only low shrubs and ground cover as the spatial definers, one can create a space by implication that is open in all directions. Such a space is airy, outward-oriented, lacks privacy, and is exposed to the sun and sky (Figure 2.8).

OPEN SPACE CREATED BY LOW SHRUBS AND GROUND COVER.

FIGURE 2.8

Semiopen space. Similar to a completely open space, a semiopen space as shown in Figure 2.9 is partially enclosed on one or more sides with taller plant materials acting as vertical walls blocking views into and out from the space. This spatial type possesses qualities similar to the completely open space but is less transparent while strongly oriented to the open sides. Such a space is often appropriate for a residential terrace where privacy is required in one direction but views are desired in another.

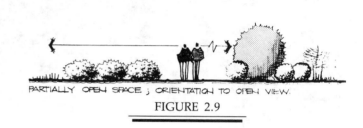

PARTIALLY OPEN SPACE ; ORIENTATION TO OPEN VIEW.

FIGURE 2.9

Canopied space. Using a mass of shade trees with a dense canopy, one can create a space that is enclosed overhead and open to the sides, as illustrated in Figure 2.10. Overall, this space has a feeling of breadth sandwiched between the overhead plane of the tree canopy and the ground plane for a person moving through and among the tree trunks. A canopied space also establishes a strong sense of vertical scale by capping the spatial height. Architecturally, this type of space is often experienced when standing in an open ground floor of a building or in a parking garage that has open sides. In the landscape, this space is characteristic of a green urban park where the understory has been removed. With the exception of filtered sun through the canopy and light seeping in from the sides, this space tends to be relatively dark during summer but open during winter. This space is cool and permits filtered views into and from it through the sides. One variation of this space is the "tunnel" space created by shade trees along a road or walk. This arrangement, shown in Figure 2.11, reinforces the linear movement of the road or path by focusing attention ahead while also permitting occasional views to the side.

CANOPIED SPACE "SANDWICHED" BETWEEN BOTTOM OF TREE CANOPY AND GROUND PLANE.

FIGURE 2.10

FIGURE 2.11

Enclosed canopied space. This space, illustrated in Figure 2.12, has the same characteristics as the canopied space just explained, but a major difference is that it is enclosed on the sides with medium- and lower-sized plant materials. This space, typical of that found in wooded forest conditions, is quite dark and oriented in upon itself, providing feelings of privacy and isolation.

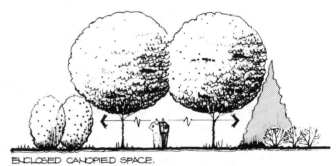

ENCLOSED CANOPIED SPACE.

FIGURE 2.12

Vertical space. Using tall, narrow plant materials, one can create an outdoor space that is vertical in orientation and open to the sky as depicted in Figure 2.13. Depending upon how much emphasis is desired on this upward movement, the space can be either open or enclosed to the sides. This vertical space has the potential of becoming almost like a gothic cathedral, lifting one's attention upward toward the sky. One possible variation of this space is created by the use of tapered plant material for the space-defining elements so that the space either expands or contracts as it becomes taller.

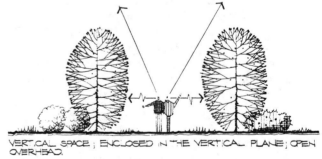

VERTICAL SPACE ; ENCLOSED IN THE VERTICAL PLANE; OPEN OVERHEAD.

FIGURE 2.13

In summary, the landscape architect can create numerous types of spatial character using only plant material as the space-defining elements. A combination of these spaces in a small park is illustrated in Figure 2.14.

In addition to being able to develop individual outdoor spaces of different qualities, the landscape

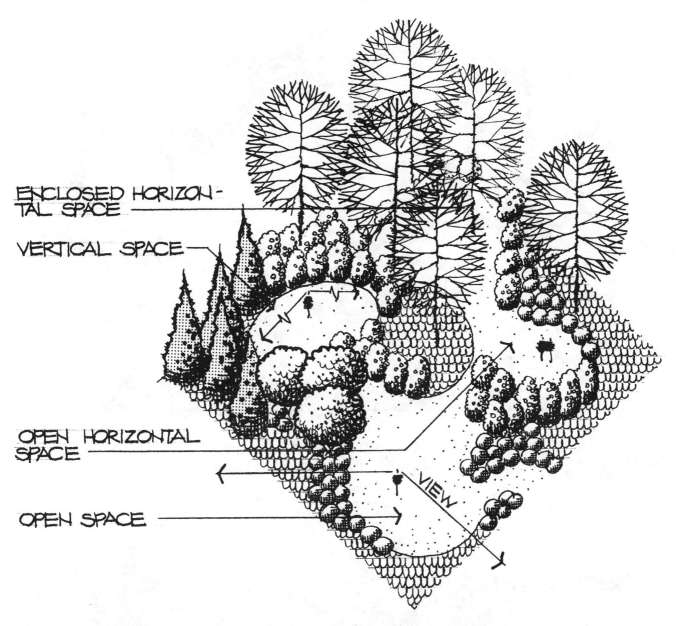

ENCLOSED HORIZON-
TAL SPACE

VERTICAL SPACE

OPEN HORIZONTAL
SPACE

OPEN SPACE

VIEW

PLAN OBLIQUE OF DIFFERENT SPATIAL TYPES.

FIGURE 2.14

architect may use plant materials to establish inter-linked sequences of spaces. As illustrated in Figure 2.15, plant materials may act as walls and doors that direct people into and through a space. While doing this, plant materials may alternately enframe and block views from the path of interconnected spaces in addition to altering the overhead canopy. Plant material can effectively "squeeze" a volume of space to give it tension and then subsequently "release" this confinement in an open area. The designer can

modulate all dimensions of spatial definition with plant material except the elevation of the ground surface itself to create pulsating and exciting spatial sequences.

To this point the discussion has centered on the use of plant materials to define space by themselves in the landscape. However, plant materials are more often than not combined with other elements to articulate space. For example, plant materials may be integrated with landform either to accentuate or to

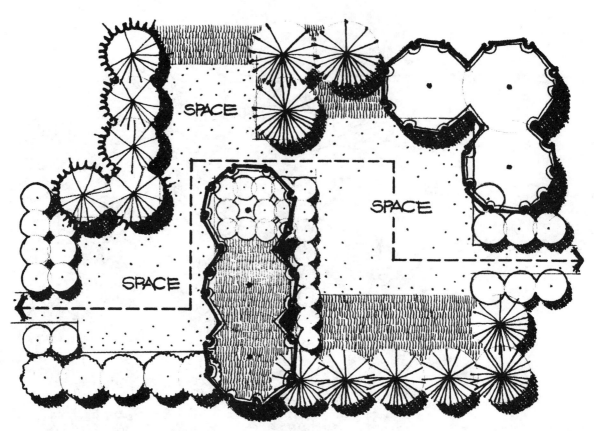

PLANT MATERIAL USED TO CREATE AND LINK A SEQUENCE OF SPACES IN AN ARCHITECTONIC FASHION.

FIGURE 2.15

FIGURE 2.16

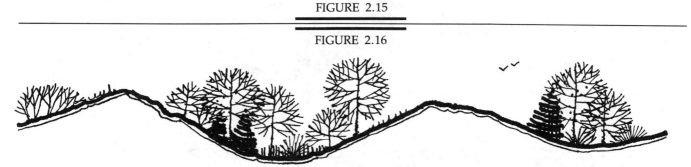

PLANT MATERIAL NEGATE SPACES CREATED BY LANDFORM.

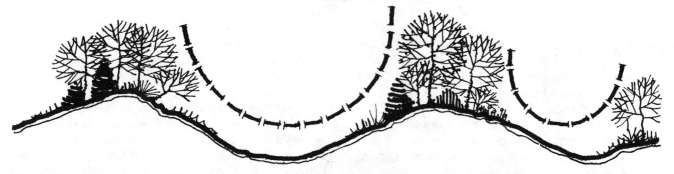

PLANT MATERIAL ACCENTUATE SPACES CREATED BY LANDFORM.

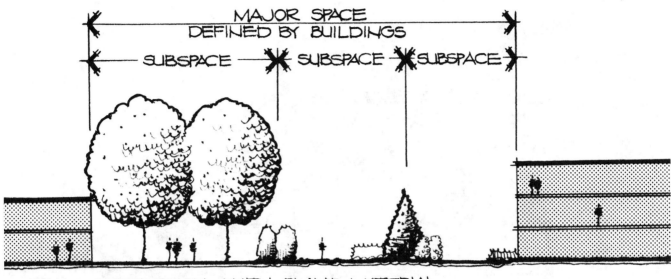

SPATIAL SUBDIVISION WITH PLANT MATERIAL.

FIGURE 2.17

negate the spatial structure established by landform on the base plane, as shown in Figure 2.16. Placed on or near the summit of a convex or ridge landform, plant materials increase the apparent height of the mass and consequently accentuate the sensation of spatial enclosure in the adjoining concave and valley landforms. Conversely, plant material placed inside a concave and valley landform on its floor or surrounding sides contradicts the space initially formed by the topography by "filling it in." Thus to

increase the feeling of space created through molding of the ground surface, plants are most effectively located on summits, ridges, and other high points, while lower areas are left more open and devoid of vegetation.

Plant material may also be used to modify the spaces created by buildings. In this application, a major function of vegetation is to subdivide larger spaces delineated by buildings into smaller spaces. A good example of this is an urban setting or uni-

FIGURE 2.18

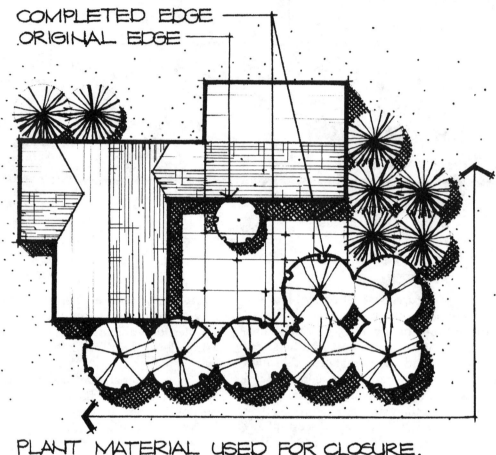

COMPLETED EDGE

ORIGINAL EDGE

PLANT MATERIAL USED FOR CLOSURE.

FIGURE 2.19

versity campus where the primary extremities of the outdoor spaces are created by the buildings. Within these hard-edged spaces, plant materials are able to provide another hierarchy of subspaces, usually more delightful and human in scale (Figure 2.17). Without this use of vegetation, most urban environments would certainly appear harsh, inhuman, and too open. A similar function of plant material occurs in a rural landscape where forest edges, woodlots, and hedgerows all subdivide the countryside into a hierarchy of spaces. A classic example of this is the rural English landscape shown in Figure 2.18.

Plant material may also be used from an architectural standpoint to complete the spatial definition and organization that has been suggested by buildings or other design elements. Two common methods for accomplishing this include the following:

1. *Closure.*[16] This term describes the completion of a spatial enclosure that has been almost, but not quite, articulated by a building or enclosing wall. A space surrounded by a building or wall on two or three sides can use vegetation for "closure" or completion of the space on its other open sides, as indicated in Figure 2.19.

[16]Gary O. Robinette, *Plants, People and Environmental Quality,* p. 23.

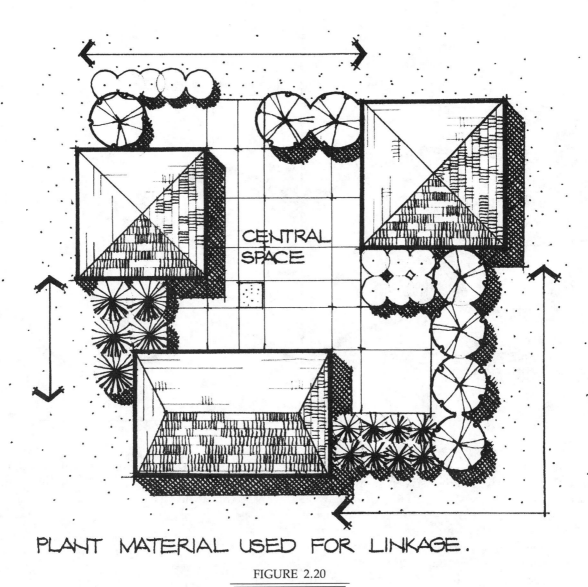

PLANT MATERIAL USED FOR LINKAGE.

FIGURE 2.20

2. *Linkage.*[17] This term applies to plant materials that finish the delineation of an outdoor space by visually connecting otherwise separate elements in the landscape. Like closure, linkage with plant material fulfills the spatial definition partially suggested by the other elements by providing more enclosure than that given only by the separate elements. As illustrated in Figure 2.20, linkage can be accomplished by massing plant material together in a somewhat linear manner between the initially isolated elements, thereby visually tying them together and finishing the spatial en-

closure. The example in Figure 2.20 shows a courtyard edge that has been started by surrounding buildings but completed by the planting. Masses of trees and shrubs visually link these separate buildings together to form a continuous spatial enclosure.

Screening. If the creation of outdoor space is one architectural use of plant material, another is to conceal unattractive objects or scenes in the environment.[18] Plant materials as vertical barriers can control views so that desirable points in the landscape

---

[17]Ibid., p. 23.

[18]Ibid., p. 24.

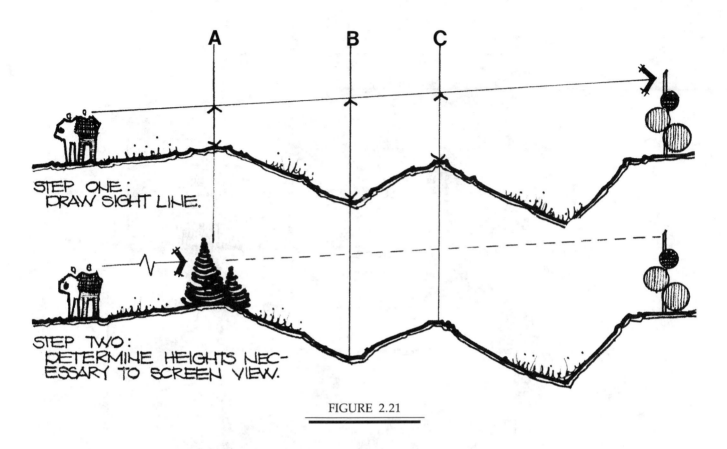

STEP ONE:
DRAW SIGHT LINE.

STEP TWO:
DETERMINE HEIGHTS NEC-
ESSARY TO SCREEN VIEW.

FIGURE 2.21

are observed while ugly points are blocked. Depending on objectives, a vegetative screen may be completely opaque to totally screen a view or it may be of various degrees of transparency to provide partial screening. To establish an effective vegetative screen, one needs first to analyze the point(s) from which the viewer will be looking, the height of the unattractive element(s), the distance between the viewer and the unsightly element, and the landform configuration. These factors collectively affect the required height, arrangement, and placement of the plant material screen. Taller is not necessarily better for screening, though it certainly might be in some situations. The best method for studying the variations of the plant screen is to draw a section along the anticipated sight line, as illustrated in Figure 2.21, and to plot accurately the eye level and height of the undesirable object within the section. By then drawing in the sight line, one can study the proper location and height of the screen. In Figure 2.21, the most effective location would be at Point A, though Points B or C might be acceptable if more of the foreground landscape were desired in the view. An additional factor to consider is the season(s) during which the plant material is to block the views. Ev-

ergreen plants are most successful for establishing a permanent wall of vegetation that prevents views throughout the year.

Privacy Control. Somewhat similar to screening is the use of plant material for privacy control.[19] Privacy control is the technique of encircling a well-defined area with plants of such a height that views into and from the space are prevented. The purpose of privacy control is to isolate the space from its surroundings, as illustrated in Figure 2.22. Thus the subtle difference between privacy control and screening is that the former encompasses and segregates a space, thereby blocking all views, while screening is the judicious placement of barriers stopping only selected views. Privacy control eliminates freedom of movement through the enclosed space, whereas screening allows movement around and through the plant material barriers. Privacy control is often a desirable design objective for an intimate sitting area or the terrace of a residence.

[19]Ibid., p. 28.

As with screening, the degree of privacy control is directly affected by the characteristics of plants used to block the views. A dense planting of vegetation over 6.5 ft (2m) tall usually provides the greatest sense of privacy. Chest-high plants produce partial privacy (but total privacy while sitting), and waist-high plants furnish little if any privacy.

Visual Plant Characteristics

Plant material used architecturally within a design to define space, establish spatial sequences, screen views, and provide privacy may also serve a number of aesthetic functions. While architectural uses concern themselves primarily with the structural aspects of a design, aesthetic uses deal principally with the visual qualities. Plant size, form, color, and texture together with compositional arrangement and relationship to the surroundings are all factors affecting the aesthetic quality of a design. The visual quality of a planting design is vitally important because a person's first response is apt to be a reaction to its appearance. A planting design may successfully fulfill other valuable functions such as creating space, modifying air temperatures, and stabilizing soil, but it will nevertheless be ill-received if it is offensive to the eye. To be successful, a planting design should be at least nondescript, if not attractive, in conjunction with accomplishing various other functions.

This section outlines the different visual plant characteristics including size, form, color, and texture along with applications and suggested guidelines for their use in designing with plant material in the landscape. Each visual plant characteristic has its own subcategories, qualities, and uses in the outdoor environment, which are discussed in the following sections.

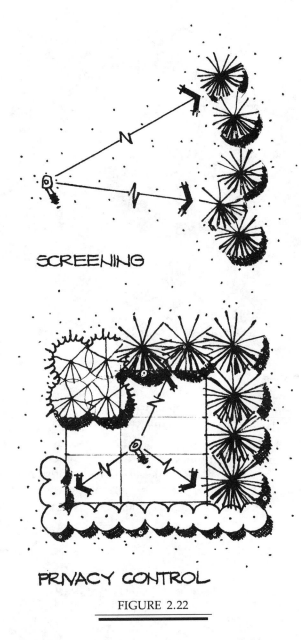

SCREENING

PRIVACY CONTROL

FIGURE 2.22

Plant Size. Size is one of the most visually significant characteristics of plant material and should be studied early in the selection of plants for a design. Plant size directly affects the scale of a space, compositional interest, and the overall framework of a design. Plant materials may be categorized according to the following sizes.

Large and intermediate trees. Based on size, the most significant plants from both a compositional and spatial standpoint within the landscape are large and intermediate trees. Large trees grow 40 ft (12m) tall or more at maturity, while intermediate trees have a maximum height of 30 to 40 ft. (9m–12m).

Examples of large and intermediate trees include sugar maple *(Acer saccharum)*, white oak *(Quercus alba)*, white ash *(Fraxinus americana)*, American beech *(Fagus grandifolia)*, and red gum *(Eucalyptus camaldulensis)*. Some functions of large and intermediate trees in the landscape are listed below.

This category of plant material are dominant visual elements because of their height and mass. Their function is similar to that of the steel and wood framework of a building: they give a composition its overall three-dimensional form by establishing the basic structure and skeleton of an out-

FIGURE 2.23

LARGE TREE FUNCTIONS AS
DOMINANT ELEMENT IN A
SMALL GARDEN SPACE.

door environment, as illustrated in Figure 2.23. Likewise, large and intermediate trees may be the first plants seen in a composition and consequently may serve as focal points (Figure 2.24) when placed among smaller plant materials. The importance of large and intermediate trees as compositional elements becomes greater as the scale of an outdoor space becomes larger. Seen across an open field or plaza, large trees are the first, and perhaps the only, plant materials noticed. Smaller trees and shrubs are seen and appreciated only after closer inspection. Therefore large and intermediate trees should generally be the first plant material located within a design because their placement will have the biggest

FIGURE 2.24

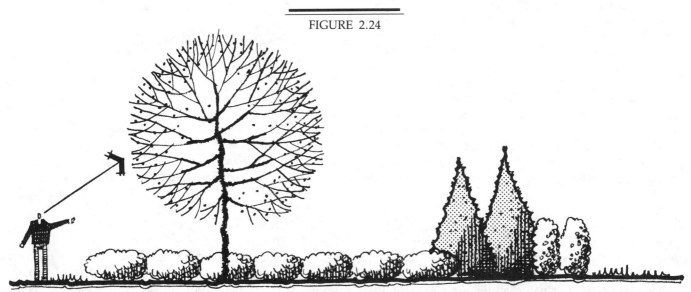

BASED ON SIZE, LARGE TREE CAN FUNCTION AS A DOMINANT ELEMENT AMONG OTHER PLANT MATERIAL.

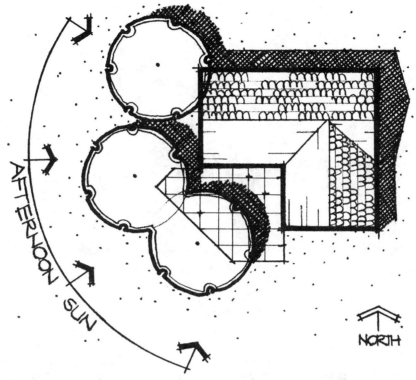

LARGE SHADE TREES SHOULD BE LOCATED ON SW, W, & NW SIDES OF BUILDINGS AND OUTDOOR SPACES TO SCREEN HOT AFTERNOON SUN.

FIGURE 2.25

impact on the appearance and feel of the entire composition.[20] Once the larger trees have been located, smaller trees and shrubs can be arranged to complement and reinforce the compositional and spatial qualities of the large and intermediate trees. Smaller plant materials provide detail at a more personalized scale within the overall framework established by the larger trees. On small sites, caution should be exercised not to overuse large trees, as they are apt to overwhelm the scale of the design and the smaller elements within it.

Another similar function of large and intermediate trees in the environment is to enclose space in the overhead and vertical planes. As previously described, the canopies and trunks of large and intermediate trees can establish ceilings and walls for outdoor rooms (Figures 2.6, 2.10, 2.11, and 2.12). The feeling of such outdoor rooms may vary somewhat depending on the actual canopy height; the

space will feel more human if the canopy is 10 (3m) to 15 ft (4.5m) above the ground or quite monumental if the canopy is 40 (12m) to 50 ft (15m) above the ground, as it sometimes is in a mature forest. Large and intermediate trees are also useful elements for subdividing expansive urban and rural spaces initially defined by buildings and landform into smaller spaces (Figures 2.17 and 2.18). Here, the height and sides of the canopy mass become critical aspects in defining the edges of space and its scale.

Large and intermediate trees may also be used in the landscape to provide shade. This is desirable for outdoor spaces and buildings in summer when temperatures can become uncomfortable where an area is directly exposed to the sun's rays. In the shade, air temperatures may be as many as 8 degrees lower than in the open.[21] In turn, the shading of a lightly constructed building can result in interior temperatures as much as 20°F lower than outside tempera-

[20]Sylvia Crowe, *Garden Design* (Funtington, England: Parkland Publishing Limited, 1981), pp. 113–114.

[21]"Study Says Trees Can Provide Cleansing Effect in Environment," *Columbus Dispatch*, p. 10.

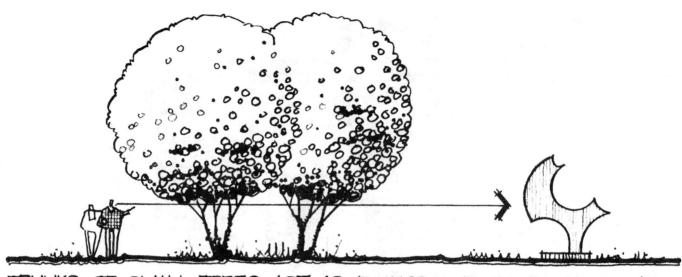

TRUNKS OF SMALL TREES ACT AS FOREGROUND TO FOCAL POINT.

FIGURE 2.26

tures.[22] To be most effective for shading, large and intermediate trees should be placed on the southwest, west, and northwest sides of the space or building to be shaded, as depicted in Figure 2.25. Because of the varying height of the sun in the sky as it moves during the afternoon, the tallest trees are required on the southwest side while shorter trees can provide adequate shade on the northwest side. Shading of air conditioners in summer can also increase their efficiency. A study by the American Refrigeration Institute has shown that shade trees can reduce the required capacity of a split-system air conditioner to cool a home by 3 percent.[23]

Small trees and ornamentals. Moving down the scale of plant size, we define small trees and ornamentals as trees that grow to a maximum height of 15 (4.5m) to 20 ft (6m). Examples of small trees include European olive *(Olea europaea),* mesquite *(Prosopis sp.),* Cornelian cherry *(Cornus mas)* that has been limbed up, and fringe tree *(Chionanthus virginnicus).* Ornamental trees include such plants as crab apple *(Malus sp.),* flowering dogwood *(Cornus florida),* and Canadian redbud *(Cercis canadensis).* Like large and intermediate trees, small trees and ornamentals have a number of potential uses in the landscape.

Small trees may define space in both the vertical and overhead planes. Depending on canopy height, small trees can imply spatial edges in the vertical plane with their trunks or they can completely enclose space in the vertical plane if their canopy mass extends below eye level. When views are afforded through the trunks and lower branches of small trees, as illustrated in Figure 2.26, they may behave as a semitransparent foreground and thus give a greater sense of depth to the space one is looking into. Overhead, the canopy of a small tree can establish the ceiling of an outdoor space that is often intimate in feeling. In some cases, the canopy may be so low as to prevent a person from walking beneath the tree. In all situations, small trees and ornamentals are appropriately used in small-scale spaces where area is limited and/or the designer desires to create a comfortably scaled spatial quality.

Small trees and ornamentals may serve as visual and compositional accents, as shown in Figures 2.27 and 2.28. This may result from a size contrast with lower plant material or from distinct form, flowers, and fruit in the case of ornamentals. Ornamental trees are logically used as focal points in places where the landscape architect desires to attract attention (near an entrance, at the terminus to a space, on a projecting point, etc.). Ornamentals may be used at the end of a linear space like a piece of sculpture or abstract sign, as in Figure 2.29, to lead and draw people through the space. Used sequentially, ornamentals can lead a person from one space to another and then on to the next. Moreover, or-

[22]Anne Simon Moffat and Marc Schiler, *Landscape Design that Saves Energy* (New York: William Morrow, 1981), p. 18.
[23]Trane Air Conditioning, letter to Jeanne Blackburn Rick, American Nurserymen, Inc., August 26, 1977.

ORNAMENTAL TREE USED AS A FOCAL POINT IN A PLANT COMPOSITION.

FIGURE 2.27

namental trees may simply be used in a design for their visual interest. Many ornamentals have four different seasons of attraction based on habit of growth, spring flowers, summer foliage, autumn color, and winter branching habit.

Tall shrubs. The next category of plant materials by size is tall shrubs, plants that grow to a maxi-

mum height of 10 (3m) to 15 ft (4.5m). In comparison with small trees, tall shrubs are not only slightly shorter but are also distinguished by the lack of a canopy. Typically, the foliage mass of a shrub extends to, or almost to, the ground while that of a small tree is located some distance above the ground, forming a canopy or ceiling over an area. Although this difference is helpful in catego-

FIGURE 2.28

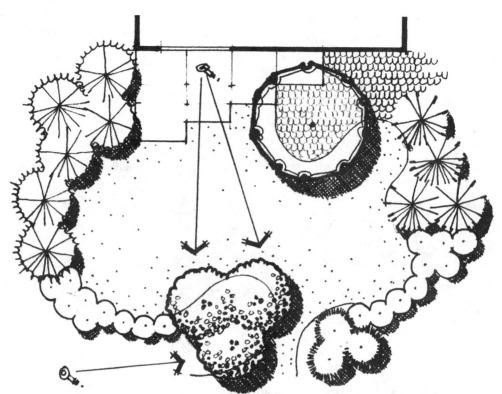

ORNAMENTAL TREES ACT AS ACCENTS FOR GARDEN SPACE AND AT-TRACTORS FOR ENTRANCE.

FIGURE 2.29

rizing plants by size, it is not always so clear in actuality, especially when many tall shrubs can be "limbed up" to create a floating canopy. Nevertheless, the distinction is made here between tall shrubs and small trees for ease of understanding. Some functions of tall shrubs in the outdoor environment are listed below.

Tall shrubs can be used in the landscape like walls to furnish spatial enclosure in the vertical plane. A space defined by only tall shrubs is contained on its sides but open above, as illustrated in Figure 2.30. Thus the feeling of such a space is apt to be light and sunny with a strong orientation upward to the sky. Tall shrubs may also create strong corridorlike

FIGURE 2.30

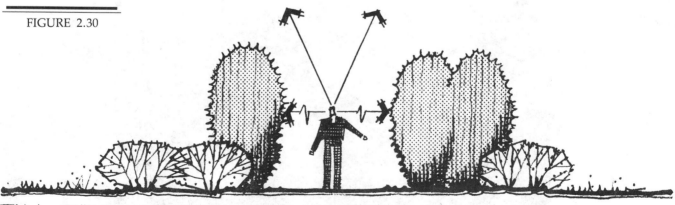

TALL SHRUBS ENCLOSE SPACE IN VERTICAL PLANE BUT ALLOW A VIEW SKYWARD.

TALL SHRUBS CAN FUNCTION AS BLINDERS AND DIRECT VIEWS TO DESIRED POINTS IN THE LANDSCAPE.

FIGURE 2.31

spaces that direct movement and the eye to a terminus, as demonstrated in Figure 2.31. The quality of enclosure can vary greatly with season if the tall shrubs are deciduous, while evergreen shrubs will keep it more consistent.

Tall shrubs may be used for both screening and privacy control. This is a popular use of tall shrubs where a soft, green barrier is desired as opposed to the hard surface of a wall or fence. As indicated earlier, careful attention must be given to the selection and placement of tall shrubs for screening and privacy control so that they perform throughout the year as required.

Tall shrubs may be used as compositional accents when contrasted against lower- or intermediate-sized shrubs. They do this particularly well if they are narrow while also possessing distinct color and texture, as illustrated in Figure 2.32.

In an opposite use, tall shrubs can act as a neutral background for other special objects placed in front of them such as a piece of sculpture or lower, flowering shrubs (Figure 2.33). Again, its ability to do this will vary depending on whether the tall shrub is deciduous or evergreen.

Intermediate shrubs. This category represents those plant materials between 3 (1m) and 6 ft (2m) tall. They may also be any shape, color, or texture. Again, their foliage mass usually extends to the ground or just slightly above it. Intermediate-sized

FIGURE 2.32

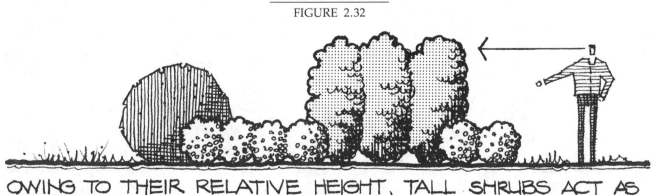

OWING TO THEIR RELATIVE HEIGHT, TALL SHRUBS ACT AS ACCENTS.

TALL SHRUBS SERVE AS A BACKGROUND TO AN ACCENT IN THE FOREGROUND.

FIGURE 2.33

shrubs serve the same types of design functions as do low shrubs, but with slightly more spatial containment. Furthermore, intermediate shrubs may act as a visual transition in a composition between tall shrubs or small trees and low shrubs.

Low shrubs. Low shrubs are the next smaller plant category in the hierarchy of plant sizes. Low shrubs are 3 ft (1m) or fewer in mature height. However, low shrubs are usually thought of as being taller than 1 ft (30 cm) because plants below this height

FIGURE 2.34

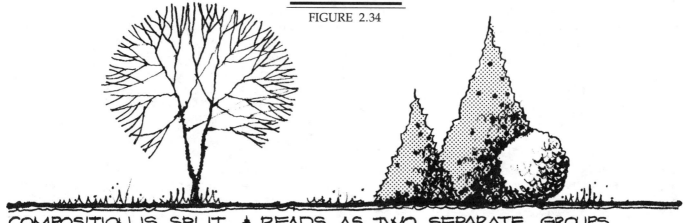

COMPOSITION IS SPLIT & READS AS TWO SEPARATE GROUPS.

SMALL SHRUBS VISUALLY LINK TWO SIDES OF COMPOSITION INTO ONE UNIFIED WHOLE.

appear and function as ground cover. Examples of low shrubs include Japanese flowering quince *(Chaenomeles japonica)*, cranberry cotoneaster *(Cotoneaster apiculata)*, Anthony Waterer spirea *(Spiraea X bumalda cv. "Anthony Waterer")*, and prickly pear cactus *(Opunta microdasys)*. Low shrubs may be placed in the landscape to accomplish the following purposes.

Low shrubs may define space or separate spaces without inhibiting views into or from them. Because low shrubs lack significant height, they articulate space more by implication than by actual physical enclosure (Figure 2.8). Thus a space that needs to be open to the sides can be defined in the vertical plane with low shrubs. A related function is the use of low shrubs along a walk or path to contain pedestrians on the walk without affecting their line of vision.

Low shrubs can be used compositionally to connect other unrelated elements visually. They do this, however, somewhat differently from ground cover. Ground cover can visually relate other elements by serving as a common base plane on which the unrelated parts are placed, whereas low shrubs function as vertical connectors similar to a low wall, as shown in Figure 2.34. Therefore low shrubs act as stronger visual links between elements in a composition when viewed from normal eye level.

A similar function is to use low shrubs as the subordinate element in a design. They can be used to contrast taller components or bring the scale of a design down to a smaller, more intimate level. Because of their size, low shrubs need to be used in large masses to be visually significant. If used in small groups (relative to the scale of the entire composition), they are apt to be lost. If overused in too many small individual masses, as illustrated in Figure 2.35, low shrubs can give a composition a spotty appearance.

Ground cover. The smallest plant category by size is ground cover. The term "ground cover" is used to describe any low or spreading plant material that reaches a maximum height of 6 (15 cm) to 12 in (30 cm). Ground cover is found with a variety of characteristics, from flowering to nonflowering and from woody to herbaceous. Examples of ground cover include English ivy *(Hedera helix)*, myrtle *(Vinca minor)*, pachysandra *(Pachysandra terminalis)*, and common ice plant *(Carpobrotus edulis)*. Ground cover can be thought of as the vegetative "rug" or floor material of an outdoor space and as such has a number of functions in design.

Like low shrubs, ground cover can be used in a design to imply spatial edges (Figure 2.2). In this regard, ground cover is often used in an exterior space

SMALL SHRUBS PLACED IN TOO MANY SEPARATE GROUPS.

SMALL SHRUBS ARE PROPERLY MASSED IN LARGER GROUPS.

FIGURE 2.35

to delineate the edges of patterns on the ground plane. Ground cover is one effective means for outlining a desired shape on the ground without using hard architectural materials. The line created by the edge of ground cover when it adjoins lawn or pavement can be visually interesting unto itself and may have the ability to captivate the eye and lead it around a space, as shown in Figure 2.36. A similar use of ground cover is to define a nonwalking surface, especially when opposed to lawn or pavement, as shown in Figure 2.37.

An additional use of ground cover to that just described is to provide visual interest based on distinct color or texture. Ground cover can be particularly

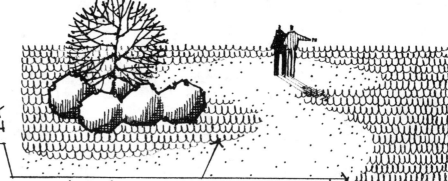

A LINE IS CREATED BY
EDGE BETWEEN LAWN
AND GROUND COVER

LINE BETWEEN LAWN AND GROUND COVER CAPTIVATES THE EYE
AND LEADS IT AROUND A SPACE.

FIGURE 2.36

FIGURE 2.37

appealing when juxtaposed to contrasting colored or textured material. This use is an important one for those ground covers that have attractive flowers or autumn color.

Different from the function just described is the use of ground cover to establish a uniform, neutral background or setting for other more obvious elements or focal points. An example of this is a bed of ground cover beneath a piece of sculpture or eye-catching ornamental tree. To serve as a neutral setting, the area of ground cover must be large enough to eliminate the visual interference of nearby elements.

As previously mentioned, another design application of ground cover is to link together visually otherwise separate elements or groups of elements into a unified whole. It can function as a common element relating to all the various parts of a composition. As shown in Figure 2.38, groups of unrelated shrubs or trees can be made to be part of the same composition by a ground cover bed that interconnects all plants into one common area on the ground plane. This is a common technique for "border planting" around the outside of an open lawn area.

A practical use of ground cover is to provide a low vegetative cover in those areas where lawn or other plant materials are impractical. Areas in awkward locations near a building that are difficult to gain access to with a lawn mower or are too dark and shady for grass are logical places for ground cover. Likewise, ground cover generally requires less maintenance than a lawn area of the same size,

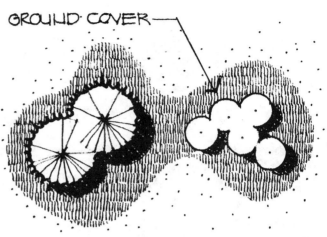

TWO GROUPS OF PLANTS ARE VIS-UALLY UNRELATED; COMPOSITION IS SPLIT.

GROUND COVER UNIFIES GROUPS OF PLANTS INTO ONE COMPOSITION.

FIGURE 2.38

once it matures. Over a long period of time, areas of ground cover can save money, time, and energy for upkeep when compared with a grass lawn.

Another related practical use of ground cover is to stabilize the soil and prevent erosion on steep slopes. It is difficult to establish a grass surface on a

slope over 4:1 in steepness and dangerous to maintain by mowing. Ground cover should be used as a substitute for lawn under this circumstance.

In summary, plant size is one of the most significant and visible of all plant characteristics, especially

FIGURE 2.39

VARYING FORM AND VALUE, BUT WITH THE SAME SIZE; LITTLE VISUAL INTEREST.

VARYING FORM, VALUE, AND SIZE (SILHOUETTE); MORE VISUAL INTEREST.

94

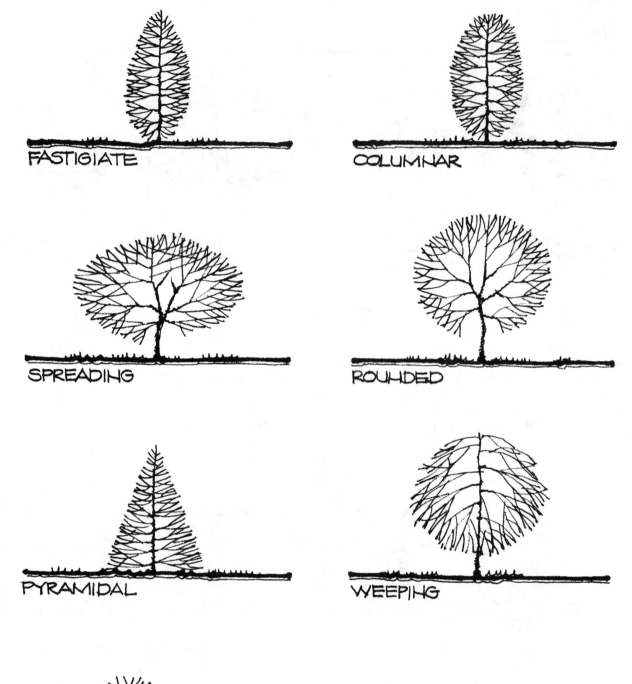

FASTIGIATE

COLUMNAR

SPREADING

ROUNDED

PYRAMIDAL

WEEPING

PICTURESQUE

FIGURE 2.40

FASTIGIATE AND COLUMNAR FORMS USED TO PROVIDE HEIGHT AND ACCENT IN A COMPOSITION.

FIGURE 2.41

from a distance. As previously indicated, plant size establishes the total structure of a planting design while the other plant characteristics provide detail and small-scale interest. The size and height of plants in a composition gives it overall uniformity or variety based on its silhouette. For example, if all the vegetation within a small garden composition is the same size, as illustrated in Figure 2.39, it will not only appear uniform but also monotonous. On the other hand, carefully planned changes in height among the plants give the composition more variety and intrigue. From a distance, alternation in plant height among a mass of plants is more obvious than a change in the other visual plant characteristics (except perhaps bright color). Consequently, plant material size should be one of the first visual plant characteristics determined in the process of planting design. Subsequently, the other qualities of vegetation can be chosen based on the selected plant sizes in the design.

Plant Form. The next visual plant characteristic to be discussed is form. The form of an individual plant or group of plants is the overall shape and habit of growth, or its silhouetted outline. While not as visually strong as size, plant form is nevertheless a key factor in establishing the structure of a plant composition, influencing unity and variety, acting as accents or backgrounds, and coordinating vegetation with the solid mass of other elements in the design. The basic types of plant forms are fastigiate, columnar, spreading/horizontal, round/globular, pyramidal/conical, weeping, and picturesque. All these different plant forms are illustrated in Figure 2.40. Each form type has its own unique characteristics and applications in design as described in the next pages.

Fastigiate. A fastigiate plant form is upright, narrow, and tapers to a point at its top. Examples include Lombardy poplar *(Populus italica nigra)*, American arbor-vitae *(Thuja occidentalis)*, and Italian cypress *(Cupressus sempervirens).* In a design, fastigiate plant forms emphasize the vertical by leading the eye skyward. They give a sense of verticality and height to both a plant mass and to a space they enclose. Used in great quantity, fastigiate plant forms may actually give the illusion that the mass or space they are in is higher than it actually is. When contrasted with lower and more rounded or spreading forms, as depicted in Figure 2.41, fastigiate plant forms act as accents and exclamation points similar to a church steeple on the skyline of a country town. Because of their ability to attract attention, fastigiate plant forms should be used judiciously in small quantities at carefully selected points. Numerous fastigiate plants should not be placed throughout a composition because they will create a "jumpy" design with too many individual focal points.

Columnar. A columnar plant form is the same as a fastigiate form except that it has a rounded top. A sentry maple *(Acer saccharum monumentale)* and Hicks yew *(Taxus media hicksi)* are examples of columnar plants. Columnar plant forms have the same design uses as fastigiate forms.

Spreading/Horizontal. This type of plant form is at least as broad as it is tall, with a generally horizontal habit. Examples are saucer magnolia *(Magnolia soulangeana)*, Washington hawthorne *(Crateagus phaenopyrum)*, and dwarf Japanese yew *(Taxus cuspidata nana).* Spreading plant forms can be used in a design to give it a feeling of breadth and extent. Spreading plant forms carry the eye along in a horizontal fashion, as illustrated in Figure 2.42, and thus may be

SPREADING FORMS GIVE A COMPOSITION A FEELING OF BREADTH AND EXTENT.

FIGURE 2.42

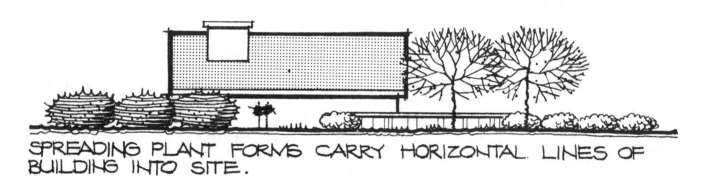

SPREADING PLANT FORMS CARRY HORIZONTAL LINES OF BUILDING INTO SITE.

FIGURE 2.43

used in a composition to connect the other forms visually, especially if the horizontal forms are sensitively repeated throughout the design. In an opposite manner, spreading plant forms may be used for contrast with the vertical fastigiate and columnar forms within a composition. Spreading plant forms tend to be at harmony with flat landforms, long lines extending across the horizon, and low horizontal building forms. Placed next to this type of building, they may extend the lines of the architecture into the surrounding site, as indicated in Figure 2.43.

Round/Globular. As the name suggests, this type of plant material form has a distinct rounded or spherical shape. European beech (*Fagus sylvatica*), silver linden (*Tilia tomentosa*), Japanese maple (*Acer palmatum*), Cornelian cherry dogwood (*Cornus mas*), and Indian laurel fig (*Ficus microcarpa*) are all examples of globular plant form. Rounded plant forms are one of the most numerous types of plant forms and therefore typically constitute the majority of plants used in a design composition (Figure 2.44). Unlike either the fastigiate or spreading plant forms, rounded plants are nondirectional and neutral in their ability to lead the eye. Therefore globular plants can be easily used to give a design unity by

their repetition throughout the composition. They can serve as the neutral, soft plant form against which the other more striking forms are opposed. Round plant forms may also be situated in a design to harmonize with and echo other curvilinear forms such as undulating landform.

Pyramidal/Conical. This type of plant form is cone-like in appearance, gradually tapering from its base to an observable point. Examples include spruce (*Picea sp.*), sweet gum (*Liquidambar styraciflua*), and katsura tree (*Cercidiphyllum japonicum*). Pyramidal plant forms are very sharp and distinct in their outline in addition to possessing an easily noticeable pointed top. Consequently, they may be used as visual accents, particularly when contrasted against lower globular forms, as shown in Figure 2.45. In addition, they may be used to echo pyramidal building forms or peaked mountain landforms. Because of this, some design theorists suggest that conical plant forms be used cautiously in visually level regions where mountains are lacking.[24] Finally, conical plant

---

[24]William R. Nelson, Jr., *Landscaping Your Home* (Urbana-Champaign, Ill.: Cooperative Extension Service in Agriculture and Home Economics, 1975), p. 98.

ROUNDED FORMS SHOULD PREDOMINATE IN A COMPOSITION.

FIGURE 2.44

PYRAMIDAL FORM USED AS AN ACCENT AMONG ROUNDED AND SPREADING FORMS.

FIGURE 2.45

forms may be harmoniously used in formal, architectonic designs where stiff, geometric shapes are appropriate.

Weeping. A weeping plant form has predominantly pendulous, or downward-arching, branches. Weeping willow *(Salix babylonica)*, weeping beech *(Fagus sylvatica pendula)*, and cranberry cotoneaster *(Cotoneaster apiculata)* are all weeping plant forms. In nature, weeping plant forms are often found in and associated with low points of ground, like the weeping willow along edges of water bodies (Figure 2.46). In a design, they can lead the eye toward the ground, a function that may be employed after the

FIGURE 2.46

WEEPING PLANT FORMS USED TO "DRIP" DOWN A WALL OR RE-
TURN THE EYE TO THE GROUND.

FIGURE 2.47

eye has been carried upward with ascending forms. Weeping plant forms may also be used at the edge of a curvilinear body of water to reflect the undulating form and to symbolize the fluid quality of the water itself. To express the weeping form of a plant, it is sometimes desirable to place it at the edge of a planter or elevated point of ground so the plant can fall or "drip" over the edge, as shown in Figure 2.47.

Picturesque. The picturesque plant form is uniquely sculptural in shape. It may be irregular, gnarled, windblown, or contorted to an unusual shape. A picturesque plant form is often a mature plant that has adapted over a long period of time to the environmental conditions present at a certain location. The plant shown in Figure 2.48 is an example of a picturesque plant form that has responded to the wind and soil conditions in a mountainous area of Arizona. Except for trained bonsai plants, most picturesque plants are the result of unique natural forces. Owing to their uncommon appearance, picturesque plant forms are best used as specimens located at a prominent point within a design. Usually no more than one picturesque plant form should be

FIGURE 2.48

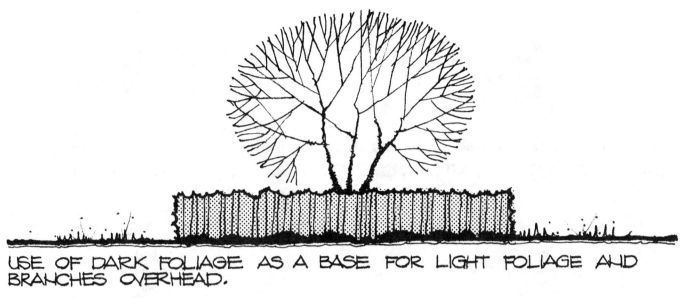

USE OF DARK FOLIAGE AS A BASE FOR LIGHT FOLIAGE AND BRANCHES OVERHEAD.

FIGURE 2.49

placed in any one area of sight at a time to avoid a busy or chaotic scene.

Naturally, not all plant materials fit neatly into the categories of plant forms just described. Some vegetation is rather nondescript in shape while others cross the lines of the various plant form types. Regardless, form is still an important visual plant characteristic, particularly when a plant is to be placed by itself or used as an accent. Plant form tends to become a little less noticeable when vegetation is massed together where individual plant shape becomes lost. In this situation the significant factor is the collective form of the entire group of plant material.

Plant Color. After plant size and form, plant color is the most notable visual characteristic of plant material. Plant color may be thought of as an emotional characteristic because it directly affects the feeling and mood of an outdoor space. Bright colors convey a light, cheerful atmosphere while dark colors portray a more somber feeling. Plant color is also significant because it is easily seen. Variations in plant color can sometimes be noticed at relatively great distances in the landscape.

Color is present in plant materials through different parts of the plant including foliage, flowers, fruit, twigs and branches, and trunk bark. In foliage the principal color is of course green, with many variations from dark green to light green including shades of yellow, blue, and bronze. Beyond this, an entire color wheel of potential hues exists in the spring and autumn foliage, flowers, twigs, and trunks.

The organization of color in a planting composition should be coordinated with the other visual plant characteristics. Plant color should be used to reinforce the function of plant size and form in a design. For instance, a plant that stands out as a focal point in a design because of size or form might also possess a color that further attracts attention. With this approach, summer foliage color along with winter twig and trunk colors are typically given the most consideration because they are present the majority of the time.[25] Flower color and autumn color, while often theatrical and memorable, are typically short-lived, lasting for no more than several weeks. It is a mistake to select a plant primarily on its flower or autumn foliage color, owing to the comparatively short duration of that characteristic.

In selecting summer foliage color, it may be advantageous to have a range of greens in a composition to give it an added dimension of appeal. A color takes on more meaning if it is opposed to another one. For example, white appears more white when placed against black, and green looks more intense when placed near red or orange. A variety of greens in a composition may also be used for other design functions. The organization of different shades of

[25]William R. Nelson, Jr., *Planting Design* (Champaign, Ill.: Stipes Publishing Company, 1979), p. 35.

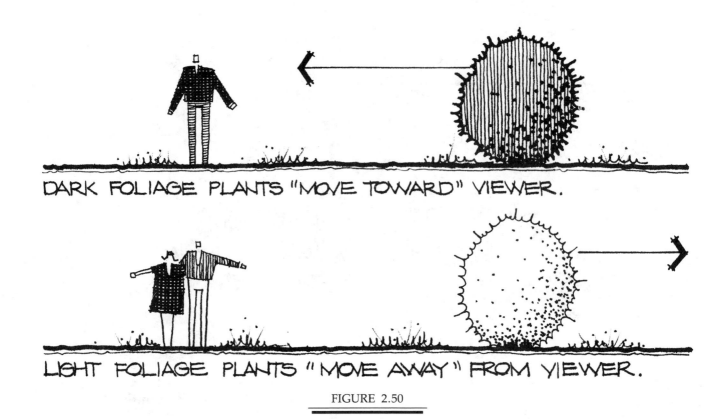

DARK FOLIAGE PLANTS "MOVE TOWARD" VIEWER.

LIGHT FOLIAGE PLANTS "MOVE AWAY" FROM VIEWER.

FIGURE 2.50

green can provide emphasis, establish unity through repetition, or visually link together various portions of the design. Darker greens typical of the Japanese yew (*Taxus cuspidata*) can provide a sense of solidity and weight to both a composition and a related space. It can act as the "anchor posts" of a design, as illustrated in Figure 2.49. Furthermore, dark greens give a quiet, peaceful, and—if overused—dismal feeling to an outdoor space, and dark hues tend to move toward the viewer. As indicated in Figure 2.50, dark colors at the end of a view seem to shorten the distance between the viewer and the object seen. Likewise, a predominance of dark colors in a space can make it feel smaller.

FIGURE 2.51

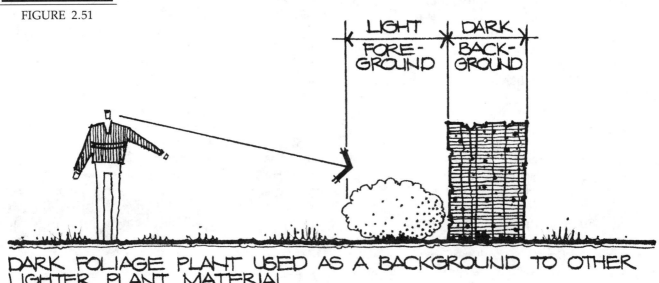

DARK FOLIAGE PLANT USED AS A BACKGROUND TO OTHER LIGHTER PLANT MATERIAL.

MEDIUM TONE GREENS SHOULD ACT AS A TRANSITION BETWEEN DARK AND LIGHT GREENS.

FIGURE 2.52

On the other hand, light green foliage can provide an ethereal, airy quality to a space. It gives a feeling of cheerfulness, gaiety, and excitement in addition to moving away visually from the viewer. When combining the various ranges of green, dark greens are logically used for the base material (owing to their visual weight), to hold the composition to the ground while lighter greens are used overhead as an expression of buoyancy (Figure 2.49). In other situations, as shown in Figure 2.51, dark-valued foliage may be used as a solid background material against which lighter, more visible colors are placed. The opposite may also be desirable in some circumstances.

In composing the plant color of a design, a neutral tone green should usually dominate with all other colors played against it. Such an impartial color can serve as the unifying thread by visually tying all other colors together, as illustrated in Figure 2.52. Contrasting greens should each occur in masses of foliage clearly distinguished from one another. Varying greens should not form too many small individual spots proportional to the overall scale of the composition or a disorganized appearance will result. Caution also needs to be used in placing unusual foliage colors such as bronze, purple, or variegated colors, as these tend to be quite noticeable because of their uniqueness. Uncommon green foliage should be reserved for a few special locations within a design. Likewise, bright flower color should also be massed and placed in only certain areas. If too many individual spots of bright color are installed in a design, it will be chaotic and disjointed. Sensitively placed flower color should be introduced for variety without distracting from the overall unity.

If green summer foliage is used as the basic compositional color within a design, then flower color and autumn color can be used as accents. Reds, oranges, yellows, whites, and pinks can all give life and excitement to design while simultaneously attracting the viewer's attention to certain points within the design. In fact, spots of bright color, if not carefully sized and located in a composition, may be so visually strong as to overpower all other plant characteristics. Areas of bright color are more appropriately used in larger quantities in open, sunny locations where the sunlight absorbs more of their brilliance than it can in shaded areas. Carefully used in shaded areas, on the other hand, bright colors can provide an area of titillation in an otherwise placid space. As previously stated, autumn foliage color and flower color should be secondary to green summer foliage.

Plant color, then, has a number of functions in an exterior space. This visual plant characteristic is generally considered to influence the unity and variety of a design in addition to the mood and feel of the space. As with other variables, plant color should be coordinated with all the other visual plant characteristics in carrying out the intended objectives of the design.

Foliage Type. Somewhat related to plant color is foliage type, which refers to the form and permanence of the foliage. In the temperate climatic zone, there

FIGURE 2.53

are three basic foliage types: deciduous, coniferous evergreen, and broad-leaved evergreen. Each has its own qualities and related potential functions in the landscape.

Deciduous. Deciduous vegetation loses its leaves in autumn and regains them in spring. Deciduous leaves are generally thin, flat, and found in numerous shapes and sizes. In the continental zone, deciduous plants constitute the predominant foliage type in terms of quantity and adaptability to varying environmental conditions. Deciduous plants occur in all shapes, colors, textures, and sizes from ground cover to majestic trees.

Common examples include cotoneasters *(Cotoneaster sp.)*, viburnums *(Viburnum sp.)*, oaks *(Quercus sp.)*, and maples *(Acer sp.)*.

Deciduous plants have several distinct functions in exterior spaces. One significant function is to emphasize the seasons. As mentioned previously, many deciduous plants have four distinct seasonal appearances and characteristics that directly affect qualities of the designs in which they are located. Deciduous plants are a dynamic element that make the climatic changes of the year more obvious and meaningful. They also provide interest as one becomes fascinated observing and marveling at the sometimes spectacular modifications in transparency, form, color, and texture that occur.

Deciduous plants serve as the primary plant material in the temperate climate zone. As such, they can function to define space in all planes, serve as accents and backgrounds, and act as the common foliage type against which evergreen and broad-leaved evergreen plants can be contrasted. In effect, deciduous plants are the "utility plant" in design, being usable for most desired functions. Besides having wide applications, some deciduous plants are selected for distinct form, flower color, or autumn foliage color. Viburnum *(Viburnum sp.)*, forsythia *(Forsythia sp.)*, honeysuckle *(Lonicera sp.)*, beautybush *(Kolkwitzia amabilis)*, dogwood *(Cornus florida)*, and crab apple *(Malus sp.)* are some examples of deciduous plants that have notable flowers that contribute to their usefulness in the landscape.

Another trait of some deciduous plant materials is their ability to allow sunlight to interact with their foliage to create a glowing effect. This phenomenon is referred to as "luminosity" and occurs when the leaves of a plant are located between the eye and the sun, as suggested in Figure 2.53.[26] When viewed from the underside and/or back, the individual leaves are seen as bright yellow-green, giving the illusion that they are internally lit. This outcome is most pronounced in the midmorning or midafternoon when the sun strikes the plant at a lower angle. The result is a radiant, shining effect that gives the understory of the plant an airy, light quality. This consequence may be desirable in locations such

[26]A.E. Bye, Jr., "What You See: Landscape Luminosity," *Landscape Architecture*, 56 (3): 207–208 (April 1966).

DIFFERENT SPECIES OF DECIDUOUS TREES CREATE HABITS OF GROWTH & APPEARANCES IN THE WINTER SEASON.

FIGURE 2.54

as sitting areas, walks, or building entrances where a shaded, protected, yet light spatial quality is desired.

One unique characteristic of deciduous plant materials is that many of them have distinct and intriguing branch habits observable during winter. This quality is as important as the texture and color of the summer foliage because deciduous plant materials have bare branches in the temperate zone for as long as they have foliage, if not longer. The density of branches, their color, and their configuration or habit of growth are all variables that need to be studied in selecting and locating deciduous plants in a design. Some deciduous plants such as the sugar maple (Acer saccharum) or amer privet (Ligustrum amurense) are densely branched and possess a distinct silhouette in winter, while others such as honeylocust (Gleditsia triacanthos) and staghorn sumac (Rhus typhina "Laciniata") have an open branching habit with an ill-defined, irregular outline.

The pattern of lines created by the branches themselves, as illustrated in Figure 2.54, is still another design consideration. Some plant materials may have noticeable horizontal lines established by their branches, such as flowering dogwood (Cornus florida) or Washington hawthorne (Crataegus phaenopyrum).

FIGURE 2.55

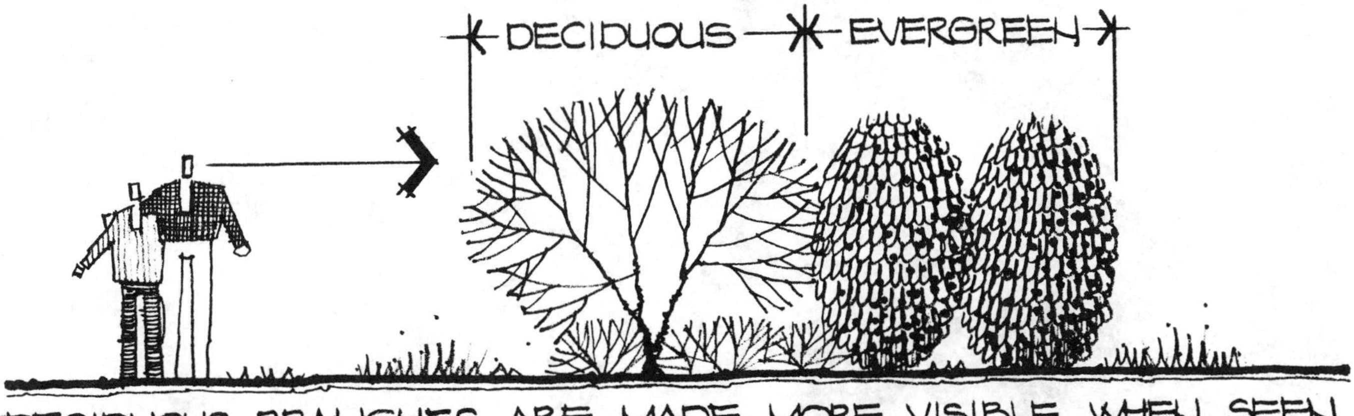

DECIDUOUS ——— EVERGREEN

DECIDUOUS BRANCHES ARE MADE MORE VISIBLE WHEN SEEN AGAINST AN EVERGREEN BACKGROUND.

Plants like American ash *(Fraxinum americana)* and European hornbeam *(Carpinus betulus)* have distinctly upward-arching branch lines, while plants like pin oak *(Quercus palustris)* have obviously downward-arching branch lines. Still other plants like crab apples *(Malus sp.)* and redbud *(Cercis canadensis)* may possess gnarled and contorted branch lines as they become old and weathered. The bare branches and their patterns can be shown off if they are placed against a dark evergreen background or other neutral setting, as portrayed in Figure 2.55. Another attractive possibility is to locate a deciduous plant so that shadows of the abstract branch patterns are either cast on areas of pavement or against a bare wall, as shown in Figure 2.56. Such shadow patterns can help relieve the monotony of a large expanse of pavement or an otherwise blank wall during the winter season.

FIGURE 2.56

Coniferous evergreen. The second general type of plant foliage is the needlelike foliated vegetation that retains its leaves throughout the year. White pine *(Pinus strobus)*, spruce *(Picea sp.)*, hemlock *(Tsuga canadensis)*, yew *(Taxus sp.)*, and juniper *(Juniperus sp.)* are examples of coniferous evergreen plants. Coniferous evergreens vary from low shrubs to tall trees of various shapes, colors, and textures. However, coniferous evergreens as a group do not have visible flowers. Like deciduous vegetation, evergreen plant materials have a number of functions based on their unique qualities.

By comparison with other types of plant materials, coniferous evergreens are, as a group, the darkest foliated of all (junipers are a notable exception). This phenomenon results because the needle foliage of coniferous evergreens absorbs much of the light falling upon it while reflecting very little. The relative dark green of evergreens is most obvious from midsummer through early spring of the following year and especially during winter, as indicated in Figure 2.57. This results in a generally massive appearance. Consequently, evergreen plant materials may be used to give visual weight and solidity to a design, as suggested in the discussion on color. They may also portray a somber, contemplative atmosphere in a space or plant material composition. However, evergreens generally should not be overplanted in any one area because they may create a funereal character in a design, as is the case in the foundation planting around many older homes. Coniferous evergreens generally should form a smaller percentage of the plants in a design compared with deciduous plant materials. The exception is regional locations where coniferous evergreens are the prevailing plant species. Here, it would be appropriate for evergreens to form the majority of plants used in a design composition.

One other principle that should be followed for evergreens in a design is that they should be grouped at various locations as opposed to scattered throughout the design because of their visual weight and obviousness during winter. Indiscriminate placement of evergreen vegetation produces a chaotic appearance, as illustrated in Figure 2.58.

Another use of evergreen plants based on their relatively dark foliage is as backgrounds to lighter colors, as shown in Figures 2.51 and 2.55. A popular application of this is to use coniferous evergreen trees and shrubs as a background to lighter flowering plants such as flowering dogwood *(Cornus florida)*, Canadian redbud *(Cercis canadensis)*, and azaleas *(Rhododendron sp.)*. These flowering plants are

FIGURE 2.57

spectacular in the spring when seen against a background of dark evergreens.

One important trait of coniferous evergreen vegetation is identified in the name itself; its foliage is relatively nonchanging and permanently green. Compared with deciduous plant material, evergreens are static and stable. Consequently, they lend a feeling of permanence to a design. They provide a timeless setting against which altering deciduous plants can be compared. The seasonal variation of deciduous vegetation is made more noticeable if certain parts of the environment such as coniferous evergreens change at a less obvious rate.

Because of their density, coniferous evergreen plant materials are effective in blocking views and air circulation. Evergreen trees are the choice vegetation to provide permanent, nonchanging screening and privacy control throughout all seasons of the year, as suggested in Figure 2.59. Furthermore, they may be located around a building or outdoor space to give it protection from chilling winds. Typically, the most advantageous location for coniferous evergreen trees to block cold winter wind in the temperate zone is on the northwest side of a building or outdoor space (Figure 2.60). Here they can reduce wind velocity up to 60 percent of its open field speed.[27] This reduction in wind velocity minimizes cold air infiltration into buildings while also cutting

FIGURE 2.58

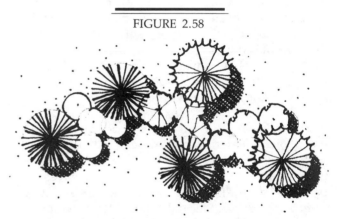

EVERGREENS ARE TOO SCATTERED & THEREFORE VISUALLY BREAK UP COMPOSITION.

EVERGREENS ARE CLUSTERED TOGETHER TO UNIFY COMPOSITION.

[27]Gary O. Robinette, *Plants, People and Environmental Quality,* p. 77.

EVERGREEN TREES MAY BE USED TO SCREEN OBJECTIONABLE VIEWS IN ALL SEASONS.

FIGURE 2.59

down on the amount of heat carried away. All in all, a properly located and designed mass of coniferous evergreen trees can produce as much as a 33 percent savings in the heating cost of a single-family home.[28] And a mass of tall evergreen shrubs placed against the wall of a building can have similar effects. Here the dense mass of shrubs acts as an added layer of insulation by creating a dead air space between the shrubs themselves and the building wall.

Before leaving the subject of deciduous and evergreen plant material, one more word needs to be said about their combination. As a general rule of thumb (without regard for specific objectives of a particular design), a proportional balance should exist between deciduous and evergreen vegetation in a plant composition. The two types complement each other by bringing out each other's best qualities. When used alone, as in Figure 2.61, deciduous plants may appear attractive enough during summer but "disappear" during winter because they lack mass and visual weight at this season. From an opposite standpoint, a design that contains only coniferous evergreen vegetation as in Figure 2.62 is apt to be dull because it is too heavy and dismal while varying little with the seasons of the year. So deciduous and coniferous evergreen plant materials are best combined to eliminate these potential problems while visually supporting each other, as in Figure 2.63.

Broad–leaved evergreens. The third general foliage type of plant material is broad-leaved evergreens, which resemble deciduous vegetation in leaf appearance but retain their foliage throughout the year. Rhododendron (_Rhododendron sp._), azalea (_Rhododendron sp._), mountain laurel (_Kalmia latifolia_), Andromeda (_Pieris sp._), and leucothoe (_Leucothoe sp._) are examples of broad-leaved evergreen plant materials. Characteristics and potential design uses of broad-leaved evergreens include the following.

Like coniferous evergreens, broad-leaved evergreens tend to possess dark green foliage. However, a number of broad-leaved evergreens possess reflective leaves, making them shiny when placed in sunlight. One potential use of broad-leaved evergreens is to lend a sparkling, luminescent quality to an open outdoor space. They can make a composition feel light and airy in a sunny location. When placed in the shade, broad-leaved evergreen vegetation may function similarly to coniferous evergreens by appearing dark and heavy.

As a group, broad-leaved evergreen plant materials are known for their spectacular spring flower. Many people place them in a design solely for their flowers. This is not necessarily the best approach because the flowers last for only a short period of time, as discussed earlier in the section on color. Rather, broad-leaved evergreen plants should be placed in a design based primarily on their foliage, with flowers considered an additional benefit. In some situations the showy flowers may be used as a focal point in the design. (This works well too for plants such as rhododendron that have coarse foliage texture because this also attracts attention.)

---

[28]Anne Simon Moffat and Marc Schiler, _Landscape Design that Saves Energy_, p. 20.

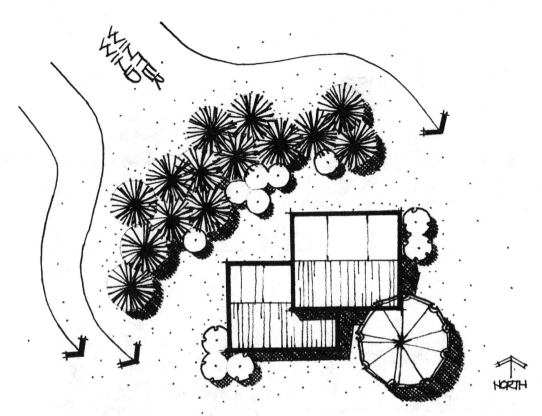

EVERGREEN TREES PLACED ON NORTHWEST SIDE OF BUILDING TO BLOCK COLD NW WINTER WIND.

FIGURE 2.60

Broad-leaved evergreens as a group are not very hardy plants. Most tend to do better in mild climates (zones 5–10) or in conditions of partial sun and shade in the temperate zone such as found on the east side of a building. Broad-leaved evergreens cannot tolerate intense hot or cold and should not be placed where they will get full sun in winter or where they will be exposed to damaging winter wind. Both conditions are apt to cause excess tran-

spiration from the leaves at times when water is not readily available to the roots. Furthermore, most broad-leaved evergreens require acid soil for proper growth, thus limiting their potential use in the landscape to areas possessing all the necessary conditions.

In summary, as we study the color of a planting design, we need to consider simultaneously the foliage type, very much an integral factor of plant

FIGURE 2.61

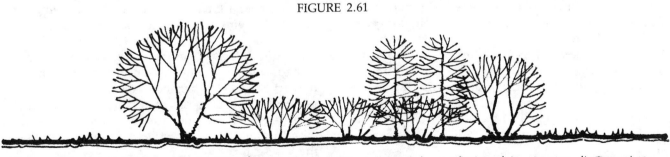

ALL DECIDUOUS PLANTING HAS NO VISUAL WEIGHT AND "DISAPPEARS" IN THE WINTER SEASON.

ALL EVERGREEN PLANTING IS TOO VISUALLY HEAVY AND
HAS NO SEASONAL VARIETY.

FIGURE 2.62

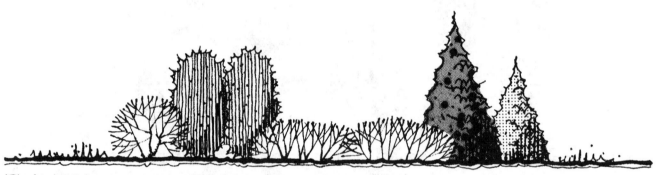

PLANTING COMPOSITION SHOULD CONTAIN A COMBINATION OF
DECIDUOUS AND EVERGREEN PLANTS.

FIGURE 2.63

color. Foliage type influences seasonal interest, visibility, and unity of a design. Foliage type also relates directly to the texture of plant materials which we discuss next.

Plant Texture. Plant texture is the visual roughness and smoothness of an individual plant or group of plants. It is influenced by leaf size, twig and branch size, bark configuration, the overall habit of growth, and the distance at which the plant material is viewed. At close range, the individual leaf size, shape, surface, and arrangement on the twig are the notable factors affecting visual texture, while the density of branches and general habit of growth are the main variables impacting texture when the plant is viewed in its entirety from a distance.[29] In addi-

tion to varying with distance, texture is also apt to alter with season in deciduous plant material. Without leaves, the textural quality of a deciduous plant during winter is different and generally more open than in summer. In some instances, as with the honey locust, the texture may change dramatically with the seasons. In summer the foliage gives the honey locust a fine, airy texture while in winter the branches themselves provide an open, rough texture.

Texture affects a number of factors in a planting composition, including compositional unity and variety, perception of distance, color tone, visual interest, and mood of a design. Plant texture is usually classified as coarse, medium, and fine (Figure 2.64), with the following properties and potential uses in the landscape.

Coarse texture. Coarse texture is usually created by large leaves, thick, massive branches (lacking

[29]Florence Bell Robinson, *Planting Design* (Champaign, Ill.: Gerrard Press, 1940), pp. 46–47.

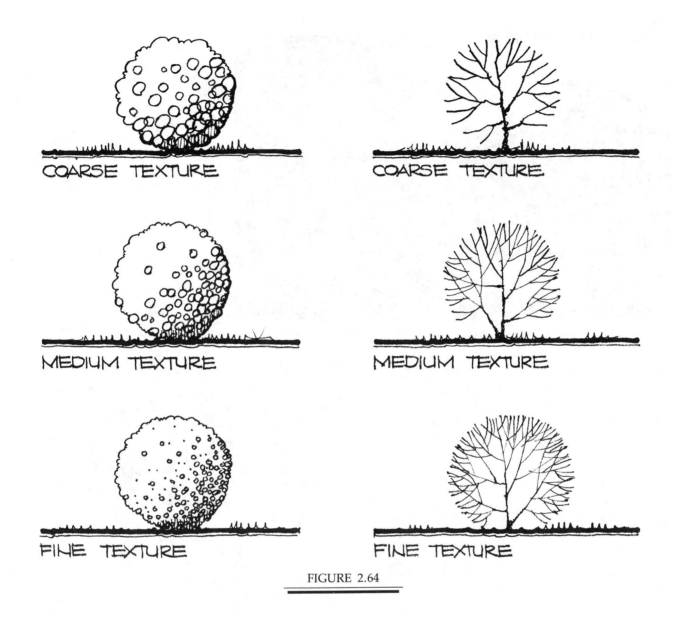

COARSE TEXTURE

COARSE TEXTURE

MEDIUM TEXTURE

MEDIUM TEXTURE

FINE TEXTURE

FINE TEXTURE

FIGURE 2.64

small, fine twigs), and/or loose open habit of growth. Plants considered to be coarse-textured include plane tree *(Platanus occidentalis)*, horse chestnut *(Aesculus hippocastanum)*, Austrian pine *(Pinus nigra)*, agave *(Agave weberi)*, saucer magnolia *(Magnolia soulangeana)*, rhododendron *(Rhododendron sp.)*, and oak leaf hydrangea *(Hydrangea quercifolia*, Figure 2.65). Some specific characteristics and functions of coarse-textured plant materials are listed below.

Coarse texture is highly visible, bold, and aggressive. Placed among medium and fine textures, coarse texture "jumps out" at the viewer and is the first texture seen. As a result, coarse texture may be used within a design as a focal point to attract and

hold attention or to give a feeling of strength. Like all other accents, coarse-textured plant materials should be carefully placed and used in moderation so as not to overpower a composition or call attention to too many individual areas.

Because of its strength, coarse texture causes the sensation of "moving toward" the viewer, making the perceived distance between viewer and plant material seem shorter than it really is, as suggested in Figure 2.66. Similarly, coarse-textured plants in quantity can make an outdoor space feel smaller than it is by visually "moving in" on the space. This may be desired where the actual physical dimensions are too large for normal human comfort but

FIGURE 2.65

undesirable where a space is tight and confined even without plant material. Caution should be exercised in locating coarse-textured plants in a small space because they can overwhelm it if overused or located improperly.

Coarse-textured plants in many instances appear more open, looser, and less distinct in outline than do finer-textured plants. Coarse-textured plants also usually have more variation of light and shade. Because of these qualities, coarse-textured plants are generally more easily used in informal settings. They are more difficult to use in formal situations that require perfect forms and precise outlines.

Medium texture. Medium texture results from medium-sized leaves and branches and/or moderately dense habit of growth. Compared with coarse tex-

ture, a medium-textured plant is less transparent and stronger in silhouette. Because the majority of vegetation has medium texture, it generally should make up the largest proportion of texture in a planting composition. Like medium-tone greens, medium texture should form the basic texture of a design, serving as a transitional element between coarse and fine textures. Medium texture can link a composition together into a unified whole.

Fine texture. Fine texture is produced by many small leaves, tiny, thin branches and twigs, and/or a tight, dense habit of growth. Honey locust (*Gleditsia triacanthos*), Japanese maple (*Acer palmatum*), white pine (*Pinus strobus*), cranberry cotoneaster (*Cotoneaster apiculata*), red bird of paradise (*Caesalpinia pulcherrima*), and Vanhoutte spirea (*Spirea vanhouttei*) are examples of plant materials with fine texture.

FIGURE 2.66

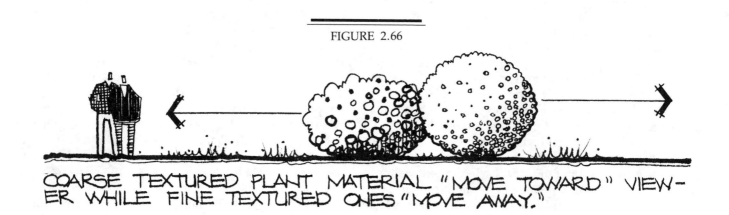

COARSE TEXTURED PLANT MATERIAL "MOVE TOWARD" VIEWER WHILE FINE TEXTURED ONES "MOVE AWAY."

Fine-textured plants have opposite characteristics and design capabilities from coarse-textured ones. Fine-textured plants are soft and delicate in appearance and consequently less obvious in the landscape. They are usually the last plants noticed in a composition (based only on texture) and are the first to be visually lost in a design as the distance between viewer and composition increases. Fine-textured plants can be appropriately introduced into a composition to act as a neutral background to more aggressive textures, to provide a refined, smooth surface character, or to add visual variety when complemented with coarse and medium texture.

Because fine-textured plants are visually less obvious in a composition, they have a tendency to "recede away" from the viewer (Figure 2.66). Therefore, when employed in quantity in an outdoor space, fine-textured plant material may give it the illusion of being larger than it is. This quality makes fine-textured plants particularly useful in tight, small spaces where the perceived edges should be permitted visually to expand only, not to contract.

Fine-textured plants often have a clearly defined silhouette and an overall smooth, solid-appearing surface owing to the quantity of small leaves and/or density of branches. (Some fine-textured plants look carefully sheared and pruned even in their natural, untouched state.) Consequently, fine-textured plants are correctly used in some settings to provide a neat, precise formal character.

As a guideline, it is best to attempt to incorporate a balanced variety of the three basic textural types within a design to make it appealing to the eye, as shown in Figure 2.67. Too little textural variation is perceived as monotonous, while too much is chaotic. This desired balance becomes most significant for smaller-scaled spaces and is progressively less important as the scale of spaces increases or as the viewer moves away from the plant material being observed. Another suggestion is to arrange the various textural types in proportionally large areas using the medium-textured plants as a transition between coarse and fine textures. Too many small areas of dissimilar textures or too sudden a change from coarse to fine texture is apt to make the composition feel disorganized and disjointed. And as with all the other visual plant characteristics, the selection and use of texture in a planting composition needs to be coordinated with plant size, form, and color in order to reinforce these other qualities.

In summary, the visual plant characteristics of size, form, color, and texture are the designer's palette of variables in designing with plant material.

FIGURE 2.67

The visual plant characteristics have a direct bearing on the order and unity of a design, visual variety and excitement, and the mood or feeling of the outdoor environment. They need to be studied carefully in creating a design and coordinated with the overall objectives of the design.

Aesthetic Uses of Plant Material

Previous sections of this chapter discussed the various functional uses of plant material in general and then, more specifically, possible architectural uses of plant material in the landscape. Based on the visual plant characteristics outlined in the preceding section, plant material can also fulfill a number of aesthetic uses.

PLANT MATERIALS COMPLEMENT ARCHITECTURE BY CARRYING LINES INTO SITE.

FIGURE 2.68

Considered from an aesthetic standpoint, plant material may be employed in exterior spaces to relate a building form to its surrounding site, unify and coordinate an otherwise discordant environment, reinforce certain points and areas in the landscape, reduce the harshness of hard architectural elements, and enframe selected views. It should be noted here that aesthetic uses of vegetation are not solely limited to plant materials as elements of decoration. Some possible aesthetic functions of plant material are described in greater detail in the following sections.

Complementors. Plant material may complete a design and furnish a sense of unity by repeating the forms and masses of a building or by extending lines of a building into the immediately surrounding site.[30] For example, the angle and/or height of a roof can be repeated using trees that are of the same height as the roof or of such a form as to carry the pitch of the roof into the site, as illustrated in Figure 2.68. Or an interior space can be extended directly into the site by repeating the ceiling height, as in Figure 2.69, with the same height of the tree canopies placed next to the building. All these techniques make the architecture and site seem visually and functionally unified in one coordinated environment.

Unifiers. Used as unifiers, plant material can serve as a common thread, visually tying together all the different components of an environment.[31] Within any given portion of the outdoor environment, plant material may act as the one element that stays the same while other elements vary. Because of its consistency in this area, vegetation unifies the otherwise chaotic scene. A good application of this function is along an urban street where each house or storefront is often different from the one next door, as suggested in Figure 2.70. Without street trees, this type of streetscape breaks apart into separate architectural pieces. A strong massing of street trees, on the other hand, performs as a common element relating to all buildings and consequently links them visually into a unified whole.

Emphasizers. Another aesthetic function of plant material is to emphasize or accentuate certain points in the exterior environment.[32] As stated earlier in this chapter, vegetation can do this by means of distinct size, form, color, or texture that is at variance with the immediate surroundings. The resulting uniqueness is highly noticeable and focuses attention on its location. It may be desirable to do this at the entrance to a site, at an intersection, near a building entrance, or in association with other visually prominent locations, as illustrated in Figures 2.71 and 2.72.

Acknowledgers. A similar aesthetic function of plant material is as an acknowledger.[33] In this capacity, plant materials point out or "acknowledge" the importance and location of a space or object in the environment (Figure 2.73). They make the space more obvious and easily recognized. Again, unique plant size, form, color, texture, or arrangement may be utilized for acknowledgment, as in the case of tall trees placed in back of a piece of sculpture.

Softener. Plant materials may be used in an outdoor space to soften or lessen the harshness and rigidity of architectonic shapes and forms.[34] Vegetation of all

---

[30]Gary O. Robinette, *Plants, People and Environmental Quality*, p. 112.
[31]Ibid., p. 113.
[32]Ibid., p. 114
[33]Ibid., p. 115.
[34]Ibid., p. 114.

113

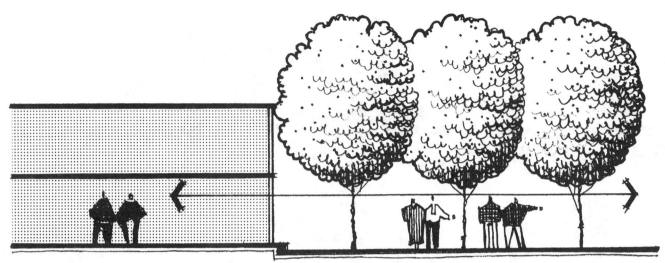

BOTTOM OF TREE CANOPY CONTINUES FIRST FLOOR CEILING INTO SITE & THUS HELPS TO UNIFY INDOORS & OUTDOORS.

FIGURE 2.69

FIGURE 2.70

STREET LACKING TREES IS UNCOORDINATED AND DISJOINTED.

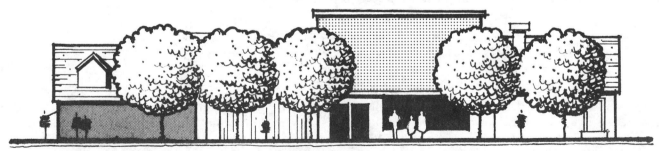

STREET TREES ACT AS UNIFIERS AND COORDINATE STREET-SCAPE THROUGH THEIR COMMONALITY.

PLANT MATERIALS USED AS EMPHASIZERS.

FIGURE 2.71

PLANT MATERIALS USED AS EMPHASIZERS.

FIGURE 2.72

PLANT MATERIALS USED AS ACKNOWLEDGERS.

FIGURE 2.73

forms and textures appears more pliant and cottony than the strict and often brazen look of bare buildings and unplanted urban settings. A space softened with plant material seems more inviting and humane than one that has not.

View Enframement. Plant materials have a direct influence on what is seen or not seen and the sequence in which the views are revealed, as pointed out in the section on architectural uses of plant materials. Because of this, plant materials may directly

PLANT MATERIAL USED TO ENFRAME A VIEW.

FIGURE 2.74

focus our attention on a particular point in the landscape by blocking out distractions to either side of the object with their foliage masses, trunks, and branches while providing an open, unobstructed view of the object itself. Used in this fashion, plant materials act as blinders and create a frame around the desired view. A classic technique for enframing a view in numerous photographs and painted landscape pictures is that of a tree trunk to one side and lower branch extending above the line of sight, as shown in Figure 2.74.

Planting Design Process and Principles

As with other physical elements used in the landscape, there are certain steps, techniques, and principles for designing with plant material. All are based upon the concept that plant materials are equally important in the landscape in meeting the objectives of the designer and solving environmental problems as do other physical design elements such as landform, buildings, pavement, and water. With this view in mind, it is critical to consider plant materials as early as possible in the design process to ensure that they fit the situation both functionally and visually. As suggested several times before, it is incorrect to study and use plant materials near the end of the design process as ornamentation or "icing on the cake" after major decisions have been made about the function, location, and form of the other physical elements in a design.

In designing with plant materials, the landscape architect typically proceeds through a number of decision-making steps referred to as the "design process." These steps proceed from the general to the specific and are outlined in greater detail in Chapter 7. The functional use, organization, placement, and selection of plant materials is an integral part of this entire process. Early phases of this process include an analysis of the site to identify problems and potentials as well as a review of the client's needs. From this the landscape architect is able to specify what elements and functions need to be included in the design, problems that need to be solved, and the intended feeling or character of the design.

Next, the landscape architect generally prepares a functional or bubble diagram that depicts the major elements and functions of the design in an abstract manner. Loosely drawn bubbles and other diagrammatic symbols are used to represent such items as spaces (outdoor rooms), walls, screens, views, and circulation. Where applicable in the design, the use of plant materials is determined for such functions as screening, shading, spatial definition, and focal points. The general location for mass planting in beds is also studied during this phase. Usually no thought is given during this phase, however, to the exact type of plant to be used (such as sugar maple or viburnum) or to the actual layout and placement of individual plants. The designer is concerned only about the location and relative size of the areas in which the plant materials are to be placed, not the arrangement within the areas. Specific forms, materials, or details of construction are unimportant at

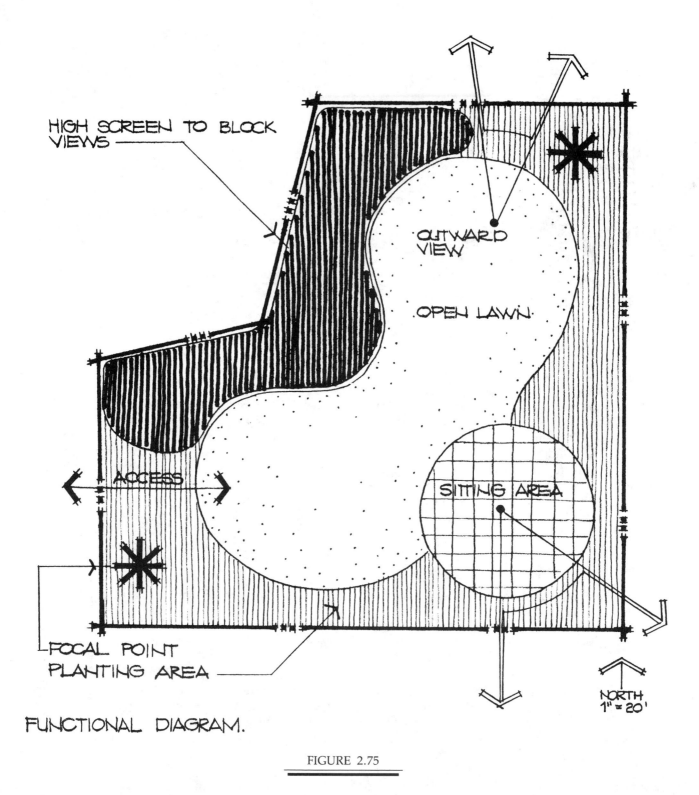

HIGH SCREEN TO BLOCK VIEWS

OUTWARD VIEW

OPEN LAWN

ACCESS

SITTING AREA

FOCAL POINT PLANTING AREA

NORTH
1" = 20'

FUNCTIONAL DIAGRAM.

FIGURE 2.75

this point. In many instances, several different alternative functional diagrams are developed in order to evaluate and select the best solution. Example of functional diagrams are shown in Figures 2.75 and 7.5.

As decisions and priorities are made about the functional diagram and as the graphic diagram itself becomes further refined, more detail can be added. Sometimes this more elaborated diagram is referred to as a "concept plan." Figures 2.76 and 7.6 are ex-

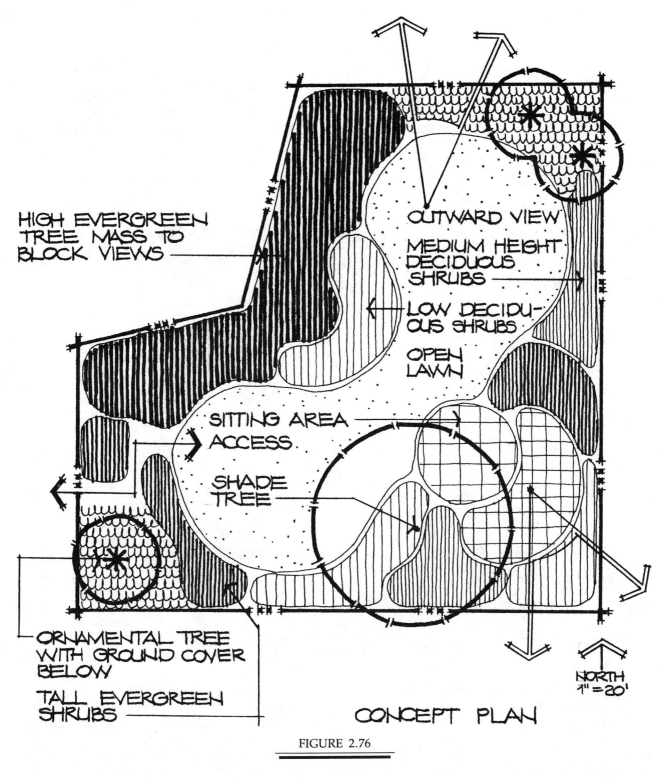

HIGH EVERGREEN TREE MASS TO BLOCK VIEWS

OUTWARD VIEW

MEDIUM HEIGHT DECIDUOUS SHRUBS

LOW DECIDUOUS SHRUBS

OPEN LAWN

SITTING AREA ACCESS

SHADE TREE

ORNAMENTAL TREE WITH GROUND COVER BELOW

TALL EVERGREEN SHRUBS

CONCEPT PLAN

NORTH 1" = 20'

FIGURE 2.76

amples of concept plans. During this phase of the process, attention is given to the conceptual layout within the planting areas themselves. Now, the landscape architect subdivides the planting areas into smaller areas or bubbles that each represent plant materials of different type, size, and form. Again, however, the designer deals essentially in broad terms. For example, the designer may choose to make one area within the planting bed tall deciduous shrubs, another area low coniferous evergreen

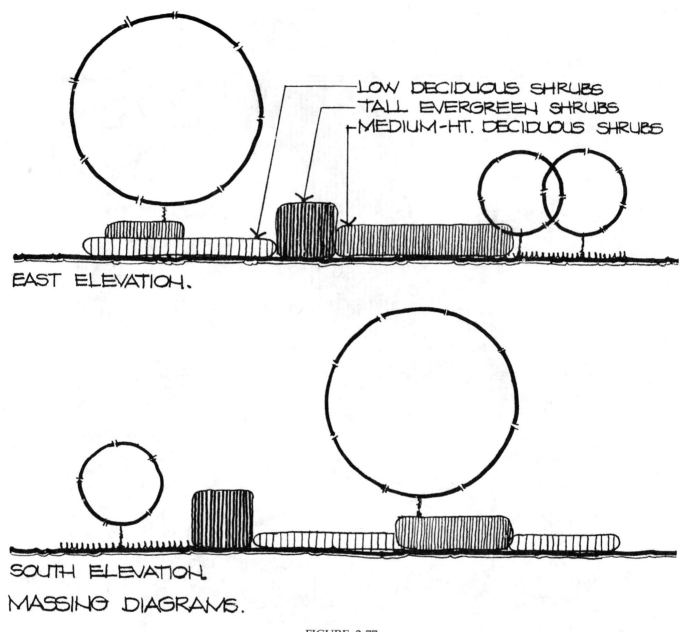

LOW DECIDUOUS SHRUBS
TALL EVERGREEN SHRUBS
MEDIUM-HT. DECIDUOUS SHRUBS

EAST ELEVATION.

SOUTH ELEVATION.
MASSING DIAGRAMS.

FIGURE 2.77

shrubs, and still another area a group of ornamental trees. The relationship among colors and textures should also be studied at this step. But still no effort is made to arrange individual plants or to identify exact species of plants. This permits the landscape architect to create the ideal relationships among the different visual plant characteristics in a conceptual fashion.

In studying the height relationships in a planting area, it is often a good idea to prepare an elevational massing diagram (Figure 2.77). The purpose of this diagram is to study the relative height of the different areas of plant materials as masses or blocks in a generalized manner similar to the concept plan itself. The elevational massing diagram or silhouette study permits the designer actually to see heights and to evaluate their relationships in a more effective manner than trying to visualize them from only the plan. As many elevational massing diagrams as possible should be prepared for different sides or

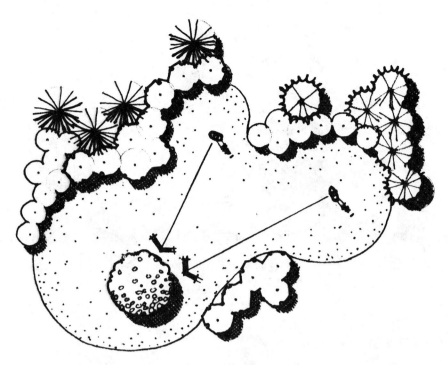

SINGLE TREE USED AS A SPECIMEN IN AN OPEN LAWN AREA.

FIGURE 2.78

viewpoints so that the planting design will be pleasing as an overall three-dimensional composition from all angles.

One critical aspect of the conceptual design stage that needs repeating is that plant materials are dealt with as masses, not as individual plants. There are several reasons for this. One is that groups of similar items in a design contribute to a sense of visual unity within a composition. This is a basic principle of design that applies equally to any design discipline whether graphic design, interior design, architecture, or landscape architecture. When the elements of a design are seen as unrelated and separate pieces, the design tends to break apart visually into competing parts. Massing or "gross collection," on the other hand, consolidates the individual parts into a unified whole.

Another reason for designing with plant materials as conceptual masses is because they are usually found this way in nature. Native vegetation organizes itself in clusters and drifts that slowly change from one species to another in response to altering environmental conditions. There is a definite sense of order and unity to the massing pattern of plant material in a natural setting. Yet within the total organization, there is constant variety of different plants changing from one group to another in a subtle manner to delight the eye. The massing of plant material in nature also affords the individual plants more mutual protection than if they were each located by themselves. Many plants grow where they do because nearby vegetation provides the light, wind, and soil conditions they require for survival. In nature, vegetation forms interdependent ecosystems in which all plants help each other.

The only time a plant should be placed in a design as a separate, individual element is when the designer wishes to attract attention to it as a specimen. A specimen plant may be a free-standing element such as the picturesque ornamental shown in Figure 2.78, which is placed in an open lawn area to function as a dynamic piece of sculpture seen from all sides. Or a specimen might be located in a mass of lesser plant material as in Figure 2.79 to act as a dominant element of the plant composition. According to our previous discussions about visual plant characteristics, the specimen plant might be columnar, pyramidal, or picturesque in form with coarse

SPECIMEN USED AS AN ACCENT IN A PLANT MASS.

FIGURE 2.79

texture and bright, showy flowers. Specimen plants should be few in a design to avoid the possibility of attracting attention to too many different points.

Having completed the conceptual organization of plant masses within the entire design, the landscape architect is able to move on to the next step of the planting design process. Now, the designer can begin to take each bubble or area of the concept plan and arrange the individual plants within it, as shown in Figure 2.80. Still, the plants are dealt with as masses (except for specimens or focal points) and arranged to fill completely all the bubble areas of the conceptual plan.

Several thoughts need to be kept in mind when organizing individual plants. First, individual plants within masses are shown as circles drawn at the appropriate scale to be about 75 to 100 percent of the plant's mature size. The landscape architect designs with plant materials for their ultimate effect and appearance, not their initial look. The application of this approach does, however, cause some initial visual problems. When planted correctly, immature nursery stock should actually be separated from one another to allow adequate room for growth. Therefore one must accept this early spottiness in a plant composition, realizing that with time the gaps between individual plants will close and disappear. Nonetheless, the gaps should not be present once the design has reached maturity. Thus, it is essential that the designer understand both the initial and the eventual mature plant size in order to correctly place

individual plants within masses in a planting composition.

Another suggestion for drawing individual plants in masses is that they should slightly overlap one another. Individual plants are usually allowed to overlap one another by one-fourth to one-third the diameter of each plant in plan, as shown on the right side of Figure 2.81, for the sake of visual unity. As stated before, a composition appears more unified when plants are viewed first as groups or masses. But a planting composition looks more disjointed and chaotic when seen as a collection of individual plants. A plant arrangement with too many individual plants is called "spotty." One additional suggestion about drawing plants in masses is that the outline around the entire mass be drawn heavier than the outline around the individual plants within the mass. This places graphic emphasis where it should be (i.e., on the mass, not the individual plants).

Still another guideline for placing individual plants in masses is to group them in clusters of odd numbers such as 3, 5, or 7—at least for groups of small numbers, as suggested in Figure 2.82. This is due to the basic design principle that odd numbers of elements produce unified compositions because the elements support and reinforce one another, whereas even numbers compete with one another owing to their easy division. In a group of three, the eye does not settle on any single element but relates to the cluster as a whole. In a group of two, the eye

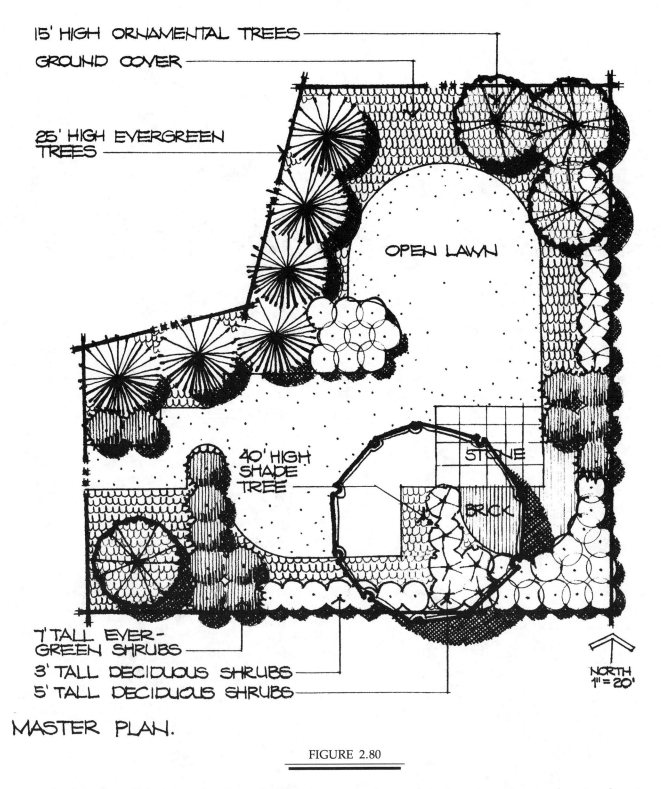

15' HIGH ORNAMENTAL TREES

GROUND COVER

25' HIGH EVERGREEN TREES

OPEN LAWN

40' HIGH SHADE TREE

STONE

BRICK

7' TALL EVER-GREEN SHRUBS

3' TALL DECIDUOUS SHRUBS

5' TALL DECIDUOUS SHRUBS

NORTH 1" = 20'

MASTER PLAN.

FIGURE 2.80

moves back and forth between the two elements because it is unable to rest on either one. Another disadvantage of organizing plants in even numbers is that this approach often requires the individual plants within the group to be of uniform size, form, color, and texture to maintain the visual unity and balance. As the designer deals with larger plants, it becomes more difficult to match size and form among them. And if one plant out of an even-numbered grouping should die, it becomes even more

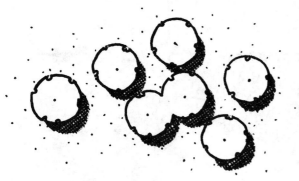

INDIVIDUAL PLANTS IN COMPOSITION ARE SCATTERED & "SPOTTY."

INDIVIDUAL PLANTS IN COMPOSITION ARE MASSED TOGETHER.

FIGURE 2.81

difficult to replace it with a perfectly matched new plant. These suggestions on the numbers of individual plants within a group are most useful when dealing with 7 plants or fewer in a mass. Above this number, it becomes difficult for the eye to distinguish between odd and even quantities.

Having massed individual plants together in groups, one needs next to consider the group-to-group or mass-to-mass relationship. The same principles apply at this level as they did for each plant within a cluster of vegetation. Groups or clusters of plant materials should also be visually connected for

FIGURE 2.82

EVEN NUMBERS OF PLANTS TEND TO SPLIT COMPOSITION.

ODD NUMBERS TEND TO UNIFY COMPOSITION

WHEN FEASIBLE, USE PLANTS IN ODD NUMBERS.

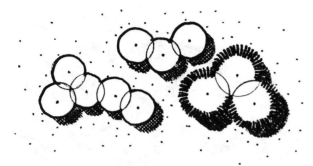

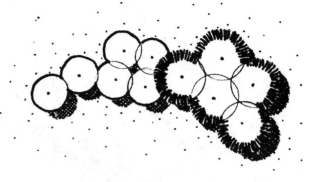

"WASTED SPACE" CREATED BE-
TWEEN SEPARATE PLANT GROUPS.

SEPARATE PLANT GROUPS ARE
MASSED TOGETHER, AVOIDING WAST-
ED SPACE.

FIGURE 2.83

the same reasons as were the individual plants within the groups. Gaps or "wasted space" between clusters of plants, as shown in Figure 2.83, should be eliminated because they are unattractive, create a disjointed appearance, and are apt to cause maintenance problems. In some compositions it is not very effective merely to have the different groups of plants touch or slightly overlap one another. Rather, it is more desirable to have the plant materials interconnect and wrap around one another to maximize the interface between the groups, as indicated in Figure 2.84. Again, this adds to the unity and cohesiveness of a composition because the separate groups of different species seem to be woven to-

gether. With this approach, the height relationships can add fascination to a composition as low plants drift in front of taller ones or as they mysteriously disappear behind a cluster of higher plant material.

When considering spacing and relative height in plan, the designer should not forget the space that exists below the tree canopies. The novice designer frequently makes the mistake of thinking the canopy viewed in plan extends down to the ground and therefore stops the placement of other lower plants at the plan edge of the tree. This creates a void below the tree canopy that disrupts the flow and continuity of the design, as shown in Figure 2.85. This wasted space is also a maintenance problem (unless

FIGURE 2.84

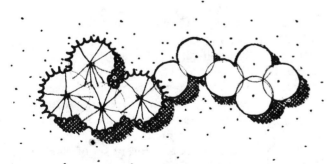

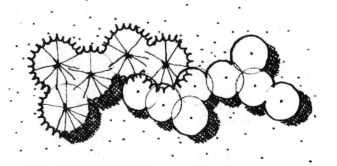

MASSES OF DIFFERENT PLANT
MATERIAL MERELY TOUCH ONE
ANOTHER.

MASSES OF DIFFERENT PLANT
MATERIAL OVERLAP & MAXIMIZE
INTERFACE BETWEEN EACH OTHER.

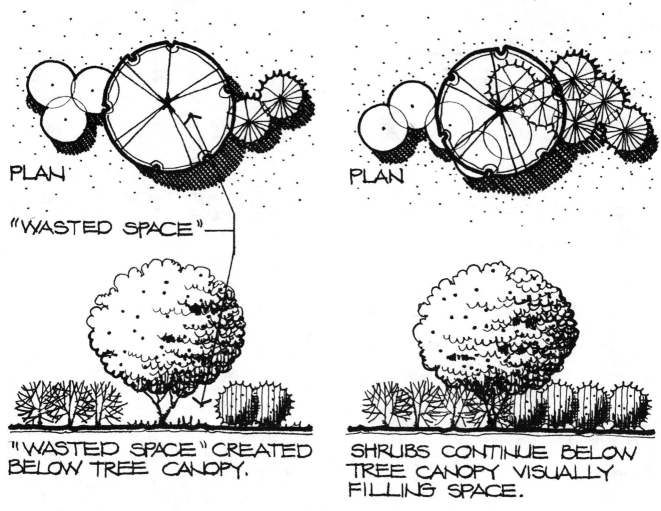

PLAN

"WASTED SPACE"

"WASTED SPACE" CREATED
BELOW TREE CANOPY.

PLAN

SHRUBS CONTINUE BELOW
TREE CANOPY VISUALLY
FILLING SPACE.

FIGURE 2.85

covered by ground cover) because access to it is apt to be troublesome. To eliminate this problem, lower plants should continue below the tree canopy unless the objective is to create a usable space there.

The organization and placement of plants in a design should be coordinated with other elements and forms in addition to other plants within the composition. The planting design should relate to landform, buildings, walls, and areas of pavement and open lawn. If designed correctly, plant material should complement these other elements by reinforcing their forms and outlines. For example, plant material should generally (though not necessarily strictly so) echo the edges of paved areas so that if one were to remove the pavement, its original shape

could still be "read" by the masses of the plant materials themselves. Consequently, plant materials should be organized in a rectilinear form around a pavement that is itself rectilinear (Figure 2.86), or in a curvilinear fashion in a plan that is free-form in character. In these instances, plants provide the third dimension to the structure and form of the plan itself. Thus it would appear incongruous to see one character of forms on the two-dimensional layout of the plan and yet a different set of forms established by the three-dimensional elements of the design.

As the landscape architect completes the first layout of the individual plants, certain parts of the design may be seen as needing changes. Conse-

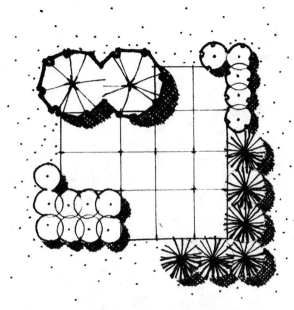

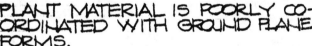

PLANT MATERIAL IS POORLY CO-ORDINATED WITH GROUND PLANE FORMS.

PLANT MATERIAL RELATES TO & REINFORCES GROUND PLANE FORMS.

FIGURE 2.86

quently, a revised plan may be prepared to include the new alterations. During the process of placing individual plants within the composition in masses or as specimens, the landscape architect also begins to study what species of plants will be used in what locations. The species of plant materials chosen for any one location should be done on the basis of the size, form, color, and texture selected earlier during the concept design stage. The designer also needs to take into account such factors as sun, wind, and soil conditions present at any one location in selecting plant species.

Some other guidelines should also be followed in choosing and locating the different species of plant material in a composition. One common species of plant material (and thus one common size, form, color and texture) should predominate in a composition in terms of quantity to further ensure unity. If one follows previously stated guidelines, this common species of plant material will typically be round in form, have medium-tone green foliage, and be medium-textured. This unifying plant species should visually carry throughout the design being repeated from one location to another. Seeing this same element at various places within the composition produces "recall" or memory of observing it be-

fore. Recall mentally unifies a design. Then, other different plant species are added to the design composition for the sake of variety, but not in such quantity or organization as to nullify the unity of the one common plant species. The total number of plant species used in planting design, as in any other discipline, should be carefully controlled so as not to become too many. Simplicity of species types can be another means for unifying a design. Some of the principles are collectively illustrated in Figure 2.87.

It is important to understand that selecting plant species or names is one of the last steps in the planting design process. As stated previously in this section, the planting design process proceeds from the general or abstract to the specific. William R. Nelson in *Planting Design: A Manual of Theory and Practice* refers to this as the "Backward Process."[35] Identifying specific names of plant materials in a design is done last to help insure the plant will first function in its location based on its visual characteristics and environmental needs for growth. This approach also aids

[35]William R. Nelson, Jr., *Planting Design: A Manual of Theory and Practice* (Champaign, Ill.: Stipes Publishing Company, 1979), p. 31.

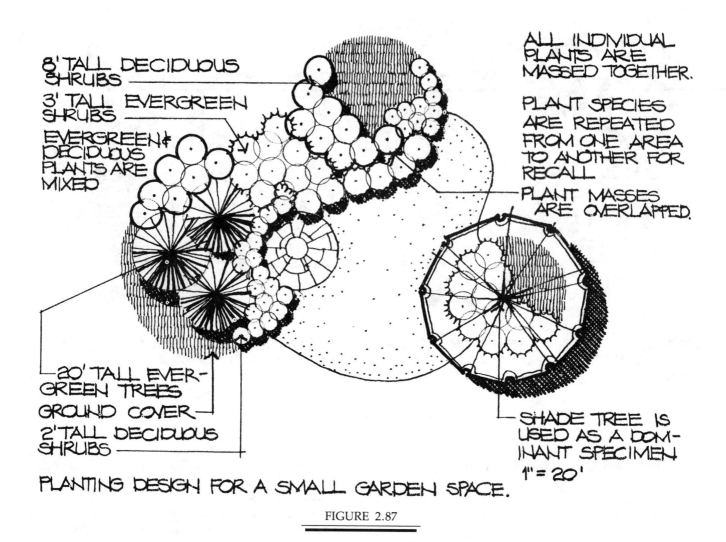

8' TALL DECIDUOUS SHRUBS

3' TALL EVERGREEN SHRUBS

EVERGREEN & DECIDUOUS PLANTS ARE MIXED

ALL INDIVIDUAL PLANTS ARE MASSED TOGETHER.

PLANT SPECIES ARE REPEATED FROM ONE AREA TO ANOTHER FOR RECALL

PLANT MASSES ARE OVERLAPPED.

20' TALL EVER-GREEN TREES

GROUND COVER

2' TALL DECIDUOUS SHRUBS

SHADE TREE IS USED AS A DOMINANT SPECIMEN 1" = 20'

PLANTING DESIGN FOR A SMALL GARDEN SPACE.

FIGURE 2.87

the designer in studying the entire composition and the relations within it before becoming too concerned with any one specific part of it. Many novice designers and lay people unfortunately have the tendency to pick the plant species first and try to fit it into the design. This process may work in some instances, but generally it makes the plant look out of context.

Summary

It can be seen that plant materials are an essential element in the design and management of the outdoor environment. Plant materials are not mere elements of decoration but serve a number of vital roles such as creating outdoor space, screening or enframing views, influencing air quality, stabilizing soil, affecting microclimate and energy consumption plus acting as compositional elements in the design of outdoor rooms. Plant materials should be studied early in the design process as an integral element with landform, buildings, pavement, and site structures. In designing with plant materials, their size, form, color, and texture should be used as a pallet of variables to meet both utilitarian and visual objectives of the design. All in all, though, plant materials must be treated as living organisms that give the outdoor environment a sense of vitality and growth.

3

Buildings

Buildings, both individually and in clusters, are the third major physical design element of the outdoor environment, after landform and plant materials. They structure and define outdoor space, influence views, modify microclimate, and affect the functional organization of the adjoining landscape. Buildings differ from other design elements dealt with in landscape architecture because all buildings have interior functions of their own that occur within the confines of their walls and/or in the adjacent site. Buildings and their environs are the primary location of most human activity including eating, sleeping, loving, child rearing, working, learning, and socializing. The objectives of this chapter are to describe the various types of outdoor spaces created by buildings, to provide some design guidelines for organizing buildings in a composition, and to outline different methods for integrating buildings and the landscape together into one well-coordinated environment.

A particularly noteworthy aspect about designing with buildings in the outdoor environment is that this process ideally involves a number of professions working together in close cooperation. Although it is the architect's responsibility to design the building and its interior spaces, it is the duty of the landscape architect to help properly site the building and design its environs. A great amount of time in the professional career of many landscape architects is spent locating and arranging buildings or in some way dealing with the interface between building and site. The siting of an individual residence, the design of a condominium complex, the layout of a college campus, and the development of an urban plaza are all examples of projects that involve coordination between architecture and the outdoor environment.

SINGLE BUILDING IS VIEWED AS AN OBJECT IN SPACE; IT IS A "FIGURE" TO BE SEEN FROM ALL SIDES.

FIGURE 3.1

The design of the building interface overlaps traditional professional boundaries and requires close cooperation between the architect and landscape architect. Neither professional should work alone with building-site interrelationship because each can contribute valuable expertise to the derivation of a sensitive design.

In dealing with the building and its surrounding site, the design professional is likely to confront one of three situations: (1) siting and collectively arranging a number of buildings on a site (a housing project, college campus, downtown urban development, office/commercial complex, etc.), (2) siting an individual building as a lone structure on a site (single-family residence, church, bank, etc.), and (3) adding onto or renovating an existing building and site.

In the first situation, the concern is the correct siting of the buildings with respect to existing constructed and natural site conditions, the outdoor spaces created by the buildings, and the functional and aesthetic relationships among the buildings themselves. When a group of professionals design a cluster of buildings, emphasis is typically placed on the integration of all the buildings and adjoining exterior spaces into the whole scheme. The design of each individual space or building is less significant unto itself than it is to the overall development.

In the second situation, siting an individual building, the concern is likely to be more focused on the building itself and the land immediately surrounding it. Here the building is treated either as a special visual focal point that stands out against its site or as a unified element blending into its setting. Many award-winning contemporary residences designed by architects fit one or the other of these circumstances.

In the third situation, the objective is commonly to add onto or alter the existing conditions in order to fulfill a revised program so that the new design appears to be a logical and sensitive extension of the older environment.

Building Clusters and Spatial Definition

By themselves, individual buildings are viewed as solid objects in the landscape surrounded by open, negative space. A single building does not create space but rather is an object in space, as suggested

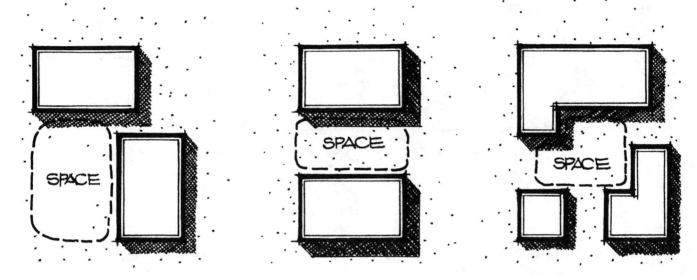

EXTERIOR SPACE IS CREATED WHEN TWO OR MORE BUILDINGS ARE CLUSTERED TOGETHER.

FIGURE 3.2

in Figure 3.1. When a group of buildings are clustered together in an organized manner, however, positively defined outdoor spaces are established in the voids between the building masses, as indicated in Figure 3.2. The collective massing of exterior building walls limits views and establishes vertical edges of outdoor rooms. The sense of enclosure is strongly implied by building walls situated on two or three sides of an area and completely delineated by building walls located on all sides.

Outdoor spaces, whose primary means of enclosure is building façades, possess some unique characteristics when compared with those spaces demarcated by more natural elements such as landform or plant material. Outdoor spaces encircled by buildings tend to be well articulated with exact sharp edges that remain fixed in place. The edges and resulting spaces are hard and nonpliable; if extended over a large area without relief, they may even become unappealingly harsh. And spaces defined by buildings lack dramatic seasonal variety in comparison with those established primarily by plant material. True, the angle of the sun and shadow patterns change during the year, with some associated varia-

tion in the feeling of the space, but the walls themselves alter little if at all.

Another unique quality of outdoor spaces defined essentially by buildings relates to the effect of windows on spatial perception. Windows produce varied spatial phenomena with changing light conditions between day and night. For a person standing in an exterior space during the day, the limits of the space seem to stop at the building façade unless there is a view into the building through a window to a lighted room. But even with this view, an exterior space seems to have well-defined boundaries. For a person inside a building during the day, views easily occur to the exterior, so that an interior space tends to "bleed" or "leak" outward, as indicated in Figure 3.3. At night, the opposite occurs. The exterior space loses its sharp boundaries for a person standing in it and tends to become ill-defined when not lit. Moreover, views into light interior spaces occur readily so that the exterior space now bleeds inward, as illustrated in Figure 3.4. On the other hand, the interior space now definitely stops at the windows for a person inside because views into the dark exterior space are weak if at all visible.

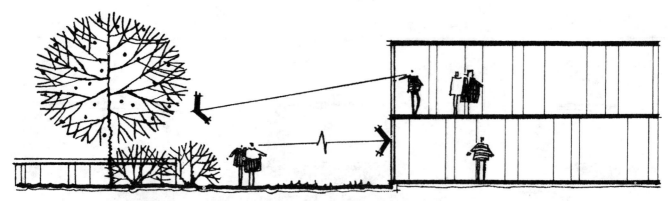

DAYTIME: VIEWS TO THE INSIDE OF THE BUILDING ARE HIN-
DERED; VIEWS TO THE EXTERIOR OCCUR EASILY.

FIGURE 3.3

The exact type and quality of spaces created by buildings, while almost infinite, does depend on the distance to building height ratio, the arrangement of the buildings, and the character of the building façades themselves. Each of these variables interacts with the others to influence the identity and feeling of the resulting space(s).

Distance to Building Height Ratio. The amount of enclosure and the resulting degree of spatial perception partially depends on the distance to height ratio between a person standing in an outdoor space and the height of surrounding building walls, just as it was previously described for both landform and plant materials. According to the standards stated by Gary Robinette in Plants, People and Environmental Quality, full enclosure occurs when the surrounding building walls create a 1:1 distance to height ratio or fill a 45-degree cone of vision (Figure 3.5).[1] A thresh-hold of enclosure occurs with a distance to height ratio of 2:1, minimum enclosure with a ratio of 3:1, and loss of enclosure with a ratio of 4:1.[2] In other words, the strongest sense of spatial enclosure is felt when a building wall fills and extends beyond the cone of vision. However, when the building is so low or a person is standing so far away as to see the building as a small part of a larger environmental context, little or no enclosure is sensed.

The distance to building height ratio also affects the feeling and use of an outdoor space in addition to influencing spatial enclosure. In Exterior Design in Architecture, Yoshinobu Ashihara analyzes the effect of the distance to building height ratio on the hierarchy of exterior to interior spaces. As illustrated in Figure 3.6, the most intimate and interiorlike space has a distance to building height ratio of between 1 and 3, while the most public and exteriorlike space has a distance to building height ratio of 6 or over.[3] A person would feel most comfortable talking to a friend in a space with a low distance to building height ratio and least comfortable in one with a high ratio.

Although a strong sense of spatial enclosure is often a design objective in arranging a cluster of buildings, care must also be taken not to create outdoor spaces where the building height and mass overpowers that scale of adjoining exterior areas. This is apt to occur when the distance to building height ratio becomes much less than 1, as in Figure 3.7. A spatial volume of these proportions seems like a deep well for the person standing inside. And the surrounding buildings themselves cannot be fully appreciated under these conditions because much of their exterior walls extend beyond the cone of vision. Some architectural theoreticians suggest that the ideal viewing distance of a building is at a distance to building height ratio of 2:1.[4] At this ratio,

[1]Gary O. Robinette, Plants, People and Environmental Quality (Washington, D.C.: U.S. Department of the Interior, National Park Service, 1972), p. 18.
[2]Ibid.

[3]Yoshinobu Ashihara, Exterior Design in Architecture, rev. ed. (New York: Van Nostrand Reinhold, 1981), p. 83.
[4]Ibid.,p. 42.

NIGHTTIME ; VIEWS TO THE INSIDE OF THE BUILDING OCCUR EASILY; VIEWS TO THE EXTERIOR ARE HINDERED.

FIGURE 3.4

the top of the building walls is seen at a 27-degree angle above the horizon (Figure 3.8).[5] Therefore an ideal distance to building height ratio for spatial enclosure without creating an uncomfortable feeling is between 1 and 3.

Plan Arrangement. Very closely linked to the factor of distance to building height ratio in defining outdoor space is the plan arrangement of the cluster of buildings. The strongest sense of enclosure occurs when the buildings are arranged as to completely surround and "wall in" a given space, thus preventing views to the outside of the space for a person standing in it. Such views, illustrated in Figure 3.9, are called "spatial leaks" and function just like the holes in any other container. The more spatial leaks there are, the weaker the perception of spatial enclosure. One method for eliminating spatial leaks when working with a multiple building layout around an outdoor space is to overlap the building façades as much as possible to prevent views into or out of the space, as shown in Figure 3.10. Spatial leaks can also be eliminated or reduced through the use of other design elements such as landform, plant material, or freestanding walls that block views, as indicated in Figure 3.11. It will be remembered from previous chapters that these other elements can be utilized for both "closure" and "linkage" of a space that has been suggested, though not completed, by the plan layout of the buildings themselves.[6]

FIGURE 3.5

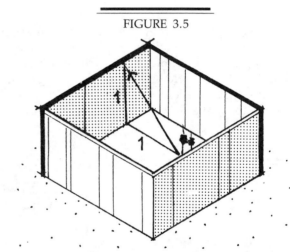

FULL SPATIAL ENCLOSURE IS PERCEIVED WITH A DISTANCE TO HEIGHT RATIO OF 1:1.

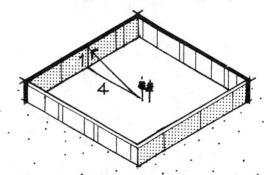

LOSS OF PERCEIVED SPATIAL ENCLOSURE OCCURS WITH A DISTANCE TO HEIGHT RATIO OF 4:1.

[5]Ibid.
[6]Gary O. Robinette, *Plants, People and Environmental Quality,* p. 23.

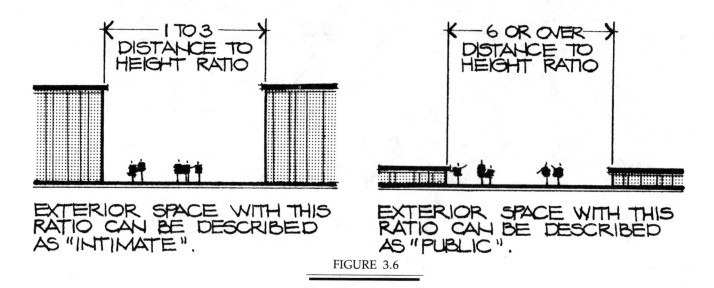

FIGURE 3.6

As shown in Figure 3.12, the weakest definition of exterior space by buildings in plan occurs when they are organized in a long row or are scattered so indiscriminately on a site that no logical perceptional relationship among them can be realized. In both these situations, there is no containment, even by subtle implication. The buildings are viewed as lone, unrelated elements surrounded by "negative" space (i.e., space without containment or focus).

While spatial enclosure is a desirable design objective, circumstances exist in which it is best to permit and even encourage views to the outside of an

FIGURE 3.7

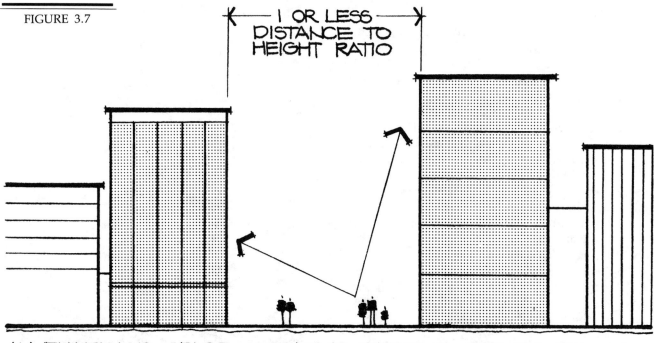

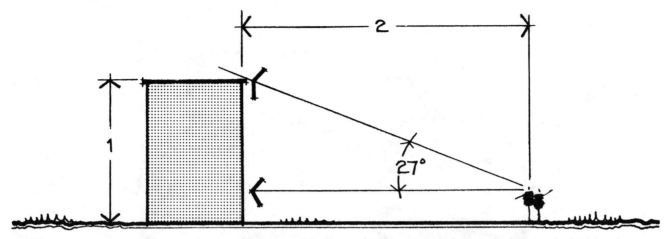

THIS DISTANCE TO HEIGHT RATIO IS CONSIDERED IDEAL FOR SPATIAL ENCLOSURE AND VIEWING A BUILDING.

FIGURE 3.8

outdoor space defined essentially by buildings. Significant features in the surrounding environment such as a river, lake, mountain range, or architectural focal point should be taken advantage of by allowing views to them. Ghirardelli Square in San Francisco, designed by Lawrence Halprin, is an example of an urban open space that has both a sense of enclosure and outward views depending on where one is standing. For a person standing in the main outdoor level of Ghirardelli Square, views are limited by the surrounding buildings and one's consciousness is limited to this space alone, as illus-

FIGURE 3.9

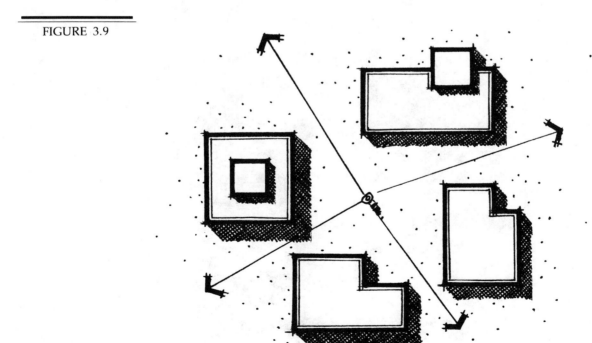

"SPATIAL LEAKS" OCCUR WHEN VIEWS EXTEND OUTSIDE AN ENCLOSED SPACE.

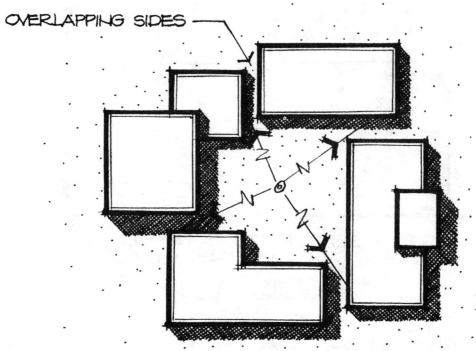

OVERLAPPING OF BUILDING SIDES MINIMIZES "SPATIAL LEAKS".

FIGURE 3.10

FIGURE 3.11

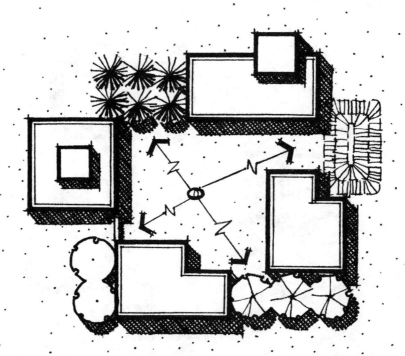

"SPATIAL LEAKS" ARE ELIMINATED THROUGH "LINKAGE" WITH OTHER DESIGN ELEMENTS.

NO SPATIAL ENCLOSURE CREATED BY BUILDINGS PLACED IN A ROW.

WEAK SPATIAL ENCLOSURE CREATED BY BUILDINGS PLACED HAPHAZARDLY ON A SITE.

FIGURE 3.12

trated in Figure 3.13. Yet as one proceeds to the upper outdoor levels and to balconies of the buildings of the upper side of the space, views open toward San Francisco Bay. Thus within a few steps, one can experience two different perceptions of enclosure while feeling part of the same outdoor environment.

The easiest method for creating outdoor space with buildings is by a simple continuous encircling wall of building façades, as indicated in Figure 3.14. This is desirable where one clearly defined space is required. Yet this may also be the least exciting and intriguing by itself, because the entire space is at

FIGURE 3.13

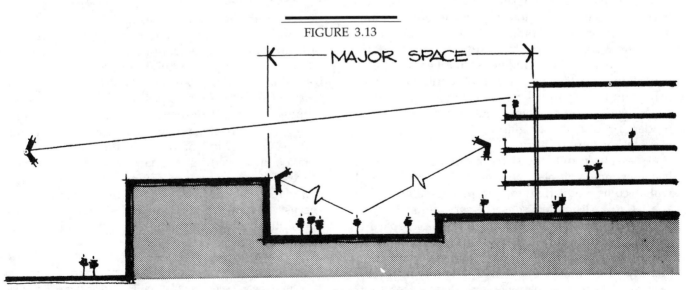

CONCEPTUAL SECTION THROUGH GHIRARDELLI SQUARE.

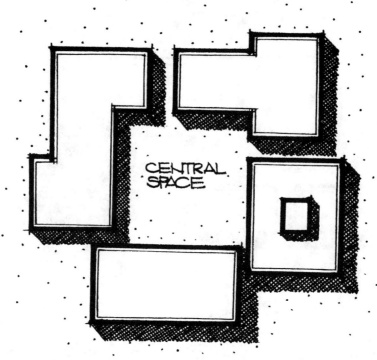

CENTRAL SPACE IS WELL DEFINED, BUT LACKS INTRIGUE; NO SUB-
SPACES CREATED.

FIGURE 3.14

once easily observed and known. Such a space is static; it lacks subspaces and implied movement. When the plan outline of surrounding building walls becomes more varied and complex with indentations and projections in the building façades, as illustrated in Figure 3.15, the resulting outdoor space takes on a richer quality with a number of implied subspaces contributing to the overall spatial fabric. For a person standing at particular points within the outdoor space, certain other points and subspaces may be hidden or partially disguised, thus establishing a sense of mystery or intrigue.

As a simple outdoor space defined by buildings becomes more complex, an inherent danger is that it will become so varied that it perceptually breaks apart into a disjointed sense of separate spaces, as in Figure 3.16. The identity of one ample space is lost to a feeling of a number of smaller spaces. Thus if the design objective is to maintain the feeling and identity of one large space with related subspaces, care must be taken to prevent the subspaces from becoming too enclosed or separated from each other. Moreover, it is a helpful design aid for one spatial

volume to dominate in size to establish a focus for the composition, as suggested in Figure 3.17. Then the smaller subspaces are unable to compete with or detract from the major space.

Another factor that influences spatial perception of central open spaces defined by buildings, and related to the distance to height ratio, is the plan horizontal dimension of a space. Paul D. Spreiregen in *Urban Design: The Architecture of Towns and Cities* has outlined the effect of distance on the feeling of outdoor space. Spaces defined primarily by buildings that are 80 ft (24m) or fewer in horizontal distance may be described as intimate (Figure 3.18).[7] In a space of this size we can distinguish detail or a human face. He further suggests that "grand urban spaces" be between 80 (24m) and 450 ft (137m).[8] The maximum distance for being able to see body action and movement is 450 ft (137m).[9]

[7]Paul D. Spreiregen, *Urban Design: The Architecture of Towns and Cities* (New York: McGraw-Hill, 1965), p. 75.
[8]Ibid.
[9]Ibid., p. 71.

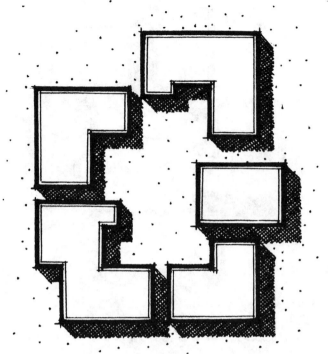

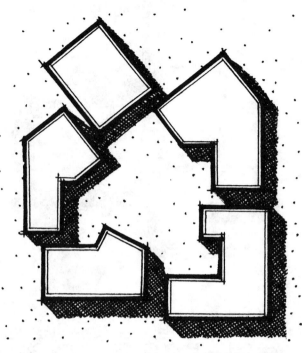

BUILDINGS CREATE MAJOR SPACE WITH RELATED SUBSPACES.

"ORGANIC SPACE" WITH RELATED SUBSPACES.

FIGURE 3.15

FIGURE 3.16

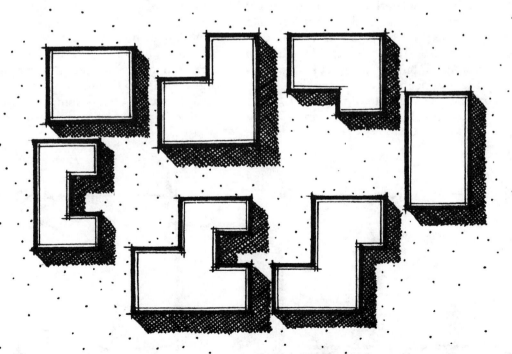

MAJOR SPACE WITH THE NUMEROUS SUBSPACES BECOMES SO COMPLEX THAT IDENTITY OF MAJOR SPACE IS LOST.

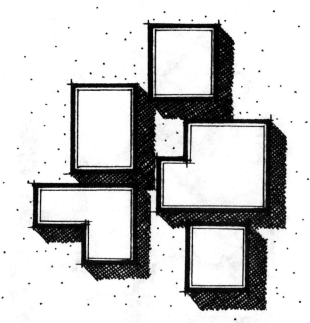

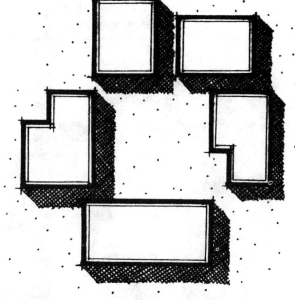

WEAK PLAN COMPOSITION; NO
DOMINANT OPEN SPACE TO ES-
TABLISH A FOCUS OF THE DE-
SIGN.

DOMINANT OPEN SPACE UNIFIES
COMPOSITION & PROVIDES A FOCUS.

FIGURE 3.17

Building Character. A third factor that affects the quality of spaces articulated by buildings is the character of the building façades that contain the space. The color, texture, detailing, and proportion of a building façade influences the personality of an outdoor space adjoining it. The space can be made to feel cold, harsh, and inhuman if the building walls surrounding the exterior space are massive, gray, and lack fine detail, as suggested in Figure 3.19. Or conversely, the same volume of space can be made

to feel delicate, light, airy, and inviting if the space-defining building walls are warm in color, finely detailed, and proportioned to the human. Many fine, thin elements in a building wall can lend a light emotion to the space itself such as in the Court of the Lions in the Alhambra in Granada, Spain. Here, the thin columns and intricate detailing furnish a light quality to the entire space. A colonnade too can produce a less bulky temperament than a wall that is a solid mass. Here, the exterior space is allowed

FIGURE 3.18

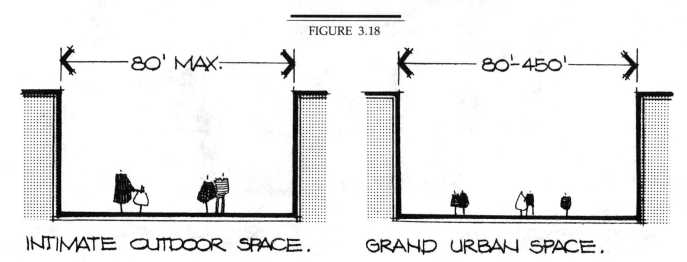

INTIMATE OUTDOOR SPACE.

GRAND URBAN SPACE.

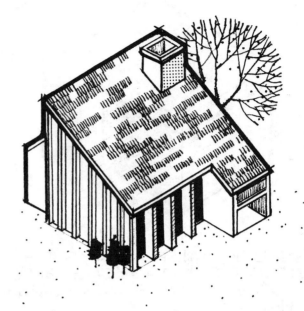

A PLAIN BUILDING BLOCK LACK-
ING DETAIL MAKES ADJOINING
EXTERIOR SPACES SEEM HARSH.

BUILDINGS THAT ARE FINELY DE-
TAILED MAKE ADJOINING EXTER-
IOR SPACES MORE HUMAN AND
PLEASANT.

FIGURE 3.19

to penetrate into and intertwine itself with the building mass, as suggested in Figure 3.20. Similarly, the solidity or transparency of the top of a building silhouetted against the sky can impress spatial character. A wall or roof silhouette that consists of a finely detailed pattern of solid and void areas along its top edge creates a lighter effect than a straight, solid edge between building and sky. And the scale of the entire building as well as its components bears upon the resulting spatial character. Building walls that are subdivided and proportioned to the size of a person, particularly at ground level as shown in Figure 3.21, give a space a more comfortable feeling than a massive wall with no relation to human size.

The use of reflective glass walls on a number of contemporary buildings is another treatment of building façades that has a dramatic effect on adjacent outdoor spaces. This wall material acts as a

FIGURE 3.20

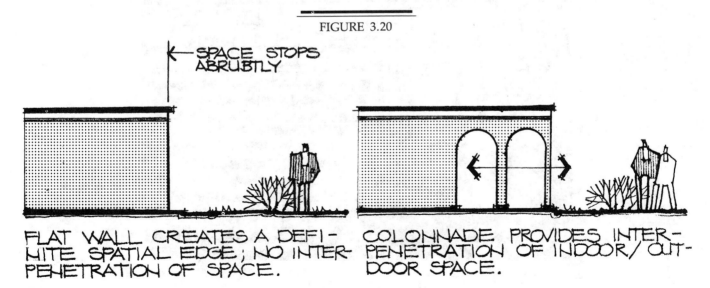

FLAT WALL CREATES A DEFI-
NITE SPATIAL EDGE; NO INTER-
PENETRATION OF SPACE.

COLONNADE PROVIDES INTER-
PENETRATION OF INDOOR/OUT-
DOOR SPACE.

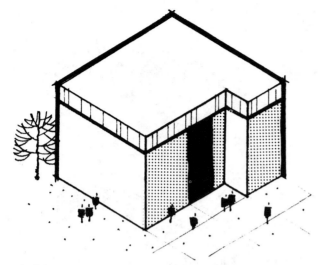

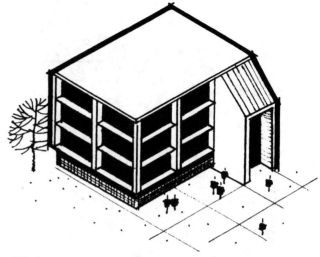

MONUMENTAL BUILDING WITH LITTLE DETAIL AND SCALE GIVES ADJOINING SPACE AN INHUMAN QUALITY.

BUILDING WITH HUMAN PROPORTIONED ELEMENTS (WINDOWS, 1ST FLOOR OVERHANG, ETC.) GIVES ADJOINING SPACE A COMFORTABLE FEELING.

FIGURE 3.21

huge mirror by reflecting the surrounding environment in the building façade. With this effect, the building is not just an object in the landscape; it becomes part of the landscape. The mirror effect of the building gives the adjoining space a property of seeming limitlessness. The actual physical edges of the space are perceptually lost and expanded by the reflection. It also has the potential of producing twisted and contorted kaleidoscopic patterns of reflection that further confuse the mind as to what is real and what is not. Well-known examples of reflective glass façades are the Hyatt Regency hotels in Atlanta (Figure 3.22), Chicago, Detroit, and Dallas.

FIGURE 3.22

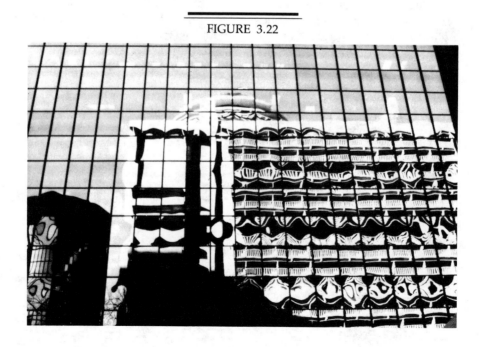

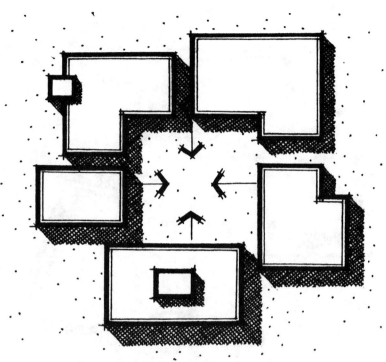

CENTRAL COMMON OPEN SPACE : SELF-CENTERED AND INWARD-ORIENTED.

FIGURE 3.23

Building Clusters and Types of Spaces

The potential plan arrangements of buildings and the types of related spaces are limitless. The possibilities are based on the environmental context, siting, objectives, and desired spatial qualities. Some of the more basic types of outdoor spaces created by buildings are described in the following sections.

Central Open Space. One very basic and common concept for composing a cluster of buildings is to group them around a central open space that relates to all the buildings in the cluster, as illustrated in Figure 3.23. This central space can be considered the spatial focus of the entire design or surrounding environment. It is the "hub" of the composition and possesses some of the same qualities as does the concave landform described in Chapter 1. Historical examples of central common open spaces include the Piazza della Signoria in Florence, Piazza del Campo in Siena, Piazza di San Pietro in Rome, and Piazza San Marco in Venice. Examples of central open spaces in the United States are the New England village green or town square, the central quadrangle of many college campuses (e.g., Harvard University, Syracuse University, University of Illinois, The Ohio State University), Rockefeller Center in New York City, and Mellon Square in Pittsburgh. All these spaces serve as the dominant space in the immediate environment and are major meeting and gathering places. They act as powerful "magnets" and destination points. Because of their spatial definition and the activity that takes place within them, they tend to be self-centered and inward-oriented.

A couple of additional notes should be made about the spatial definition of the central open space. We pointed out earlier that the strongest sense of spatial enclosure was achieved when views or spatial leaks out of space were minimized. Two examples of this concept are the Piazza della Signoria in Florence and the Piazza del Campo in Siena. Views through and from these two historically significant medieval open spaces are limited because they were organized on "windmill" or "whirling square" layouts.[10] As shown in Figure 3.24, streets

---

[10]Norman T. Newton, *Design on the Land: The Development of Landscape Architecture* (Cambridge: Harvard University Press, 1971), p. 134.

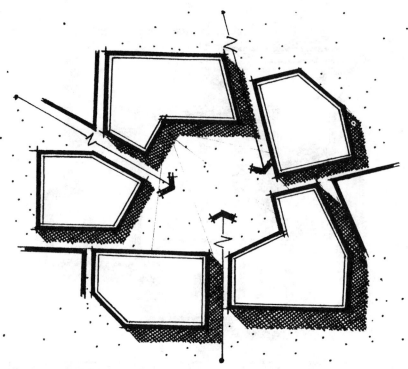

"WIND MILL" OR "WHIRLING SQUARE"; VIEWS AND MOVEMENT INTO THE SPACE STOPPED.

FIGURE 3.24

FIGURE 3.25

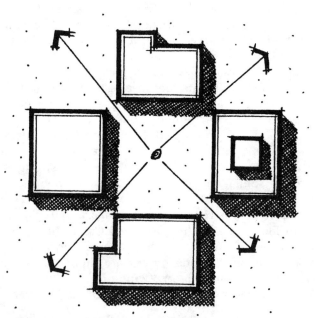

OPEN CORNERS CREATE A WEAK FEELING OF SPATIAL ENCLOSURE.

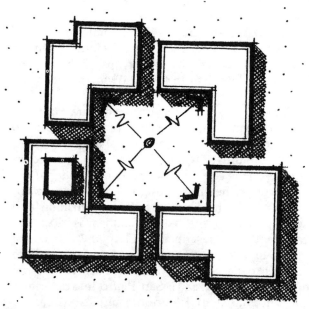

CLOSED CORNERS CREATES A STRONG SENSE OF SPATIAL ENCLOSURE.

that enter this type of open space "dead end" there; they do not pass directly through. Consequently, these spaces have a strong sense of containment. Not only does this plan organization contribute to strengthening the enclosure of the spaces, but it also forces the pedestrian entering the space to experience or even stop in the space. A person cannot simply pass through by continuing along the edge between two openings. The pedestrian is encouraged to walk through, not by, the space.

Inherent in many of the windmill layouts is enclosure of the central open space at the corners. When the corners of a central open space are open as they often are at street intersections or between two separate buildings facing 90 degrees to each other (Figure 3.25), the space is defined only by flat planes of the enclosing buildings. Both views and space spill outward through the corner openings. Yet when the building walls themselves fill and turn the corner of a central open space, there is a much stronger sensation of enclosure.[11] The corners turn the eye inward and keep views within the central space.

One further thought about a central open space is that its identity is strongest when the "hollowness" of the space is reinforced. To do this, the central portion of the space should indeed be left open. Any planting of trees or the placement of other objects should be kept to the perimeter of the space. The least desirable thing is to place a large, space-occupying solid object in the middle of the space, as illustrated in Figure 3.26. When this is done, a spatial "doughnut" results. The quality of the central open space is lost and replaced by a more linear space that revolves around the solid center. One other concept for accentuating a central open space is to slope or step it down toward the middle. In effect, this places a concave landform on the base plane of the central open space and makes the openness of the space more obvious.

Focused Open Space. While the concept of the enclosed central open space is appropriate in some situations, it is unsuitable in others. As in Figure 3.27, circumstances exist in which it is desirable to allow a space defined by a cluster of buildings to be open on one side to take advantage of views to a prominent feature in the landscape outside the space itself. When one portion of the building walls surrounding an open space is lacking, the space created

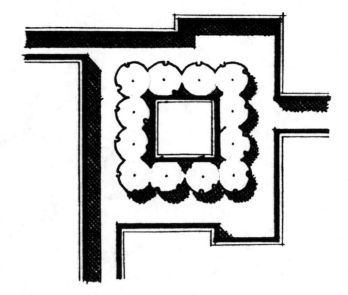

UNDESIRABLE: OPENNESS OF SPACE IS LOST BY PLACEMENT OF SOLID MASSES IN THE MIDDLE.

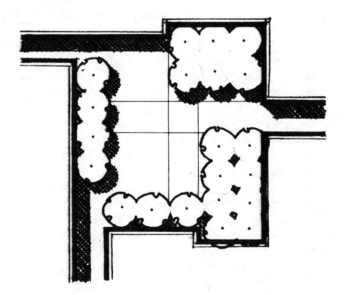

DESIRABLE: OPEN QUALITY OF SPACE IS REINFORCED BY PLACEMENT OF OTHER ELEMENTS AROUND THE EXTERIOR.

FIGURE 3.26

---

[11]Yoshinobu Ashihara, *Exterior Design in Architecture*, p. 79.

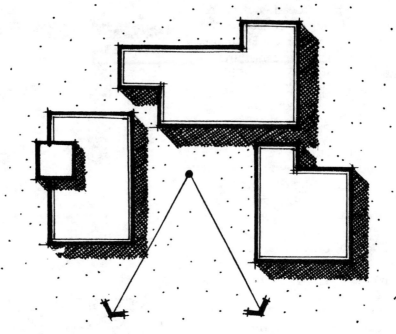

FOCUSED OPEN SPACE; BUILDING CLUSTER HAS STRONG DIRECTION AND ORIENTATION TO OPEN SIDE.

FIGURE 3.27

will be directed toward the opening. Remember from earlier discussions on landform that space, like water, flows toward the point of least resistance. Because of the strong orientation of a focused open space, every attempt should be made to maintain the sense of direction in the organization of other elements such as plant material or landform within the overall space.

When organizing the buildings around a focused open space, one caution is not to make the open side too proportionally large or the feeling of spatial identity and enclosure will be lost. The objective in creating a focused open space should be to define the space adequately with sufficient encircling building walls while still permitting some views outward from the space.

Channeled Linear Space. A channeled linear space is the third type of exterior volume that can be created by the clustering of buildings. This type of space is proportionally long and narrow, with openings at one or both ends, as shown in Figure 3.28. A channeled linear space is generally straight and does not bend around corners or disappear. Standing in this type of outdoor space, a person can readily see either end. Most downtown urban streets in the

United States are examples of this linear space, as is the Mall in Washington, D.C.

One of the noteworthy qualities of a channeled linear space is that it is a space for movement with the focus of the space centered at either end. When standing in this type of space, a person's attention is "squeezed" and "channeled" between the long linear sides, as in Figures 3.29 and 3.30. In fact, the open ends of the space take on significantly more importance than the vertical planes along the two sides. Owing to the visual prominence of the open ends, it is incorrect to attempt to compete with the termini of a channeled linear space by adding attractors along the edges, as is often done with the placement of signs or other objects of interest. These elements merely fight one another and the spatial ends. It is better to acknowledge the foci of the space and eliminate disruptive competition along the length of the channeled linear space. This type of space can be successfully used in the environment to direct attention to significant landmarks such as a piece of sculpture or an architectural feature.

Organic Linear Space. Another fundamental type of linear space that can be created by clusters of buildings is an organic space. It differs from the chan-

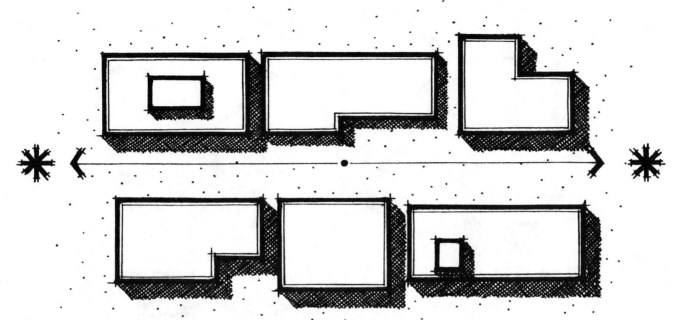

CHANNELED LINEAR SPACE; ATTENTION IS DIRECTED TOWARD THE ENDS OF THE SPACE.

FIGURE 3.28

neled linear space in that it is not a simple, straight space from one point to another but rather continues around corners and frequently disappears out of sight, as illustrated in Figure 3.31. This spatial type may also include a linked sequence of separate spaces. Many streets in European medieval villages or towns of today fit this classification of space (Figure 3.32). While walking through this type of space, a person's focus and concentration is constantly changing. Commonly, one's attention is directed to-

FIGURE 3.29

FIGURE 3.30

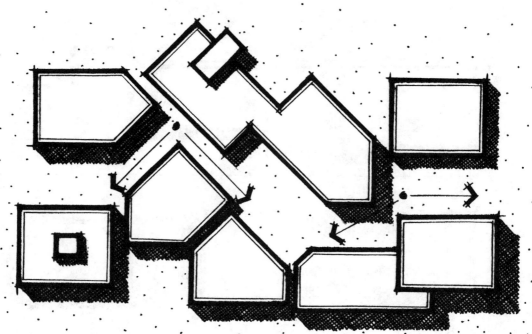

ORGANIC LINEAR SPACE : VIEWS AND FOCUS CONSTANTLY CHANGE
AS ONE MOVES THROUGH THE SPACE.

FIGURE 3.31

FIGURE 3.32

ward the ends of the subspace in which he or she is standing; as one then walks toward and arrives at this point, a new leg of the space, previously unseen, comes into view and now concentration is redirected to a new terminus. This sequence of events repeated again and again walking through an organic linear space can make it an enchanting experience because a sense of anticipation is provided by wondering what "lies around the corner." A person is enticed to seek out the unknown, and in doing so, is rewarded by changing views and spatial surprises, as suggested in Figure 3.33.

These four spatial types just described are not usually created or found as isolated entities. They are frequently juxtaposed next to one another to form a much larger sequence of spaces with each of the parts contributing to the experience of the whole. In this situation, the identity and essence of each type of space can be emphasized by its position with respect to an opposing spatial type. For example, the static, containing quality of a central, common open space can be made more apparent if a person must move through a tight linear space to gain access to it. Buildings, as do any other design element, can create a series of expanding (release) and contracting (tension) volumes linked by views, materials, or other common threads of unity (see

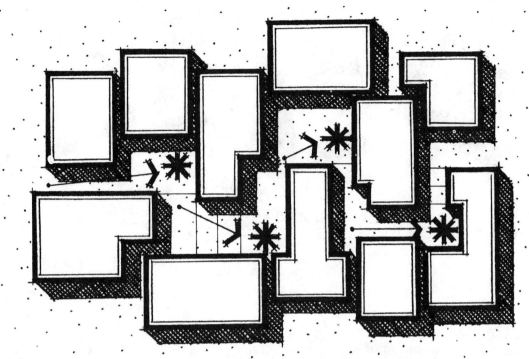

ORGANIC LINEAR SPACE PROVIDES OPPORTUNITIES FOR SUR-
PRISES; FOCAL POINTS HIDDEN AROUND CORNERS ARE
SUDDENLY DISCOVERED.

FIGURE 3.33

also Chapter 4 on Pavement). In the final analysis, it is the accumulated linkages of spaces that provide the life and emotion of the outdoor environment.

Design Guidelines for Building Clusters

How a given cluster of buildings is organized in the landscape depends on a number of factors including existing site conditions, functional relationships between buildings, required uses or activities in the adjoining site, intended characteristics of the outdoor spaces, and basic principles of design composition. Some design suggestions have already been made in this chapter about creating outdoor space. A number of other basic compositional guidelines also need to be taken into account.

In plan, the designer should strive to provide a sense of order so that a meaningful relation appears among the building masses as well as the spatial volumes they create. The least-ordered organization occurs when the buildings are placed indiscriminately on the site with no effort to coordinate relationships among them, as in Figure 3.34. This approach, though desirable for some situations, typically results in a chaotic, fragmented composition. One of the simplest and most commonly utilized concepts to achieve compositional order is to place the buildings in the cluster at right angles to one another (Figure 3.35). This solution is automatically ordered without any additional attempts to create a sense of logic and has the added advantage of being easy to lay out on paper and in the field.

Yet the system of right-angle relationships does have potential drawbacks. If overused, it becomes too predictable and monotonous, as illustrated by the ever present grid layout of most urban street systems in the United States. Spatial surprises or dramatic building relationships are lacking. In building clusters that are linear in their overall layout, variation can be given by pushing some of the building masses forward and some back in relation to each other, as illustrated in Figure 3.36. This estab-

WEAK RELATION AMONG BUILDINGS; A CHAOTIC COMPOSITION RESULTS FROM UNCONTROLLED ORIENTATIONS.

FIGURE 3.34

lishes subspaces in association with the building offsets and breaks the monotony of a long continuous row.

Another alternative to the rigidity of a completely rectilinear layout is to carefully place some of the building masses in the composition at angles to each other, that are not 90 degrees, as in Figure 3.37. This interjects a degree of variety into the layout. This procedure, however, must be compatible with both the context and the objectives of the design. If handled by a skilled and knowledgeable designer, the entire building composition may be accomplished with only nonninety-degree angular relationships. Again, this approach is more organic, though we hope not less ordered, than the totally right-angled scheme.

FIGURE 3.35

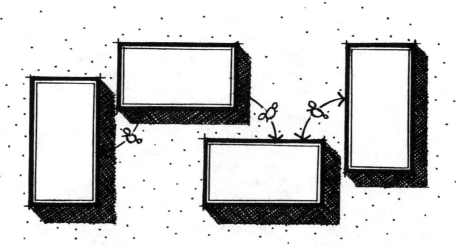

INDIVIDUAL BUILDINGS ARE VISUALLY RELATED TO EACH OTHER BY 90° RELATIONSHIPS.

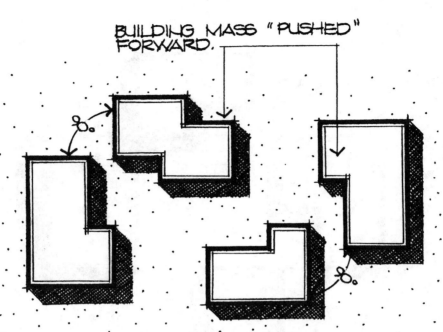

SPATIAL VARIATION AMONG THE 90° RELATIONSHIPS IS CREATED BY PUSHING & PULLING BUILDING MASSES.

FIGURE 3.36

FIGURE 3.37

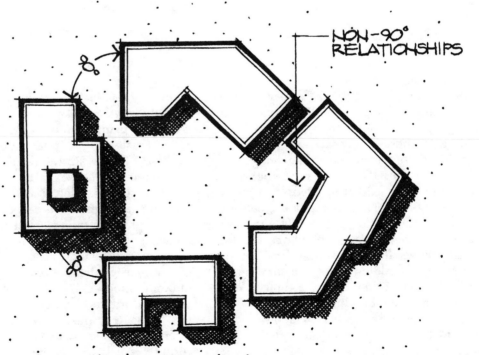

SPATIAL VARIATION CREATED IN BUILDING COMPOSITION BY SOME NON-90° RELATIONSHIPS.

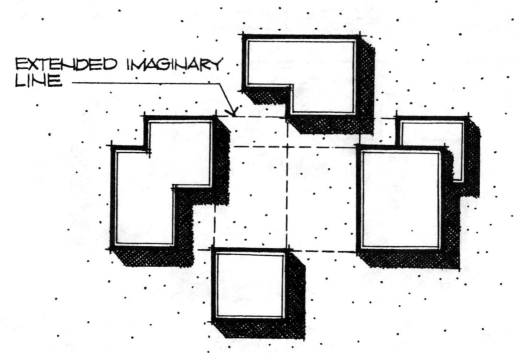

EXTENDED IMAGINARY LINE

BUILDINGS IN THE CLUSTER ARE RELATED TO EACH OTHER BY EX-
TENDING IMAGINARY LINES FROM EDGE OF ONE BUILDING TO AN-
OTHER.

FIGURE 3.38

When working with any of these schemes, one can strengthen the building-to-building association in a cluster by directly relating the forms and lines of one building to those of nearby buildings. One way to accomplish this is by extending imaginary lines outward from the edges of a given building and then aligning them with the edges of nearby buildings, as in Figure 3.38. This method creates a solution that has a thoughtful and readily apparent visual alliance between adjacent buildings in the cluster. It also allows for a maximum amount of views out of any one building into the central open space without their being blocked by a directly opposing wall of an adjacent building.

On the other hand, there are certain disadvantages as well to this system of aligning buildings. This technique of relating building edges to each other allows spatial leaks out of a cluster and con-

sequently results in a weakly defined outdoor space. And this method, like the rectilinear layout, is sometimes too planned and logical in its order. To counteract these two potential problems, it is sometimes advisable to overlap the relationship between opposite facing building walls, as in Figure 3.39. This provides a sensation of spatial tension for a person walking through the area between the two buildings. The overlapping creates a stronger feeling of spatial enclosure within the central open space of the building cluster.

Another guideline for the plan arrangement of building modules, such as individual townhouse units that are to be massed together into one building, is again to overlap the units to maximize their interface, as shown in Figure 3.40. Any corner-to-corner association between modules should be avoided because such a relationship creates a point

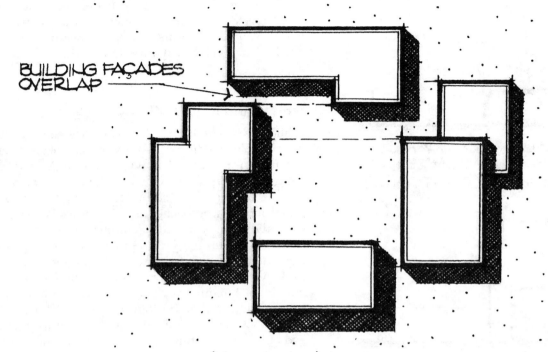

BUILDING FAÇADES OVERLAP

TO CREATE A STRONGER SENSE OF SPATIAL ENCLOSURE WHEN EXTENDING IMAGINARY LINES, BUILDING FAÇADES ARE OVERLAPPED.

FIGURE 3.39

FIGURE 3.40

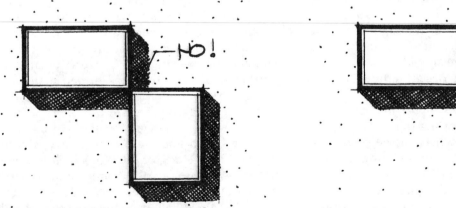

NO!

UNDESIRABLE: INDIVIDUAL BUILDING MODULES ARE PLACED CORNER TO CORNER.

OVERLAP

DESIRABLE: INDIVIDUAL BUILDING MODULES ARE OVERLAPPED.

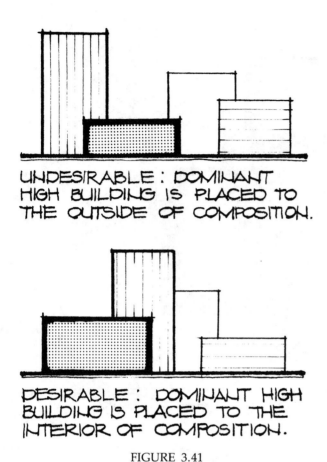

UNDESIRABLE: DOMINANT
HIGH BUILDING IS PLACED TO
THE OUTSIDE OF COMPOSITION.

DESIRABLE: DOMINANT HIGH
BUILDING IS PLACED TO THE
INTERIOR OF COMPOSITION.

FIGURE 3.41

of tension on plan and is structurally unsound in terms of the building construction.

The building-to-building interrelation needs to be studied in height as well as plan for a successful compositional solution. Again, although there are many possibilities to the height organization of a multiple building cluster, one should include a comparatively tall building in the design to function as a dominant element. All other buildings, then, in the cluster should relate to and support this dominant building. A suggestion in locating this commanding building is to place it somewhere in the middle of the composition with the other building masses gradually gaining height as they are placed closer to it, as in Figure 3.41. As a result, lower buildings are generally located near the perimeter of the grouping and taller buildings are situated to the inside. This concept creates a gradual transition from low to high and places the focus more to the interior of the composition, where it can be properly supported by the

surrounding building masses. If the tallest building is located too close to the outside of the cluster, the design solution appears out of balance because too much visual weight is placed to one side.

Siting Individual Buildings

While the discussion to this point has concentrated on multiple building schemes, the landscape architect must frequently deal with the siting of individual buildings as lone architectural elements on a site as well. In siting isolated buildings, one of two basic philosophical approaches usually prevails: (1) treat the building as a positive sculptural element set off from its surroundings, or (2) treat the building as an element to be blended harmoniously into its environs. According to the first concept (Figure 3.42), the individual building is designed to be an attractive, eye-catching focal point (figure) contrasted against a neutral setting (ground). It is a statement of human and object dominating the environment. The site development in this case is minimum in order to quietly support but not compete with or overpower the building. A building placed by itself in an open field and the contemporary white façaded residence in a wooded setting are examples of this design concept. To be successful, no other building or noticeable constructed element should be in the same field of vision as the individual building so that it is clearly recognized as the element of importance.

The second concept for siting an individual building is at the opposite end of the philosophical spectrum because it emphasizes the coordination of the building with its site (Figure 3.43). This approach is based on the theory that the building should be an integral part of the site with the two conceived as a continuum. Here, people and their development are viewed as being part of nature. An effort is made to eliminate any distinction between what is building and what is site. Site character and materials are repeated in the building itself to blend the two together. Site development in this concept is apt to be more extensive than in the figure/ground relationship described above. Examples of this second approach to the siting of buildings include Falling Water at Bear Run, Pennsylvania, and Taliesin West near Scottsdale, Arizona, both designed by Frank Lloyd Wright. Neither of the two conceptual methods for siting an individual building is necessarily more correct than the other; the one to follow depends on the context and objectives of the particular design project.

INDIVIDUAL BUILDING CONTRASTED AGAINST ITS SITE.

FIGURE 3.42

INDIVIDUAL BUILDING BLENDED IN WITH ITS SITE.

FIGURE 3.43

Relating Buildings to a Site

There are a number of concepts and principles for visually and functionally relating buildings, both as individual elements and as clusters, to their surrounding site in order to achieve a totally cohesive design solution. As with all other design guidelines, they need to be evaluated anew each time a project is undertaken and applied only when suitable.

Landform. One factor that must always be taken into account when relating buildings to a site is landform. Landform, as discussed in Chapter 1, affects the visual and functional relationship between buildings and the site, as well as drainage. Generally, it is easier and more economical to locate a building on a relatively level site than on one with sloped or irregular landform. On a level site, costs of building construction and extending utilities to it are less than on steeper sites. And as pointed out previously, the building layout can be much more flexible on a comparatively level site. Nevertheless, these initial costs and advantages of building on level land should be weighed with the longer-term costs of destroying valuable cropland that is so often located on relatively level sites before development.

On level landform, a building can be integrated into its site by extending outward in a number of

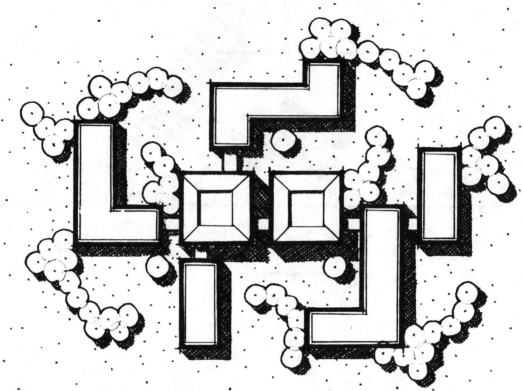

BUILDING BECOMES AN INTEGRAL PART OF SITE BY BUILDING WINGS WHICH EXTEND INTO SITE LIKE ARMS.

FIGURE 3.44

directions, as in Figure 3.44. These extensions of the building act like arms that reach out to hold onto and encompass part of the site. A visually level site also lends itself to both excavation and mounding that can be undertaken to relate a building to the adjacent environment. As in Figure 3.45, both spaces or solid land masses can be created to complement the architecture and carry selected building forms into the site.

As the ground surface becomes progressively steeper, it becomes more difficult and expensive as well as visually less stable to locate a building. The exact way a building relates to a sloped site depends on the steepness of slope as well as program objectives. Three common techniques for siting a building on more gentle slopes (3 to 8 percent) are illustrated

in Figure 3.46. One typical method is to terrace the ground to simulate a flat site. The uphill portion of the site where the building is to be located is excavated and filled in on the downhill portion to create a level base for the building. As the slope becomes steeper, retaining walls may need to be incorporated on the uphill and/or downhill side to minimize the amount of cut and fill required to establish the level terrace. In essence, retaining walls help minimize site disturbance. Another way the building can be related to a sloped site is by a split-level first floor. This permits the building to be placed into the slope in a steplike fashion with some of the grade change taken up in the building itself. With this concept, part of the building structure actually functions as a retaining wall. For a building like a row of attached

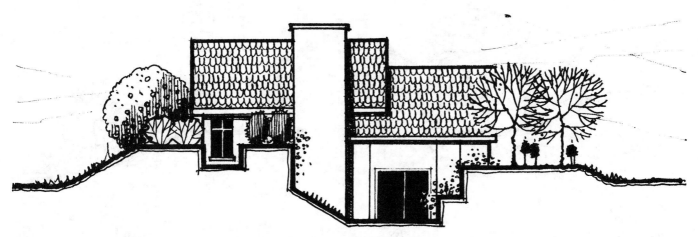

BUILDING BECOMES AN INTEGRAL PART OF SITE THROUGH MOUNDING AND EXCAVATION.

FIGURE 3.45

townhouses, the split between levels can occur between the individual units in the cluster. All these concepts for stepping a building with the slope minimize cut and fill in comparison with the terracing approach. And the stepping technique is often the most successful for expressing the influence of the slope and for making the building appear as if it were indeed a natural part of the slope.

On steeper slopes (10 to 15 percent), the split-level method may be taken one step farther so that there is an entire story difference between the uphill and downhill sides, as shown in the top half of Figure 3.47. The uphill side will have one less story exposed above ground than the downhill side with the building built into the slope. A common example of this is a house with one story facing the uphill side and two stories facing downhill. In this situation, a person is able to walk out of the basement on the downhill side.

One last concept for siting a building on a very steep slope is to support the building structurally above the lower ground elevation, as illustrated in the bottom half of Figure 3.47. By means of pole construction or other support, the building is elevated above the ground with minimal if any change in the contour of the existing ground plane. This concept, while costly, is appropriately used in loca-

tions where the site is either too steep or sensitive (like a wooded area) to grade. This concept also lends itself to dramatic architectural solutions with a portion of the building cantilevered over the site.

The plan layout or footprint of a building placed on a slope should also respond to the difficult topographic conditions. Remember from earlier discussions of valleys and ridges that buildings should be long, narrow, and sited parallel to the contours to blend in with these landform types (Figure 3.48). Such building plans express the directionality of the slopes and minimize the amount of grading required in fitting the building to the ground. Conversely, a building will contrast with a slope to a greater degree as it becomes less elongated in plan and/or is placed perpendicular to the contours of the slope. The one situation where a building can be compact and yet fit into the slope is at the end of a ridge or point of topography. Here the building plan can be more rounded or U-shaped to relate to the bend of the contours, as shown in Figure 3.49.

After locating a building on any of the slope conditions just described, one must give additional attention to the ground directly adjacent to the base of the building. For all conditions, the ground immediately around the base should slope away for at least a short distance so that surface drainage like-

156

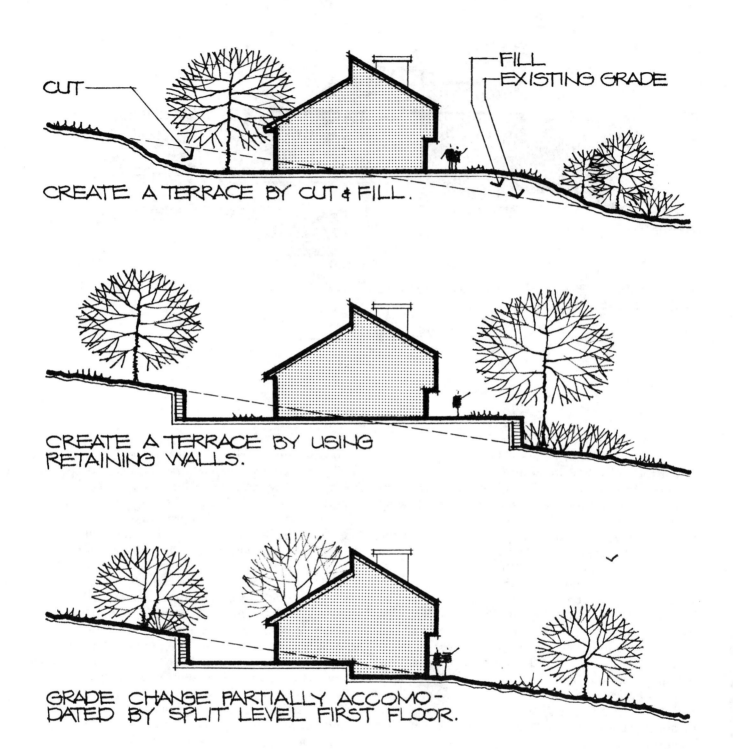

CUT

FILL
EXISTING GRADE

CREATE A TERRACE BY CUT & FILL.

CREATE A TERRACE BY USING
RETAINING WALLS.

GRADE CHANGE PARTIALLY ACCOMO-
DATED BY SPLIT LEVEL FIRST FLOOR.

THREE METHODS FOR ADAPTING A BUILDING TO A GENTLE
SLOPE.

FIGURE 3.46

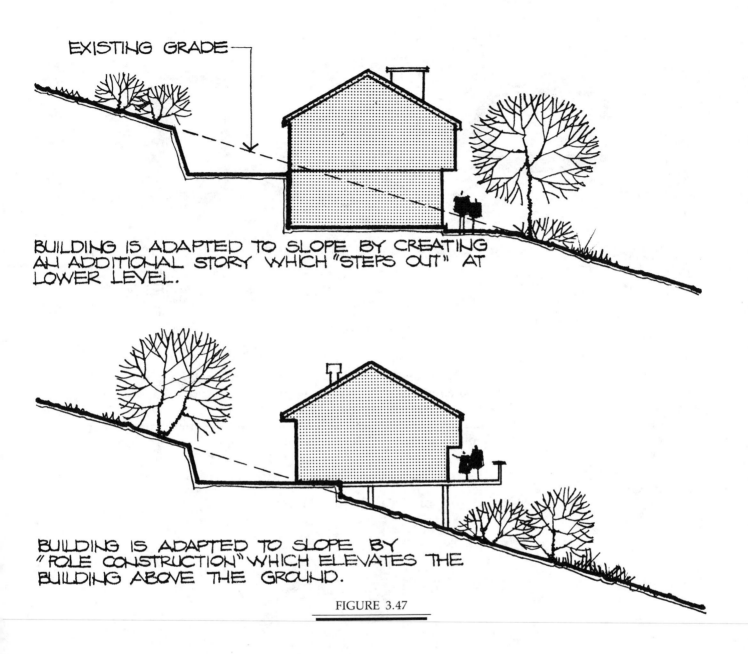

EXISTING GRADE

BUILDING IS ADAPTED TO SLOPE BY CREATING AN ADDITIONAL STORY WHICH "STEPS OUT" AT LOWER LEVEL.

BUILDING IS ADAPTED TO SLOPE BY "POLE CONSTRUCTION" WHICH ELEVATES THE BUILDING ABOVE THE GROUND.

FIGURE 3.47

wise flows away from the building to keep the walls and floors of the building dry. On sloped sites such as that illustrated in Figure 3.50, this means a swale or low area must be located on the uphill side of the building between it and the slope to catch the water flowing down the slope and divert it around the building.

On the level site, the designer has several choices for relating the first floor (or ground floor) of a building to the outside ground level (Figure 3.51). One common method is to locate the first floor six inches

or more above the outside ground elevation (while also sloping the ground away from the building for drainage). This method safely places the main floor above any possible inflow of water. If a basement is part of the building, this approach also reduces the amount of excavation required. The disadvantage of this method is that it tends to emphasize the dichotomy between indoors and outdoors because the grade change acknowledges the separation between the two. The inside floor elevation and outside ground level do not link together as one continuous

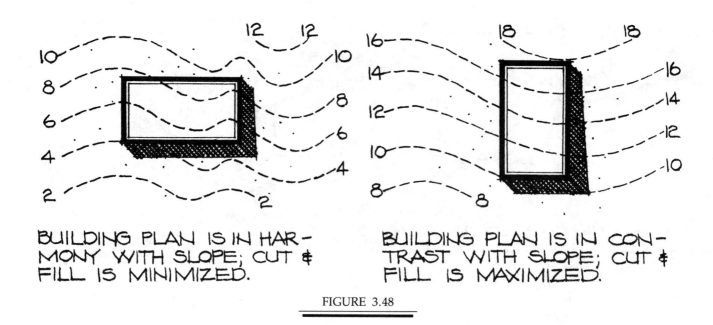

BUILDING PLAN IS IN HAR-
MONY WITH SLOPE; CUT &
FILL IS MINIMIZED.

BUILDING PLAN IS IN CON-
TRAST WITH SLOPE; CUT &
FILL IS MAXIMIZED.

FIGURE 3.48

plane but instead are split by the grade change. Therefore a second means for relating the first floor of a building to the ground level immediately around it is to locate both at the same elevation so that they do flow together, strengthening the inter-

connection between inside and outside. A related advantage of this concept is the ease of access for wheelchairs or people with walking disabilities. Again, though, ground surface immediately outside the building must slope away from it to force the

FIGURE 3.49

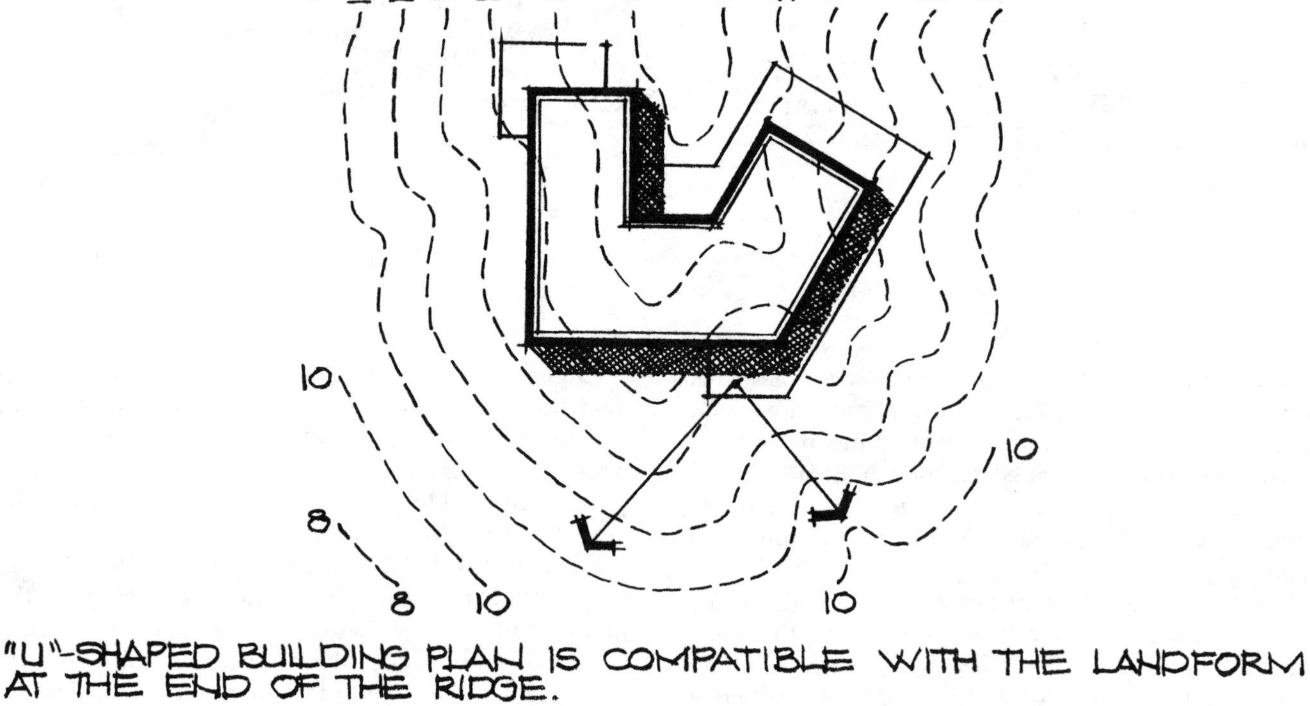

"U"-SHAPED BUILDING PLAN IS COMPATIBLE WITH THE LANDFORM
AT THE END OF THE RIDGE.

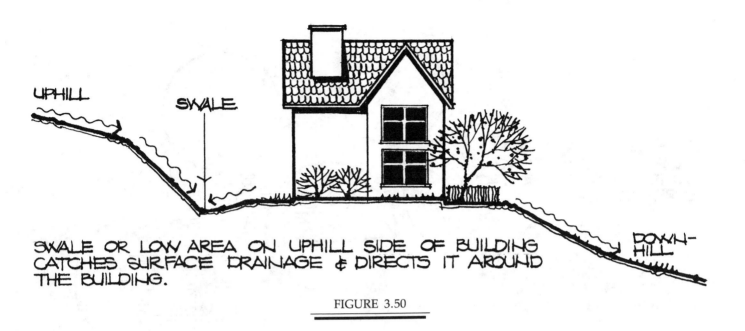

SWALE OR LOW AREA ON UPHILL SIDE OF BUILDING
CATCHES SURFACE DRAINAGE & DIRECTS IT AROUND
THE BUILDING.

FIGURE 3.50

surface drainage to do the same. The disadvantage
of this concept is the possibility of flooding in heavy
rains or in situations where water drains too slowly
away from the base of the building.

Plant Material. Another factor to deal with in relating a building to its site is plant material. In coordinating buildings and plant material, there are two
areas of concern: (1) relating a building or group of
buildings to existing plant material on a site, and (2)
relating buildings to a site by the correct placement
of new or introduced plant material. In the first situation, the possible extremes of existing vegetation
conditions in the temperate zone are the wooded
condition and open field condition.

There are a number of techniques for integrating
a building into a wooded or forest environment
based on a philosophy of minimal disturbance.
Wooded areas are sensitive ecosystems with a number of design constraints. They have limited ground
area available for buildings (without cutting down
trees), cannot tolerate compaction of the ground surface or major change in the elevation of the ground
plane, and are dark and shaded during summer.
Consequently, buildings located on a wooded site
should be designed to respond to these constraints,
as suggested in Figures 3.52 and 3.53. A building
sited in a wooded area should be compact in plan

FIGURE 3.51

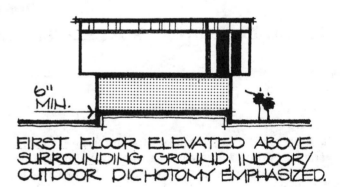

FIRST FLOOR ELEVATED ABOVE
SURROUNDING GROUND; INDOOR/
OUTDOOR DICHOTOMY EMPHASIZED.

FIRST FLOOR LEVEL WITH SUR-
ROUNDING GROUND; INDOOR/OUT-
DOOR DICHOTOMY MINIMIZED.

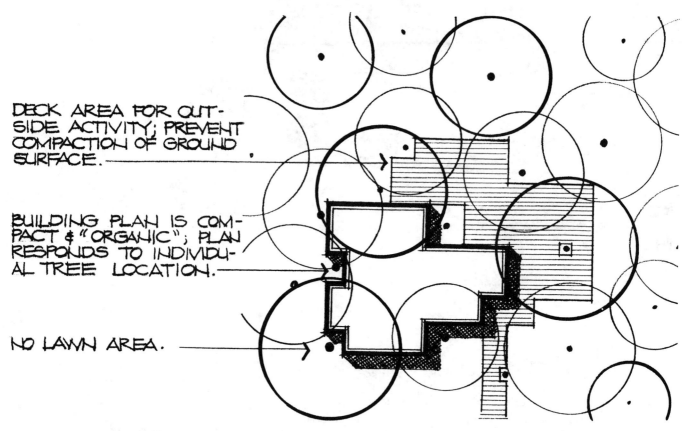

DECK AREA FOR OUT-
SIDE ACTIVITY; PREVENT
COMPACTION OF GROUND
SURFACE.

BUILDING PLAN IS COM-
PACT & "ORGANIC"; PLAN
RESPONDS TO INDIVIDU-
AL TREE LOCATION.

NO LAWN AREA.

PLAN; BUILDING LOCATED IN WOODED AREA.

FIGURE 3.52

layout in order not to take up too much ground area. The less ground area covered, the fewer the number of trees that have to be cut down. To provide for needed floor area, a building should be organized vertically in a multistory arrangement. A proportionally tall building takes up less ground area and visually echos the verticality of the trees. Besides being compact, the plan layout must be flexible and organic to respond to the location of individual trees. In most instances a plan that is modular or preplanned before being sited requires more trees to be cut down than one tailored to respond to the individual trees at a specific site.

Furthermore, buildings located in wooded conditions should ideally be constructed with their first floor slightly elevated above ground, as is the case of a house built with pole construction. This is sug-

gested in order to minimize the amount of excavation and grading required in the construction of the building. For pole-constructed buildings, excavation is essentially limited to the individual locations of the poles. The remainder of the ground surface in the vicinity of the building can be left reasonably undisturbed. In a similar vein, walks or outside living areas associated with the building should be constructed as wood decks also elevated above the ground. Again, this minimizes excavation, reduces compaction of the ground surface, and allows surface drainage to filter through the decking to the ground below.

When buildings are placed in an open field, other concepts are suggested for relating them to the site. Owing to the lack of constraints created by trees, the buildings can be much more flexible in their plan ar-

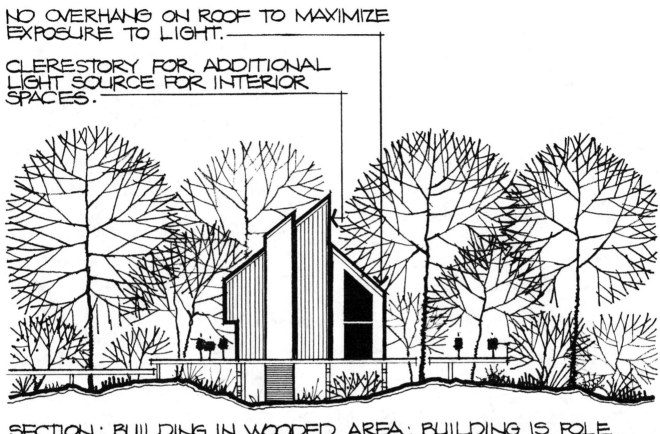

NO OVERHANG ON ROOF TO MAXIMIZE EXPOSURE TO LIGHT.

CLERESTORY FOR ADDITIONAL LIGHT SOURCE FOR INTERIOR SPACES.

SECTION: BUILDING IN WOODED AREA; BUILDING IS POLE CONSTRUCTED TO MINIMIZE EXCAVATION; AND BUILDING IS TALL & NARROW TO MINIMIZE GROUND COVERAGE.

FIGURE 3.53

rangement (assuming other factors such as soil, slope, drainage, and the like also permit this). Buildings located in open fields can be more sprawling and low in profile as long as topography permits. Changes in the ground plane can occur more easily and with less disturbance in an open field than in a woodland. Because of the lack of trees in an open field, exposure to the sun becomes a problem during summer. To provide sun protection, shade trees and large roof overhangs on the buildings are required. Some of these concepts are shown in Figure 3.54.

The way introduced plant materials are selected and located, especially in an open field condition, also influences the integration of a building into its site. Remember from Chapter 2 that plant material can be used to complement the architecture of a building. Vegetation can relate a building to the sur-

rounding site by carrying lines, forms, and spaces into the site, as shown in Figure 2.68. Recall that a roof line or wall mass can be extended into the adjoining site by masses of plant material that repeat lines and masses of the building itself. Or the ceiling of an interior space can be extended into the site through the use of tree canopies that are approximately the same height as the interior so that exterior spaces are made to seem as if they were related portions of one overall, unified design.

Building Design. The design and layout of the building itself also influences its integration into the site. Factors that should be taken into account include the functional relation between indoors and outdoors, the interpenetration of space between building and site, and the use of windows. Of these

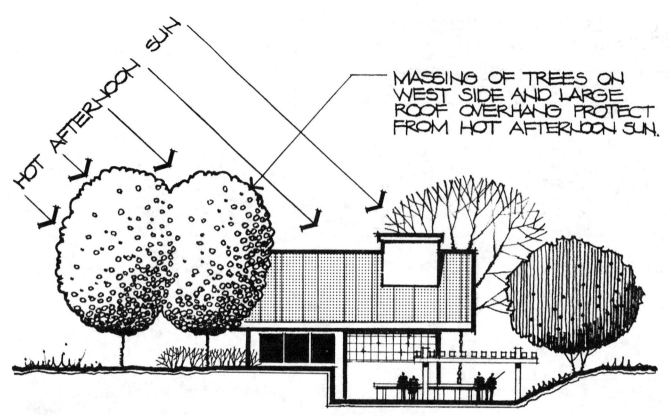

HOT AFTERNOON SUN

MASSING OF TREES ON WEST SIDE AND LARGE ROOF OVERHANG PROTECT FROM HOT AFTERNOON SUN.

SECTION: BUILDING IN OPEN FIELD AREA; BUILDING IS LOW & SPRAWLING; ALTERATION OF GROUND LEVEL CAN OCCUR WITHOUT RESTRICTION.

FIGURE 3.54

different considerations that affect the relation of a building to its site, certainly the functional organization is one of the more critical. It is essential that the interior use in a certain area of a building is compatible with the exterior function immediately outside in the site.

Ideal functional relationships between indoors and outdoors can be described and illustrated with a single-family residence. For instance, a typical single-family residence can be divided into two primary functions: living quarters and the work/storage area. The kitchen, portions of the basement, and the garage represent the work/storage areas, while the remainder of the house can be considered the living quarters. The living quarters can be further subdivided into public and private areas: eating, social, and entertainment areas are public, while sleeping and bathroom areas are private. To permit the house to properly relate to the site, the outdoor functions should be located so they are next to compatible indoor functions, as illustrated in Figure 3.55. For example, outdoor storage, garden, and work areas should relate to the garage and the kitchen. The outdoor living and entertaining area should ideally be placed next to either the family room or the living room. Outdoor entertainment should not be located near bedrooms because of potential party noise. Likewise, it would be awkward to have to walk through the outdoor entertaining area to get to the work or garden area. These ideal functional relationships between inside and outside a single-family residence are nothing more than logical arrangements.

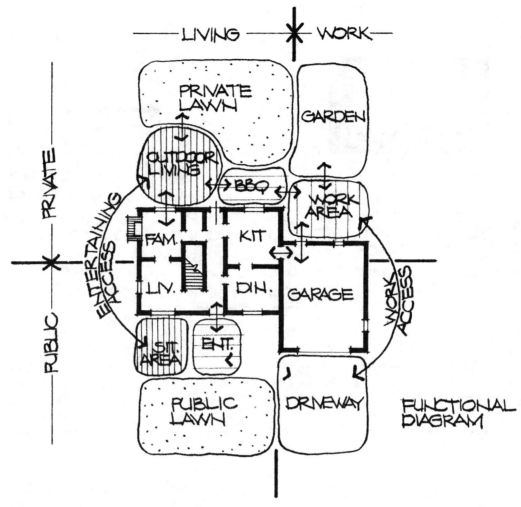

INTERIOR AND EXTERIOR SPACES SHOULD HAVE IDEAL FUNC-
TIONAL RELATIONSHIPS SO THE BUILDING AND SITE FIT ONE
ANOTHER.

FIGURE 3.55

Yet how many times have you experienced a home that did not work well because of poor functional relationships between house and site? The same thinking that is applied to relating the functions of a residence to its site should also apply to all buildings and site regardless of type or scale.

Another architectural aspect that affects the relation between building and site is space. A building that is a simple, flat planed box has a weaker spatial relation to its site than one that allows the exterior space to interpenetrate the building mass. In a flat planed building, the separation between indoor and outdoor space is clean and definite. There is no interlocking of the two spatial volumes. The building is seen more as an object sitting on the site than one interacting with and becoming part of the site. However, when portions of the building mass are pushed inward or pulled outward, indoor and outdoor space begin to interpenetrate each other. The building mass and the adjoining outside space become like interlocking hands or pieces of a puzzle. Graphic examples of this concept are illustrated in Figures 3.56

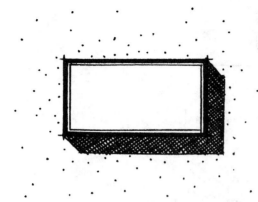

SIMPLE BUILDING PLAN HAS A
WEAK RELATION WITH SITE; NO
INTERPENETRATION OF SPACE
WITH SITE.

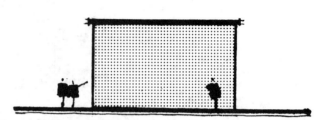

SIMPLE BUILDING MASS HAS
NO INTERPENETRATION OF SPACE
WITH SITE.

FIGURE 3.56

and 3.57. With the interconnecting of indoor and outdoor space, the division between building and site begins to blur. The building and site become one total integrated environment rather than two separate entities placed next to each other.

One other architectural solution that contributes to fostering the continuity between the inside and the outside of a building is maximizing the amount of window area, which in turn permits strong visual linkage between indoors and outdoors. Windows act as physical barriers but not visual or psychological ones. Windows allow outdoor spaces and elements

FIGURE 3.57

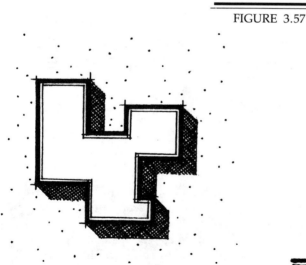

BUILDING PROJECTIONS IN PLAN
"HOLD ONTO SITE"; STRONG IN-
TERPENETRATION OF SPACE EX-
ISTS BETWEEN BUILDING AND
SITE.

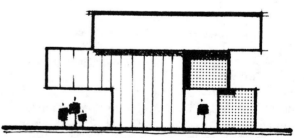

COMPLEX BUILDING MASS HAS
STRONG INTERPENETRATION OF
SPACE WITH SITE.

FIGURE 3.58

to become visually part of the indoors for a person sitting or standing inside a building, as shown in Figure 3.58. The ultimate use of glass for this purpose is the famous glass house designed by Phillip Johnson in New Canaan, Connecticut, in which the entire exterior façade is glass. Here, site elements such as trees become the true spatial edges of the house.

Transition Space. A concept for relating a building to its site that is very similar to interlocking indoor and outdoor space is the provision of a transition space at building entrances. A transition space diminishes the break between indoors and outdoors and allows a person entering or leaving a building to make the change between them in a gradual manner. It is undesirable to force a person to move abruptly between two different settings because this establishes both a physical and a psychological separation between the two. Rather, it is advisable to create a space that is neither indoors nor outdoors, allowing for a slow change between the two. In addition to this, a transition space is necessary to physically separate an entrance from other areas and functions such as a pedestrian walk. It is inconvenient and dangerous to permit a door to open directly onto a walk because of the congestion that results and the possibility of a person walking or running into the open doors (Figure 3.59).

A transition space can be created by partially delineating an area outside a building entrance with plant material, walls, mounding, and/or distinct pavement pattern, as shown in Figure 3.60. An additional option is to create a space by extending the upper floors of the building over the first floor entrance area. This space, while physically outside, is protected from the weather and produces an interconnection between building mass and exterior space, as discussed in the previous section.

A critical factor in organizing a transition space is the placement of a grade change. As stated before, the strongest sense of continuity between interior and exterior spaces results when the inside floor and the ground immediately outside a building are at the same elevation. Therefore, if a set of steps is needed to accommodate a grade change, it should be either located a short distance from the building on the outside or placed a short distance inside, as in Figure 3.61. The steps should not be placed right at the door because this eliminates any interior/exterior unity and is dangerous for opening or closing the door. It is not safe to require a person to open a door while simultaneously making a step up or down.

Walls. Both retaining and freestanding walls may be utilized to visually and functionally relate a building to its site. Particularly effective in this regard are

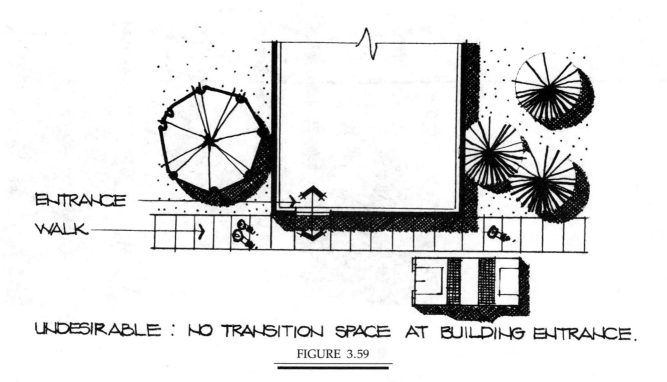

UNDESIRABLE : NO TRANSITION SPACE AT BUILDING ENTRANCE.

FIGURE 3.59

walls that extend out into the site from the building. Extended building walls can act like arms that reach out and hold onto the site, as suggested previously for building layout. This technique also diminishes the distinction between where the building ends and the site begins. The two "melt together." Another use of either freestanding or retaining walls is to repeat the material in the building façade in the walls located throughout the site as shown in Figure 3.62. This establishes visual "recall" and visually links the building to the other walls in the immediate environment.

FIGURE 3.60

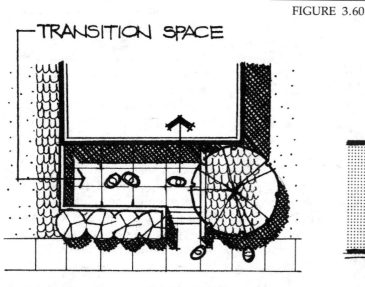

TRANSITION SPACE CREATED BY ELEVATION CHANGE, WALL AND PLANT MATERIAL.

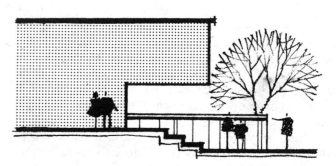

TRANSITION SPACE CREATED BY BUILDING OVERHANG AND WALL EXTENSION.

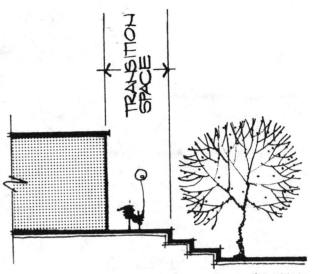

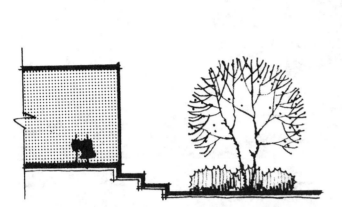

UNDESIRABLE : STEPS ARE LO-
CATED TOO CLOSE TO THE EDGE
OF BUILDING.

DESIRABLE : STEPS ARE LOCATED
AWAY FROM BUILDING EDGE,
THEREBY CREATING A TRANSI-
TION SPACE.

FIGURE 3.61

FIGURE 3.62

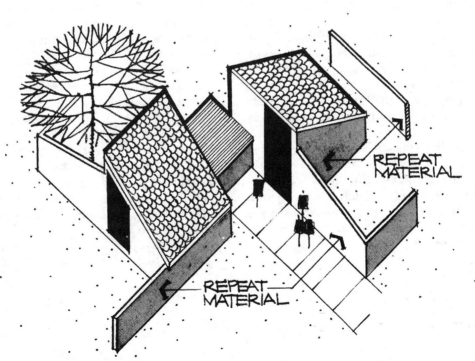

WALLS ARE EXTENDED OUTWARD INTO SITE AND MATERIALS
ARE REPEATED TO REINFORCE UNITY WITH SITE.

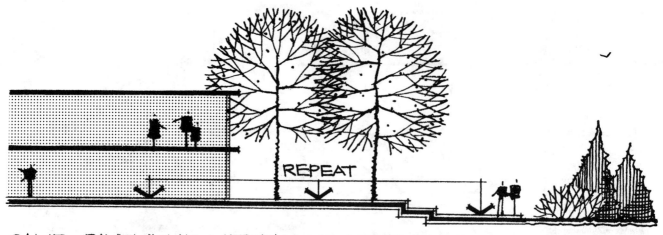

SAME PAVEMENT MATERIAL IS USED IN BOTH INTERIOR AND EXTERIOR SPACES TO UNIFY THE TWO.

FIGURE 3.63

Pavement. Pavement is still another design element that can be employed to unify a building and its site. As discussed more extensively in the next chapter, lines and patterns in an area of pavement next to a building should relate directly to the form and lines inherent in the building itself. Pavement patterns can be made to correlate with building corners, doors, window edges, and window mullions in order to enhance the visual relation between a building and hard surfaces, as illustrated in Figure 4.19. Or the pavement material can be the same as that on the building façade as a method for unification. Brick, stone, and concrete are materials successfully repeated between building wall and adjacent pavement. Another similar concept is to repeat the material used on the floor inside the building as a pavement material outside the building. This works especially well when the same material extends outside a building at the same elevation with only a glass window or door demarking the boundary be-

tween inside and outside. Figure 3.63 illustrates the application of some of these concepts.

Summary

As one of three major elements in the landscape, buildings and their associated land area are critical in the organization and character of the outdoor environment. In clusters, buildings are able to create outdoor spaces that vary from a small courtyard to an urban plaza of some grandeur. The exact character of an outdoor space established primarily by buildings depends on the plan arrangement of the buildings in addition to their size and fenestration. Within the framework of defining outdoor spaces, effort should be made to visually and functionally coordinate a building with its site by proper treatment of landform, repetition of materials, plan arrangement of the buildings, and transition spaces at building entrances.

4

Pavement

The overall framework of most outdoor spaces, whether large or small, formal or informal, urban or rural, is created by landform, plant materials, and buildings, as already discussed. These major design elements, both individually and collectively, create outdoor spaces by affecting the ground plane, vertical plane, and overhead plane. Within this spatial framework, the use and organization of elements on the ground plane itself becomes an important aspect in completing the spatial definition and feeling, as well as fulfilling other desired utilitarian and aesthetic uses.

Pavement, water, and vegetative surfaces such as lawn, ground cover, annuals, or low shrubs are all different elements that may be integrated into the ground plane to achieve various design objectives. Of these, pavement stands out as the one "hard" structural element. This chapter discusses the compositional and functional uses of pavement in the landscape and the different types of pavement that can be used along with the aesthetic and functional characteristics of each.

Pavement is any hard natural or artificial surface material consciously placed on the ground plane of an outdoor space to establish a durable surface while also satisfying design objectives. Examples of pavement include gravel, brick, tile, stone, concrete, asphalt and, in some cases, wood decking.

Pavement has several characteristics that set it apart from other ground surface materials. First, as has been pointed out, pavement is a hard, comparatively nonpliable surface material. As such, it is relatively fixed and nonchanging. Plant material and water, on the other hand, are quite variable over time. Because of pavement's rather permanent quality, it is a good structural material to support intense uses on the ground plane and establish fixed ground areas that remain the same over time. A classic example of the durability of pavement is the Appian Way, constructed by the Romans from Rome south to Brindisi. This road, begun in 312 B.C., still can be seen and used in some sections. Besides its permanence, pavement is able to define exact edges of shapes and forms on the ground plane while lawn and ground cover edges must be constantly trimmed or contained with another material to achieve similar results.

Another general characteristic of pavement is that it is a relatively expensive ground surface material, particularly in comparison with vegetative ground surfaces. For example, brick on a sand base costs about $5.44 per sq ft (930 sq cm) installed (exact cost, of course, varies with geographic location),[1] 4-in (10 cm) thick Portland cement concrete costs about $2.81 per sq ft for an area 1,000 sq ft or less,[2] and 2 1/2-in (6.5 cm) thick stone in a random ashlar pattern on a sand bed costs about $8.50 per sq ft.[3] On the other hand, a sodded lawn area costs about $0.21 per sq ft in northern areas of the United States and seeded lawn costs about $0.04 per sq ft installed for an area 1,000 sq ft (90 sq m) or less.[4]

While initially more costly than vegetative surfaces for material and installation, pavement often holds an advantage over a longer period of time in terms of cost. Pavement typically is less expensive to maintain than either lawn or ground cover. Although not totally maintenance free, pavement does not require mowing, watering, or fertilization. Nationally, Americans spend about $12 billion a year to maintain about 20 million acres (about 8 million hectares) of lawn.[5]

Pavement is not without its disadvantages despite its wide potential applications in outdoor spaces. Pavement tends to be much hotter than vegetative ground surfaces exposed to the sun. Near the ground surface itself, it may be as much as 5 to 6 degrees F. hotter over pavement than over lawn or ground cover.[6] To compound this problem, more sunlight is usually reflected from pavement surface than from a surface of vegetation, causing disturbing glare. As one illustration, concrete reflects about 55 percent of the sunlight that falls on it, while average vegetation reflects 25 percent.[7]

Another negative quality of some pavement types is that they are impermeable to percolation of water. Consequently, they create more surface runoff than would occur from a lawn, grassland, or woodland. Used in great quantities such as in urban areas, this quality of impervious pavement can cause flooding and erosion downstream owing to the great volume of runoff.

Finally, pavement can give an impersonal, barren quality to the outdoor environment if overused or poorly detailed. Many urban areas suffer from ever present, inhuman expanses of hard paving.

Functional and Compositional Uses

As with the other physical landscape architectural design elements, pavement has a number of potential functional and compositional uses in the landscape. Some of these functions are singular while most occur simultaneously with one another. Many of these uses can be reinforced through the sensitive and coordinated use of the other design elements.

Accommodate Intense Use. Probably the most obvious functional use of pavement is its ability to accommodate constant, intense use on the ground plane without immediate deterioration. Paved surfaces, compared with lawn or ground cover areas, can withstand considerable wear and tear without loss of character or erosion of subsurface soil layers. Similarly, pavement can accommodate wheeled vehicles more easily than other ground surface materials. On foot, a person can go almost anywhere, yet in a wheeled vehicle, a person is generally restricted to pavement or stable earth surfaces. Furthermore, pavement can perform throughout the year in all weather conditions. Of course, one of the big disadvantages of lawns is that they cannot be submitted to concentrated use nor can they be used in wet weather when they are easily converted into a muddy quagmire. In dry weather pavement prevents wind erosion and dust that result from barren earth surfaces. In addition, pavement that is adequately engineered may be subjected to considerable

[1]Kathleen W. Kerr, ed., *Cost Data for Landscape Construction*, 1982, 3rd annual ed. (Minneapolis: Kerr Associates, 1982), p. 168.

[2]Ibid., p. 170.

[3]Ibid., p. 172.

[4]Ibid., p. 86.

[5]Ted Williams, "The Joe-Pye Weed is Always Taller in the Other Person's Yard," *Audubon* 83(4): 108 (July 1981).

[6]Charles McClenon, ed., *Landscape Planning for Energy Conservation* (Reston Virginia: Environmental Design Press, 1977), p. 50.

[7]*Window Design Strategies to Conserve Energy*, National Bureau of Standards Building Science Series 104 (Washington, D.C.: U.S. Department of Commerce, National Bureau of Standards, 1977), pp. 1–15.

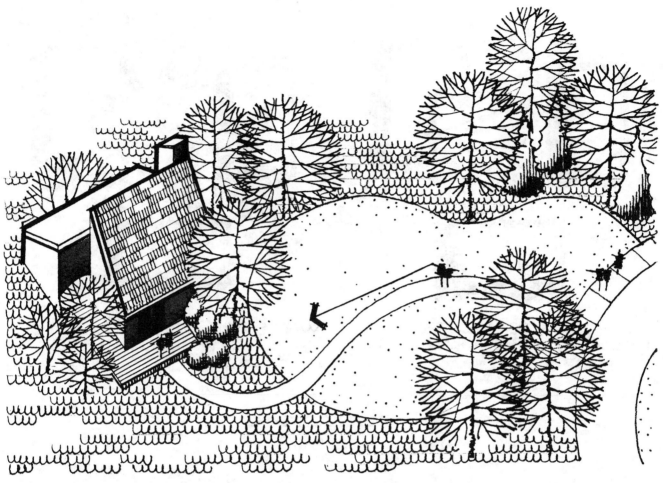

A RIBBON OF PAVEMENT CAN BE USED TO LEAD THE EYE AND PROVIDE DIRECTION BETWEEN POINTS IN THE LANDSCAPE.

FIGURE 4.1

structural pressure such as that produced by the weight of a truck. Pavement, if properly constructed, can do all of this without undue maintenance.

Provide Direction. A second function of pavement is to give direction and indicate movement when used as a thin strip or in a linear manner on the ground plane. Pavement can suggest movement in several ways. First, pavement can indicate where and how to move from one point to another by leading the eye and keeping the pedestrian or vehicle "on track." This works especially well when the ribbon of pavement is placed on a vegetative background such as a lawn or countryside. Examples of linear

configurations of pavement used to give direction are a road in the countryside, a walk leading up to the front door of a house or public building (Figure 4.1), paths in a park, and walks leading across large open spaces on college campuses. All these examples tell a person where to walk or drive.

The use of pavement to suggest direction of movement works well when the ribbon of pavement follows a logical path of movement but becomes a problem when the route of movement is too circuitous, making it easier to take "short cuts." This problem can be prevented in park or campus settings if "desire lines" can be anticipated and plotted on plan, as in Figure 4.2. The walks, then, should generally reflect these "desire lines" to eliminate the

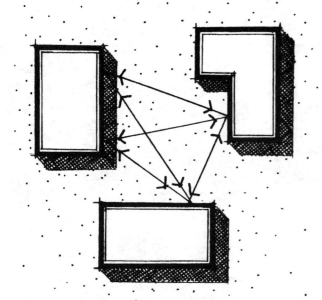

"DESIRE LINES" PLOTTED BE-
TWEEN MAJOR ENTRANCES OF
BUILDINGS.

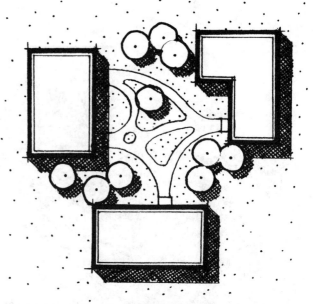

WALKS ARE DESIGNED AND LO-
CATED TO REFLECT DESIRE
LINES.

FIGURE 4.2

FIGURE 4.3

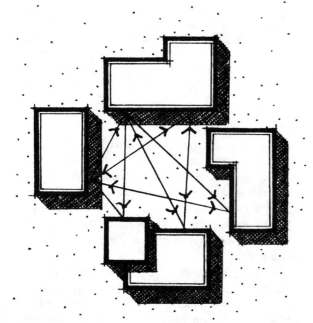

URBAN SPACE WITH NUMEROUS
"DESIRE LINES" LOCATED BE-
TWEEN BUILDINGS.

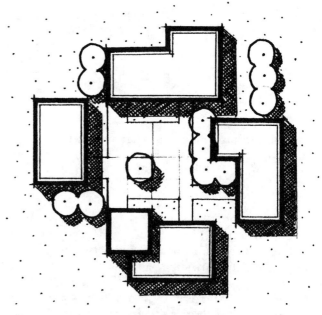

PAVED PLAZA ACCOMMODATES
THE NUMEROUS PATHS OF MOVE-
MENT WHILE MAINTAINING UN-
ITY.

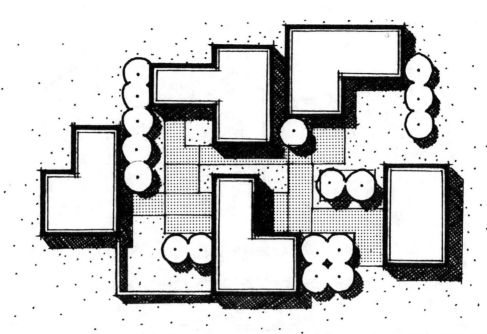

A STRONG PAVEMENT PATTERN CAN DIRECT AND LEAD PEDESTRIANS
BETWEEN ADJOINING SPACES IN AN URBAN SETTING.

FIGURE 4.4

need for cutting across the grass. If numerous desire lines are found within a particular space, as in Figure 4.3, it might be advantageous to provide a large plazalike expanse of pavement to allow more freedom of movement and produce a unified layout. Too many paths of pavement dissecting an open lawn area can break it up into numerous poorly related spaces.

The concept of directing movement with pavement also applies in hard-surfaced urban settings, where it is sometimes desirable to pilot the pedestrian through a sequence of spaces. The visual and physical connections among adjoining open spaces in urban environments are frequently ill-defined and unknown to the first-time visitor. In this situation, a thread of pavement that is distinctly different from its surroundings can physically link the various open spaces together and subtly direct a pedestrian through them by means of its commonality, as illustrated in Figure 4.4. When leaving this particular pavement and crossing onto a different material, the pedestrian experiences a new direction of movement.

The layout of linear segments of pavement not only affects the practical aspects of circulation but the more subtle character of movement as well. For example, the path may be smooth and flowing, con-

noting a casual, pastoral feeling; rectilinear and rigid, indicating a formal, controlled quality of walking; or angular and irregular, suggesting an erratic, nervous means of circulation, as indicated in Figure 4.5. A direct path from one point to another suggests a formal, strong relation between the two points, while a meandering link indicates an incidental relation. Each of these characteristics has its appropriate place of application. Therefore the designer should carefully select the desired feeling of movement before settling on a particular layout.

Suggest Rate and Rhythm of Movement. Besides suggesting direction, a linear layout of pavement can influence the rate and rhythm of movement, as indicated in Figure 4.6. The wider a ribbon of pavement is, the more casual the rate of walking can be. On a relatively wide path, a person can get out of the way of others and stop to observe a particular point. Or the person can slowly meander from side to side of the walk, taking in different scenes along the way. As the width of pavement narrows, one is forced to continue to move ahead with little opportunity to stop without getting entirely off the pavement. These characteristics can be further reinforced if the wider area of pavement is also somewhat rough, making rapid movement difficult and the

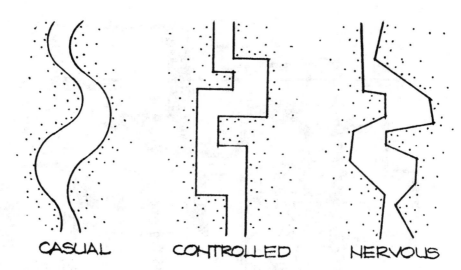

CASUAL   CONTROLLED   NERVOUS

FORM OF LINEAR PAVEMENT INFLUENCES CHARACTER OF MOVE-MENT.

FIGURE 4.5

narrow area of pavement made smooth to accommodate easy, fast movement.

The rhythm of moving along a linear path can also be influenced by the design and layout of pavement. Where a pedestrian places a foot and how far apart individual steps are taken are two aspects of the rhythm of walking. Both these factors can be affected by the spacing between blocks of pavement or distance between expansion joints, by material variation, or by the width of pavement. For example, equal spacing of stone blocks along a path can establish a regular cadence by which a pedestrian can measure time and progression through space, as indicated in the left portion of Figure 4.7. For a different effect, the spacing might be closer between some stones and farther apart between others so that the pedestrian's rhythm is short and quick at one point and long and slower at another, as in Fig-

FIGURE 4.6

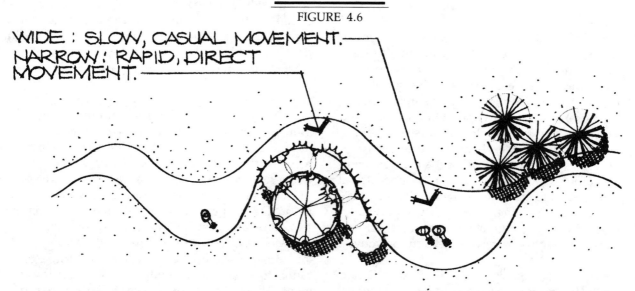

WIDE : SLOW, CASUAL MOVEMENT.
NARROW : RAPID, DIRECT MOVEMENT.

RATE AND TYPE OF MOVEMENT IS AFFECTED BY PAVEMENT WIDTH AND LAYOUT.

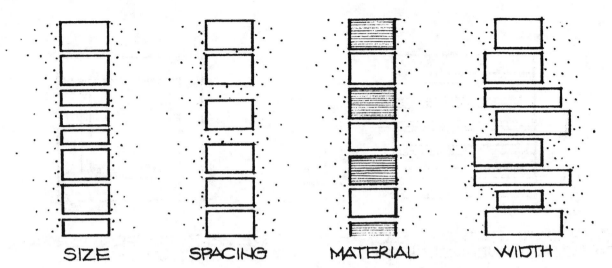

SIZE   SPACING   MATERIAL   WIDTH

RHYTHM OF MOVEMENT CAN BE INFLUENCED BY THE ABOVE VARI-
ABLES.

FIGURE 4.7

ure 4.7. Likewise, a strip of pavement that alternates between wide and narrow as it progresses between two points establishes a rhythm of tension and relief suggesting rapid and slow movement. And alternating the pavement materials in a repeating pattern also creates a sensation of rhythm as one moves along a walk.

Create Repose. A use of pavement opposite to giving direction is to create a sense of repose and rest. Pavement can suggest a stationary experience when it occurs in relatively large, nondirectional forms or patterns, as illustrated in Figure 4.8. Nondirectional, static forms of pavement or pavement patterns are appropriate for stopping and resting areas along a

FIGURE 4.8

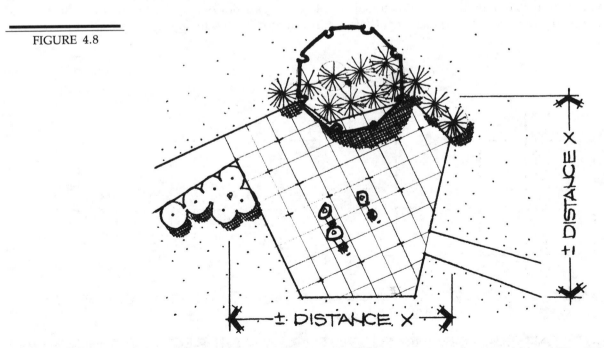

A NONDIRECTIONAL AREA OF APPROXIMATELY EQUAL PROPORTIONS
CAN PROVIDE A SENSE OF REPOSE.

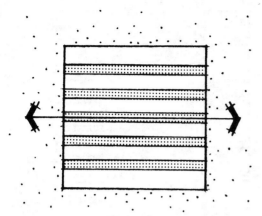

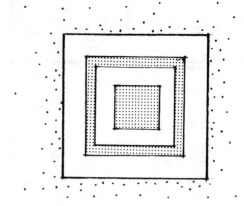

PAVEMENT PATTERN SUGGESTS DIRECTION AND MOVEMENT.

PAVEMENT PATTERN IS STATIC AND NONDIRECTIONAL.

PAVEMENT PATTERN CAN INFLUENCE MOVEMENT OR NONMOVEMENT THROUGH A SPACE.

FIGURE 4.9

path or for central meeting spaces in the landscape.

In creating a sense of repose with pavement, careful consideration must be given to the choice of the pavement material as well as to the pattern in which it is laid out so that it clearly says "stop" when placed in the context of adjoining paths of movement, as suggested in Figure 4.9. In some situations, a simple change of material in the nondirectional space is enough to reinforce its purpose. In other cases, a static pavement pattern is also necessary to accent the stationary quality of the space. These same thoughts apply at an intersection of walks. Various possibilities and results are illustrated in Figure 4.10.

Indicate Uses on the Ground Plane. Pavement, and its changes from one space to another, can be used in outdoor spaces to signify varying uses and func-

FIGURE 4.10

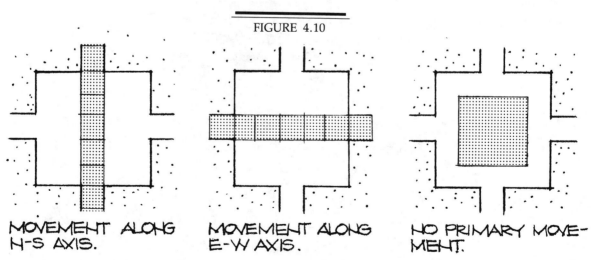

MOVEMENT ALONG N-S AXIS.

MOVEMENT ALONG E-W AXIS.

NO PRIMARY MOVEMENT.

PAVEMENT PATTERN USED TO SUGGEST PRIMARY DIRECTION THROUGH AN INTERSECTION.

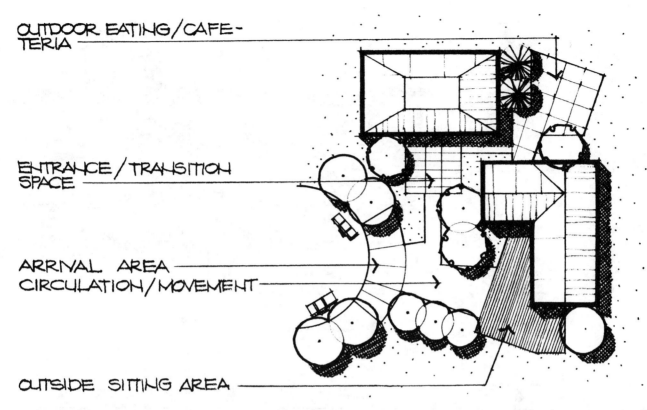

OUTDOOR EATING/CAFE-
TERIA

ENTRANCE/TRANSITION
SPACE

ARRIVAL AREA
CIRCULATION/MOVEMENT

OUTSIDE SITTING AREA

DIFFERENT PAVEMENT MATERIALS ARE USED TO REINFORCE THE
PARTICULAR FUNCTIONS OF INDIVIDUAL OUTDOOR SPACES.

FIGURE 4.11

tions on the ground plane.[8] It has already been stated that changes in pavement can identify differences between movement, rest, sitting, gathering, focal area, and so forth. By altering color, texture, or the pavement material itself, as in Figure 4.11, a separation of uses and activities can be implied from one space to another. One rule of thumb suggests that pavement be altered from one area to another in a design only if the use also varies. If use or activity is to remain the same, then the pavement should also remain constant.

One application of this potential function is to use a change in pavement to indicate a hazard for pedestrians. As in Figure 4.12, a dangerous area along a walk such as an automobile crossing can be indicated by a variance in the pavement material. The pedestrian should notice this deviation and be warned of a different use of the walk at this point. Likewise, the pedestrian crossing in a street can be denoted by a change in the pavement of the crosswalk itself. Before the days of painted street lines, a change in pavement material was a common method for signifying a pedestrian crosswalk. An example of this, shown in Figure 4.13, is found in such New England villages as Nantucket, where large, smooth slabs of granite were used to identify crosswalks. This still has its applications and is more attractive than the ever present painted crosswalk. A common method for pointing out the dissimilarity between pedestrian and vehicular circulation is to use a relatively smooth pavement for the pedestrian surface and a rougher material for the vehicular surface. The smoother surface is easier for the pedestrian to walk on while the coarser pavement is readily observed in

[8]Vincent J. Bellafiore, "Pavement in the Landscape: The Design and Construction of Surfaces for Pedestrian Spaces," in *Handbook of Landscape Architecture Construction*, Jot D. Carpenter, ed. (McLean: The Landscape Architectural Foundation, 1976), p. 596.

HAZARD

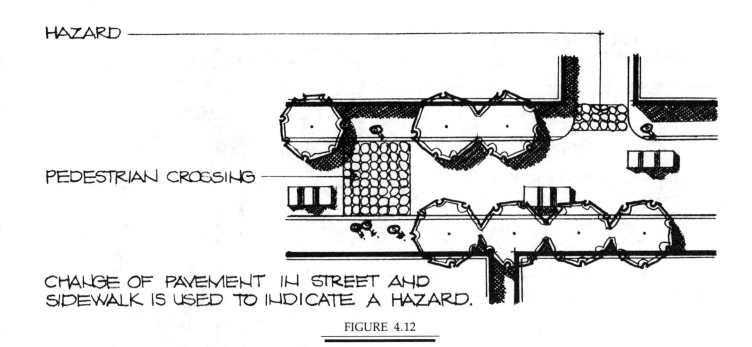

PEDESTRIAN CROSSING

CHANGE OF PAVEMENT IN STREET AND
SIDEWALK IS USED TO INDICATE A HAZARD.

FIGURE 4.12

FIGURE 4.13

contrast to it. In addition, the rugged surface slows vehicles down, a desirable objective in pedestrian areas.

Influence Scale. Another functional and compositional use of pavement in exterior spaces is to influence scale.[9] The texture of pavement material, the size of individual paving blocks or modules (as in flagstone and brick), and the size and spacing of paving patterns are all factors that affect the perceived scale of a paved area. Larger, more expansive patterns give a space a sense of being ample in scale, while smaller, tighter patterns are likely to make a space feel diminished and intimate, as in Figure 4.14. Pavement patterns involving brick or stone bands, for instance, can be applied to large areas of concrete or asphalt to reduce the apparent scale of these areas and provide visual relief from these potentially drab materials, as illustrated in Figure 4.15. The patterns introduced into the primary pavement material will actually subdivide the total space into smaller, more easily perceived subspaces. When using a pattern of contrasting material on the ground plane, the difference of color and texture should generally be quiet and subtle in order to contribute to the unity of the pavement. The more striking the pattern becomes, the more attention it demands, competing with other elements in the overall design.

[9]Ibid., p. 594.

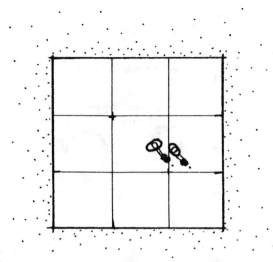

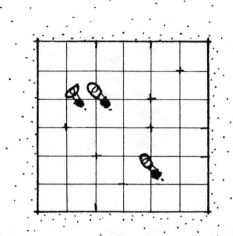

PAVEMENT PATTERN CREATES A SENSE OF LARGE SCALE.

PAVEMENT PATTERN CREATES A SENSE OF SMALL SCALE.

PAVEMENT PATTERN USED TO INFLUENCE SCALE OF OUTDOOR SPACE.

FIGURE 4.14

FIGURE 4.15

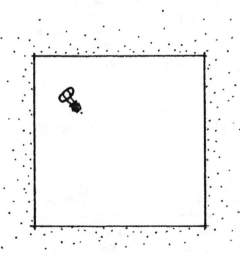

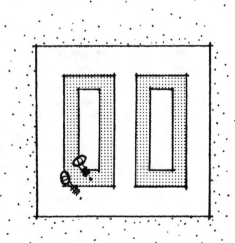

LARGE EXPANSE OF PAVE-MENT WITHOUT A SENSE OF SCALE.

PATTERN OF BRICK/STONE PROVIDES A SENSE OF SCALE.

PAVEMENT PATTERN USED TO INFLUENCE SCALE OF OUTDOOR SPACE.

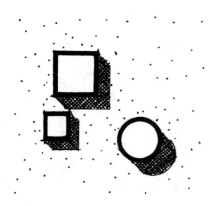

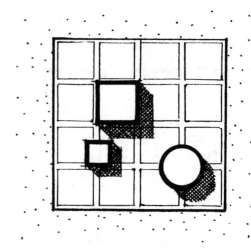

WEAK RELATION AMONG ELE-
MENTS.

STRONG PAVEMENT PATTERN
UNIFIES ELEMENTS WITH COM-
MON BACKGROUND.

PAVEMENT CAN BE USED TO UNIFY AND COORDINATE ELEMENTS IN
THE LANDSCAPE.

FIGURE 4.16

Provide Unity. Already touched upon is the use of pavement to provide unity in a design. It can do this by acting as a common material to which all other elements and spaces of the design relate.[10] The entire composition can be linked by the common pavement even though other elements vary greatly in scale and character, as suggested in Figure 4.16. Pavement can best function as a unifier when it possesses a distinct or unique pattern, making it easily recognized and remembered. This use of pavement is successfully applied in urban environments to visually unify a complex of buildings and related outdoor spaces. One example of this application is the Embarcadero Center in San Francisco. Here, a circular pattern of small tile pavers shown in Figure 4.17 is everywhere in the center including indoors and outdoors. People easily recognize that they are at Embarcadero Center by the paving material and know immediately that they have left the center when another pavement appears. Similar uses of strong pavement patterns are found in other urban centers.

Serve as a Setting. Pavement may be used in the landscape to act as a neutral setting to other more visually prominent elements. Used in this manner, pavement may be thought of as a blank tabletop or an empty sheet of paper on which notable elements acting as focal points are placed. Pavement can function as a neutral setting to buildings, sculpture, potted plants, displays, benches, and so forth. Pavement that is to function as a background should be visually quiet; it should not contain bold patterns, coarse texture, or any other attention-holding quality that would compete with the primary elements to be seen.

Establish Spatial Character. One use of pavement mentioned previously is to establish and reinforce spatial character. The paving material used in a design along with its surface and edge details can have a significant impact on the feeling of the outdoor spaces in which it is used. Different pavement materials and patterns can create and reinforce such diverse spatial feelings as refined, rugged, quiet, aggressive, urban, or rural. In terms of specific materials, brick has the ability to give a warm, inviting feeling to a space, angled flagstone provides an

---

[10]Ibid., p. 592.

FIGURE 4.17

irregular, informal atmosphere, and concrete can give a cold, impersonal sensation. The material and pattern of pavement in a design should be partially chosen for the feeling desired. It would be incorrect to use asphalt in a space meant to be warm and friendly.

Provide Visual Interest. One last use of pavement in the landscape that can easily be incorporated with other functions is to serve as an element of visual interest. As people walk through a space, their attention naturally gravitates downward toward the ground plane. People tend to pay a great deal of attention to what is underfoot and immediately in front of them. Thus the visual quality of pavement is an important factor in determining the intrigue and fascination with a design. In some instances, pavement material and pattern may be selected solely for eye appeal. A distinct paving pattern can not only provide visual stimulus but can also create a strong sense of place as it does in the Piazza San Marco in Venice and the Piazza del Duomo in Milan. Furthermore, a striking pattern may be a special point of appeal for upper story windows that look down on the floor of a nearby outdoor space.

Design Guidelines for Pavement

As with landform and plant materials, a number of design guidelines should be considered when using pavement in the landscape. They should be weighed with the overall objectives of a design and utilized accordingly.

As with any other design element, the number of materials used in a given area of a design should be simplified to help insure unity. Too much variation in a pavement material and/or pattern can easily create visual chaos and disorder. One pavement material should dominate in a design, as in Figure 4.18, with other materials added for visual contrast and variety as well as suggesting other uses on the ground plane. The one dominant material can be used throughout different locations of a design in order to establish unity and recall.

The selection of pavement material and the design of the pavement pattern should be undertaken simultaneously with the selection and organization of the other elements of a design to help insure that the pavement is visually and functionally integrated into the entire scheme. It is not a desirable procedure to select and design the pavement as an afterthought late in the development of a design solu-

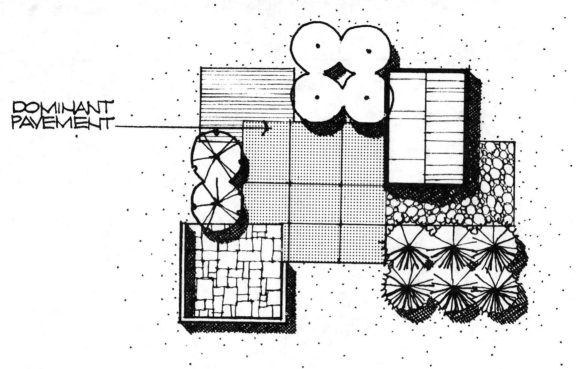

DOMINANT PAVEMENT

ONE PAVEMENT MATERIAL SHOULD DOMINATE IN A DESIGN.

FIGURE 4.18

tion. While selecting a paving pattern, one should study it in both plan and eye-level perspective. In plan, attention should be given to creating a visually attractive pattern and to coordinating it with other elements of the design including adjoining pavement materials, buildings, planters, lighting, drop inlets, tree wells, and benches, as shown in Figures 4.19 and 4.20. If treated correctly, the pavement should appear to relate strongly to all these design elements in a thoughtful, planned manner. When adjoining areas of pavement change pattern without a third transitional material, the patterns and lines of the two should match and align with each other. This is especially true when dealing with the scoring lines and expansion joints of concrete or the lines and mortar joints found in stone and tile pavement. The lines and pattern of one material should carry on into those of adjoining pavements, as in Figure 4.21. Similarly, the edges and lines of a building should be coordinated with the pavement next to the building so that it visually connects to the pavement, as in Figure 4.19.

The pavement pattern should be studied in eye-level perspective in addition to the plan itself because this is how most people will actually perceive it. From eye level, the pattern often appears quite different than it does in plan. Lines parallel to the line of sight converge, while lines perpendicular to the line of sight "pile up" on one another as they become farther from the viewer, as in Figure 4.22. Moreover, the observed pattern may change as one moves through a space gaining varying vantage points. Unfortunately, most designers rely too heavily on the plan alone, failing to use a perspective study. Without the study, the designer may on occasion be surprised that the pattern does not appear as intended after it has been constructed.

The pavement selected for a particular space should also be suitable for the type of intended use, anticipated intensity of use, and desired spatial character. Cost usually has some bearing on what pavement is selected. From a practical standpoint, no pavement material lends itself equally well to all possible functions and activities. For example, it is

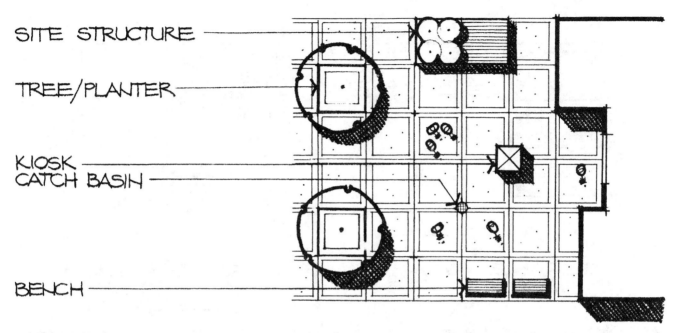

SITE STRUCTURE

TREE/PLANTER

KIOSK
CATCH BASIN

BENCH

PAVEMENT PATTERN IS COORDINATED WITH BUILDING AND SITE ELEMENTS.

FIGURE 4.19

FIGURE 4.20

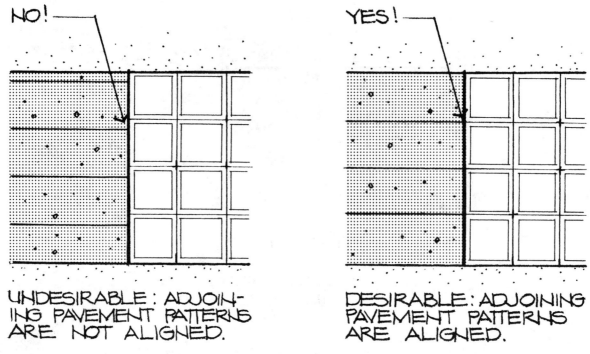

NO!

YES!

UNDESIRABLE: ADJOIN-
ING PAVEMENT PATTERNS
ARE NOT ALIGNED.

DESIRABLE: ADJOINING
PAVEMENT PATTERNS
ARE ALIGNED.

ADJOINING PAVEMENT PATTERNS SHOULD BE ALIGNED WITH
EACH OTHER.

FIGURE 4.21

easier to walk on smooth surfaces such as concrete or asphalt than rough materials such as gravel or irregular fieldstone. Likewise, pavement surfaces cannot be loose or have any bumps or indentations if they are to accommodate wheeled vehicles such as bicycles or baby strollers. And some pavement materials adapt better than others to different shapes of paved areas. For instance, concrete is easier to use in free-form shapes than brick or tile.

As indicated in the previous sections of this chapter, different pavements have different visual characteristics. Some are more formal and appropriate in public spaces while others are better suited to private, residential situations. The particular pavement for any space should be selected based on a number of considerations.

Another guideline for using pavement in the landscape is that it should not be changed from one area of a design to another without a specific purpose. As stated earlier, an alteration of pavement material between areas usually signifies a shift in use or, in some cases, a change in ownership and control. Regardless of the exact purpose, a change in

pavement symbolizes to the user that the circumstances of the situation have also varied.

When converting pavement material or pattern for specific reasons, several other factors need to be considered. First, some design theorists recommend that pavement not vary in the same plane, as indicated in Figure 4.23. In other words, if pavement is to be different in two adjoining spaces, there should also be a level change to separate and demark the two pavement types. The level change functions as a transition and avoids the potential problem of having the two pavements directly abut each other. If a level change is not feasible for separating two pavements that are next to each other, then another approach can be taken. This is to introduce a third, visually neutral material in between the first two adjoining materials. The third material visually separates the two materials by a short distance and prevents incompatible patterns and lines from touching each other. This technique is particularly necessary if the first two pavement materials are distinctly different or visually clashing when placed directly next to each other, as in Figure 4.24.

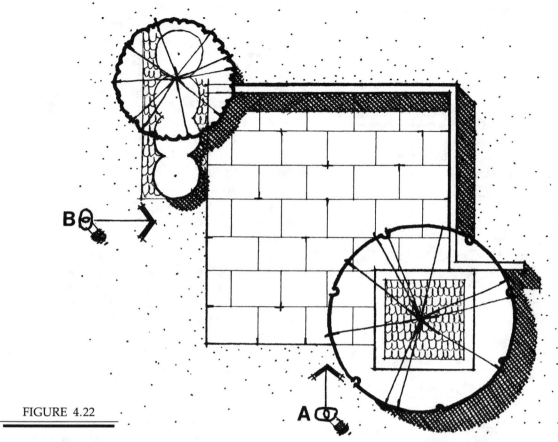

FIGURE 4.22

PLAN VIEW: PRE-CUT STONE BLOCKS ARE ORGANIZED IN AN ASHLAR PATTERN.

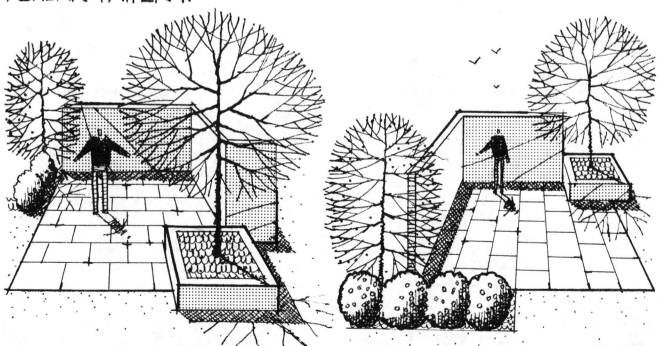

A: THIS VIEW EMPHASIZES THE WIDTH OF THE SPACE.

B: THIS VIEW EMPHASIZES THE DEPTH OF THE SPACE.

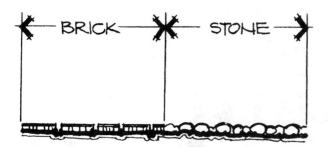

UNDESIRABLE: DIFFERENT
PAVEMENT MATERIALS AD-
JOIN EACH OTHER ON THE
SAME LEVEL.

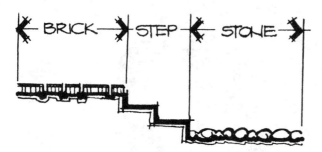

DESIRABLE: DIFFERENT PAVE-
MENT MATERIALS ARE SEP-
ARATED BY A LEVEL CHANGE.

FIGURE 4.23

One last design guideline for using pavement in the outdoor environment is that smooth-textured pavement should generally predominate within a space because it is quieter and visually less aggressive. This is usually desirable so the pavement does not detract from other elements of a design. Rough-textured pavements can be used in smaller quantities for accent and variety.

Basic Pavement Materials

There are numerous pavement materials available for use in the landscape. Generally they fall into three major groups: (1) loose pavement such as gravel, (2) unit pavers such as brick, tile, or stone, and (3) adhesive pavement held together by a binding agent as in Portland cement concrete or asphalt. Each of these categories and specific types of pavement have their own unique characteristics and potential uses in landscape architectural design, as will be discussed in the following pages. As with other design elements, it is useful to have a good grasp of these qualities before attempting to design with pavement.

Loose Pavement: Gravel and Its Variations. Gravel, one of the least expensive pavement materials, is available in a range of shapes, sizes, and colors.

FIGURE 4.24

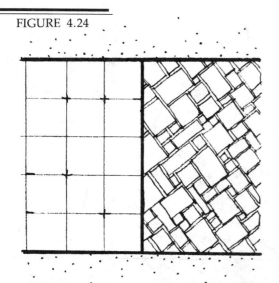

UNDESIRABLE: SHARP-
LY CONTRASTING PAVE-
MENT MATERIALS DIRECT-
LY ADJOIN EACH OTHER.

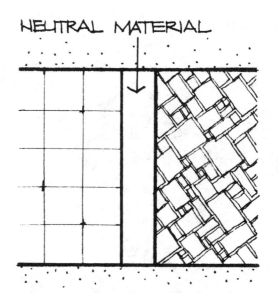

NEUTRAL MATERIAL

DESIRABLE: A THIRD
NEUTRAL MATERIAL ACTS
AS A TRANSITION BETWEEN
CONTRASTING PAVEMENTS.

Gravel can be either whole or crushed. Whole gravel obtained from direct excavation is usually smooth and rounded. Crushed gravel, as the name implies, is formed by crushing larger stone and is rather angular and sharp-sided. Gravel may vary in size from about ¼ in (.6cm) across ("pea gravel") to coarser material about 2 in (5cm) across. In color gravel varies from almost pure white to black, with many tones of brown and gray in between.

As a pavement, gravel has several advantages. One is that it allows surface runoff to percolate through to the underlying soil. From an ecological standpoint, this is good because it helps to replenish ground water and to supply plant material with needed moisture. Furthermore, the less runoff that occurs from a paved area, the less the chance that erosion and flooding will occur downstream. Gravel also requires less expense in terms of drainage facilities like drop inlets and pipes because there is not as much runoff as with concrete and asphalt surfaces. All in all, gravel is economically and ecologically expedient.

Gravel does have drawbacks as a pavement material. By its very nature, gravel is loose and therefore needs to be contained by other elements. Metal edging, wood, or the side of another pavement such as concrete can be used to hold gravel in its intended locations, as suggested in Figure 4.25. Figure 4.26 shows the use of metal edging to contain a gravel

walk in a courtyard next to an office building. In Great Britain, it is common to find gravel in depressed walks contained simply by earthen and sod sides. By itself, gravel is a poor material to define the outline of a form on the ground plane because it is so easily disturbed with heavy use. This characteristic also results in a maintenance problem because there is frequently a recurring need to rake or sweep gravel back into its proper place. Figure 4.27 shows the maintenance problem of gravel near the Mall in Washington, D.C. Moreover, it is difficult to rake leaves or remove snow from a gravel surface because the individual stones are easily picked up.

Another disadvantage of fine or small aggregate-sized gravel such as pea gravel is that it is an inappropriate pavement material to use on slopes because it may wash away with surface runoff during a storm. Here again, containment by means of steps or terracing is necessary. Finally, gravel has the potential of being a difficult surface to walk on, especially for women in high heels or people with physical disabilities that affect walking. This is especially true when the gravel surface has excessive depth and/or is not adequately compacted. Both these conditions result in loose and unstable gravel, making the walking experience very similar to that of walking on soft sand; a person must exert a great deal of physical effort and be constantly on the offensive to keep balance.

FIGURE 4.25

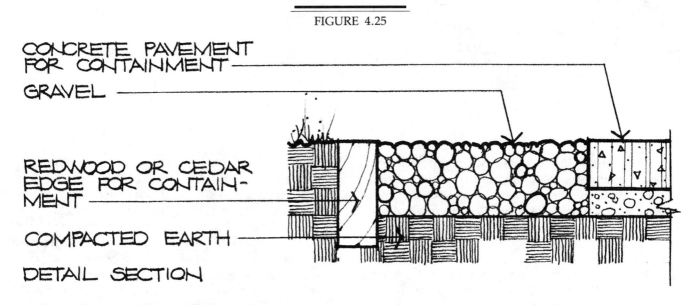

CONCRETE PAVEMENT FOR CONTAINMENT

GRAVEL

REDWOOD OR CEDAR EDGE FOR CONTAINMENT

COMPACTED EARTH

DETAIL SECTION

GRAVEL SHOULD BE CONTAINED ALONG ITS EDGES FOR CONTROL.

FIGURE 4.26

FIGURE 4.27

Despite these inconveniences, gravel does have several potential applications and functions in the outdoor environment. Its loose, textured quality allows it to be appropriately used in informal and rural settings to portray a naturalistic character. Similarly, gravel can be used to provide textural interest and contrast on the grand plane as in Figure 4.28. Yet gravel can also be used more formally if it is well contained with exact edges. At one point in time gravel was used in the sculpture garden at the Hirshhorn Museum in Washington, D.C., as well as in the adjoining Mall between the Capitol Building and the Washington Monument.

Despite gravel's potential instability, it can still be used as a walking surface if it is well contained, has a stable base, and is of a fine granular size. Pea gravel properly compacted and placed on a firm base provides a fine-textured yet safe walking surface. Large, expansive areas of pea gravel for walking are used in the formal settings along the Mall in Washington, D.C., at Hampton Court in England, and at Versailles in France.

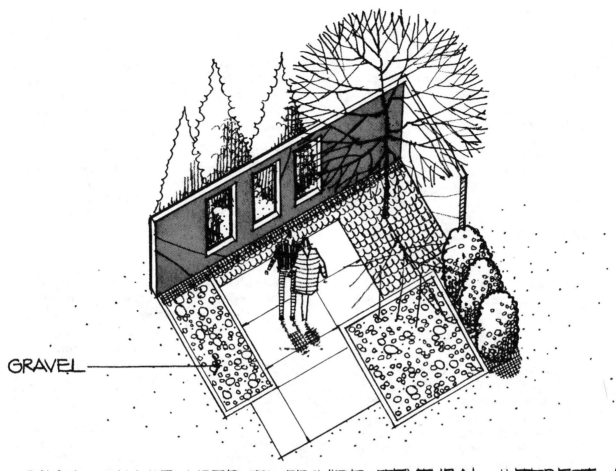

GRAVEL

GRAVEL CAN BE USED TO PROVIDE TEXTURAL INTEREST AND
CONTRAST ON THE GROUND PLANE.

FIGURE 4.28

One variation of gravel that eliminates its negative aspects as a walking surface is Epoxy Gravel (manufactured under the trade name of Prairie Film®). Epoxy gravel consists of individual pebbles bound together into a fixed mass by epoxy glue. However, open air space exists throughout the mass, allowing water to percolate through. At first glance this pavement type looks like gravel but with a shiny coating. Epoxy gravel is used mostly as a stable, fixed walking surface in regions of warmer climate where frost does not disturb or crack the pavement.

Another use of gravel in the landscape is as a pavement material in free-form or odd-shaped ground forms. Like concrete and asphalt, gravel is a fluid pavement medium that can adapt to any shape or form in which it is placed. In this way it is of course different from brick or stone, which must be painstakingly cut to fit curves or odd shapes.

Finally, gravel can be used as a surface material in areas where it is difficult to grow lawn or ground cover because of shade or lack of moisture. A common application of this is beneath an overhang of a building. Another adoption is in the desert Southwest, where decomposed granite is a popular ground surface material often used in place of lawn and ground cover. Decomposed granite is very compatible with other materials found on the desert floor and, of course, it does not require watering. In other more temperate climates, however, it is generally not advisable to substitute gravel for a mulch or ground cover around the base of plants. Whereas this may be a maintenance-reducing technique, it also creates a harsh environment for most plants except those native to the desert. Gravel can greatly intensify the heat at the base of a plant and cause root damage.

Unit Pavers. *Stone.* Stone, brick, and tile are examples of unit pavers. Of these, stone is the one type that is a natural as opposed to manufactured material. While it must often be quarried or cut, the stone itself is formed by the forces of nature. Stone is a very diverse material; it has a number of geological origins and is available in many sizes, shapes, and earth tone colors. It is also one of the more expensive pavement materials. The material itself is costly and the installation of stone is labor-intensive. The various ways by which stone may be categorized and described are outlined in the following paragraphs along with a description of their possible uses in the design of exterior spaces.

Three basic geological origins of stone are sedimentary, metamorphic, and igneous.

Sedimentary Stone. Sedimentary stones are formed from material deposited at the bottom of large water bodies over a long period of time and are composed of small granular particles that have solidified together from outside pressure. (Sedimentary stones include sandstone and limestone.) Sedimentary stones are porous and soft by comparison with other types of stone and consequently easily cut. As a pavement, they can be worn down with intense use and may stain or weather. Limestone is especially susceptible to chemical weathering. However, both sandstones and limestones make suitable pavements for pedestrian areas.

Metamorphic Stone. Metamorphic stone is rock of any origin that has been transformed by intense pressure. Consequently, metamorphic stone is extremely hard and durable. It is also quite heavy and expensive. Marble is a well-known metamorphic stone used only in limited amounts as a pavement because of its expense and difficulty to cut.

Igneous Stone. Igneous stone is rock formed by the cooling of hot molten material. It is similar to metamorphic stone in its strength and durability. A well-known igneous stone is granite, a popular pavement material because of its strength and endurance. Although heavy and difficult to cut, granite does make a good pavement material for areas subject to intense use and wear or in locations exposed to unusual weathering. Granite can be cut and obtained in a variety of sizes, depending on its function and intended appearance. One popular size of granite used as a pavement material is referred to as a "granite set." Each granite set is a block that measures about 3 in (7.5 cm) on a side and is typically massed together with other blocks in one of several patterns to cover a ground area.

The three geological types of stone may be further classified by where they are found and how they are cut. Under this system of classification, the five general types are fieldstone, riverstone, cobblestone, flagstone, and cut stone. These types are illustrated in Figure 4.29.

Fieldstone. Fieldstone is stone of any size and shape found at or near the earth's surface in individual pieces. It has been generated from the breakup of bedrock or other larger stones in the region. Fieldstone is not quarried and therefore tends to be very irregular in shape and size. It is typically used as found, with no cutting or finishing. Fieldstone is a difficult material to use for pavement because individual pieces are hard to fit together while the surface itself is often rough and oddly sloped. Fieldstone is most appropriately used in informal and infrequently used spaces where an imperfect naturalistic quality is desired. Unless carefully selected and fit together, fieldstone is generally not a proper pavement material for public spaces.

Riverstone. Riverstone is stone that has been worn and generally rounded by the action of running or falling water. Riverstone is readily found in many rivers of the western United States, particularly those that receive runoff from glaciers or large quantities of snow. The riverstone, most useful as a pavement surface is usually only 1½ to 3 in (3.8 cm to 7.5 cm) in size; it is massed together as an aggregate bonded by mortar or sand. Despite the smoothness of individual stones, an aggregation of riverstones is usually rough and texturally appealing. Riverstone may be used to signify nonwalking surfaces, provide textural contrast to concrete or flagstone, or furnish a strong tactile appeal, as shown in Figure 4.30. Riverstone pavement is also commonly used in the bottom or along the sides and edges of pools for its texture and natural association with water. Figure 4.31 shows this use of riverstone in the base of the fountain in Point Park in Pittsburgh.

FIELDSTONE

RIVERSTONE

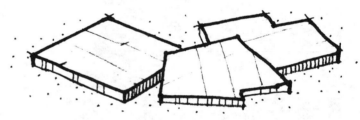

FLAGSTONE

COBBLESTONE

CUTSTONE

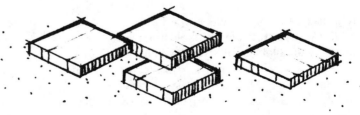

TYPES OF STONE.

FIGURE 4.29

192

Pavement

FIGURE 4.30

FIGURE 4.31

Cobblestone. A type of stone very similar to riverstone is cobblestone. Cobblestone is also rounded from wearing by moving water but generally flatter in its overall proportions. And it is typically 3 in (7.5 cm) across or wider.[11] The name cobblestone is sometimes misused in association with Belgian block. Belgian block is granite cut into rectangular bricklike blocks, whereas cobblestone is rounded and used as it is found. Historically, cobblestone has been used extensively as a street pavement. Figure 4.13 shows cobblestone as a street pavement in Nantucket, Massachusetts. Cobblestone is rather difficult to walk on because of its size and texture. It is also a difficult surface to

drain, especially on flatter slopes, because of its irregularity. Therefore cobblestone is best used for the same functions as riverstone but where a coarser appearance is desired.

Flagstone. Flagstone is any stone that is layered, allowing it to be split into relatively thin (3/4 in to 2 in) (1.8 cm to 5 cm) slabs or "flags." Flagstone is usually quarried and therefore should not be confused with fieldstone. Examples of flagstone include slate and bluestone. Once stratified, it can be cut into any shape desired from several inches to several feet across. As illustrated in Figure 4.32, flagstone may be cut into rectangles, squares, triangles, or irregular shapes (these irregular shapes are confused with fieldstone) and used accordingly in various patterns.

[11]Ibid., p. 622.

FLAGSTONE

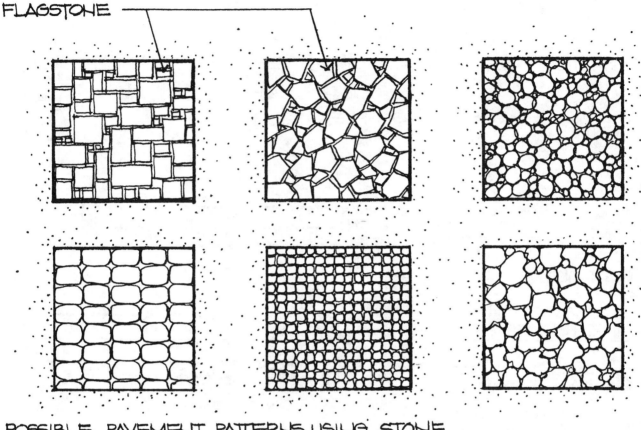

POSSIBLE PAVEMENT PATTERNS USING STONE.

FIGURE 4.32

Flagstone is a smoother, more refined material than fieldstone and may be used in a number of situations based on its shape and color. Flagstone cut in rectangular shapes is appropriately used in formal or urban settings where straight lines are prevalent, while irregularly shaped or angled flagstone is easily applied in informal or naturalistic circumstances. No matter what its shape, flagstone may be placed on either a flexible base such as sand or crushed limestone or on a solid base such as concrete, as shown in Figure 4.33. The construction method for a given situation depends on cost and intended use. A flexible base is the less expensive and is appropriate for pedestrian use or light use in nonpublic areas. A flexible base also has the advantage of permitting some surface runoff to percolate down through the joints to subsurface soil layers. Flagstone laid on a flexible base can readily be removed to allow for excavation for pipes and wires. After installation of the utility, the stone pavement can be replaced with little indication of disturbance.

Cut Stone. As the name suggests, cut stone is stone that has been chiseled or sawn to a desired size and shape. There are two kinds of cut stone: (1) stone cut into blocks and (2) stone cut into thin slabs called "pavers." The two common pavement materials made from cut stone blocks are the previously mentioned granite sets and Belgian block, illustrated in Figure 4.34. Granite sets are approximately 3 in (7.5cm) on a side and, like flagstone, may be placed on either a flexible or a solid base to

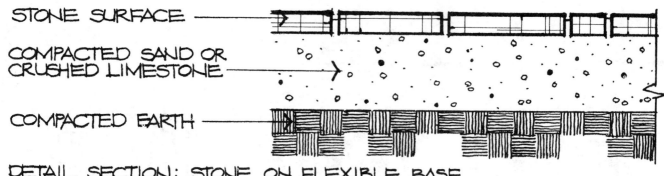

STONE SURFACE

COMPACTED SAND OR
CRUSHED LIMESTONE

COMPACTED EARTH

DETAIL SECTION: STONE ON FLEXIBLE BASE.

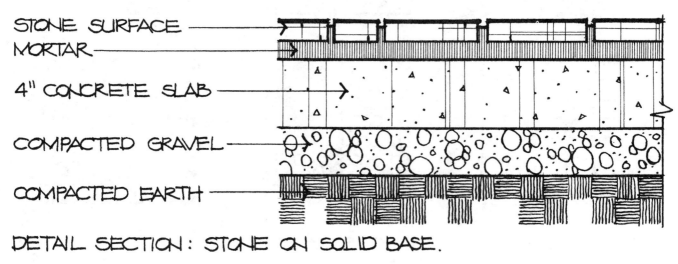

STONE SURFACE
MORTAR

4" CONCRETE SLAB

COMPACTED GRAVEL

COMPACTED EARTH

DETAIL SECTION: STONE ON SOLID BASE.

FIGURE 4.33

give a strongly textured surface. Belgian blocks may be used for similar purposes as granite sets but with a rougher visual texture.

Thin cut stone, or pavers, can be obtained in a variety of sizes and colors depending upon source. Pavers may also be placed on either a flexible or a solid base, depending on budget and anticipated intensity of use. Visually, pavers resemble flagstone and may be used in situations where the same size unit paver are desired throughout the pavement area or where it is necessary to repeat a certain pattern within an area, as in Figure 4.35. The difference between flagstone and pavers is that flagstone is custom cut at the job site to fit each individual placement, while pavers are precut off the job site to a standard or fixed size.

The wide range of possible stone characteristics available to the designer indicates the almost limitless number of patterns and applications that stone can be used for in exterior spaces. In fact, one of the challenges in working with stone is the creative development of visually appealing two-dimensional patterns, as shown in Figures 4.32, 4.34, and 4.35. With a multitude of potential patterns, stone may be used to furnish all the design applications outlined previously and be applied to strengthen any spatial quality from formal to informal, urban to naturalistic, and intimate to monumental. Another range of possibilities exists when stone is combined with other pavement materials such as brick or concrete.

Brick. The second type of unit paver is brick. Brick differs from both gravel and stone in that it is

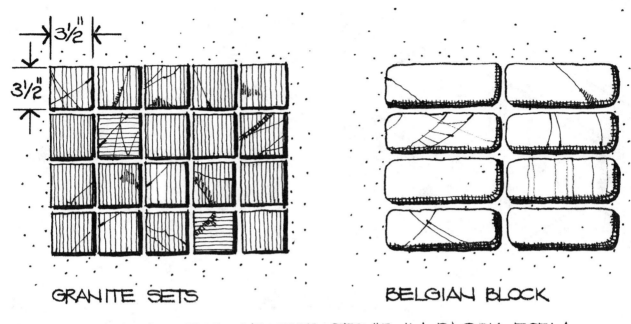

3½"

3½"

GRANITE SETS   BELGIAN BLOCK

TWO COMMON TYPES OF CUT STONE IN BLOCK FORM.

FIGURE 4.34

FIGURE 4.35

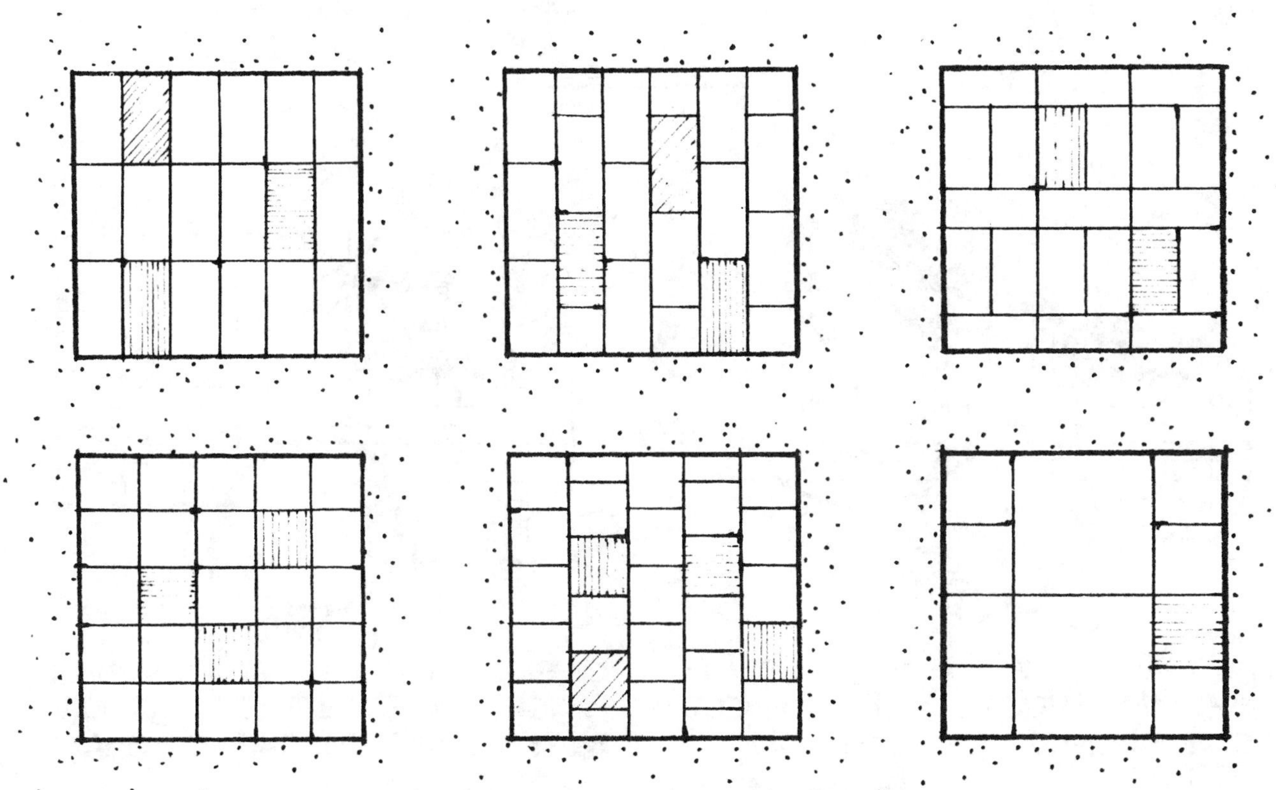

POSSIBLE PAVEMENT PATTERNS WITH CUT STONE.

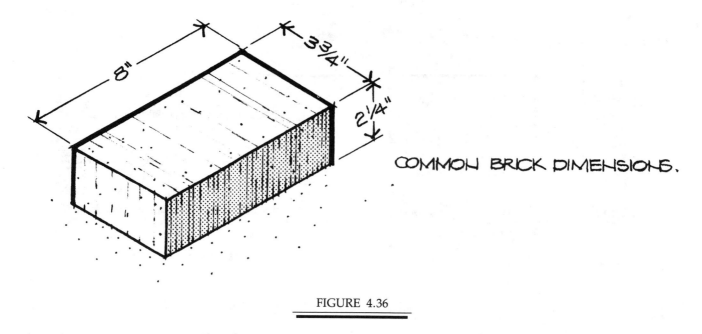

COMMON BRICK DIMENSIONS.

FIGURE 4.36

manufactured. It is produced from molded or extruded clay that is then fired in a kiln. The higher the temperature at which brick is fired, the harder the brick that results. Consequently, brick that is to be used as an exterior pavement must be fired to extremely high temperatures. Soft brick is not acceptable because it breaks apart from wear and frost action.

Brick too possesses a number of design characteristics, but it is not as diversified a material as stone. One of the distinguishing qualities of brick is its warm, friendly color. Although clay red is the most common color, brick is also available in a range of other earth tones. Brick, by itself or in combination with other materials, effectively gives an exterior space an inviting, attractive quality based on its

FIGURE 4.37

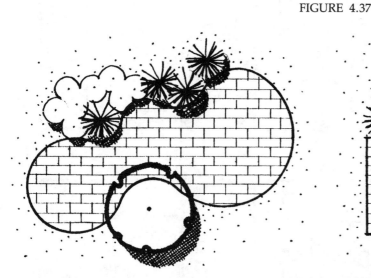

UNDESIRABLE: NUMEROUS INDIVIDUAL BRICKS MUST BE CUT TO CONFORM TO EDGE OF FREE-FORM SHAPE.

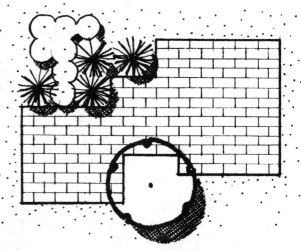

DESIRABLE: FEW INDIVIDUAL BRICKS MUST BE CUT TO CONFORM TO RECTILINEAR SHAPE.

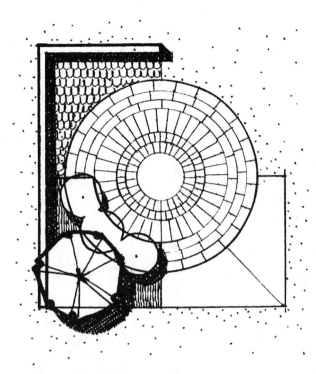

BRICK USED IN CIRCULAR PATTERNS.

FIGURE 4.38

color. This characteristic of brick is especially attractive when brick is integrated with cold, drab materials such as concrete.

Another characteristic of brick is that it is modular; that is, it is manufactured in a common fixed shape and size that is then repeated throughout a design. As illustrated in Figure 4.36, the standard brick is rectangular and measures 2¼ in x 3¾ in x 8 in (about 5.7cm x 9.5cm x 20cm). The modular quality of brick limits its flexibility somewhat because one is restrained to the standard shape and size. Any size or form that deviates from this standard requires a specially molded brick or one that is cut to fit the odd shape. For this reason, brick is most conveniently used for rectilinear forms and patterns on the ground plane. As indicated in Figure 4.37, brick does not usually adapt easily to curvilinear or free-form shapes because they require a great deal of cutting and shaping along the edges of the forms. However, brick can be used in radiating or circular patterns where the radius is generous enough to allow individual bricks to be used without cutting, as in Figure 4.38.

One other potential drawback of brick pavement is that it does not work well in regions of significant snowfall, especially if the joints between individual bricks are wide or uneven. Snow is apt to become compacted into the joints or texture of the brick itself, making it difficult to keep the surface clean. And snow plowing can destroy a brick pavement constructed on a flexible base.

Despite some of the restrictions for working with brick, it may be used in a number of patterns. Like stone, brick has exciting possibilities for the creation of visually attractive two-dimensional patterns. Some of the more common brick patterns are illustrated in Figure 4.39. Of these, probably the most widely used pattern is the running bond because of its ease of layout and installation. It is also a very directional pattern because of the long lines established by the rows of bricks. One suggestion for using running bond is to align the rows of brick perpendicular to the primary line of sight across an area of pavement, rather than parallel to the line of sight, as in Figure 4.40. The reason for this suggestion is that any imperfections in laying the bricks in rows

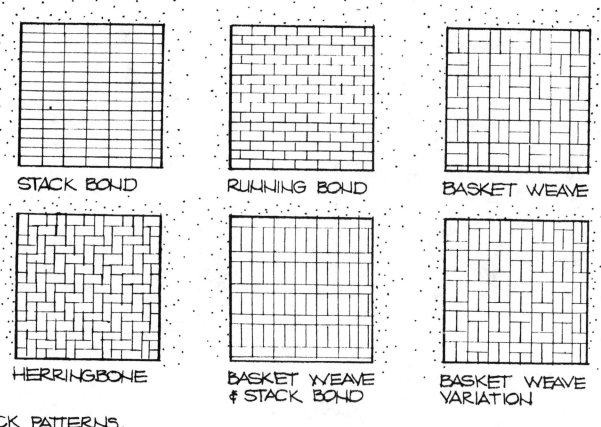

STACK BOND   RUNNING BOND   BASKET WEAVE

HERRINGBONE   BASKET WEAVE & STACK BOND   BASKET WEAVE VARIATION

BRICK PATTERNS.

FIGURE 4.39

FIGURE 4.40

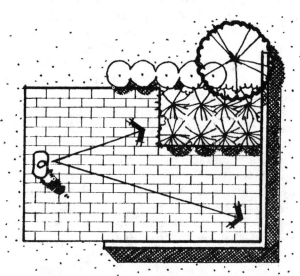

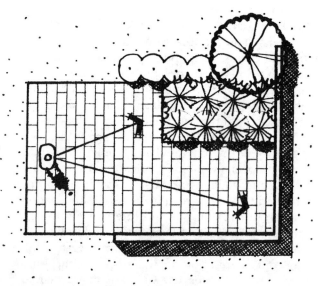

UNDESIRABLE; PRIMARY VIEW OF BRICK PATTERN SHOULD NOT OCCUR PARALLEL TO BRICK COURSES.

DESIRABLE; PRIMARY VIEW OF BRICK PATTERN SHOULD OCCUR PERPENDICULAR TO BRICK COURSES.

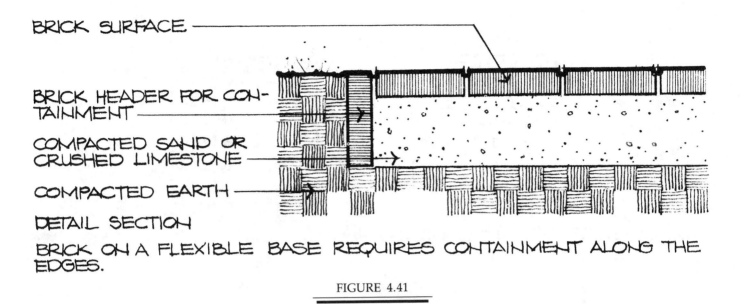

BRICK SURFACE

BRICK HEADER FOR CON-
TAINMENT

COMPACTED SAND OR
CRUSHED LIMESTONE

COMPACTED EARTH

DETAIL SECTION
BRICK ON A FLEXIBLE BASE REQUIRES CONTAINMENT ALONG THE
EDGES.

FIGURE 4.41

are much easier seen when looking down the rows than when looking across them.

As already alluded to, brick pavement has abundant functions and applications in the exterior environment. It may be used from small, intimate gardens to large urban plazas such as that adjacent to Boston City Hall. Brick pavement is particularly helpful in furnishing a personal feeling in space regardless of scale because of its color and size. Brick may aid in modifying the monumental scale of a plaza because people can relate directly to the size of each individual brick. Likewise, brick pavement may visually connect a brick building or wall to its surrounding site or it may simply be utilized for its visual qualities. Brick pavement is able to connote a historical flavor because of its extensive use in such locations as Philadelphia and Williamsburg.

With all these uses, brick pavement may be constructed in a similar fashion as stone pavement. Brick may be placed on either a flexible base (sand, crushed limestone, or fine gravel) or a solid base (concrete). The advantages and disadvantages of brick on sand versus concrete are the same as those for stone. However, when brick is located on a sand base, a stable edge is needed to contain the brick and sand in a manner like gravel, as illustrated in Figure 4.41. Otherwise, the edge of a brick pavement on a sand base easily breaks apart and requires constant maintenance.

Interlocking brick. Another type of unit paver very similar to brick is interlocking brick. Some refer to this material as a stone, but it is actually manufac-

tured like a brick. It is called interlocking brick because the shape of each module permits it to be interlocked or connected to adjoining units much like pieces of a puzzle. Interlocking brick is available in several different shapes including one that is rectangular in much the same proportions as a standard brick and others that are more square and octagonal. Some of these shapes are illustrated in Figure 4.42. This pavement material may also be obtained in a variety of colors: tan, pink, red, gray, and light blue.

Interlocking brick can be used in the landscape for similar functions and situations as both stone and brick. Whether a designer selects stone, brick, or interlocking brick for a given area of pavement will depend on the desired color, texture, and pattern in addition to intended function and available budget. One advantage of interlocking brick over stone and normal brick is that it is generally a more durable pavement for vehicular traffic. The interlocking brick is an extremely dense material and therefore is able to support a great deal of weight, even though it is usually laid on a flexible base. The material's density also inhibits the infiltration of both water and salt.

Tile. A fourth type of unit paver is ceramic tile, which is best described as a thin version of brick and is sometimes simply referred to as a "thin paver." Tile's thickness may range from about ½ to ⅝ in (1.2cm to 1.6cm). It is manufactured as an extruded or hand-molded clay unit fired at temperatures in excess of 2,000 degrees F. Compared with brick, tile is denser and stronger and therefore more resilient to wear as well as to freeze/thaw and thermal shock.

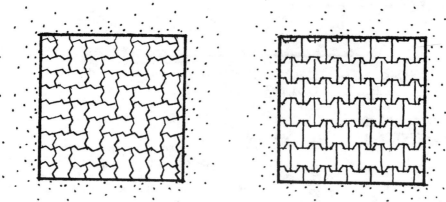

EXAMPLES OF INTERLOCKING BRICK.

FIGURE 4.42

FIGURE 4.43

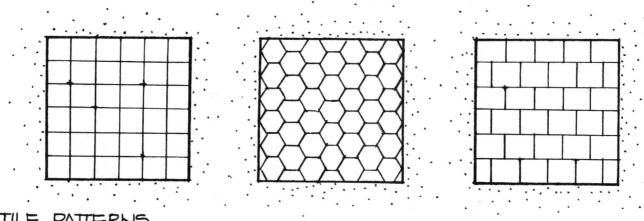

TILE PATTERNS.

Tile is also easier to handle and install because of its relatively light weight. Unlike brick, tile must always be placed on a hard base like concrete for its structural support. Thus tile may be thought of as a veneer pavement. Tile comes in a variety of sizes including rectangular, square, and hexagonal, as illustrated in Figure 4.43. Some rectangular tile has the same proportions as brick and so looks just like brick when installed as a pavement surface. Tile is also available in a variety of earth tones and finishes. Unlike brick, tile is available in a variety of glaze finishes that provide the designer with an additional palette of surface treatments to work with. A disad-

vantage of some types of tile is that they can be slippery to walk on when wet. Tile may be used as a pavement in many situations but is particularly suitable to outdoor spaces where a smooth, refined, almost polished look is desired. Tile is also a good pavement to use to visually relate indoors and outdoors. On the ground plane in adjoining indoor and outdoor spaces, tile can join the two spaces visually together (Figure 3.63).

Adhesive Pavement. *Portland cement concrete*. Portland cement concrete, commonly referred to simply as "concrete," is one of several different adhesive

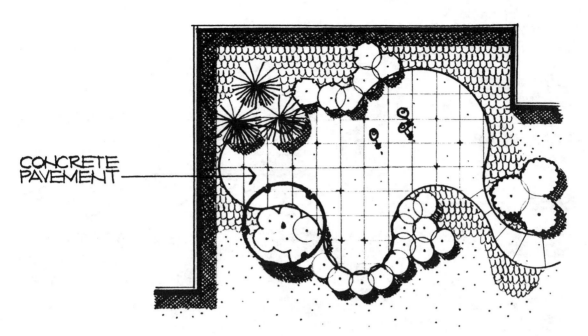

CONCRETE PAVEMENT

OWING TO ITS INITIAL PLASTICITY, CONCRETE IS VERY SUITABLE FOR FLOWING, FREE-FORM AREAS OF PAVEMENT.

FIGURE 4.44

pavements used in the outdoor environment. Adhesive pavements are so named because they consist of small aggregates held together in a pavement mass by an adhesive or binding material. Technically, Portland cement concrete is a mixture of Portland cement, sand (aggregates), and water. (Note that cement is an ingredient of concrete, not a pavement in its own right). A chemical reaction called hydration occurs between the cement and the water to create the binding agent that holds the aggregates together. This combination hardens within a few hours and continues to strengthen over a span of many years if it is mixed and treated properly. This hardening process is referred to as "curing."

There are two general ways Portland cement concrete is used as a pavement in the landscape. The first is cast-in-place and the second is precast. Cast-in-place concrete is as the name suggests; the concrete is placed in its wet, plastic state into the form or area that it is to occupy on the site itself. As precast pavement, the concrete is placed into a given set of molds to create pavement blocks of various standard sizes and shapes much like cut stone. Precast concrete pavement is typically prepared away from the job site.

As a cast-in-place material and before it hardens, Portland cement is a plastic medium that can flow and adapt to any configuration. Concrete molds itself to the exact shape of the form in which it is placed to create, in effect, a mirror image of the containing form. Consequently, concrete can be much more easily used for free-form pavement shapes than either stone or brick, as suggested in Figure 4.44. Recall that cut stone and brick consist of nonconforming modules of a fixed size and shape. The initial plastic state of concrete permits patterns to be imprinted into its surface. Besides this characteristic, concrete is a durable surface material; it can withstand constant, heavy use without harm. Furthermore, concrete is less expensive than either stone or brick. This results from the low cost of the raw material and its efficiency in covering large areas quickly. Its strength and comparatively low cost account for its wide use as a pavement. One last advantage of concrete is that it does not require much maintenance. Any needed upkeep or repair usually stems from poor construction or the action of salt.

One distinct characteristic and design factor of Portland cement concrete is the presence of expansion joints and scoring lines. As shown in Figure

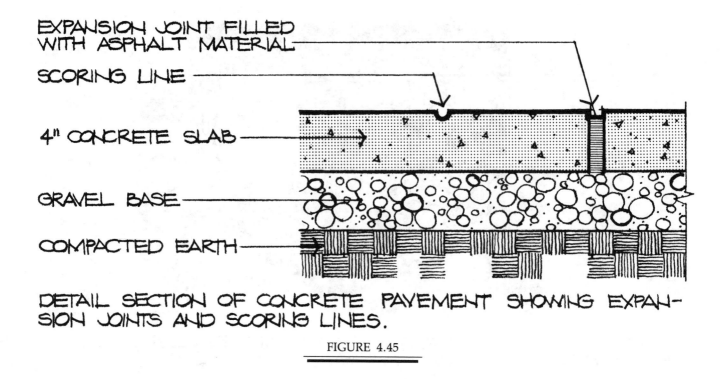

EXPANSION JOINT FILLED WITH ASPHALT MATERIAL

SCORING LINE

4" CONCRETE SLAB

GRAVEL BASE

COMPACTED EARTH

DETAIL SECTION OF CONCRETE PAVEMENT SHOWING EXPANSION JOINTS AND SCORING LINES.

FIGURE 4.45

4.45, an expansion joint (also called an "isolation joint") is a vertical division in the concrete extending the depth of the slab. In essence, an expansion joint is a space separating adjoining slabs of concrete, allowing them room to expand and contract without structural damage. This space is usually filled with an asphalt-treated or rubberized material. Redwood or cedar dividers used as an integral part of the pavement pattern also function as expansion joints. Expansion joints are an absolute necessity for an extensive area of pavement; a concrete pavement lacking them is subject to heaving and cracking. Generally, expansion joints should be placed a maximum of 30 ft (9m) apart on roads, walks, and other large paved areas.[12] Scoring lines (sometimes called "control joints") are also cuts in the surface of concrete pavement. As indicated in Figure 4.45, scoring lines extend only 1/8 to 3/16 in (.3cm to .5cm) deep into the surface and do not divide the concrete slab into physically separate pieces. From a construction standpoint, the purpose of scoring lines is to provide a line of weakness to "control" the location of pos-

sible cracks. The absence of scoring lines permits a concrete pavement to crack indiscriminately in a haphazard pattern. Some experts suggest scoring lines be placed a maximum of 20 ft (6m)[13] from one another in any direction. Therefore there are apt to be more scoring lines than expansion joints within any given area of concrete paving.

Both expansion joints and scoring lines are an important and integral design factor of Portland cement concrete pavement. Besides the structural functions just described, they provide visual rhythm, texture, scale, and intrigue for an area of concrete pavement, as suggested in Figure 4.46. Furthermore, they are a key factor in relating concrete pavement to adjoining pavements and/or structures, as indicated earlier in this chapter. Their plan arrangement is easily dealt with for rectilinear forms, as in Figure 4.47, but becomes more difficult for curvilinear forms where their location needs to be coordinated with center points and radii associated with the outer edge of the paved area. When designing the configuration of expansion joints and scoring lines with curved paved areas, one of the most important

---

[12]Harlow C. Landphair and Fred Klatt, Jr., *Landscape Architecture Construction* (New York: Elsevier North Holland, 1979), p. 208.

[13]Ibid.

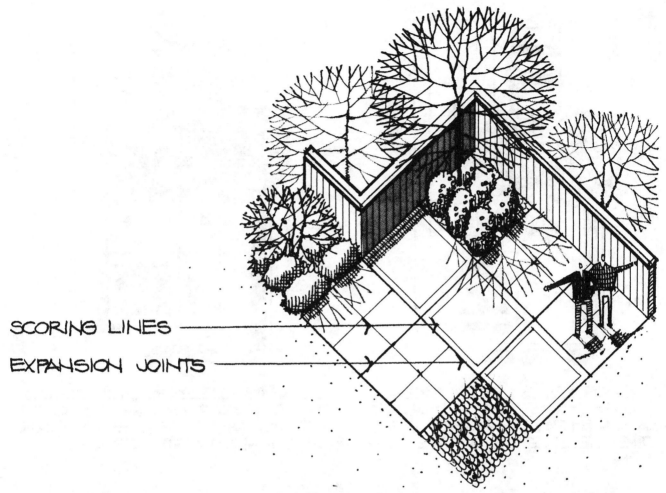

SCORING LINES ——————————

EXPANSION JOINTS ——————————

EXPANSION JOINTS AND SCORING LINES PROVIDE TEXTURE
AND SCALE IN CONCRETE PAVEMENT.

FIGURE 4.46

objectives is to avoid creating acute angles between the expansion joints themselves or with the edges of the concrete pavement. As much as possible, expansion joints should intersect the edge of pavement at a right angle. Some desirable and undesirable layouts of expansion joints in curved pavement areas are shown in Figure 4.48.

Portland cement concrete pavement has some drawbacks. For one, concrete has a high albedo; that is, it is very reflective when exposed to direct, intense sunlight. Particularly during summer or in sunny regions such as Florida and Arizona, it can be uncomfortable to walk across concrete pavement because of its brightness and reflected heat. Another disadvantage of concrete pavement is that it does not allow water to percolate through it. As a result it has greater runoff, requiring more drop inlets, pipe, and the like than an equal area of pervious gravel, stone, or brick. Another problem of concrete mentioned previously is its potential deterioration from salt used to melt ice and snow during winter. Pockmarks and chipping occur on concrete pavement that has not been cured properly and has been covered with salt in winter. Of course, the most sig-

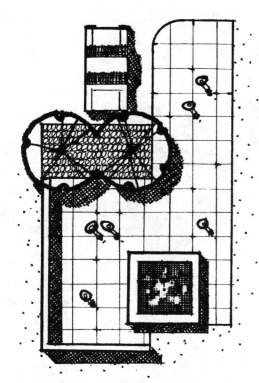

UNDESIRABLE: EXPANSION
JOINTS HAVE WEAK VISUAL RE-
LATIONSHIP WITH EDGES OF
OTHER ELEMENTS IN THE DE-
SIGN.

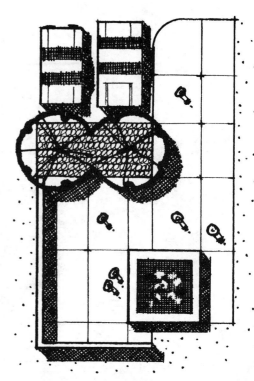

DESIRABLE: EXPANSION JOINTS
HAVE STRONG VISUAL RELATION-
SHIP WITH THE EDGES OF OTHER
ELEMENTS IN THE DESIGN.

FIGURE 4.47

nificant disadvantage of concrete paving is its uninviting, drab color. The dull gray of concrete has very little visual appeal by itself.

Despite this uninspiring color, there are a number of methods by which the visual appearance of Portland cement concrete can be enhanced. One means is to integrate it with other materials such as stone or brick that not only provide relief from the monotony of the concrete but also furnish contrasting colors and textures (Figure 4.49). These additional materials can be arranged in intriguing patterns to complement the concrete. A second means for improving the visual quality of concrete is applying a broom finish before the surface has completely hardened. A broom finish gives the surface a rough, sandpaperlike appearance that is visually more appealing and more slip-resistant when wet.

A third way for improving the aesthetics of concrete is to imprint patterns into the surface while it is still wet. Different patterns of stamps are available for creating imitations of brick, stone, and tile. One widely used type of imprinted concrete is available under the trade name of Bomanite®. When the right color is added to the concrete mix as well, the resulting concrete pattern is often difficult to distinguish from the material it is imitating. The advantage of imprinted concrete other than visual improvement is that the imitation pavement material is usually cheaper than the "real" material. The disadvantage is that the imprinted concrete is a fake.

Finally, color may be added to concrete mix to improve its appearance. This approach, nevertheless, is not entirely satisfactory because it is difficult to control the exact amount of pigment in a concrete

UNDESIRABLE ; EXPANSION
JOINTS MEET EDGE OF
PAVEMENT AT ACUTE AN-
GLES.

DESIRABLE ; EXPANSION
JOINTS MEET EDGE OF
PAVEMENT AT RIGHT AN-
GLES.

FIGURE 4.48

mix and to make it consistent from one batch to an-other. Besides, color in concrete has a tendency to fade over time.

One other variation of concrete used to create a visually attractive pavement surface with most of the attributes of concrete is exposed aggregate concrete. This is a special type of concrete in which surface aggregates of the mix are exposed to give a textured, gravellike appearance, as illustrated in Figure 4.50. The aggregates that are exposed may be added di-rectly to the concrete mix or spread over and embed-ded in the surface after it has been floated for the first time. In both cases, mortar covering the aggre-gates is washed and/or brushed away to reveal the surface aggregates before the concrete has com-pletely hardened. Different sizes and colors of ag-gregates are available depending on the visual effect

desired. Exposed aggregate concrete is more expen-sive than normal concrete but nevertheless is well used in intimate garden spaces, pedestrian areas where a strong tactile effect is required on the ground plane, or in pavements where a gravellike texture is required without the disadvantages of gravel, as suggested in Figure 4.51. Exposed aggre-gate concrete can even be used in formal outdoor spaces if it is well detailed. This type of concrete is not a good pavement to use where snow removal by plowing is required because this usually damages the aggregate surface.

As indicated previously, a second general type of concrete pavement is precast concrete. In this form, concrete can be molded into units or modules of many different sizes and shapes. Common precast concrete pavement units are square or rectangular.

206

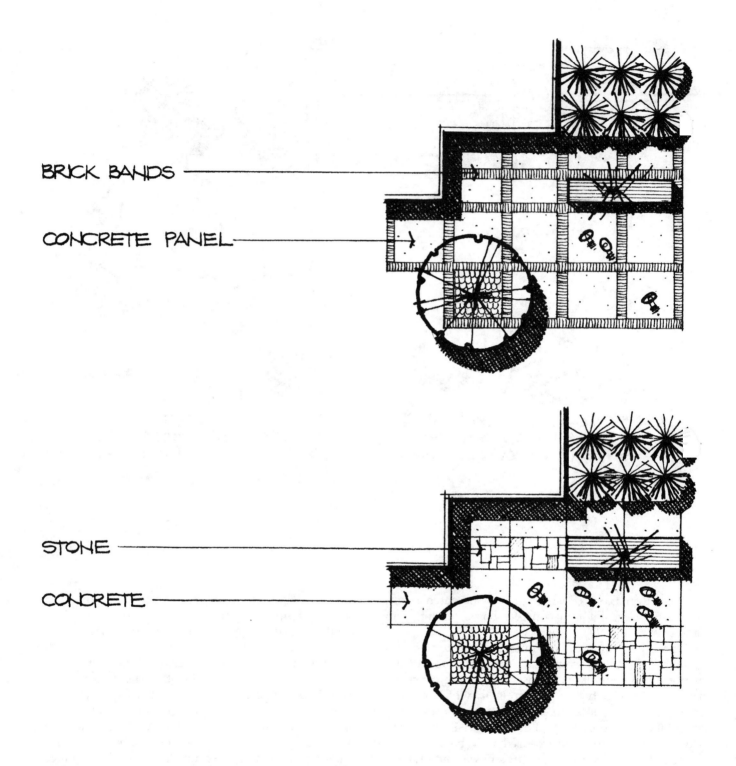

BRICK BANDS

CONCRETE PANEL

STONE

CONCRETE

TECHNIQUES FOR ENHANCING THE APPEARANCE OF CON-
CRETE PAVEMENT.

FIGURE 4.49

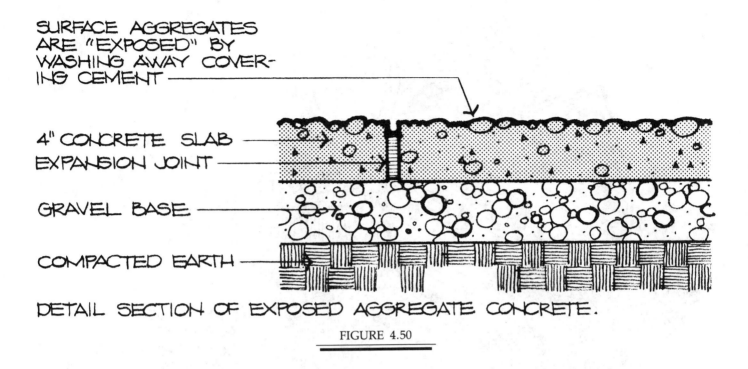

SURFACE AGGREGATES ARE "EXPOSED" BY WASHING AWAY COVERING CEMENT

4" CONCRETE SLAB
EXPANSION JOINT

GRAVEL BASE

COMPACTED EARTH

DETAIL SECTION OF EXPOSED AGGREGATE CONCRETE.

FIGURE 4.50

Others are octangular, round, or triangular. Precast concrete pavers can be used very much like stone or brick to establish a pavement surface. Another use for precast concrete units, illustrated in Figure 4.52, is to space them in lawn areas so that the turf forms a joint between adjoining paver units. This method can establish a strong visual effect resulting from the pattern of light concrete contrasted against the dark green of the grass. This use of precast concrete units is good for areas where only light pedestrian use occurs or as a transition between areas of solid lawn and solid pavement.

One unique type of precast concrete paving unit is designed to integrate grass or ground cover with pavement in a grid. Referred to by various names such as "grassy grids" or "grass pavers," the individual precast concrete units are formed to have a grid pattern of holes built into them that extend entirely through the depth of the unit, as in Figure 4.53. When placed on the ground as a pavement surface, the holes or voids are filled with earth and planted with grass or ground cover. As a result, the pavement has a grid pattern of square blocks of concrete (though other patterns are also available) with grass or ground cover in between when seen from the surface (Figure 4.54). This type of precast con-

crete is appropriately used where hard, stable pavement is needed but without the appearance of a solid mass of pavement. Overflow parking areas, infrequently used service roads or transitional areas between concrete and lawn are possible uses. From an environmental standpoint, one advantage of grassy grids is that they permit surface water to percolate through them much like through gravel. This reduces the amount of runoff from the pavement area and diminishes the need and cost for catch basins and a subsurface storm water system.

Bituminous concrete (asphalt). The second type of adhesive pavement used extensively in the outdoor environment is bituminous concrete, or simply "asphalt." Asphalt consists of small aggregates (about ¼ in or smaller) bound together in a mass by a petroleum-based bituminous adhesive. Structurally asphalt differs from concrete because it is a flexible pavement material. Asphalt actually moves and flexes when pressure is placed on it.

One trait asphalt has in common with Portland cement concrete is its plastic quality. Asphalt too can conform to any shape on the ground, making it suitable for free-form configurations as well as more rigid ones.

EXPOSED
AGGREGATE
CONCRETE CAN
PROVIDE A
COARSE
GRAVEL-LIKE
TEXTURE ON THE
GROUND PLANE
IN INTIMATE
GARDEN SPACES.

FIGURE 4.51

FIGURE 4.52

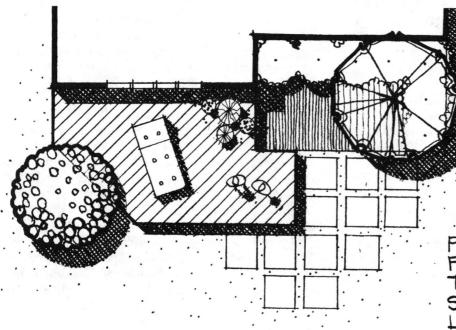

PRECAST CONCRETE
PAVERS CREATE
TRANSITION AND
STRONG PATTERN IN
LAWN AREA.

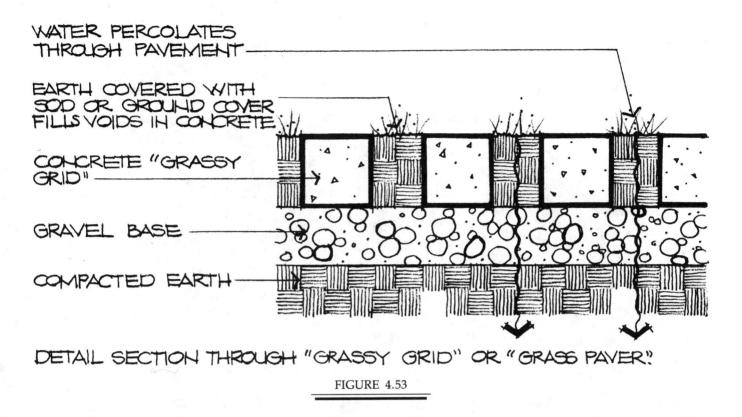

WATER PERCOLATES
THROUGH PAVEMENT

EARTH COVERED WITH
SOD OR GROUND COVER
FILLS VOIDS IN CONCRETE

CONCRETE "GRASSY
GRID"

GRAVEL BASE

COMPACTED EARTH

DETAIL SECTION THROUGH "GRASSY GRID" OR "GRASS PAVER."

FIGURE 4.53

An advantage of asphalt over Portland cement concrete in free-form is that it does not require forming or expansion joints. Moreover, asphalt does not need attentive workmanship for finishing or curing and is an easier pavement material to work with in construction than concrete.

Asphalt does, however, require more maintenance than Portland cement concrete. Periodically, its surface should be covered with a bituminous coating to seal it and prevent destructive wear. One other drawback of asphalt is that it has a tendency to break apart somewhat along the edges of a pavement area. This can lead to unsightliness plus additional need for maintenance.

As an aesthetic pavement material, asphalt is not a popular material in terms of its color and character. Most people do not find asphalt visually pleasing as a pedestrian pavement. Yet the dark color of asphalt has positive points in that it tends to blend in with the base plane of dark lawns and ground cover. It is not a visually noticeable pavement on a dark background such as Portland cement concrete or light stone. And the dark color creates little reflection from the sun, though this quality also causes a significant heat buildup.

Asphalt has numerous possible uses in exterior spaces. As illustrated in Figure 4.55, its plasticity makes it suitable for flowing pedestrian walks on campuses or in parks, as long as the pavement is kept a minimum of 8 ft wide. Pavement less wide than this cannot be laid by machine but must be done by hand at greater expense. Asphalt can be attractively utilized in other situations by combining it with other pavement materials or imprinting patterns into its surface before it has hardened. As with Portland cement concrete, large metal stamps can be used to create impressions in various sizes and shapes. Asphalt is not the best material to use in small, intimate spaces because of its impersonal quality and because it is more efficiently installed in large expanses. Still, asphalt should be considered in the list of potential pavement materials for outside use.

Summary

Pavement fulfills both aesthetic and utilitarian functions in the exterior environment. It may simply be used to accommodate intense use on the ground plane and structurally support pedestrian and vehicular circulation. Beyond this, however, pavement may provide an exterior space with a desired feeling and character owing to its color, texture, and pat-

CONCRETE
GRASS

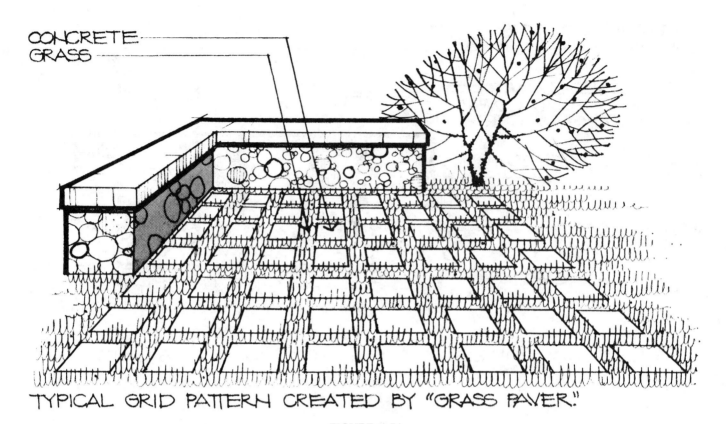

TYPICAL GRID PATTERN CREATED BY "GRASS PAVER."

FIGURE 4.54

FIGURE 4.55

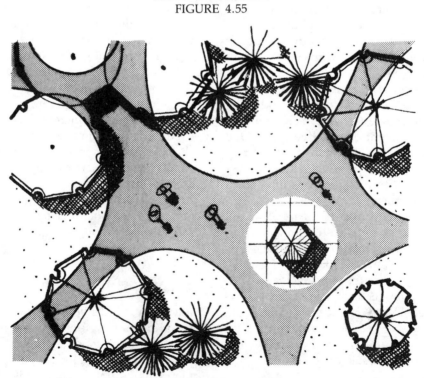

ASPHALT PROVIDES A DARK-VALUED PAVEMENT THAT IS SUITABLE FOR FLOWING, CURVILINEAR WALKS AND FORMS. NOTE LACK OF EXPANSION JOINTS.

tern. A space may be made to feel formal and urban or casual and intimate based on the pavement material chosen. Pavement can be used in the landscape to direct movement, affect visual scale, provide identity, or establish patterns of visual appeal. Because of its wide range of uses, a great deal of thought should be given to the choice of pavement material. It is important to understand the different types and characteristics of stone, brick, tile, Portland cement concrete, and asphalt so the right material is selected for the intended use and appearance. Whatever pavement material is used, it must be coordinated with all the other elements of the design.

5

Site Structures

Not all visual and functional objectives can be satisfied through the use of landform, plant materials, buildings, and pavement in the outdoor environment. Often the intent of the landscape architect is best accomplished by utilization of other physical design elements such as site structures. Site structures can be defined as three-dimensional constructed elements in the landscape that fulfill specific functions within the larger spatial context collectively established by landform, plant materials, and buildings. Site structures are "hard," fixed, and relatively permanent features in the outdoor environment. Examples of site structures include steps, ramps, walls, fences, and sitting elements. Gazebos, overhead trellises or sun shelters, decks, and small buildings are also site structures, although they are not discussed in this chapter. As can be seen from the list of examples, site structures are small-scaled "architectural" elements with diverse characteristics and uses.

This chapter discusses the varied characteristics, functions, and design guidelines for steps, ramps, walls, fences, and sitting elements in the outdoor environment. However, the chapter does not outline technical information required for the detailing or construction of these site structures. Other sources should be consulted for this knowledge.

Steps

In the landscape, there frequently is a need to move pedestrians and others from one elevation to another on the ground plane in a safe and efficient

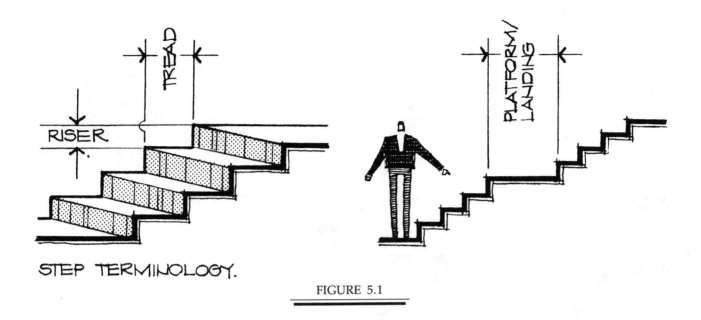

STEP TERMINOLOGY.

FIGURE 5.1

manner. Steps and ramps are the two elements used to accomplish this. Both provide a hard, permanent surface that allows people to move up and down an incline in a planned, structured fashion.

Steps have several distinct advantages and disadvantages in the landscape compared with ramps. One attribute of steps is that they provide a series of level surfaces where a person can find "sure footing" and maintain a sense of balance while negotiating a level change. Steps help maintain a feeling of equilibrium on a slope. Another advantage of steps is that they require relatively small horizontal distances to cover a vertical elevation change. While the exact horizontal distance varies with the step dimensions and the grade change, it will always be considerably less than that required by a ramp. Figure 5.18 illustrates this difference. Thus steps are comparatively efficient in their space utilization, an essential characteristic in tight, confined sites. This is one reason why steps are so much more widely used than ramps. Furthermore, steps can be constructed with a variety of materials, allowing them to be visually adaptable to almost any situation. Stone, brick, concrete, wood, railroad ties, and even gravel if properly contained are all possible step materials. Steps also serve a number of other functions in the landscape besides accommodating a grade change. Some of their other uses are discussed later in this chapter.

The major disadvantage of steps is that they cannot be negotiated by wheeled vehicles such as baby strollers, bicycles, and wheelchairs. Besides this, steps are often difficult to use for the elderly or people who have walking handicaps. The elevation change between individual steps can be too much to negotiate for individuals with certain walking disabilities. For these people, steps act as "barriers" preventing free, unimpeded movement through the environment. Unfortunately, many areas of the exterior environment are inaccessible to wheeled vehicles or persons with walking disabilities because of the presence of steps. The landscape architect should be constantly reminded that when steps are included in a design, they create an obstruction unless an alternative means of access is provided for individuals who cannot use steps.

Another disadvantage of steps for all users is that they can become dangerous when covered with snow or ice. This has long been known in regions of the country receiving heavy snowfall. Here, steps of extensive length and/or width are often closed or barricaded to a narrow, usable area during winter. Large expanses of outdoor public steps are not as appropriate in high snowfall regions as they are in more moderate climates because of the potential hazard.

When designing with steps, several terms should be known and used: tread, riser, landing, and platform. These terms are graphically shown in Figure 5.1. The "tread" is the horizontal plane or surface of the step on which a person's foot is placed. The tread is often referred to as the "step" by lay people. The "riser" is the vertical portion of a step, or the height. In any given set of steps, there is always one more riser than the number of treads if one discounts the pavement surface at the top and bottom of the steps. A "landing" or "platform" is a compar-

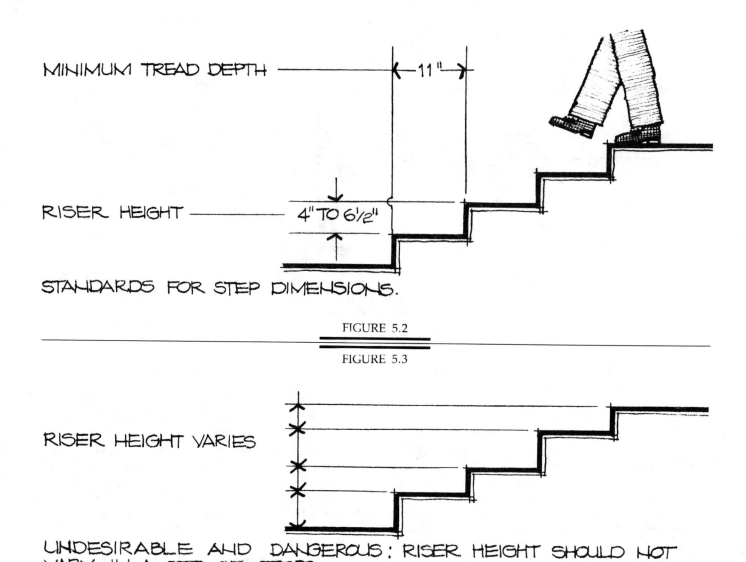

MINIMUM TREAD DEPTH ──────── ←── 11" ──→

RISER HEIGHT ──────── 4" TO 6½"

STANDARDS FOR STEP DIMENSIONS.

FIGURE 5.2

FIGURE 5.3

RISER HEIGHT VARIES

UNDESIRABLE AND DANGEROUS: RISER HEIGHT SHOULD NOT VARY IN A SET OF STEPS.

atively large, level area between two series of steps. A landing serves as a resting area and visually breaks up a long flight of steps.

The dimensions and the relationship between treads and risers in a set of steps are key factors in determining the comfort and safety of walking up and down them. The tread/riser design determines where a person's foot is placed, plus both the horizontal and vertical distances needed in moving the foot to the next step. Although people perhaps do not take note of a set of steps that poses no problem in walking up or down, everyone has at one time or another discovered a set of steps that were awkward to negotiate. Poorly designed steps are apt to make a person skip, double-step, or jump from one tread to another. An extremely poor riser-to-tread relationship can be a hazard.

In developing dimensions for treads and risers in an outdoor setting, several thoughts should be kept in mind. First, the scale of outdoor spaces is different from that of interior spaces because of actual physical dimensions and the larger size of the space-defining elements themselves. Outdoor spaces generally are bigger than indoor spaces. Second, climatic variation is a real limiting factor directly influencing safety. Rain, snow, and ice all make walking outside more dangerous than walking inside. Consequently, steps located outside should be wider but less steep than those located inside to adapt adequately to the difference in spatial scale and climate.

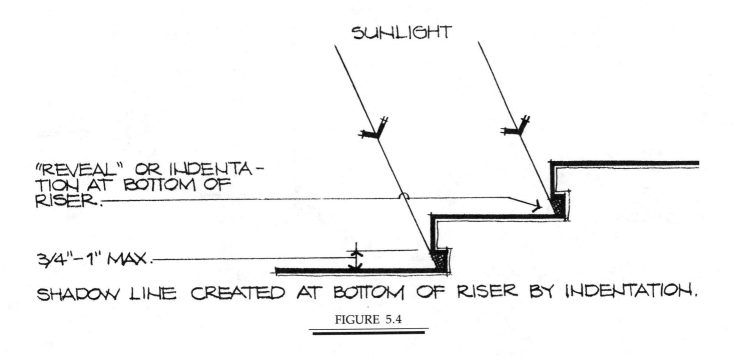

SUNLIGHT

"REVEAL" OR INDENTA-
TION AT BOTTOM OF
RISER.

3/4"–1" MAX.

SHADOW LINE CREATED AT BOTTOM OF RISER BY INDENTATION.

FIGURE 5.4

A commonly applied guideline for the riser-tread relationship is twice the riser plus the tread should equal 26 in (66cm) (2R + T = 26 in (66cm)).[1] This guideline has evolved from those sets of steps actually found to be comfortable to walk up and down for the stride of an average person. With this guideline, a 6-in (15cm) riser would be compatible with a 14-in (35.5cm) tread and a 5 ½-in (14cm) riser would be best associated with a 15-in (38cm) tread. As can be seen from these dimensions, the taller the riser, the shallower the depth of the tread. Other formulas and concepts have also been developed based on experience or design objectives. Regardless of which approach is employed for arriving at riser and tread dimensions, a riser should be a minimum of 4 in (10cm) and a maximum of 6 ½ in (16.5cm) in height,[2] as indicated in Figure 5.2. Below 4 in (10cm) a riser becomes dangerous because it is too insignificant a dimension to be easily perceived outdoors. When not readily seen, a riser can cause a person to trip and fall. Risers below 4 in (10cm) would also require too many treads for any given elevation change. Above 6 ½ in (16.5cm) tall, risers become difficult to walk up for the elderly, small children, and others who have a short stride.

The dimension of the risers in a set of steps should remain constant throughout a given flight. If riser height varies, as in Figure 5.3, the pedestrian must pay constant attention to each foot placement, which increases the chance of an accident. One additional factor relating to risers is the use of a shadow line as an integral part of the riser. A shadow line can be created on the bottom portion of the riser if a small indentation is provided at this position, as shown in Figure 5.4. A shadow line is useful because it strengthens the form of the stairs and makes them more obvious from a distance. Do not make the indentation too high or deep so as to create an area where a foot can become jammed and caught by the space.

Another consideration in the design of steps besides size of individual risers is the number of risers that should be located in any given set of steps. At a minimum, a set of steps should never have just one riser because such an elevation change in a walking surface is also apt not to be noticed and cause the pedestrian to trip and fall. This problem is compounded when the steps are constructed of the same material as the adjoining pavement. This makes the step blend in with its surroundings and even more difficult to see. Changes in elevation along a walking surface should be significant enough to be easily recognized, allowing the pedestrian time to adjust pace and foot placement. Depending on circumstances, the minimum number of risers in a set of steps may vary between 2 and 3.

[1]Reader's Digest, *Reader's Digest Practical Guide to Home Landscaping* (Pleasantville, New York: The Reader's Digest Association, 1972), p. 201.
[2]The American Society of Landscape Architects' Foundation, *Barrier-Free Site Design* (Washington, D.C.: U.S. Department of Housing and Urban Development, 1975), p. 29.

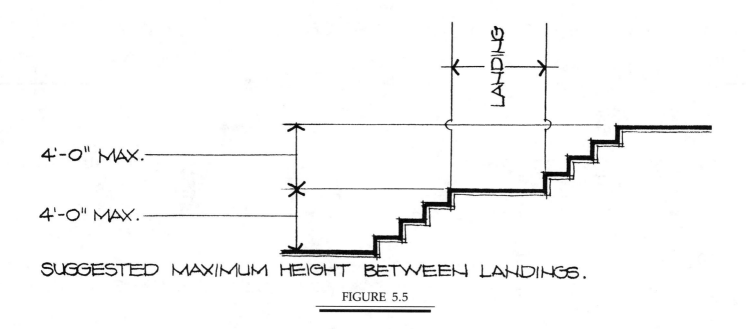

4'-0" MAX.

4'-0" MAX.

SUGGESTED MAXIMUM HEIGHT BETWEEN LANDINGS.

FIGURE 5.5

FIGURE 5.6

At the other end of the scale, the maximum number of risers used in a set of steps should be such that the height between landings is not more than 4 ft (122cm) for unprotected steps and 6 ft (183cm) for protected steps (Figure 5.5).[3] There are several reasons for the logic of this guideline. First, a set of steps that exceeds this suggested limit is dangerous and tiresome to climb, particularly for those who have difficulty in walking. Second, a lengthy, high set of steps tends to appear visually massive and psychologically imposing when viewed from the lower elevation. A person looking at such a set of steps may well feel tired and defeated even before taking the first step. In fact, some people may be turned away by an overly high set of steps.

Platforms or landings can break the visual and psychological monotony of a group of steps, making the elevation change easier to traverse. A landing can provide a rest for both the eye and the legs. An example of landings that make a set of steps seem gradual and easy to negotiate is shown in Figure 5.6. The location of a landing or landings within a flight of steps can also influence the visual and walking rhythm. The landing acts as a pause in the repetitious beat of the individual steps and can have different rhythmic effects, depending on where it is

[3]Ibid.

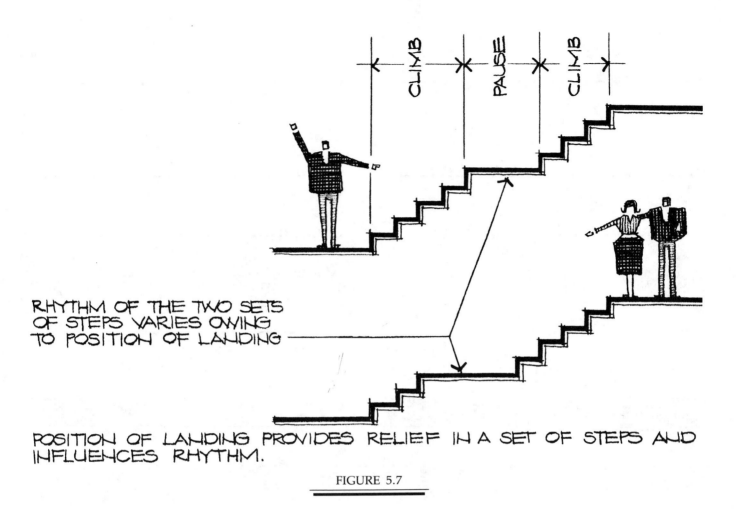

RHYTHM OF THE TWO SETS OF STEPS VARIES OWING TO POSITION OF LANDING

POSITION OF LANDING PROVIDES RELIEF IN A SET OF STEPS AND INFLUENCES RHYTHM.

FIGURE 5.7

placed in a set of steps, as in Figure 5.7. The placement of landings influences the sequence of views as one progresses up a flight of steps, as pointed out in the discussion on uses of landform (Figure 1.76).

Although both riser and tread dimensions should be selected in conjunction with each other, the tread depth should nevertheless be at least 11 in (28cm) (Figure 5.2).[4] This dimension is required in order to accommodate the foot length of the average person. A tread fewer than 11 in (28cm) in depth is difficult and hazardous to walk on because only part of the foot can be placed on any one step.

Another consideration for the treads in a set of steps is their plan arrangement. Whenever possible for a confined path of movement, the treads should be located perpendicular to the primary direction of movement, as indicated in Figure 5.8. They should not be situated at an angle or askew to the principal movement because it is more awkward to walk up or down a flight of steps sideways than at right an-

gles to them. Similarly, the tread orientation and depth should not vary in any set of steps unless they are in an open plaza or variation is itself a recurring characteristic of the steps. Inconsistent changes can easily catch the pedestrian by surprise and increase the possibility for accidents. In an open plaza, riser height and tread depth can vary somewhat more easily because movement is less confined and more casual. The width of a flight of steps should depend on their context and anticipated volume of use. The more people who are to use a given set of steps, the wider they should be. For two-way traffic, the suggested minimum width is 5 ft (152cm).[5]

Still another design and safety aspect of steps is the use of cheekwalls and handrails. As illustrated in Figure 5.9, "cheekwalls" are the walls located on the sides of a set of steps to serve as a transition

---

[4]Ibid.
[5]Ibid., p. 30.

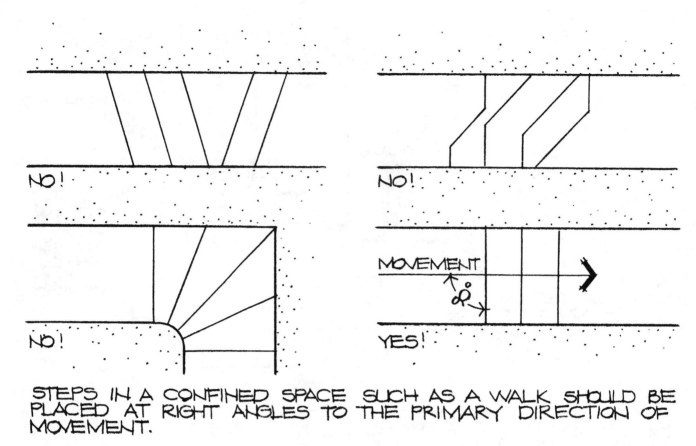

STEPS IN A CONFINED SPACE SUCH AS A WALK SHOULD BE PLACED AT RIGHT ANGLES TO THE PRIMARY DIRECTION OF MOVEMENT.

FIGURE 5.8

between the steps themselves and the accompanying slope. Cheekwalls visually end the steps, act as retaining walls to hold back the slope from the steps, and help contain pedestrians' feet on the steps. Cheekwalls may be designed in one of two general ways. The first is to keep the top of the cheekwall at a constant elevation above the height of the uppermost riser, as shown in the left side of Figure 5.10. With this design, the difference in height between the steps and the top of the cheekwall is least near the top of the steps and most at the bottom. The second alternative is to allow the cheekwall to fall at a gradient approximately equal to that of the steps, as shown in the right side of Figure 5.10. With this second method, the height difference between the top of the cheekwall and the steps remains about the same at the top of the steps as at the bottom.

An element often associated with a cheekwall is a handrail. A handrail provides something to hold onto and steady oneself while going up or down the steps. Handrails on large expanses of steps also contain and control movement up and down the steps. Handrails may be located on top of or along the inside of cheekwalls, depending on the height of the cheekwall and the appearance desired. Handrails may also be placed independently of cheekwalls and allowed to stand by themselves. For convenience of holding, handrails should be located 32 (81cm) to 36 in (91.5cm) above the nose of the treads in a set of steps, as illustrated in Figure 5.11.[6] In addition, the handrail should extend about 18 in (46cm) horizontally beyond the nose of the top and bottom treads in a set of steps to allow a person to hold the handrail a short distance before and after actually going through the motions of moving up or down the steps. Usually it is desirable to have at least one handrail per set of steps for safety, especially in public areas. For wide expanses of steps, as in Figure 5.12, handrails should be located at 20-to 30-ft (6 to

[6]Ibid., p. 31.

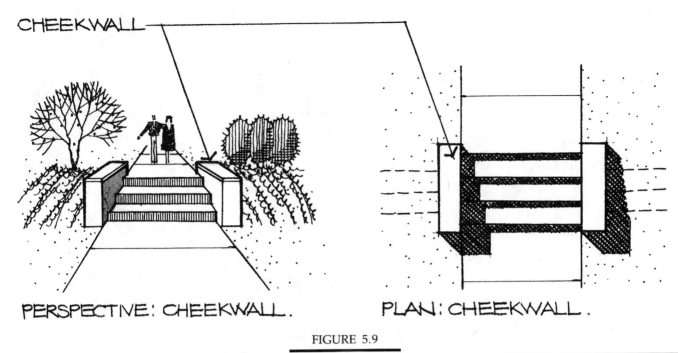

PERSPECTIVE: CHEEKWALL.

PLAN: CHEEKWALL.

FIGURE 5.9

FIGURE 5.10

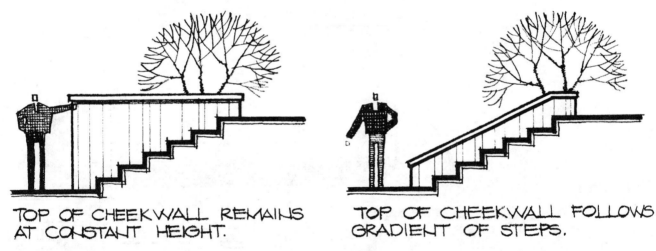

TOP OF CHEEKWALL REMAINS AT CONSTANT HEIGHT.

TOP OF CHEEKWALL FOLLOWS GRADIENT OF STEPS.

TWO ALTERNATIVE WAYS FOR DESIGNING CHEEKWALLS.

9m) intervals across the width of the steps.[7] Handrails are not as necessary for steps that have only a few risers or are located in private or infrequently used outdoor spaces.

In addition to the practical aspects of accommodating grade changes between two areas in the landscape, steps serve a number of other functions as well. Steps can define the limits of an outdoor space by implication if not by actual physical enclosure. As indicated in Figure 5.13, a small elevational change reinforced by steps between two adjoining areas is able to suggest the spatial separation between them. Steps indicate where one space ends and another begins. Somewhat associated with their potential space-defining qualities is the ability of steps to act

[7]Ibid.

220

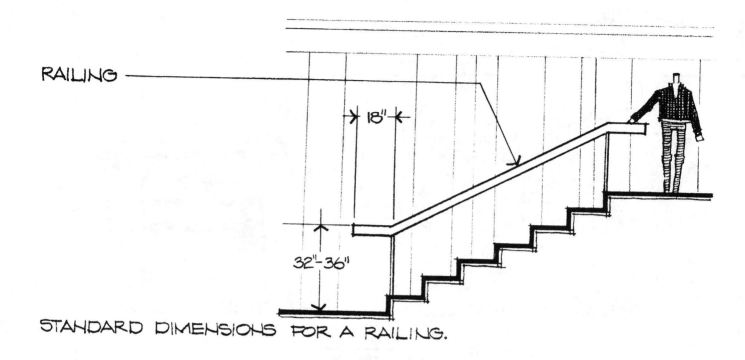

RAILING

18"

32"-36"

STANDARD DIMENSIONS FOR A RAILING.

FIGURE 5.11

FIGURE 5.12

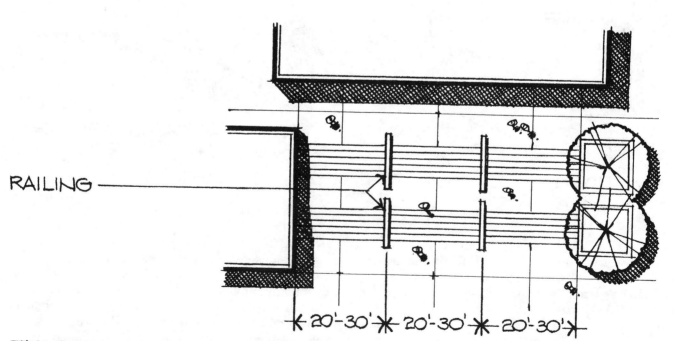

RAILING

20'-30' 20'-30' 20'-30'

STANDARD DIMENSION FOR LOCATION OF RAILING IN A
WIDE EXPANSE OF STEPS.

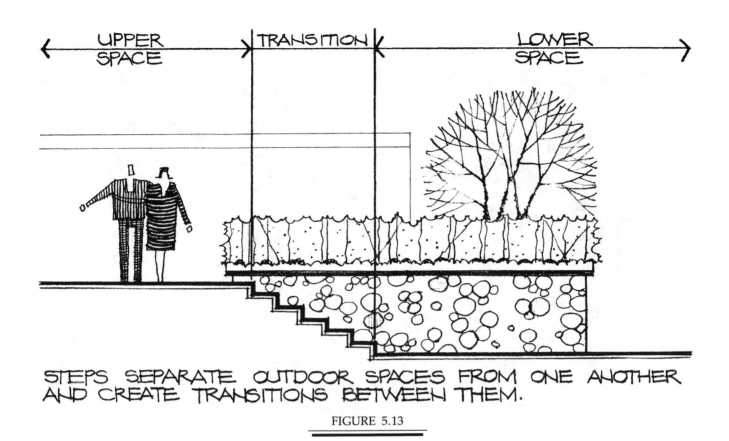

STEPS SEPARATE OUTDOOR SPACES FROM ONE ANOTHER AND CREATE TRANSITIONS BETWEEN THEM.

FIGURE 5.13

as gateways or doors between adjoining outdoor rooms. While moving through the landscape, steps suggest to people that they are in the process of leaving one space and entering another. In this sense, steps are transition elements that allow for a gradual but noticeable change from one space to the next.

From an aesthetic standpoint, steps can accomplish several uses in the outdoor environment. One aesthetic function is that steps can act as a focal point or accent at the end of a walk, as illustrated in Figure 5.14. They provide a point to walk toward or attract the eye. This quality of steps can be reinforced through associated planting and use of walls. Another aesthetic quality of steps is that they create strong horizontal lines in outdoor spaces. These lines may be effective in establishing a sense of stability because of their horizontality or they may provide visual fascination that results from the abstract pattern of repeating lines. As in Figure 5.15, the pattern of lines created by steps in an unconfined setting such as an open plaza can emulate contour lines

of a hard, abstract landform. Not only do these lines capture the eye and carry it around a space, but they also can become dynamic elements because of their changing appearance from varying sun and shadow. The pattern of steps in Lovejoy Plaza in Portland, Oregon, and in Manhattan Square Park in Rochester, New York, both designed by Lawrence Halprin, are two examples where the lines established by steps have been used as a significant visual element in the overall designs.

Still another potential function of steps in the landscape is as casual sitting surfaces (Figure 5.16). This use of steps is most effective where the steps face onto a busy public walk or street or in urban multipurpose spaces where area and benches are limited. People enjoy watching other people and activity. So whenever properly sited, steps can act like stadium bleachers for an audience. There are numerous examples of steps used for sitting and observation, but a classical one is on the front steps of New York City row houses. Here, steps are social gathering points. Another example of steps used in this

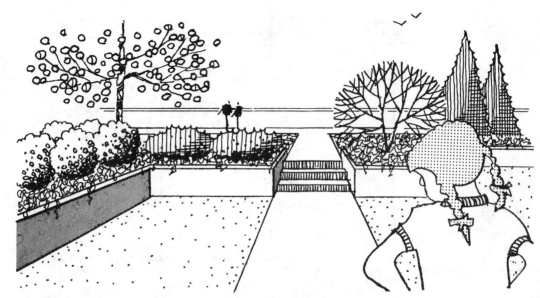

STEPS CAN SERVE AS A FOCAL POINT AT THE END OF A WALK.

FIGURE 5.14

FIGURE 5.15

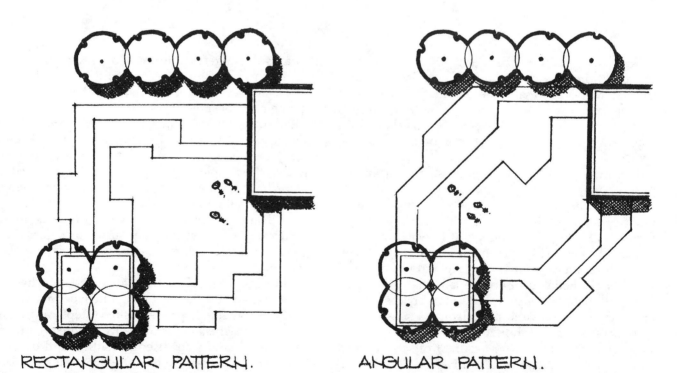

RECTANGULAR PATTERN.   ANGULAR PATTERN.

STEPS CAN BE USED IN LARGE PLAZA SPACES TO PROVIDE AT-
TRACTIVE PATTERNS OF LINES ON THE GROUND PLANE.

FIGURE 5.16

manner, shown in Figure 5.17, is found in Robson Square in Vancouver, British Columbia. At lunchtime people sit randomly in small conversation groups throughout the area on the expansive steps of the complex.

Ramps

Ramps are the second major means for moving the pedestrian from one level to another on the ground plane. As alluded to earlier, the most important advantage of ramps compared with steps is that they permit freedom of movement through the environment for most potential users. Ramps are an integral factor in "barrier-free" site design. Ramps allow the pavement surface to flow through a series of spaces as a continuous, unbroken element. It should be noted, however, that some people find ramps more difficult to walk on because of the sloped surface. For these people, steps may actually be easier to negotiate.

The notable disadvantage of ramps is that they require a proportionally large horizontal area to take up a given elevation change with the proper gra-

FIGURE 5.17

224

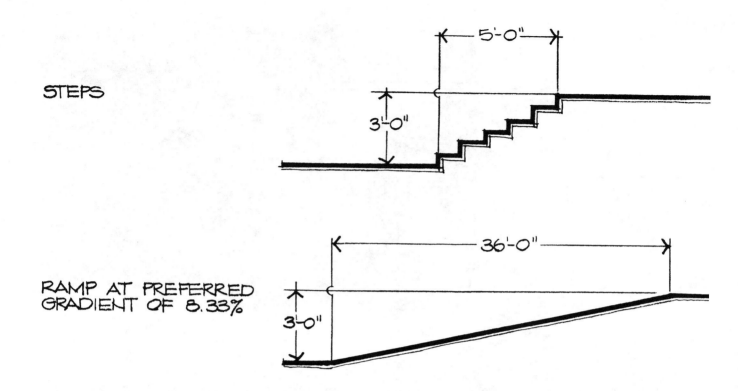

STEPS

5'-0"

3'-0"

RAMP AT PREFERRED
GRADIENT OF 8.33%

36'-0"

3'-0"

RAMPS REQUIRE SUBSTANTIALLY MORE HORIZONTAL DISTANCE
TO ACCOMMODATE A GIVEN ELEVATION CHANGE THAN STEPS DO.

FIGURE 5.18

FIGURE 5.19

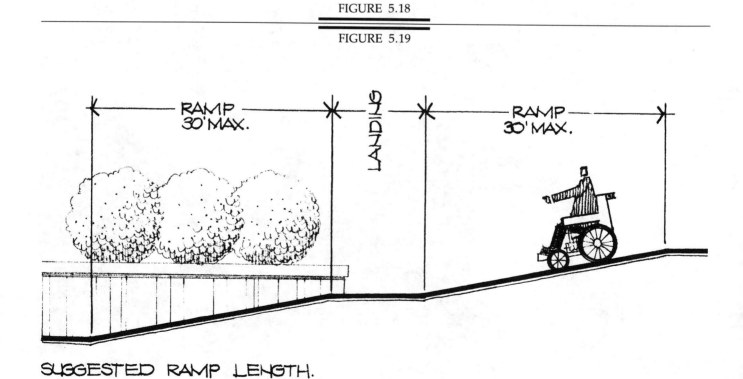

RAMP
30' MAX.

LANDING

RAMP
30' MAX.

SUGGESTED RAMP LENGTH.

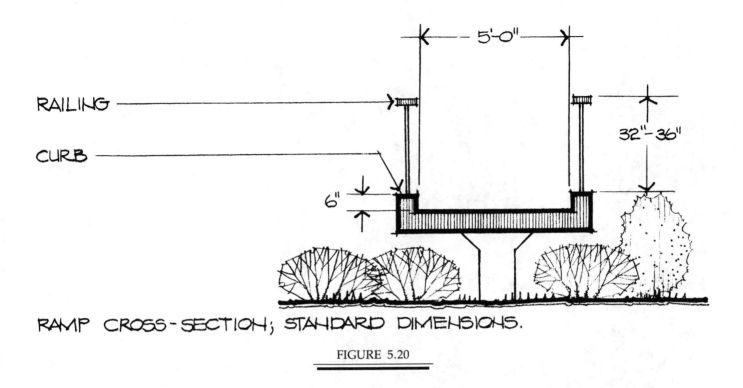

RAILING

CURB

6"

5'-0"

32"-36"

RAMP CROSS-SECTION; STANDARD DIMENSIONS.

FIGURE 5.20

dient. (An example is given in the next paragraph.) In areas where space is limited, ramps must sometimes be contorted to awkward twists and turns to achieve the required distance and gradient. Another disadvantage of ramps is that they can become perilous when wet unless the ramp floor is constructed from a textured, nonslip material. Visually, ramps may look unsightly and misplaced because of their length. When not sensitively designed, ramps often look like afterthoughts or add-ons (which they are in some cases).

As with steps, there are several guidelines for the design of ramps. First, the ramp gradient, or degree of the floor slope, should not exceed an absolute maximum of 8.33 percent, or 12:1.[8] Thus, as an example, a ramp would need a horizontal distance of 36 ft (12m) just to take up a 3-ft (1m) vertical elevation change at the preferred 1:12 maximum slope, as in Figure 5.18. A flight of stairs on the other hand would require only between 5 (152cm) and 6 ft (183cm) of horizontal distance to achieve the same vertical change in elevation. This again points out

the comparatively vast amount of area necessary for ramps. The need for landings also contributes to the length of ramps. Landings provide resting areas and visually counter long stretches of ramp as they do in sets of steps. For long ramps, as in Figure 5.19, the maximum length of ramp between landings should not exceed 30 ft (9m), with landings themselves a minimum of 5 ft (152cm) in length.[9] The minimum width for a ramp should be the same as that for steps and based on whether there is to be one-way or two-way traffic. The sides of a ramp should have at least 6-in (15cm) curbs with a handrail to contain people on the ramp, as illustrated in Figure 5.20. The railing height and placement should be the same as that for steps (32 to 36 in (81–91.5cm) above the floor surface). One further consideration relating to the placement of a ramp is that it should be as much as possible located on primary, direct lines of movement. Ramps should not require users to go out of their way. Finally, the location and layout of a ramp should be decided as early as possible in the development of a design because of the study it requires for properly integrating it with other ele-

[8]Robert D. Loversidge, Jr., ed., *Access for All; An Illustrated Handbook of Barrier-Free Design for Ohio,* 2nd ed. (The Ohio Governor's Committee on Employment of the Handicapped, Columbus, Ohio, 1977, 1978), p. 59.

[9]The American Society of Landscape Architects' Foundation, *Barrier-Free Site Design* (Washington, D.C.: U.S. Department of Housing and Urban Development, 1975), p. 27.

FIGURE 5.21

FIGURE 5.22

FIGURE 5.23

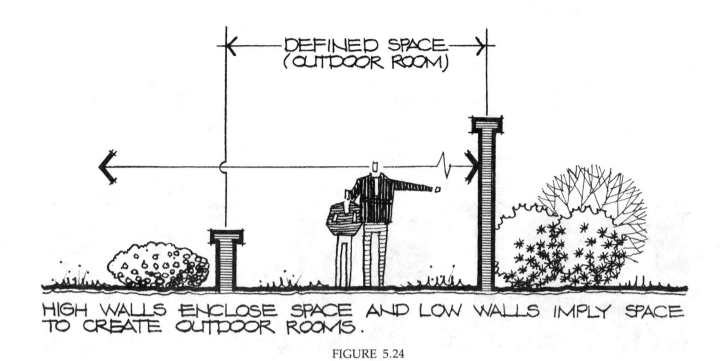

HIGH WALLS ENCLOSE SPACE AND LOW WALLS IMPLY SPACE TO CREATE OUTDOOR ROOMS.

FIGURE 5.24

ments of the design. A ramp should appear as a well-coordinated element within the total design scheme. One innovative way for integrating steps and ramps together was created in the design of Robson Square in Vancouver, British Columbia. Figures 5.21, 5.22, and 5.23 show the way the ramps were coordinated with the steps and the resulting zig-zag pattern.

Walls and Fences

Another form of site structures in the outdoor environment are walls and fences. Both establish hard, architectural vertical planes in the landscape with a number of utilitarian and visual functions. Walls are generally defined as vertical planes constructed of stone, brick, or concrete and may be further categorized as either freestanding or retaining walls. Freestanding walls stand essentially by themselves with a minimum of connections to other elements. Freestanding walls are self-supporting. Retaining walls, on the other hand, hold back a slope or volume of earth from a lower elevation, as described in the next section. Fences can be defined as freestanding vertical planes constructed of either wood or metal. Fences are typically thinner and less massive than walls. Both walls and fences have a number of design possibilities and functions in the outdoor environment, some of which are defined below.

Define Space. Freestanding walls and fences are able to define and enclose space in the vertical plane, as suggested in Figure 5.24. The exact manner in which they do this depends on their height, material, and detailing. The more solid and taller the walls and fences, the greater the sense of spatial enclosure. As described previously for both landform and plant materials, walls and fences create a full sense of spatial enclosure when a 1:1 distance to height ratio is established between the viewer and the height of the wall or fence. Consequently, the strongest feeling of outdoor space is produced by walls and fences over 6 ft (183cm) tall. Low walls, like low shrubs, define space more by implication than actual physical enclosure.

Walls and fences create spaces that are slightly different in character from spaces defined primarily by landform and plant materials. Walls and fences provide hard, well-defined vertical planes rather than soft, sometimes pliable boundaries such as plant materials give. Thus the spaces themselves are much more clearly articulated with precise, exact edges. Similarly, walls and fences tend to be more permanent and less changing in creating space than are plant materials. Spaces formed essentially by walls and fences have less seasonal variation or alteration from year to year. They are more stable. Nevertheless, when walls and fences are carefully juxtaposed with plant material, they can establish an

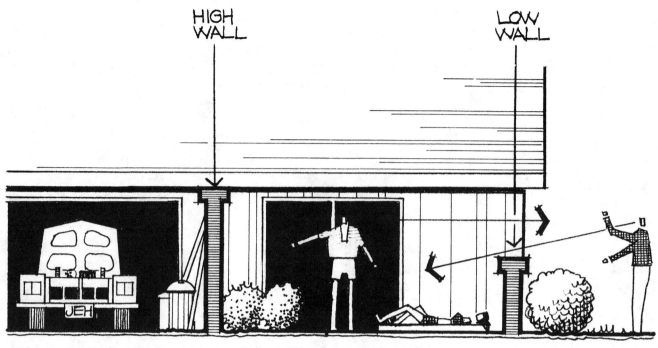

HIGH WALL PROVIDES PRIVACY IN LIMITED SPACE; LOW WALL CAN PROVIDE PRIVACY WHILE SITTING BUT PERMIT VIEWS WHEN STANDING.

FIGURE 5.25

attractive contrast between the artificial qualities of the wall and the fence and the naturalistic characteristics of the vegetation.

Screen Views. Walls and fences that define space also affect views into and out from an outdoor space. Walls and fences may be used to totally block views on the one hand or partially screen views in varying degrees on the other. The design and layout of the wall or fence depends on the effect desired.

Tall (over 6 ft (183cm)), solid walls are most effective in providing total screening as might be required around a parking lot, along a roadway, or around unsightly industrial equipment. Tall vertical

FIGURE 5.26

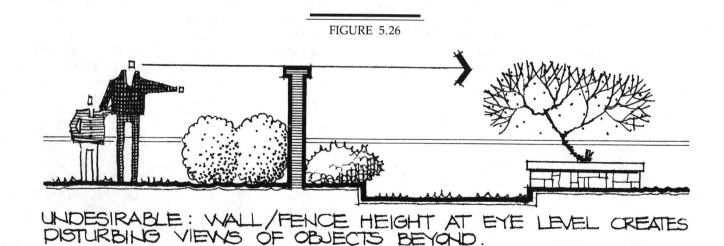

UNDESIRABLE: WALL/FENCE HEIGHT AT EYE LEVEL CREATES DISTURBING VIEWS OF OBJECTS BEYOND.

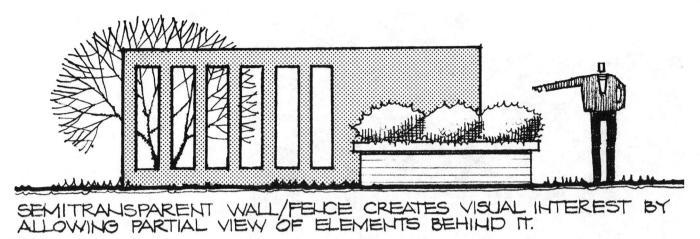

SEMITRANSPARENT WALL/FENCE CREATES VISUAL INTEREST BY ALLOWING PARTIAL VIEW OF ELEMENTS BEHIND IT.

FIGURE 5.27

planes are also appropriate for creating privacy as is often necessary for the outdoor living area of single-family or multifamily residences (Figure 5.25). People usually want to use their outdoor spaces without the feeling of being looked at. Walls and fences may be more efficient in furnishing privacy in these circumstances than either landform or plant materials because walls and fences are narrower and take up less space. Tall shrubs used to screen views may be two feet or more in width, whereas a fence or wall needs to be only a few inches wide. Although a tall wall or fence is generally required for total privacy, a lower wall or fence may be adequate in circumstances where privacy is needed only for people sitting or lying down. Whatever the particular needs in stopping views, a wall or fence should not be designed so that its top is at eye level, as in Figure 5.26. This creates a disturbing feeling of almost but not quite being able to see. A person's reaction to this is to move the eye level up or down to avoid the half-and-half view. For privacy a wall or fence should extend above eye level, not just stop at eye level.

In some situations it may be desirable only to partially screen a view, as suggested in Figure 5.27. This might be done if the view is not totally offensive or if it is desired to tease the viewer with a small, incomplete look at the overall scene. A person intrigued by a partial view will often move through a space to a position where more if not all of the scene can be fully viewed. A view can be partially screened by a wall or fence that is made semitransparent by openings or spaces in the material of the wall or fence, as shown in Figures 5.28 and 5.29. These voids not only permit some views through the wall but may also actually be of interest unto themselves because of their size, proportion, and interaction with light and shade. Openings and spaces may also be used to make a wall or fence less massive and heavy in appearance.

Separate Functions. Another use of walls and fences closely related to creating space and screening views is to separate adjoining uses from each other. Sometimes it is necessary to place dissimilar and even incompatible uses next to each other in the organization of a design's functions. Walls and fences, as do the interior walls of a building, allow these unlike uses to occur without interfering with each other. For example, a wall can be used to separate a quiet sitting area from the noise and confusion of a parking lot next door. The wall around the sculpture garden in the Museum of Modern Art in New York City allows people to enjoy the serenity of the garden with a minimum of interference from the surrounding city environment. Low stone walls and hedgerows separate pastures from other pastures, crops, roads, and uses throughout the English countryside.

In separating functions, walls and fences also identify territoriality and provide security for the spaces they enclose.[10] Walls and fences can reinforce

[10]See also Oscar Newman, *Defensible Space* (New York: Macmillan, 1972).

FIGURE 5.28

FIGURE 5.29

the location where one property ends and another starts by establishing a permanent barrier on the boundary. The familiar saying "good fences make good neighbors" suggests that clear identification of and division between properties avoids territorial disputes and clearly indicates to individual owners where their domain begins and ends. Before a wall or fence is erected on a property line in a residential setting, especially in the front yard, local zoning codes should be reviewed. Many municipalities have strict restrictions on height and location of vertical barriers in the front yard area.

In addition to simply acknowledging a boundary, walls and fences can also provide security by keeping people and animals either in or out of a given area of land. Historically, medieval villages in Europe often had a tall fortress wall around the community for protection against intruders. The Great

FIGURE 5.30

Wall of China is another classic example. Today walls and fences are used for similar purposes to protect property from vandalism and other unwanted activity. And in some cases, as around a swimming pool, walls and fences fulfill a need for safety. The wall in Figure 5.30 at the Hyatt Regency in Atlanta is intended to serve this function. From an aesthetic standpoint, the challenge to the designer is to make attractive and "uninstitutional" walls and fences erected for security. Security fences such as a chain link fence can look stark and harsh if not integrated with other elements such as plant material.

Modify Climate. Freestanding walls and fences may also be used in the landscape to minimize the negative effects of both sun and wind. High walls and fences may be used to cast shade onto a building or outdoor space at those times of the day when the sun angle is low, such as early morning or late afternoon and evening. As suggested in Figure 5.31, a wall or fence is most efficient when located on the west and northwest side of a building or outdoor space in order to screen against the hot late afternoon sun in summer. A wall or fence on the west and northwest side of a building, whether by itself as in Figure 5.31 or integrated with plant material, can prevent heat buildup in the building's walls and consequently produce lower interior temperatures.

A wall or fence is least effective as a sun screen when placed on the south side of the area to be shaded because the high sun angle at noon will cast a minimum amount of shadow to the north side of the wall or fence.

Besides screening low sun, walls and fences may be used to block wind. When wind is blocked from an area, the "sensible temperature" (the temperature perceived by a person) goes up because of a decrease in windchill. The exact way a wall or fence affects wind depends on its design. At first thought, a solid wall or fence would seem to be the best for screening wind from an area. Yet research and field observation have proven this not to be true. Actually, a solid wall or fence as shown in Figure 5.32 creates an eddy of downward and reverse-flowing wind on the lee side.[11] So for maximum protection against the wind, a wall or fence, like the vegetative windscreen discussed in Chapter 2, should contain some openings in its plane to allow a portion of air to flow through and uphold the wind flowing over the top. The most effective screen over the greatest distance has been found to be a louvered fence with the louvers tilted upward.[12] There are a number of possible variations on fence designs with different

[11]Charles McClenon, ed., Landscape Planning For Energy Conservation (Reston, Virginia: Environmental Design Press, 1977), p. 121.
[12]Ibid.

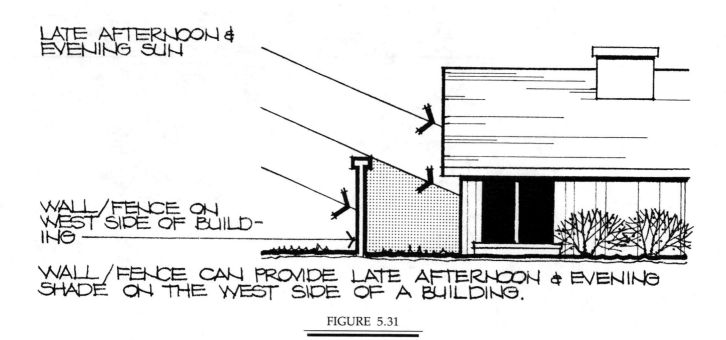

LATE AFTERNOON &
EVENING SUN

WALL/FENCE ON
WEST SIDE OF BUILD-
ING

WALL/FENCE CAN PROVIDE LATE AFTERNOON & EVENING
SHADE ON THE WEST SIDE OF A BUILDING.

FIGURE 5.31

FIGURE 5.32

UNDESIRABLE : SOLID FENCE
CREATES TURBULENCE AND
DIRECTS WIND DOWNWARD.

DESIRABLE : UPWARD-TILTED
LOUVERED FENCE DIRECTS
WIND UP AND OVER SPACE.

resulting patterns of wind flow through and over them. Each needs to be studied before selecting the one best suited for any given situation. As to location, the most effective position depends on the purpose of the wall or fence. To provide protection against the cold winter wind in the temperate zone, the best location is on the west and northwest sides of the area to be screened (Figure 5.33). This is the same as the preferred position for sun protection. A fence or wall located here will provide both summer sun and winter wind protection. Along a seashore the location of a wall or fence may vary depending on local conditions.

In a similar but somewhat opposite sense, walls and fences can be used to direct summer breezes into an outdoor space to take advantage of the cooling effect of moving air during this season. Walls and fences may be located actually to direct and funnel summer breezes into an outdoor space from the southwest direction in the temperate climate zone, as shown in Figure 5.34. In the design of the fence itself, slats or louvers may be oriented to direct the breeze toward a place where people may be sitting or standing. However, do not use horizontal louvers pointed downward because the breeze will also be directed downward. The result will be that dust, leaves, and other particles on the ground will be stirred up and carried through the air.

233

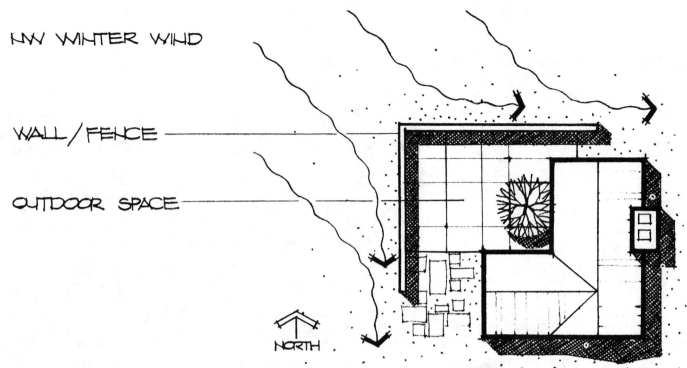

NW WINTER WIND

WALL / FENCE

OUTDOOR SPACE

NORTH

WALL/FENCE ON NORTHWEST SIDE OF OUTDOOR SPACE AND
BUILDING CAN HELP TO DIVERT WINTER WIND.

FIGURE 5.33

FIGURE 5.34

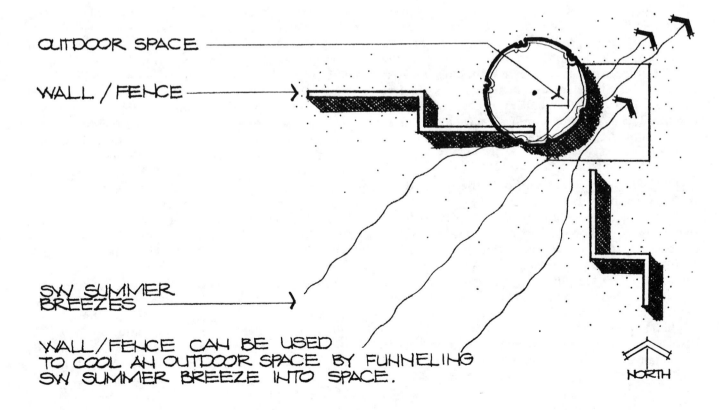

OUTDOOR SPACE

WALL / FENCE

SW SUMMER
BREEZES

WALL/FENCE CAN BE USED
TO COOL AN OUTDOOR SPACE BY FUNNELING
SW SUMMER BREEZE INTO SPACE.

NORTH

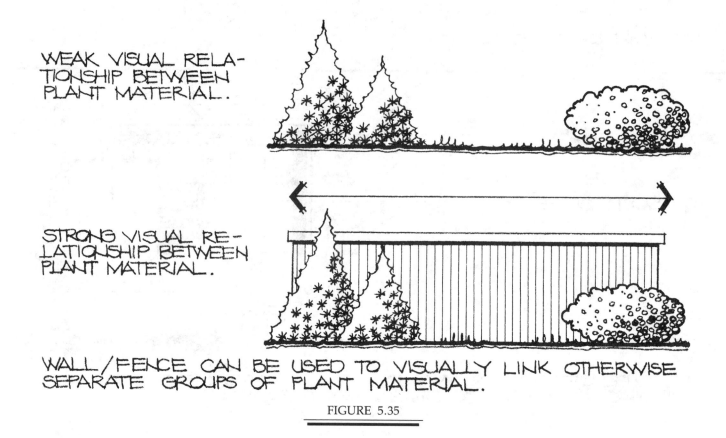

WEAK VISUAL RELA-
TIONSHIP BETWEEN
PLANT MATERIAL.

STRONG VISUAL RE-
LATIONSHIP BETWEEN
PLANT MATERIAL.

WALL/FENCE CAN BE USED TO VISUALLY LINK OTHERWISE
SEPARATE GROUPS OF PLANT MATERIAL.

FIGURE 5.35

Sitting Elements. Low freestanding walls and sometimes low fences can be used as seats while serving
other functions as well. This use of walls has the
greatest application in heavily used urban spaces or
other outdoor spaces where it is not desirable to
clutter the environment with many benches required
to accommodate large numbers of people. To serve
comfortably as a sitting surface, a wall should be
about 18 in (46 cm) above the ground and 12 in (30.5
cm) wide.

Visual Elements. In addition to all these varied potential functions just described, freestanding walls
and fences can also fulfill a number of visual uses in
the landscape. They may act as neutral, nonchanging backdrops to other positive highlights in a space
such as attractive plant material or a piece of sculpture. Used for this purpose, the wall itself should
not demand too much attention or it is likely to compete with the element in the foreground. Another
aesthetic application of walls and fences in the outdoor environment similar to that of plant material is
to visually connect and unify otherwise unrelated

elements. For instance, a freestanding wall can relate
two isolated groups of plant material by acting as a
common background that visually links the vegetation masses together, as shown in Figure 5.35. Similar to this design function is the use of walls to coordinate a building to its surrounding site. By
carrying a building wall and material into the site, a
wall can perform as an "arm" of the building reach-
ing out to embrace the site. This helps to unify the
building and site into a total coordinated environment, as illustrated in Figure 3.62. Last of all, another use of freestanding walls and fences is as elements of visual interest all by themselves. As one
example, the plan layout of a wall or fence may
move in, out, and around a space, intriguing the eye
with altering direction and varying patterns of light
and shadow, as it does in the right half of Figure
5.36. A serpentine wall has these qualities. The detailing of materials used in the construction of the
wall or fence is another means for establishing visual
appeal in a wall or fence. Again, patterns can be created that work with varying materials or with the
interaction of light and shadow. An additional

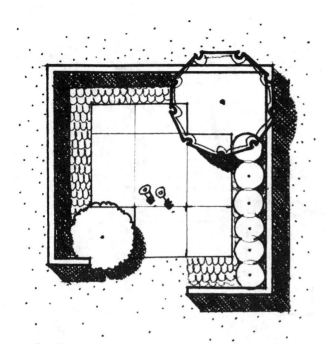

SIMPLE WALL LAYOUT PRO-
VIDES LESS VISUAL AND SPA-
TIAL EXCITEMENT.

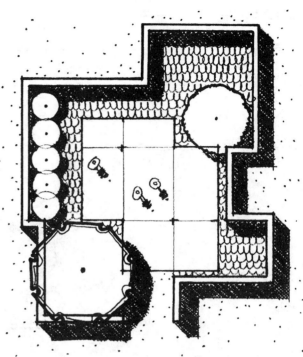

WALL MOVES IN AND OUT A-
ROUND SPACE TO PROVIDE
VISUAL AND SPATIAL INTRIGUE.

FIGURE 5.36

means for providing visual fascination is painted graphics. This may vary from graffiti to a well-conceived mural. The use of "supergraphics" on walls in urban settings has evolved into an art form in its own right through the use of bright, bold colors and designs applied to large, massive walls.

Retaining Walls

As identified earlier, the second general type of wall used in the landscape is the retaining wall. The principle function of a retaining wall is to hold back a portion of higher ground from a lower one. A retaining wall permits two elevation levels to be placed adjacent to each other with an abrupt vertical change between them. Thus a retaining wall saves space compared with a gradual slope placed between two different levels. To hold earth adequately and safely, a retaining wall needs to be properly engineered and constructed. Whenever feasible, it should be built fewer than 4 ft (122 cm) in height to prevent costly reinforcing and construction techniques. If a retaining wall is to exceed this height, it is advisable to

consult a civil engineer. Another suggestion is to slightly pitch the wall toward the slope as it increases in height to help reinforce its stability, as shown in Figure 5.37. This pitch is called a "batter." For drainage a slight swale should be made in the earth at the top of the wall to prevent surface drainage from washing over the wall and down its face. "Weep holes" should be placed at given intervals in the wall to permit subsurface seepage to move through the wall without causing damage.

While holding back earth, a retaining wall may also serve other uses as well. Like freestanding walls, retaining walls are able to define space and spatial edges, provide a background to other elements, connect buildings to their surrounding sites, and act as attractive aesthetic elements by themselves. Compared with slopes, retaining walls establish sharp, distinct edges and planes that tend to be more prominent from a visual standpoint. Slopes tend to be softer and less visually aggressive than retaining walls. Another possible application of retaining walls is for seating. Used for this purpose, a retaining wall, like a freestanding wall, should be 16

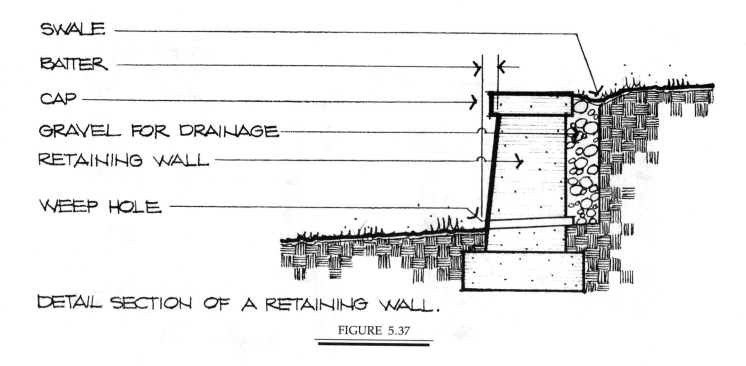

SWALE
BATTER
CAP
GRAVEL FOR DRAINAGE
RETAINING WALL
WEEP HOLE

DETAIL SECTION OF A RETAINING WALL.

FIGURE 5.37

(40.5cm) to 20 in (51cm) in height with a 12 in (30.5 cm) wide cap or top to provide enough seat space.

Design Guidelines

A number of aesthetic considerations apply to most walls and fences no matter what their specific type or material of construction. In the design of walls or fences, three primary elements typically make up the constructed vertical plane: (1) base, (2) wall or fence surface, and (3) cap or top, as graphically depicted in Figure 5.38. A similar kind of division into three major areas can also be found on other structural elements such as columns or building façades. The base provides a transition between the wall or fence and the ground and visually establishes a feeling of support for the vertical plane to rest on. The exact detailing of the base depends on how much attention or prominence is required to bring to the base. Where no emphasis is desired, the wall or fence surface may extend to and into the ground with no base at all. When the objective is to reinforce the base, it may be designed as a distinct element from the wall or fence surface. In this situation it may be made wider than the vertical plane above so that it is more easily seen and provides a visually sturdy resting place for the wall or fence surface. Generally, the base should establish a strong horizontal line for visual stability. This is most signifi-

cant when walls or fences must be located on a sloped ground surface, as in Figure 5.39. In this situation, it is usually best to have the base step up or down the slope in a series of horizontal segments. When the base is allowed to parallel the slope, the angled baseline that results tends to establish a visually unstable support for the rest of the wall or fence. Another approach for dealing with slopes in association with walls is to eliminate the base altogether and allow the ground to fall directly along the wall surface.

The wall or fence surface constitutes the major portion of the vertical plane. This surface can be handled in an infinite number of different ways. The exact detailing of any given wall or fence surface should depend on aesthetic, spatial, functional, and budgetary objectives. However, some general thoughts should be kept in mind. The method of construction and the type of material used in the wall or fence surface directly affects the visual direction and texture of the wall or fence. For example, if the material in the surface forms strong horizontal lines such as those created by rows of bricks or horizontal louvers in a fence, as in the left side of Figure 5.40, then the wall or fence will appear more elongated and stretched out. This same kind of surface can also emphasize level landform, relate to strong horizontal lines in adjoining buildings, or contrast columnar plant material or other upright elements

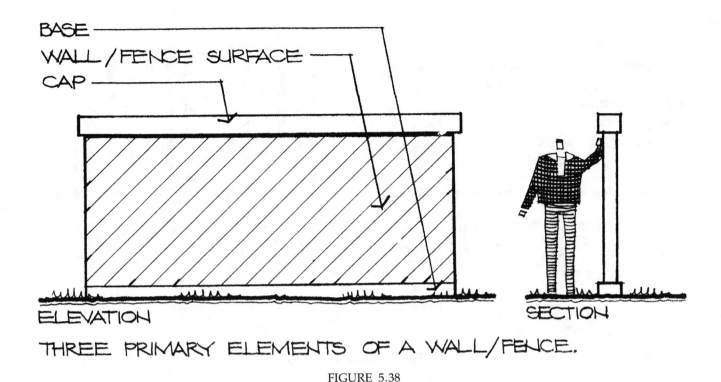

BASE

WALL/FENCE SURFACE

CAP

ELEVATION

SECTION

THREE PRIMARY ELEMENTS OF A WALL/FENCE.

FIGURE 5.38

juxtaposed with them. In an opposite approach, walls or fences that have distinct vertical lines in their surface will appear taller and more compact in length, as in the right side of Figure 5.40. In the case of fences whose posts are an integral visual element in the fence, the posts not only emphasize the vertical, but their spacing establishes a rhythmic pattern of repetition. The rhythmic pattern can help unify a space and elements in the foreground as well as establish scale. Posts placed close together can create a sense of small or intimate scale, while posts spaced farther apart can provide a feeling of larger scale.

FIGURE 5.39

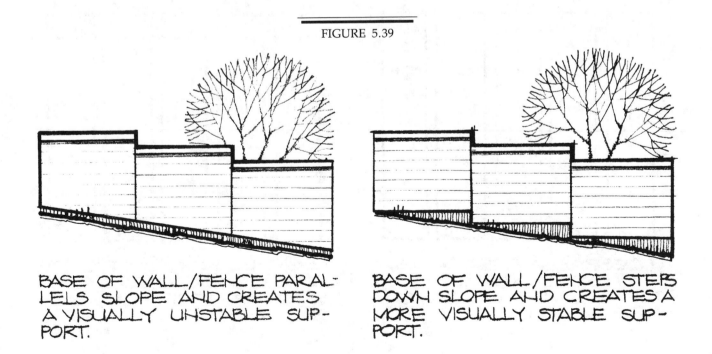

BASE OF WALL/FENCE PARALLELS SLOPE AND CREATES A VISUALLY UNSTABLE SUPPORT.

BASE OF WALL/FENCE STEPS DOWN SLOPE AND CREATES A MORE VISUALLY STABLE SUPPORT.

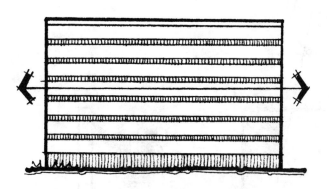

HORIZONTAL MATERIAL PATTERN MAKES WALL/FENCE APPEAR STRETCHED AND ELONGATED.

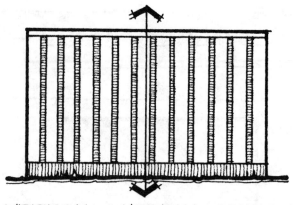

VERTICAL MATERIAL PATTERN MAKES WALL/FENCE APPEAR TALL AND COMPACT.

FIGURE 5.40

FIGURE 5.41

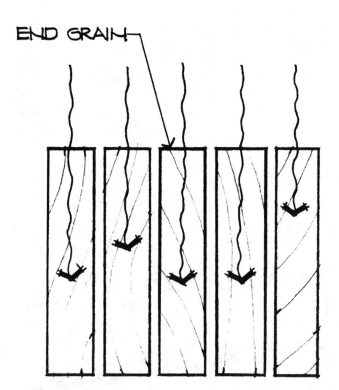

END GRAIN

UNDESIRABLE : END GRAIN OF WOOD IS EXPOSED AT TOP ALLOWING WATER TO SEEP IN.

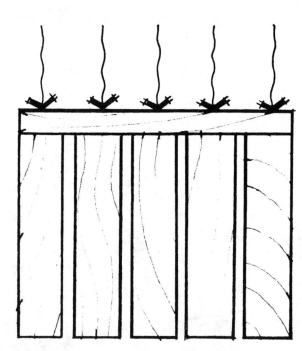

DESIRABLE : END GRAIN OF WOOD IS PROTECTED BY CAP WHICH PREVENTS WATER FROM SEEPING IN.

And as with plant material, the overall texture of a wall or fence surface influences scale. Surfaces that have coarse texture such as large stone visually move toward the viewer, while finer textures recede.

The cap or top is the third major portion of a fence or wall. The cap serves two essential functions, one practical and one visual. From a utilitarian standpoint, the cap covers the body of the wall or fence and prevents infiltration of water. In the case of walls, water that seeps into the internal areas can freeze and expand during colder seasons of the year. For fences constructed of vertical wood members, a cap serves a similar purpose. The end grain of a piece of wood such as a 2×4 is the most vulnerable to water penetration. When this portion of a piece of wood sticks up in the air, as in Figure 5.41, rain and snow can easily seep into the wood and cause it to rot. A cap on a wood fence prevents this undesirable action from occurring. Visually, a cap on top of a wall or fence finishes and completes the appearance of the vertical plane. In a way, the cap contains the wall or fence surface and prevents it from visually moving off into space. And a cap, like the base, typically establishes a noticeable horizontal line that can be silhouetted against a background. For emphasis, the cap is often visually heavier and wider than the wall or fence surface below. Where the cap extends out over the vertical surface, a shadow can be cast on the surface below, further accentuating the cap.

Wall and Fence Materials

As indicated earlier, freestanding walls, retaining walls, and fences can each be constructed out of a wide range of potential materials. Some of the more common materials include stone, brick, concrete, iron, and wood. A more detailed description of the characteristics and potential uses of these materials in fences and walls follows.

Stone. Stone of different sizes, shapes, and geological origins may be used in both freestanding and retaining walls. Stone is typically used in walls to furnish a rough, naturalistic character even though a diversity of appearances from highly textured and irregular to smooth and refined can be created, depending on type and pattern of stone used. Still, compared with other possible materials, stone is most suitable for providing an earthy gray or brown tone in a strong textural pattern. Stone is perhaps most appropriately used in walls that are intended to be solid. Rarely is stone used in a wall that is required to be partially transparent.

The different visual qualities of stone walls aside, stone is generally used in walls in one of two ways: (1) uncut (or fieldstone) or (2) cut. In its uncut state, fieldstone is used to give a wall a rough, irregular look. This pattern, sometimes referred to as a "rubble pattern," is most appropriately used in a naturalistic or pastoral setting as an expression of the surroundings. Fieldstone may also be used in walls located in more formal settings as an element of contrast. Cut stone, on the other hand, is commonly used in situations that require a more controlled and formal quality. As in pavement, stone may be cut into any number of sizes and shapes, depending on the desired visual effect. Rectangular patterns or "ashlar patterns" are used most because they are easier to construct. Some of these various patterns of stone walls are illustrated in Figure 5.42.

Both freestanding and retaining walls of either fieldstone or cut stone may be constructed by either of two methods: (1) masonry or wet wall and (2) dry wall. In a masonry wall the individual stones are held together by mortar. This wall tends to be more stable and permanent, yet also more expensive than a dry wall. In some instances, concrete or concrete block is used as the core of the wall with stone mortared to this core as a veneer (Figure 5.43). The resulting appearance may be no different from an entirely stone wall.

A dry wall is one in which no mortar or any other binder is used. The individual stones are skillfully fitted together to form a stable mass held in place by gravity and the fit of each stone to the next. It requires a sensitive craftsman to construct a dry wall to be structurally and visually acceptable. Depending on how closely the individual stones fit, a dry wall can provide a more noticeable texture than a masonry wall because of the lack of mortar filling the individual joints. A strong pattern of light and shade can be achieved by working with the voids between stones. A dry wall is best in circumstances where it will not receive unusual physical wear such as would occur if it were used as a sitting wall. A dry stone wall should not be built to excessive height or it might fall down. Generally speaking, the higher a dry wall is, the wider its base must be for structural support.

Brick. Brick is another wall material. As in pavement, brick provides a warm, refined urban quality. Brick typically creates a smoother, more polished wall surface than stone. Brick can also be used in a wall to visually relate it to brick façades of adjoining or nearby buildings, thus helping to unify building and site.

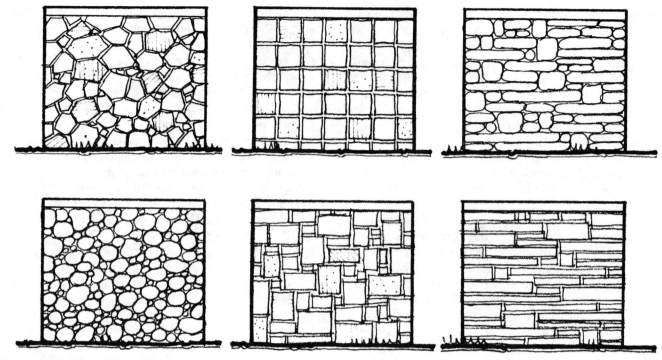

STONE PATTERNS IN WALLS.

FIGURE 5.42

FIGURE 5.43

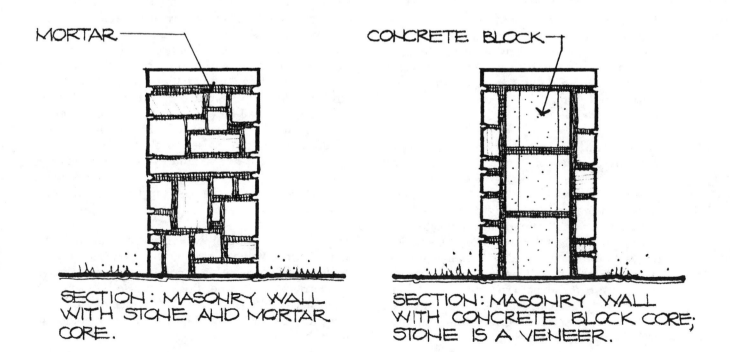

MORTAR

CONCRETE BLOCK

SECTION: MASONRY WALL WITH STONE AND MORTAR CORE.

SECTION: MASONRY WALL WITH CONCRETE BLOCK CORE; STONE IS A VENEER.

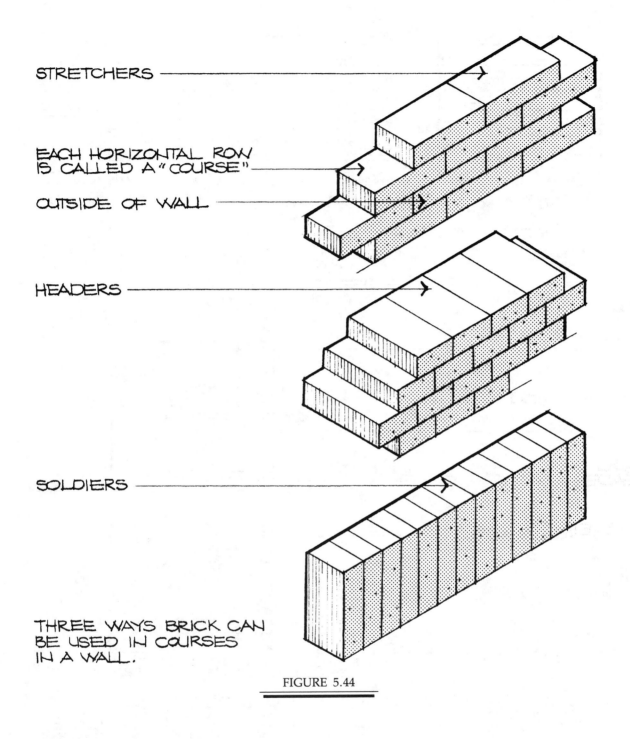

STRETCHERS

EACH HORIZONTAL ROW
IS CALLED A "COURSE"

OUTSIDE OF WALL

HEADERS

SOLDIERS

THREE WAYS BRICK CAN
BE USED IN COURSES
IN A WALL.

FIGURE 5.44

As in pavement, brick can be employed in walls in a number of potential patterns. All patterns are based upon the different possible ways for arranging brick in "courses," or horizontal rows. Within each course, individual brick can be used in one of three basic ways as (1) stretchers, (2) headers, or (3) soldiers (Figure 5.44). When used in a course as a "stretcher," a brick is laid flat with one of its long thin sides facing the outside surface of the wall. A "header" is a brick placed in the wall perpendicular to the course so that one of the ends of the brick makes up the wall surface. Bricks used as headers in a course are laid flat and may alternate with stretchers or make up an entire course themselves. A "soldier" is a brick laid on its end with one of its long, thin sides placed vertically to the outside of the wall. Soldiers are sometimes used as a base course of a brick wall.

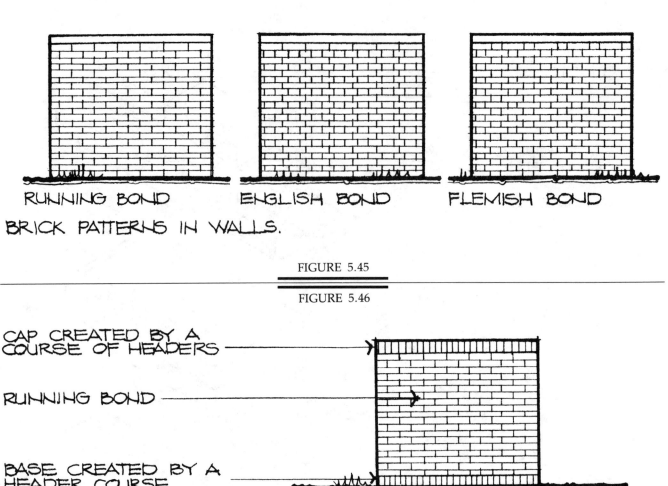

RUNNING BOND　　　ENGLISH BOND　　　FLEMISH BOND

BRICK PATTERNS IN WALLS.

FIGURE 5.45

FIGURE 5.46

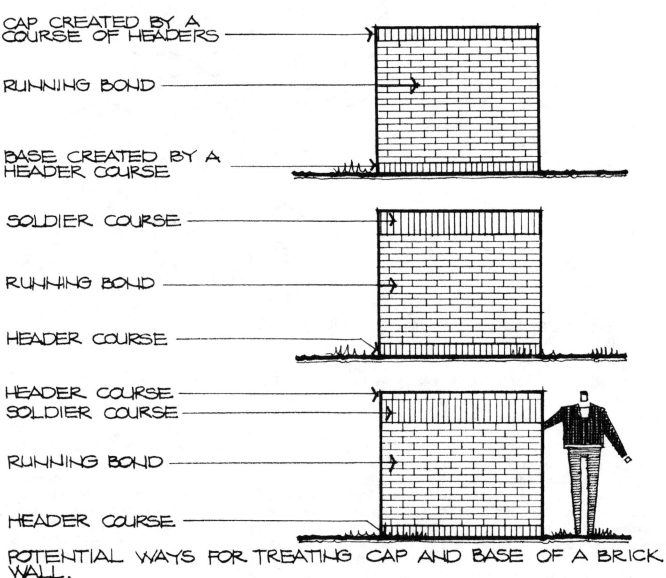

CAP CREATED BY A
COURSE OF HEADERS

RUNNING BOND

BASE CREATED BY A
HEADER COURSE

SOLDIER COURSE

RUNNING BOND

HEADER COURSE

HEADER COURSE
SOLDIER COURSE

RUNNING BOND

HEADER COURSE

POTENTIAL WAYS FOR TREATING CAP AND BASE OF A BRICK WALL.

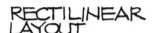
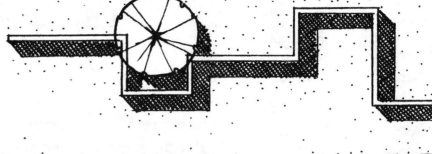
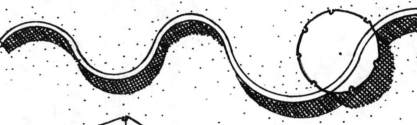

INITIAL PLASTICITY OF CONCRETE PERMITS IT TO BE FORM-
ED IN MANY TYPES OF LAYOUTS.

FIGURE 5.47

The most common pattern of brick in a wall is the running bond pattern, where each brick in a course is used as a stretcher offset from the one above and below it. Other patterns including the English bond and Flemish bond can be created using brick as both stretchers and headers in the same course (Figure 5.45). And still other patterns can be produced by either indenting or protruding bricks from the overall wall surface in a regular, repeating manner. As do stone walls, brick walls usually require a cap to seal their top from rain and snow and to visually "finish off" the wall top. A common cap for a brick wall is a row of headers or soldiers along the top. A brick wall can also be capped with either stone or concrete. Some of these alternatives are illustrated in Figure 5.46. All brick walls are masonry walls regardless of specific size or function.

Portland Cement Concrete. Portland cement concrete may be used in both freestanding and retaining walls. As in pavement, Portland cement concrete can be utilized as either cast-in-place or precast material. When concrete is used as cast-in-place, it has the unique characteristic of being highly flexible in terms of both plan layout and surface treatment. This is a result of concrete's initial plastic state, which allows it to conform to any form in which it is placed. The layout of a cast-in-place concrete wall can be rectilinear, curved, or irregular (Figure 5.47). Appealing wall patterns and textures can be produced by the configuration of the construction forms in which Portland cement concrete is placed or by the treatment of the surface once the forms have been removed. For example, the shape of the forms may create indentations and/or protrusions in the

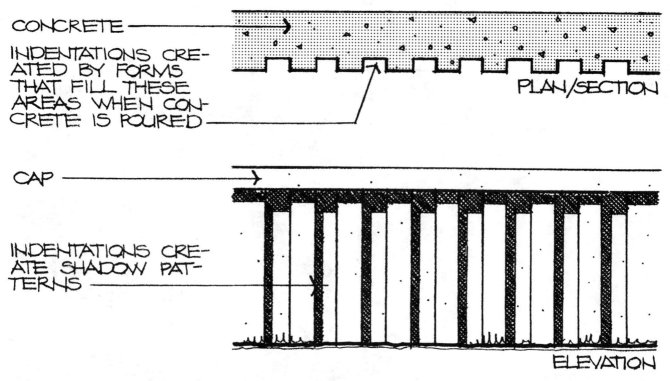

CONCRETE

INDENTATIONS CREATED BY FORMS THAT FILL THESE AREAS WHEN CONCRETE IS POURED

PLAN/SECTION

CAP

INDENTATIONS CREATE SHADOW PATTERNS

ELEVATION

PLASTICITY OF CONCRETE ALLOWS PATTERNS AND INDENTATIONS TO BE MADE IN ITS SURFACE.

FIGURE 5.48

FIGURE 5.49

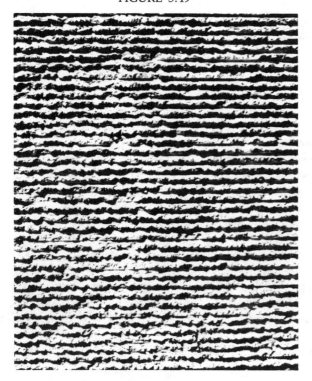

wall surface. These pushes and pulls in the wall surface can create striking patterns of light and shadow, as seen in Figure 5.48. Or a wood texture can be imprinted in the concrete by using rough-sawn wood forms. After the forms have been taken off, the aggregates in the concrete can be exposed to give the surface a rough texture or the surface can be hammered or chipped to provide other effects, as shown in Figure 5.49. Despite the cold gray color of concrete walls, the many possible patterns and textures can make concrete walls extremely appealing. The cost of a Portland cement concrete wall is generally less than that of either a stone or brick wall because less labor is involved in constructing a cast-in-place concrete wall.

The second way Portland cement concrete can be used in walls is as a precast material. Precast concrete, like brick, is available as modular units of different sizes, shapes, colors, and textures. A wall constructed from precast concrete units actually has more similarities to a brick wall than a poured concrete wall in terms of construction methods, potential uses, and general appearances. The modular na-

DECORATIVE BLOCK WALLS.

FIGURE 5.50

ture of concrete units does not have the flexibility of poured concrete in terms of shape or plan layout. But precast concrete units can be used in different patterns and in semitransparent walls where spaces and voids are left in some predetermined design.

Precast concrete units are available in a variety of sizes and appearances. It would be impossible to attempt to list and describe all of them here; however, some types are more common than others, including the standard concrete block, slump block, and decorative block. The standard concrete block, which measures 8 in × 8 in × 16 in, (about 20cm × 20cm × 40cm) is used most for structural walls in the construction of buildings. Concrete block is not used by itself to any large extent in the landscape owing to its unappealing gray color and the feeling that it is "unfinished" by itself. But concrete block is used more frequently as an internal structural component of both stone and brick walls (Figure 5.43). In this situation, the stone and brick are used as a veneer. A similar use is to cover the concrete block with stucco to create a more appealing surface texture and color.

Slump blocks, a cross between concrete block and adobe brick, are actually concrete blocks but look like adobe brick. This material is used in the Southwest for solid screen walls. Decorative block is a general term that describes the numerous precast units that are molded into attractive forms. Some of these are rather simple, while others are quite ornate with various shaped spaces in them. Decorative blocks are most appropriate where a semitransparent wall is required or where it is desired to have the wall surface itself take on visual prominence. Examples of decorative block are shown in Figure 5.50.

Wood. Still another material that can be used for both walls and fences is wood. Wood provides a range of visual effects, from rustic and naturalistic to smooth and formal, depending on its finish. The advantage of using wood in the vertical plane compared with other materials is that it is comparatively lightweight and thin. A wood fence, for example, does not require the same amount of structural support as does a stone or brick wall of the same height. The cost of a wood fence is considerably less than that of a stone or brick wall. Furthermore, the materials required to build a wood fence are generally readily available. The disadvantage of using wood is that it is not as durable or permanent as other materials. It requires periodic maintenance to prevent it from weathering or rotting from exposure to moisture. The particularly vulnerable part of a wood vertical plane is the portion that comes into contact with the ground. This should be kept as dry as possible through good drainage. Another limitation of wood is that it must usually be used in straight lines and planes. It is difficult to make wood conform to curves or other irregularities, unlike concrete or stone.

Because of the wide range of sizes and lengths of available wood timber and the relative ease of cutting it to custom shapes, wood can be used in a freestanding vertical plane in almost any manner desired. A wood fence may be completely solid or almost totally transparent with an entire range of variations in between (Figure 5.29). A wood fence can appear very heavy and massive or quite light and delicate. Wood may be placed vertically in a fence to accentuate height or horizontally to reinforce length. As pointed out before, when the posts of a fence are a visible part of it, the placement has

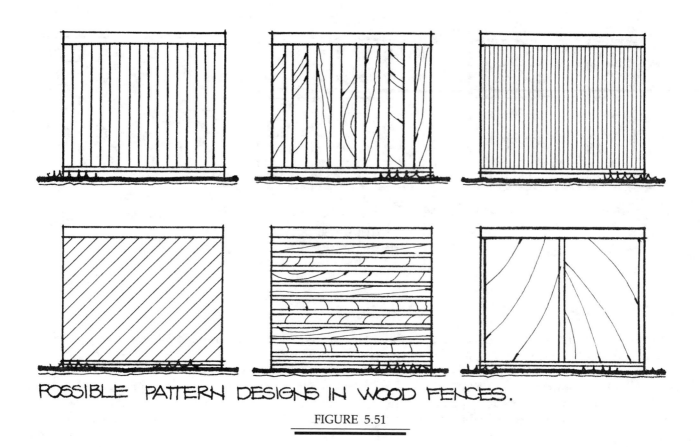

POSSIBLE PATTERN DESIGNS IN WOOD FENCES.

FIGURE 5.51

a direct impact on the visual rhythm and scale of the fence. Figure 5.51 illustrates different fence designs.

Wood in the form of heavy timbers may be used for retaining walls too. Here, wood such as Wolmanized® timber must be pressure-treated to prevent it from rotting. The reason why wood might be used in retaining walls is to provide a gray or stained texture near the ground or to blend the retaining wall in with wood in nearby structures such as decks, fences, or the siding of a building. In addition to pressure-treated timbers, railroad ties may be used in retaining walls too. Although railroad ties have been successfully used in many designs, a word of caution needs to be expressed about their use in all situations. For some untrained designers and lay people, railroad ties have been used as a panacea for all conditions requiring a retaining wall. The result has frequently been the use of railroad ties in situations where they are aesthetically inappropriate to their environmental context. Railroad ties are best used for retaining walls in a rustic or pastoral setting, not an urban or formal one.

Wrought Iron. One other material for fences is wrought iron. Wrought iron is best used where a transparent screen is desired and/or decorative division between spaces is needed. Within the fence surface, wrought iron may be used in simple, straight lines or bent to form elaborate patterns, as in Figure 5.28. Wrought iron, partially owing to its cost and historical use, is employed more in formal settings. Because of its normal black color (though it may be painted other colors), wrought iron can best display its intricate patterns when placed in front of a light background. Similarly, dramatic effects can be created when either sunlight or artificial light shines through the wrought iron fence from the background, as suggested in Figure 5.52.

Seating

Seating in the form of benches, walls, planters, or other elements is another type of site structure that directly affects the comfort and enjoyment of an exterior space. The most obvious role of seating in the

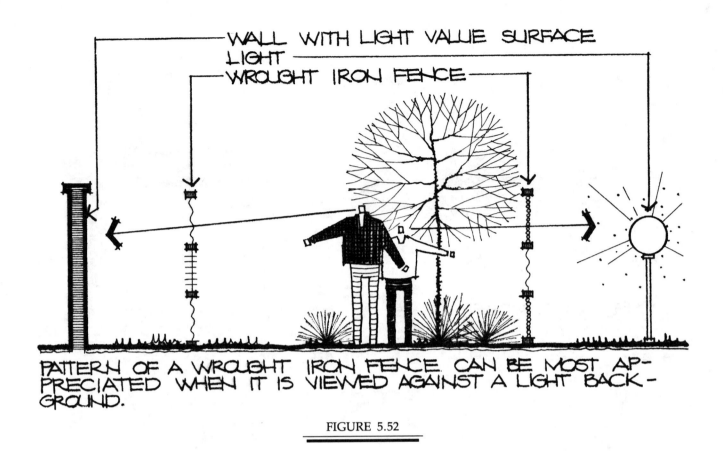

WALL WITH LIGHT VALUE SURFACE
LIGHT
WROUGHT IRON FENCE

PATTERN OF A WROUGHT IRON FENCE CAN BE MOST AP-
PRECIATED WHEN IT IS VIEWED AGAINST A LIGHT BACK-
GROUND.

FIGURE 5.52

exterior environment is to serve as a clean, dry, sta-ble surface on which to sit. Besides this, elements of seating may act as objects that aid one to rest or wait, converse, observe, and study or eat, either sin-gly or collectively.

Rest or Wait. In any urban or rural situation where extensive walking or athletic activity is anticipated, seating should be provided so people can get off their feet and rest. For example, a bench or other seating element provides a welcome opportunity to rest and catch one's breath when located along a hiking trail or city street where hard pavement read-ily causes sore feet. Another similar use of seating occurs just outside a building where a place to sit allows a person to rest from activities and duties in-side. A short breath of fresh air gained outside can sometimes do wonders to revive one's energy. Benches, sitting walls, or planters located adjacent to a major building entrance may further provide a convenient place to sit and wait for an acquaintance to arrive or leave the building. Such a convenient

meeting place can be reinforced by an element upon which to sit and rest.

Converse. Besides being a place to rest or wait, seat-ing may also be a location for conversation and dis-cussion among a small group of people. While con-versation can occur on seating at any location or arrangement, some designs are more conducive to it than others. Seating arranged in a small cluster al-lowing people to face one another, as shown in Fig-ure 5.53, encourages conversation more than a linear arrangement where a person must turn awkwardly to the side to talk. Consequently, a single park bench or a group of them placed side by side along a walk is not the ideal layout for conversation. Fur-thermore, conversation is easier in locations that are quiet and afford some degree of privacy. This is not to say, however, that a space must be totally isolated or enclosed in order for conversation to occur.

Observe. Many people enjoy sitting down simply to watch the world go by. In fact, one of the most in-

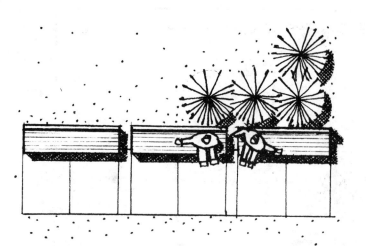

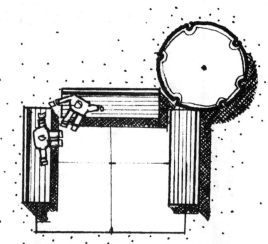

A LINEAR ARRANGEMENT IS NOT CONDUCIVE FOR FACING ANOTHER PERSON & DISCOURAGES CONVERSATION.

A "U" SHAPE ARRANGEMENT ALLOWS PEOPLE TO FACE ONE ANOTHER & ENCOURAGES CONVERSATION.

FIGURE 5.53

teresting activities for some individuals is to observe other people. For seating to be used in this manner, it should be installed near, but not directly in, an area of major activity. As an example, seating situated along a major walk, on a busy corner, or overlooking a plaza would be ideal for observing others. Moreover, observation is enhanced if the seating is

placed on a slightly higher elevation than the activity area permitting those sitting down a good vantage point.

Study or Eat. Seating offers convenience for studying and eating. Seating for studying is of course most appropriate on a campus or other academic

FIGURE 5.54

OFTEN A PERSON FEELS UNCOMFORTABLE SITTING IN A LOCATION WHERE OTHERS CAN LOOK AT HIM FROM BEHIND.

SEAT LOCATED WITH A WALL IN THE BACKGROUND PROVIDES A PERSON WITH A SENSE OF SECURITY.

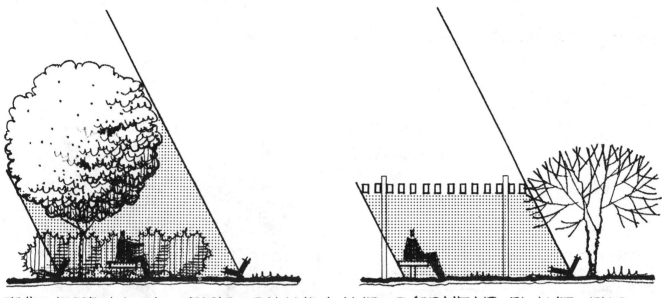

THE BOTTOM OF TREE CANOPY AND OVERHEAD PLANE PRO-
VIDE SCALE AND SHADE FOR A SEATING AREA.

FIGURE 5.55

setting where some students prefer to sit on benches to read, as opposed to lying on the grass or propping up against a tree. Seating furnishes a dry surface on which to place extra books and papers and supplies a spot to eat a brown bag lunch or takeout food purchase. Both studying and eating can be aided if tables are furnished with the seating.

There are several design and location considerations for all seating regardless of which function it is to accommodate. One suggestion, as stated above, is to place seating to the side of major activity or circulation rather than directly in it. A person can feel uncomfortable when surrounded by commotion. It is best to tuck seating into a protected corner or simply to the edge of an activity area. Likewise, people may tend to feel more at ease if the seating is placed against some other element such as a wall or mass of plant material, as suggested in Figure 5.54. Although this is not always possible or even desirable, some individuals feel ill at ease when their back is turned to an open space or when they feel they are in a "fishbowl."

Another desirable, though not always feasible, characteristic of a seating area is a location beneath a shade tree or other overhead plane. The canopy of the tree provides a comfortable scale by limiting the

height of the space while also furnishing shade, as shown in Figure 5.55. However, some seating might still be placed in a more open area of the site so that users can choose from either sunny or shady conditions. There are those days of the year when it is indeed enjoyable to sit in the sun. Although in the temperate zone people do not use outdoor seating as much in late fall, winter, and early spring as in summer, climatic factors of this time of year should still be appraised. Seating is used more in these off-seasons if it is placed on the southern side of the building where it can benefit from the warmth of the sun. In addition, seating should be protected from the chilling effects of the winter wind. To be used during fall, winter, and spring, seating should not be located on the northern side of a building or in a wind corridor. The ideal conditions for the location of seating in terms of microclimate are illustrated in Figure 5.56.

From a visual and aesthetic standpoint, seating should appear as a thoughtful, integrated element of the total design. The design, location, and coordination of seating with other elements should be given as much attention as other aspects of the design. Unfortunately, seating is sometimes not thought about until late in the development of a de-

NW WINTER WIND ———————→

TALL EVERGREEN SHRUBS
BLOCK NW WINTER WIND

LARGE TREE PROVIDES
AFTERNOON SHADE
SEATING

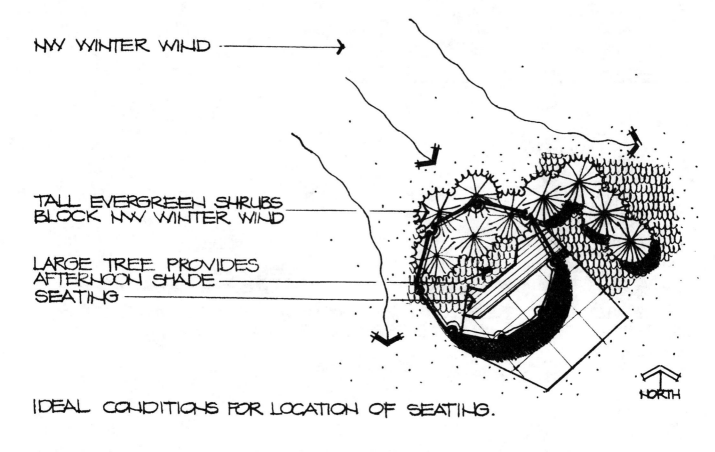

NORTH

IDEAL CONDITIONS FOR LOCATION OF SEATING.

FIGURE 5.56

FIGURE 5.57

UNDESIRABLE : SEATING IS
NOT INTEGRATED WITH OTHER
FORMS, IT IS AN "ADD-ON."

DESIRABLE : SEATING IS AN
INTEGRAL ELEMENT IN THE
OVERALL DESIGN.

FIGURE 5.58

sign. A notable offender is the park bench that is ordered from a catalog and then randomly placed in the design. This solution, while often necessitated by budget constraints, is usually an afterthought that detracts from the overall design. The form of the seating should be coordinated with other elements and shapes in the design so that it properly fits in with them. For example, a curved seat should be placed in a curvilinear design, an angular seat in

an angular design layout, and so on (Figure 5.57). Such ideal solutions are expensive because they require on-site, custom construction. In coordinating the form of seating with other aspects of a design, it may be advisable in some instances to have the seating function as a low wall around a space, as in Figure 5.58. Here, the bench also serves as a railing at the water's edge in Sausalito, California.

One approach to seating that differs from the

FIGURE 5.59

MODULAR SEATING: SAME ELEMENT REPEATED THROUGHOUT SPACE

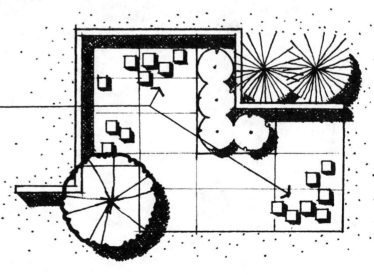

MODULAR SEATING.

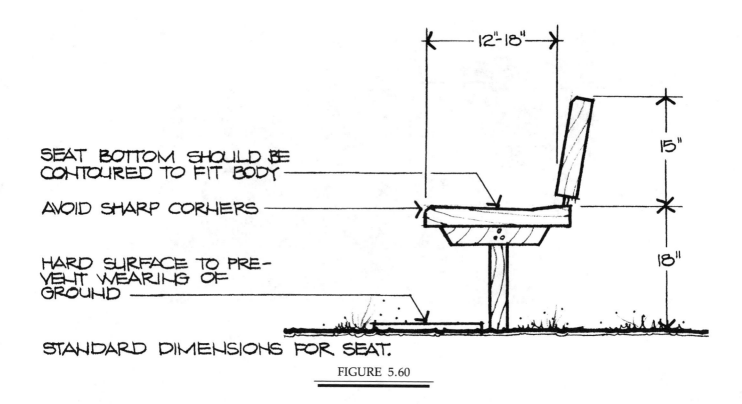

SEAT BOTTOM SHOULD BE
CONTOURED TO FIT BODY

AVOID SHARP CORNERS

HARD SURFACE TO PRE-
VENT WEARING OF
GROUND

STANDARD DIMENSIONS FOR SEAT.

FIGURE 5.60

FIGURE 5.61

common linear seat or cluster of seats is modular seating. This type of seating utilizes the same unit seat repeated throughout the seating area in an organic arrangement, as shown in Figure 5.59. A modular seating layout permits individual seating, group seating, conversation, and orientation in a direction selected by each individual user. One problem of conventional benches is that they force a person to sit facing a certain predetermined direction. Modular seating, on the other hand, furnishes a choice of directions. More options can be established in a modular seating cluster if the height of the individual seats varies or if tablelike surfaces are included in the design. Even though modular seating has a number of advantages, it is not appropriate everywhere because of its character and its taking up a large area of space.

A critical factor in designing seating is to utilize correct dimensions so that each seat will be comfortable. The average seat should be between 18 (46cm) and 20 in (51cm) above ground level for adults and 12 (30.5cm) to 18 in (46cm) wide, as shown in Figure 5.60.[13] If the seat is to have a back, it should extend

---

[13]The American Society of Landscape Architects' Foundation, *Barrier-Free Site Design*, pp. 59–60.

above 15 in (38cm) above the height of the seat surface. Both the seat surface and the seat back should be subtly contoured to fit the shape of the body. In some cases the designer may want to build armrests into the seat 6 (15cm) to 9 in (23cm) above the seat surface. Underneath the seat surface enough space should be left to allow legs and feet to be placed somewhat below the seat. Thus all seat legs or other structural support should be recessed at least 3 (7.5cm) to 6 in (15cm) in back of the front edge of the seat. If the seat is not to be placed on pavement, a hard surface or gravel should still be placed directly below the seat to prevent dirt or mud patches that form from repeated wear of the area.

Seating can be constructed out of most any material, but wood is generally an appropriate material for the seat surface because of its warm, personal character and its availability. A simply designed wood bench is shown in Figure 5.61. Stone, brick, and concrete can also be employed for the seat surface but have the disadvantage of becoming unbearably hot when exposed to summer sun and winter cold. Stone, brick, and concrete also do not dry readily after a rain if they are improperly pitched. All these materials can be detailed and assembled in a variety of ways to fit the desired character of the design context.

Summary

Steps, ramps, walls, fences, and seating are elements that enhance the spatial quality and livability of the outdoor environment. In the context of larger, more dominant elements such as landform, plant materials, and buildings, site structures can be thought of as smaller-scale detail elements that reinforce and complement the more substantial aspects of the outdoor environment. Steps and ramps facilitate movement from one ground elevation to another, walls and fences subdivide space and provide structural detail, and seating makes outdoor spaces seem more human by furnishing places to rest and observe. The sensitive use of site structures makes the landscape more inhabitable and responsive to human needs.

6

Water

Water is yet another physical design element used by landscape architects in the design and management of the exterior environment. Water is a highly varied design element and may take on such diverse forms as flat, quiet pools, falling water, and jets of water. Water may be used in the landscape as a purely aesthetic element or it may be employed for such utilitarian functions as cooling the air, buffering sound, irrigating the soil, or providing a means of recreation. This chapter discusses the unique characteristics of water, visual and other functions of water in the outdoor environment, and the different forms in which water may be used in landscape architectural design.

Water has a number of unique, distinguishing qualities compared with the other design elements discussed in previous chapters. Water is one of the most magnetizing and compelling of all design elements. Few people can ignore or fail to react to its presence in the outdoor environment. Humans seem to be instinctively drawn toward water for both utilitarian and visual reasons. From a very practical viewpoint, people need water for survival just as they require air, food, and shelter. Perhaps the desert oasis best epitomizes the essential role water plays in sustaining life. It is easy to forget this basic human need because modern technology has made water so readily available in most industrialized nations of the world. Yet from an historical perspective, many early cities and villages in this country, as well as in others, were originally settled at the edge of a river, stream, lake, spring, or well out of necessity. Boston, New York, Albany, Philadelphia, Pittsburgh, and Baltimore in the east, and Chicago, Detroit, St. Louis, and Cincinnati in the Midwest are all cities that have a strong historic link to water. For our ancestors living in these communities, water was not only a necessary commodity for survival but also provided a source of food, transportation, and recreation. Even today we are reminded of water's critical role by examining its availability in many of the western and southwestern states of this country. In some urban areas, such as Tucson, Arizona, future growth will be directly influenced by water availability.

Besides this need to be near water to support life, people are emotionally lured toward water for its sight, sound, and recreational uses. Water in most any condition (unless polluted) holds a special visual appeal magnetizing people to it. This is best indicated by the almost complete development of most shorelines and the related high real estate value of shoreline property. As of the late 1960s, over one-third of the population in the United States lived in coastal counties, with the growth rate within one mile of shorelines increasing at more than three times the national rate.[1] For some people, this desire to live at the water's edge outweighs the potential hazards such as flooding and wave damage. Each year there is extensive property damage and loss of life resulting from a careless wish to be near a body of water. In fact, 35 million people or more in this country are at major risk from flooding.[2]

In addition to simply being attracted to water, people have a strong innate temptation to interact with water. Humans have a deep desire to touch and feel water or even become totally immersed in it for fun and recreation. This urge is perhaps most strongly exhibited by small children who instinctively enjoy playing with water. Without understanding the potential dangers of water, children delight in touching and manipulating it. Long periods of time can be spent splashing water about or interacting with it. Even most adults have a difficult time walking up to the edge of a body of water without touching it. Sooner or later, a hand or foot reaches out to test the water and perhaps splash it about.

Water also has a therapeutic effect. It can be hypnotic in capturing and holding the senses of sight and sound. Watching and listening to water along the shore of a lake, river, or stream can carry a person's awareness away from the reality of the moment to a more restful and peaceful state of mind. The rhythmic repetition of waves washing ashore or the continuous gurgle of a brook can be soothing and calming. So effective is the sound of water on a person's mood that the sound of ocean waves was produced for commercial sale on a record album in the early 1970s. The cut was titled "The Psychologically Ultimate Seashore"[3] and was supposed to fill a listener's living room with the tranquilizing sound of waves along a seashore.

Besides these characteristics, water also has a definite romantic quality. Over time, numerous songs, poems, novels, and motion pictures have been based on a romantic theme of water either as the primary setting or as an essential element of the plot. "La Mer" by Debussy and "South Pacific" by Rodgers and Hammerstein are musical compositions where water plays a central role in the score. And how many photographs or postcards have you seen where water provides a dramatic setting for a sunset or an embracing couple? Even advertisers have attempted to benefit from the romantic appeal of water by showing their product (cars, shampoo, soft drinks, etc.) against a background of a lake or ocean. Water possesses an undeniable emotional attraction for people, with numerous implications as to how, when, and where it is used in the design of exterior spaces.

General Characteristics

Water possesses several physical properties that influence the purpose and method by which it can be used in landscape architectural design.

Plasticity. Water is obviously a liquid (except when frozen), having no shape unto itself. Its form is determined by the characteristics of its container. Thus the same volume of water can have an infinite number of different qualities, all depending on the size, color, texture, location, and so forth of the container. In a sense, a person designs with water by designing the container. Consequently, to create a certain water characteristic, one must first directly design the type of container that will in turn produce the desired result with the water. Because water is a highly plastic element, its particular form and appearance in any given situation is the direct result of the influence of gravity. For instance, flowing water is attempting to reach a point of stability with gravity while still water expresses an equilibrium with gravity.

---

[1]Water Resources Council, *The Nation's Water Resources* (Washington, D.C.: The First National Assessment of Water Resources Council, 1968).

[2]Robert Kales, "Planning for Hazards," *Landscape Architecture* 65 (2) 165 (April 1975).

[3]"The Psychologically Ultimate Seashore," *Environments; New Concepts in Stereo*—Disc 1 (Atlantic Recording Corporation, NY).

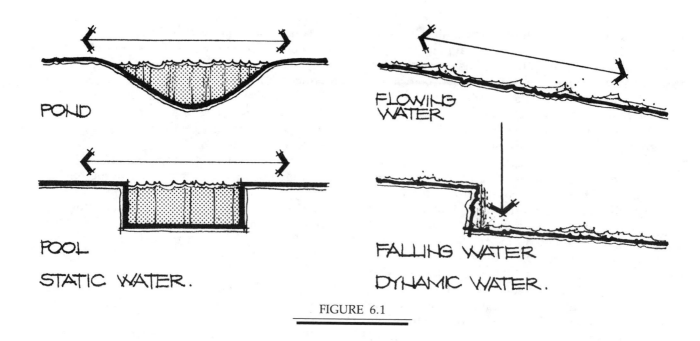

FIGURE 6.1

Motion. As just alluded to, water may be classified into two general categories according to its motion: static (quiet, nonmoving) or dynamic (moving, changing). These two types are graphically expressed in Figure 6.1.

Static water. Static, quiet water is found in lakes, ponds, pools, or gently flowing rivers. It is peaceful, relaxing, and mellow in character with a soothing effect on human emotions. Static water is visually placid, and this quality may allow and encourage the mind to think in an uninterrupted manner. Again, this type of water expresses a balance and equilibrium with the force of gravity. Historically, the static body of water was an important element in both the French Renaissance gardens of the seventeenth century and the English landscape gardens of the eighteenth century. Although their containing form varied, the static water in both these styles was used as a neutral, reflective element encouraging contemplation. More will be said later in this chapter about other potential design uses of static water in the outdoor environment.

Dynamic water. The second general type of water according to its motion is moving, flowing, or falling water such as is found in rivers and streams or cascading down waterfalls. Jets of water may also be classified as another type of dynamic water. This type of water has opposite characteristics from those of static water. Dynamic water is energetic and emotionally stimulating. It easily captures the attention of the eye and may be accompanied by sound emitted through the motion of the water. Dynamic water has the potential of being exciting and dramatic as a result of its sound and its interaction with color and light. Dynamic water is not, but is attempting to be, at balance with gravity. The greater the imbalance with gravity, the faster the movement of dynamic water. Historically, dynamic water was an important element in the Italian Renaissance gardens in the sixteenth century and at Versailles in the form of water jets. Dynamic water has numerous possible uses in design but is most easily used as an attractive point of interest. Other possible uses of dynamic water are outlined in later sections of this chapter.

Sound. As already mentioned, another characteristic of water is its ability to emit sound when it is in motion or when it abruptly strikes a fixed object or surface. Depending on the amount of movement and volume of water involved, numerous possible sounds can be produced that complement and enhance the visual aspects of an outdoor space. Moreover, water sound can be used to influence human emotions; it may calm and soothe on the one hand or excite and inspire on the other. The ceaseless, rhythmic motion of waves against a shoreline may be quiet and peaceful, while the roar of a waterfall may be motivating. Some of the common sounds

FIGURE 6.2

created by water include trickle, dribble, bubble, gurgle, roar, gush, splash, and babble.

Reflectivity. Another significant characteristic of water is its ability both literally and figuratively to reflect its environmental setting. In a quiet, static state, water can function as a mirror, repeating an image of its surroundings (land, vegetation, buildings, sky, people, etc.) on the base plane. Under ideal conditions, when the surface of the water is glass-smooth, the reflected image may be so precise as to make the distinction between it and reality difficult to decipher, as in Figure 6.2. This photograph gives only one clue as to which is the actual side of the picture and which the reflected. When the water surface becomes ruffled by a breeze or other disturbance, it loses the exact detail of the reflection. Instead, the image now takes on a quality of an impressionistic or abstract painting with forms and color mottled, but still understandable.

In addition to actually reflecting the visual image of its adjoining environment, a body of water figuratively reflects the characteristics of its container and surroundings by responding to the following factors.

Slope (gravity). As previously stated, water in the form of a river or a stream directly responds to the

degree of slope on which it is located. Any slope causes water to move, with its speed intensifying as slope steepness increases. With higher rates of movement, the visual attraction of water as well as the sound produced become greater. Moving water is a potential source of energy as well as a force of erosion.

Container shape and size. Because of its fluid state, a given volume of water expands outward until it is stopped and contained by an upward slope or vertical wall. Water takes on the shape of any container in which it is placed. For example, the edge traced by a body of water is irregular when the containing edges push inward and outward in a random pattern. Or the water outline is straight when the containing edge is a smooth plane. The size of the container influences all water but has a noticeable effect on the characteristics of flowing water. For instance, a constant volume of flowing water can be rather placid in a wide container or channel but quite turbulent when funneled through a narrower channel because of the increased resistance, as suggested in Figure 6.3.

Container roughness. The material and texture of the containing surfaces have an influence on the appearance and movement of water too. A given vol-

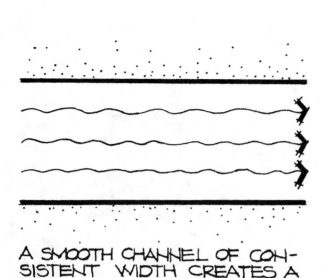

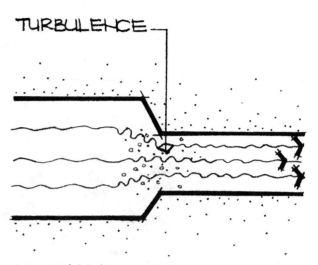

A SMOOTH CHANNEL OF CON-
SISTENT WIDTH CREATES A
SMOOTH, CALM FLOW.

AS CHANNEL WIDTH DECREAS-
ES AT A GIVEN POINT, TURBU-
LENCES INCREASES.

FIGURE 6.3

ume of water flowing through a channel of a fixed size moves easily and quietly when the channel sides and bottom are smooth and free of obstacles. Yet the same volume of water will flow in a slower, more turbulent manner in the same channel size when the container surface is rougher and more highly textured. This fact is often one of the reasons cited for the engineered "channelization" of a meandering brook to allow the water to move faster and "more efficiently." Unfortunately, natural animal and fish habitats are lost, infiltration of water into the ground is diminished, and erosion is increased from channelization.

Temperature. As is well known, water often has a dramatic change from a liquid to a solid state because of seasonal temperature changes between summer and winter. This also creates a notable alteration in the appearance of water as well. A quiet, static body of water that may appear dark while in a fluid state will appear light and glazed when frozen. Likewise, moving water often produces sculptural and unique formations as it freezes. Such natural beauty is even more stunning as it interacts with sunlight.

Wind. Wind, as mentioned earlier, is still another environmental factor governing the character of water. The surface of a flat water body may vary from a mirrorlike plane to a stormy tumult of white-capped waves, with many variations in between depending on the presence and severity of wind. In fact, the surface texture of a flat, nonmoving water body can be considered a direct result of wind.

Light. Light interacts with water to influence its visual character and mood. Water can vary from a glittering and sparkling element when moving or falling to a sullen black mass when in a quiet state under a dark sky. Under certain conditions water can take on the qualities of fine cut glassware or transparent plastic that twinkles and radiates arrows of reflected light. Under other conditions water may appear as a solid dark mass absorbing much of the light that strikes it. Consequently, numerous emotional responses from joyous and cheerful to gloomy and funereal can be evoked by water as a result of the interaction of water with light.

Several conclusions can be drawn from the influence of the factors cited above on water. First, water by itself has no distinct design properties other than that it is a liquid.[4] Instead, all the visible character-

[4]E. Byron McCulley, "Water—Pools and Fountains," in *Handbook of Landscape Architectural Construction*, Jot D. Carpenter, ed. (McLean, Virginia: The Landscape Architecture Foundation, Inc., 1976) p. 480.

istics of water are directly dependent on exterior factors (just outlined) that bear on and affect it. Water must depend on its environmental context for its particular qualities. Change the forces in the environmental setting and you also alter the characteristics of water in that setting. Thus we may say water is both literally and figuratively reflective of its surroundings.

A second conclusion from the impact of the many influencing factors on water is that it is a highly varied and flexible design element. It has no constant and is not apt to be exactly the same from one time to another. Again, it changes according to external influences affecting it. Therefore water can provide another dimension of interest in a design because of its ability to change outside the control of the designer. The challenge for the designer is to understand sufficiently the factors that influence water's appearance to be able to manipulate them properly to create the desired visual effect.

General Uses of Water

Water has numerous possible functions in the design and maintenance of exterior spaces. Some uses relate directly to the visual aspects of a design, while others pertain to more utilitarian requirements. Nonaesthetic functions of water are outlined in this section; visual uses of water in design are discussed in a later section.

Consumption. Water is of course used for both human and animal consumption. Although this use may not pertain to all designs, certain athletic fields, campgrounds, parks, and so on require water as an essential consumable element to support the facility. With this need, the water source, method of transport, and means for making it available to the user become critical design decisions.

Irrigation. A common utilitarian use of water is irrigation of field crops, lawns and gardens, park space, and the like. For dry regions of the country like California, Arizona, New Mexico, and Colorado, irrigation is essential to support a lush growth of plants. Irrigation is also a means for reducing maintenance because a program of fertilization can be carried on through liquid solvents in the irrigation system at much less time and cost than conventional methods. An irrigated site including a lawn area can withstand heavier use than a nonirrigated site because grass and other plant material can be maintained in a much more healthy condition when watered.

There are three general types of irrigation: (1) spray irrigation, (2) flood irrigation, and (3) drip irrigation. Spray irrigation, the most common type, is accomplished by spraying an area from fixed spray heads located strategically throughout the area of irrigation. The pipes needed to support this type of system are permanently located below ground. As the name implies, flood irrigation is accomplished by literally flooding an area of ground with one to two inches of water. To flood irrigate, the area to be irrigated must be contained with slopes or low berms. Drip irrigation, the third form, provides water to a plant by a slow, continuous drip of water from plastic tubing located on the ground's surface. Drip irrigation is best used for individual locations, such as single plants, rather than for broad areas such as lawns. Compared with the other two types of irrigation, drip irrigation is the most efficient and least wasteful of water.

Climate Control. Water may be used in the outdoor environment to modify air and ground surface temperatures. It is well known that a large body of water at the regional scale can modify air temperatures in the surrounding land areas. Large bodies of water warm up and cool off slowly so that they are normally cooler in the summer and warmer in the winter than adjacent areas of land. This causes local temperatures of land next to large water bodies to be different from that of the general region. For instance, this phenomenon raises the average January temperature about 5 degrees F. in the Great Lakes region. Conversely, the average July temperature of this same area is decreased about 3 degrees F. owing to the lakes.[5] In terms of daily temperature variations, breezes will move from the water body onto the land during the day with a resulting cooling effect when the land heats up in comparison with the water. Such a breeze can produce as much as a 10 degree F. drop in air temperature.[6]

Water at a smaller site scale can fulfill similar functions. Evaporation of moisture from a surface will lower the temperature of that surface and in turn the air temperature in its vicinity. Thus if water is present in a pool or fountain, or is constantly sprayed over a surface, the surrounding air temper-

---

[5]Helmut Landsberg, "Climate and Planning of Settlements," Convention Symposium I, *Urban and Regional Planning*, The American Institute of Architects, Washington, D.C., May 1950. Cited by Victor Olgyag, *Design with Climate; A Bioclimatic Approach to Architectural Regionalism* (Princeton, N.J.: Princeton University Press, 1963), p. 51.

[6]Victor Olgyay, *Design With Climate*, p. 51.

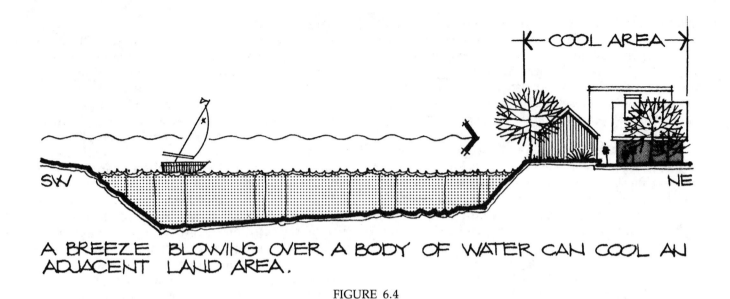

A BREEZE BLOWING OVER A BODY OF WATER CAN COOL AN ADJACENT LAND AREA.

FIGURE 6.4

ature will be lower than if water were lacking. The cooling effect of water can be enhanced if wind is directed over and through an area of water into an activity space where people are present, as shown in Figure 6.4. Spanish Moorish gardens such as at Alhambra used this principle as a method of air-conditioning both their indoor and outdoor spaces.

Sound Control. Water may be used in outdoor spaces as a sound buffer, especially in urban environments where there is apt to be high noise levels from cars, people, and industry. In these circumstances, sound generated from falling or moving water can begin to mask these noises in the immediate area of the water to create a more peaceful atmo-

FIGURE 6.5

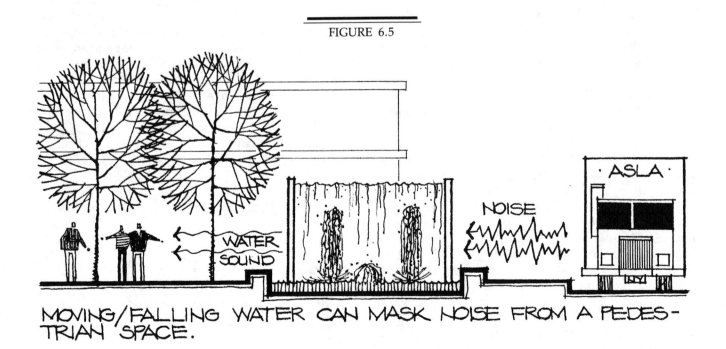

MOVING/FALLING WATER CAN MASK NOISE FROM A PEDESTRIAN SPACE.

sphere, as suggested in Figure 6.5. One example of water used partially for this function is in Paley Park in New York City. A wall of falling water in this minipark located in midtown Manhattan generates a loud sound that conceals the traffic noise of the street for visitors standing or sitting in the park. Because of this sound buffer, one easily forgets the commotion of the city in the relaxing background. Other examples of falling water that disguise noise in urban settings are located in Freeway Park in Seattle, Washington, designed by Lawrence Halprin, and in Robson Square in Vancouver, British Columbia, designed by Robert Zinser of Arthur Erickson Architects (Figure 6.26).

Recreation. Another popular use of water in the landscape is for recreation. Water can be used for swimming, fishing, boating, scuba diving, sailing, water skiing, and ice skating. These recreational uses of water account for intense use of lakes, rivers, streams, and oceans throughout the country. Landscape architects become involved in the planning and design of all types of water recreational facilities, from private backyard pools to regional lakes and ocean fronts. In addition to the planning and design of the body of water itself, the landscape architect is apt to participate in the design of associated support facilities such as bathhouses, marinas, picnic areas, and lodges. Related to the development of a water body for recreational use is the concern for its wise use and preservation. Recreational uses of water are proper and enjoyable only as long as the water resource is treated with care and sensitive management.

Visual Uses of Water

Water can be used in the outdoor environment for a number of visual functions in addition to the more general uses just outlined. The process for integrating water in the landscape for visual uses should be similar to that employed for the other design elements. That is, the landscape architect should first decide what functions water is to fulfill in an outdoor space and subsequently analyze what type and character of water meets these desired functions. This procedure is critical because of the potentially highly varied character of water, which permits infinite possible visual uses. Some of the more common visual functions of water based on its type of motion and character are described below.

Flat, Static Water. Water can be used in the outdoor environment as a flat, quiet water body in the form of either a pool or a pond depending on the shape and character of the container.[7]

Pool. "Pool" is a term used for a body of water of any size placed in a hard, well-defined constructed container.[8] A pool is apt to be geometric in shape but is not limited to symmetrical or pure geometric forms (circle, square, triangle, trapezoid, etc.). Historically, examples of pools of water can be found in the Court of Myrtles at Alhambra, at the Taj Mahal, in the gardens of Vaux-le-Vicomte, and in the Parterre D'Eau (Water Parterre) at Versailles. More contemporary examples of pools include the expanse of quiet water at the Christian Science Headquarters in Boston and the long, narrow basin at Las Arboledas, Mexico, designed by Luis Barragan.

The exact shape of a pool used in a design depends on the setting and other design determinants of form and character. The important factor is that a pool appears constructed, not natural or soft, as illustrated in Figure 6.6. Consequently, a pool is most appropriate in urban spaces where hard planes and edges predominate or in other circumstances where an expression of humans controlling nature is appropriate. Pools may be used in the outdoor environment for the following purposes.

A pool of quiet, still water may be used as a plane of reflection for the sky and/or nearby elements such as buildings, trees, sculpture, and people. By means of the reflected image, a person is able to see these other elements in a new and fascinating way that is possible only by looking into the plane of water, as in Figure 6.7. The viewer is provided with a new point of perspective.

Reflecting pools also provide planes of either light value or dark value, depending on the sky condition, the surface of the container itself, and the location of the viewer. On a light, sunny day, for instance, a reflective pool is apt to appear bright and shiny in contrast to dark areas of lawn or pavement. These shimmering pool surfaces in turn create a light, weightless quality in opposition to the heavy massiveness of other areas of ground plane. At times this effect can give the feeling that there are holes or voids in the solid mass of the earth.

---

[7] E. Byron McCultey, "Water—Pools and Fountains," in *Handbook of Landscape Architectural Construction*, Jot D. Carpenter, ed. (McLean, Virginia: The Landscape Architecture Foundation, 1976), p. 481.
[8] Ibid.

POOLS ARE STATIC BODIES OF WATER IN HARD, GEOMETRIC FORMS.

FIGURE 6.6

To maximize the reflective ability, several factors must be considered. First, the size and location of the pool should be studied with respect to the viewer's position(s) and the object(s) to be reflected. For a single object, the reflective pool should be placed in front of the object to be reflected, between the

object and the viewer (Figure 6.8). The length and width will then depend on the size of the object itself and the amount of it that one wishes to mirror. The required dimensions should be studied by means of section drawings and by applying the principle that the angle at which the sight line strikes the

FIGURE 6.7

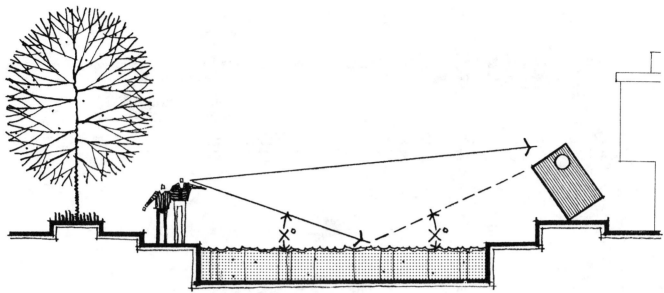

POOLS USED FOR REFLECTION SHOULD BE PLACED BETWEEN
VIEWER AND OBJECT TO BE REFLECTED.

FIGURE 6.8

FIGURE 6.9

A PERSPECTIVE CAN BE USED TO STUDY THE IMAGE IN A POOL
OF WATER.

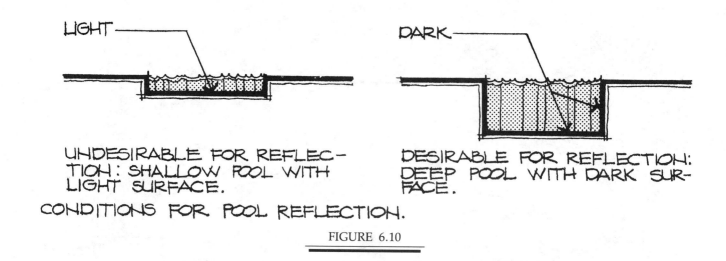

UNDESIRABLE FOR REFLEC-
TION: SHALLOW POOL WITH
LIGHT SURFACE.

DESIRABLE FOR REFLECTION:
DEEP POOL WITH DARK SUR-
FACE.

CONDITIONS FOR POOL REFLECTION.

FIGURE 6.10

water surface is the same as the angle of reflection. Perspectives should also be employed, as in Figure 6.9.

Another consideration is the depth of the pool and the tone of its containing surfaces. To enhance reflection, the surface of the pool should appear as dark as possible. This can be accomplished by increasing the depth of the pool and/or making the containing surface dark in value. An effective means for accomplishing the latter is to paint the inside

pool walls black or dark blue. As the pool becomes more shallow and/or the containing surface becomes lighter in value, perception of reflected images on the water surface becomes more difficult, as indicated in Figure 6.10.

Still other factors that affect reflectivity are the level of the water surface in the pool and the character of the water surface itself. To provide maximum reflectivity, the water level should be relatively high in the pool. This establishes maximum expo-

FIGURE 6.11

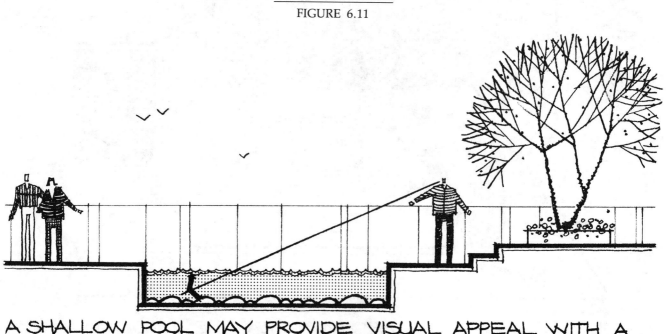

A SHALLOW POOL MAY PROVIDE VISUAL APPEAL WITH A
TEXTURED AND PATTERNED BOTTOM.

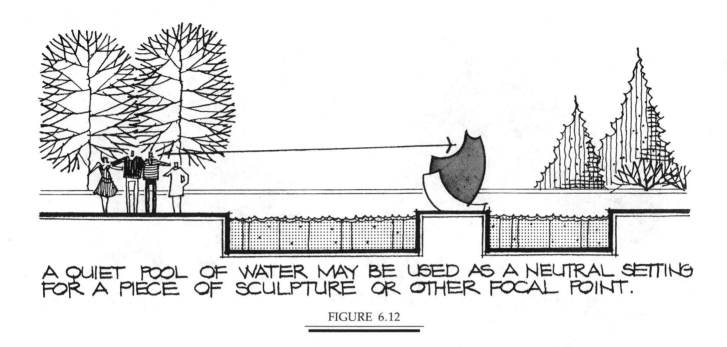

A QUIET POOL OF WATER MAY BE USED AS A NEUTRAL SETTING FOR A PIECE OF SCULPTURE OR OTHER FOCAL POINT.

FIGURE 6.12

sure of the water surface to the surroundings and cuts down on the amount of shadows cast by the pool sides. The water surface of a reflecting pool should be kept free of movement and clear of obstacles like algae or debris that would interfere with reflection. And last, a suggestion is to keep the shape of a reflecting pool rather simple to prevent it from visually competing with the reflection in the water's surface.

If a pool of water is not to function as a reflective body, it may take on special visual quality based on the treatment of its containing surface. The containing surfaces, particularly the pool bottom, can be designed with appealing patterns through the use of attractive materials, paint, and texture, as suggested in Figures 6.11 and 6.40. The bottom of the pool at the base of the large fountain jet in Point Park, Pittsburgh, for instance, contains a repeating "fish scale" pattern created by river stones (Figure 4.31). Painted stripes and designs are a unique way to create additional interest along the bottom and sides of a residential swimming pool. All the designs on the bottoms and sides of a pool acquire another dimension of visual quality when they interact with the pool water, its movement, and light filtering down through the water. The image of the patterns becomes blurred and distorted as the result of surface movement caused by wind or other disturbances.

Weird and twisted kaleidoscopic images of the original pattern often ensue under these circumstances.

A static pool of water can be used as both a neutral background and foreground to other elements and focal points in the outdoor environment, as in Figure 6.12. Like areas of lawn, ground cover, or pavement, a quiet surface of water can provide an unobtrusive setting for a piece of sculpture, a building, a unique tree, or a fountain jet. And in doing this, the water surface is able to reflect an image of the central element, thereby accentuating its sight as well as providing a different visual experience of the element, as shown in Figure 6.7. As suggested previously, the shape and appearance of a pool that is to fulfill this purpose should be unobtrusive in order not to take attention away from the object being visually supported.

Pond. The second general type of flat, static water is the pond, which differs from a pool by being designed to appear natural or seminatural.[9] Nevertheless, a pond may be either constructed or natural to the site. The shape of a pond is typically free-form or curvilinear, as shown in Figure 6.13, and consequently is most appropriately located in rural or

[9]Ibid, p. 482.

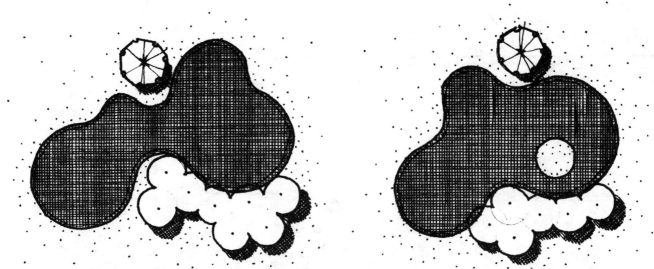

PONDS ARE STATIC BODIES OF WATER IN SOFT, CURVILINEAR OR NATURALISTIC FORMS.

FIGURE 6.13

FIGURE 6.14

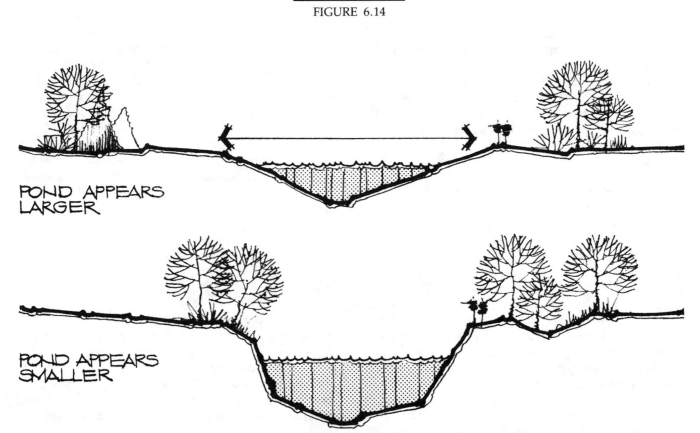

POND APPEARS LARGER

POND APPEARS SMALLER

STEEPNESS OF SLOPES SURROUNDING A POND INFLUENCES THE PERCEPTION OF SIZE.

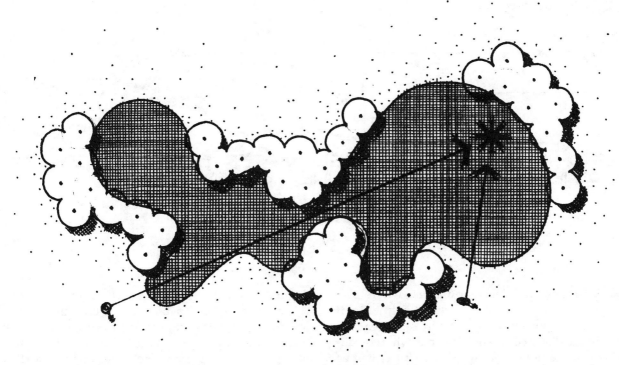

A POND MAY VISUALLY LINK AND UNIFY THE LANDSCAPE BY "RE-CALL" OF VIEWS FROM DIFFERENT VANTAGE POINTS; A SENSE OF MYSTERY MAY ALSO BE CREATED WHEN ENTIRE POND CANNOT BE SEEN FROM ANY ONE POINT.

FIGURE 6.15

parklike settings. A pond of a given size can be made to seem larger if the containing slopes are gentle, or smaller if the containing slopes are steeper, as shown in Figure 6.14. In essence, the sides of a pond act as spatial edges affecting perception and views. A pond may accomplish all the functions previously outlined for pools in addition to the following.

A pond may be used to create a feeling of repose and tranquility in an outdoor space. A pond is more effective in doing this than a pool because of the pond's soft, peaceful forms. When combined with visually rounded and flowing landform and with naturalistic plantings typical in the English landscape gardens such as those found at Stourhead or Blenheim, ponds are able to reinforce the bucolic feeling of undisturbed serenity.

Closely associated with a pond's feeling of repose is its ability to serve as a reference plane in the landscape. Because a pond's surface is a level plane, it provides a common point throughout its layout to judge and compare relative heights of nearby landforms and tree masses. To serve this function, however, it is critical that the pond occupy the natural low area of a site. When a pond is located in an elevated position relative to other surrounding areas of the site, it acquires an uneasy feeling of tension with the lower elevations. A pond is not able to serve properly as a reference plane when situated too high in a site.

A pond may be used in the landscape to establish a unifying link between different areas of the environment, as illustrated in Figure 6.15. Water in any setting is readily noticed because of its visual contrast to other elements in the outdoor environment. Consequently, its visual strength can tie together discordant parts of a design composition and link them through its commonality. This use of a pond is especially effective when it is the dominant element or focal point of a particular portion of the landscape. The unifying function of a pond is most use-

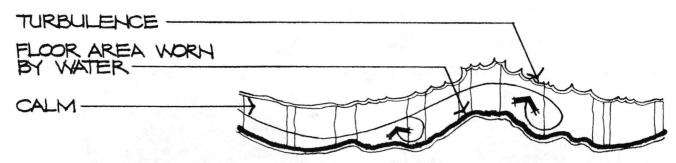

TURBULENCE

FLOOR AREA WORN
BY WATER

CALM

SECTION THROUGH STREAM BED: WATER BEHAVIOR RESPONDS
TO CONFIGURATION OF CHANNEL BOTTOM & SIDES.

FIGURE 6.16

ful in a large site covering many acres, where size alone can divide an area into unrelated segments. If a viewer sees a portion of a pond in one area and then travels a distance to another area where a different part of the pond is seen, the two areas will be unified by the viewer mentally "recalling" the view of the pond at the earlier location.

Figure 6.15 also shows another potential function of a pond that is closely associated with the one just described. The view of a pond from certain points can be used to provide intrigue and lead a person through a sequence of outdoor spaces. A sense of mystery and fascination is created when a portion of a pond or lake is seen disappearing behind a hill or clump of trees, like a path or road that winds out of view. In all these similar situations, the viewer is enticed to solve the puzzle of what is unseen and out of view by traveling to a different point where a new view is provided of that which was previously only glimpsed.

Flowing Water. The second general form that water may take in the outdoor environment is that of flowing water. "Flowing water" is any moving water confined to a well-defined channel. Flowing water results when the channel and its bottom are sloped, allowing the water to move in response to gravity. Streams, creeks, and rivers are natural examples of flowing water. It should be noted that flowing water does not include the category of falling water where water drops abruptly from a higher elevation to a lower one. Flowing water is best used in outdoor spaces as a kinetic element to express movement, direction, and energy.

As a visual element, flowing water can be de-

signed to create different effects in the outdoor environment related to the design objectives and the context of the project. The behavior and characteristics of flowing water depend on volume of water, steepness of slope, channel size, and properties of channel bottom and sides. As mentioned earlier in this chapter, a relatively smooth flow of water can be achieved by a channel, lined with a slick material, that is a constant width and depth. Such a character of flowing water is suitable for a peaceful or casual environment where the water needs to be a neutral element.

A more turbulent effect of flowing water can be created where the channel alters back and forth between wide and narrow, the channel bottom is steeply pitched, and/or the channel is composed of rough materials such as rocks and boulders. These factors, either separately or collectively, establish obstacles for water to strike and flow around with resulting turbulence, white water, and sound.

To be able to create different visual effects with agitated flowing water, it is helpful to understand some of the mechanics of water moving through a channel. For example, a "roller coaster" arrangement of alternating valleys and crests along the channel bottom forces water flowing along the channel to move down and up in correspondence to the relief, as illustrated in Figure 6.16. As the flowing water moves over each crest, it is forced to move faster to get over the obstruction. Owing to the increased speed at these points, more pressure is created here. As a result, these crests are subject to wear at a faster rate than the valleys that are less exposed to the flow. In plan, the same principles apply. Elements or points that project into the volume of mov-

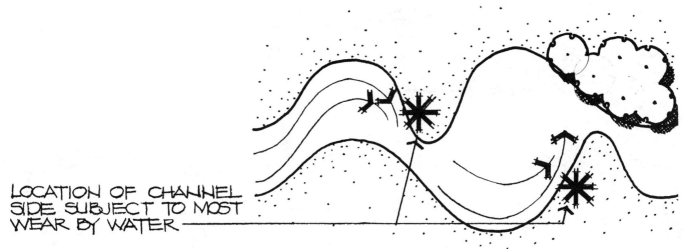

LOCATION OF CHANNEL
SIDE SUBJECT TO MOST
WEAR BY WATER ————————

OUTSIDE OF CHANNEL SUBJECT TO WEAR BY FLOWING WATER.

FIGURE 6.17

FIGURE 6.18

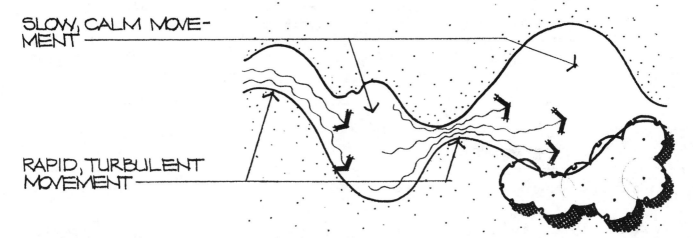

SLOW, CALM MOVE-
MENT ————————

RAPID, TURBULENT
MOVEMENT ————————

CHARACTER OF MOVING WATER PARTIALLY DEPENDS UPON
CHANNEL WIDTH.

ing water act as barriers deflecting the water away from and around them, as shown in Figure 6.17. Again, these projections receive intense wear from the moving water.

Flowing water also reacts to channel width. A constant volume of water moves more slowly in a wide channel than in a narrow one, as indicated in Figure 6.18, and turbulence is apt to result if the transition between wide and narrow channel sizes is abrupt. Roughly flowing water can furnish a boiling, white water effect that is more eye-catching and loud than smoothly flowing water. It is very likely to be a stimulating element in the landscape that attracts people to it to watch and listen. Therefore roughly flowing water is suitable in those outdoor spaces where activity and motion are desired. In natural settings, roughly flowing water is also a challenging recreational resource for canoeing or

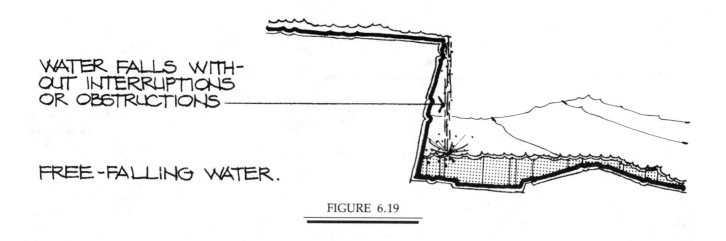

WATER FALLS WITH-
OUT INTERRUPTIONS
OR OBSTRUCTIONS

FREE-FALLING WATER.

FIGURE 6.19

rafting. The New River in West Virginia, the Yough-iogheny in Pennsylvania, and the Colorado River are known for their white water rapids.

Falling Water. The third form of water in the land-scape is falling water, which occurs when water moves over and down a sudden drop in the eleva-tion of the channel. Falling water expresses the forces of gravity even more dramatically than flow-ing water and therefore is often a noticeable focal point in the outdoor environment. There are three basic types of falling water: (1) free-fall, (2) ob-structed flow, and (3) sloped fall.

Free–fall. As the name implies, this type of falling water drops directly from one elevation to another in an uninterrupted manner, as illustrated in Figure 6.19. The character of free-falling water depends on volume, velocity, height of fall, and edge condition over which the water falls. The possible combina-

FIGURE 6.20

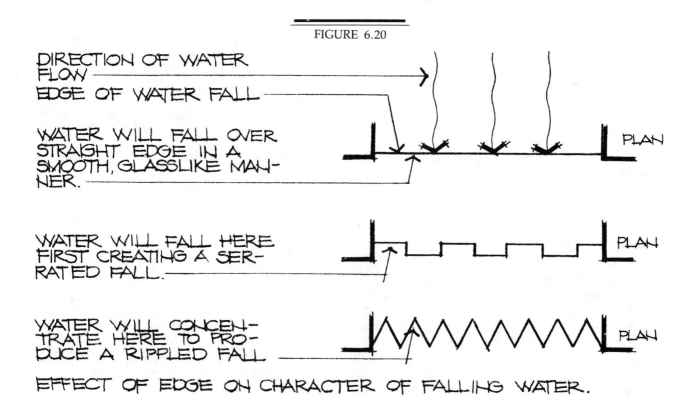

DIRECTION OF WATER
FLOW
EDGE OF WATER FALL

WATER WILL FALL OVER
STRAIGHT EDGE IN A
SMOOTH, GLASSLIKE MAN-
NER.

WATER WILL FALL HERE
FIRST CREATING A SER-
RATED FALL.

WATER WILL CONCEN-
TRATE HERE TO PRO-
DUCE A RIPPLED FALL

EFFECT OF EDGE ON CHARACTER OF FALLING WATER.

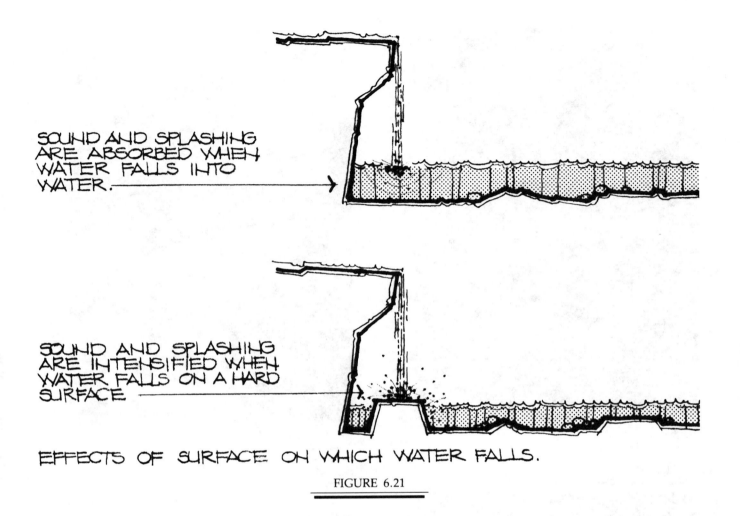

SOUND AND SPLASHING
ARE ABSORBED WHEN
WATER FALLS INTO
WATER.

SOUND AND SPLASHING
ARE INTENSIFIED WHEN
WATER FALLS ON A HARD
SURFACE

EFFECTS OF SURFACE ON WHICH WATER FALLS.

FIGURE 6.21

tions of these variables suggest the many different appearances and sounds that can be created with falling water from an almost inconspicuous dribble of a garden brook to the monumental roar of Niagara Falls.

As one design variable, the edge over which the water falls should be carefully studied to create the desired effect, particularly with small volumes of water. The effects of different edge conditions on falling water are indicated in Figure 6.20. A perfectly smooth edge causes water to cling to its surface and fall in an unwrinkled sheet that looks like a stretched piece of clear cellophane. An excellent example of this is found at the edge of the large reflective pool at the Christian Science Headquarters in Boston. A rougher edge concentrates the water at certain points and produces a rippled result in the falling water. When the edge becomes very rough and erratic in combination with a relatively large volume of water, a white water effect is created.

As suggested in Figure 6.21, another variable that influences the sight and sound of free-falling water is the surface on which the water falls. When the falling water strikes a hard surface such as rock or concrete, it creates a distinct splashing effect with water deflected in all directions. A sharp splattering sound also results from such a condition. When water falls into a pool at the base of the fall, part of the movement of the fall is absorbed by the pool so that the amount of splashing is slightly less than when it falls on a hard surface. The sound emitted when water falls into water tends to be a deeper, fuller-bodied one compared with water falling on a fixed surface.

Another design variable that can be worked with is the position of the falling water with respect to light. When a strong light source such as the sun is behind the falling water as in Figure 6.22, the falling water often takes on a sparkling, crystalline quality that adds to the visual appeal.

FIGURE 6.22

FIGURE 6.23

FIGURE 6.24

Examples of free-falling water in the landscape are numerous. Natural examples include Niagara Falls, the Upper Falls and Tower Falls in Yellowstone National Park, and Bridal Veil Falls in Yosemite National Park. Still other examples are shown in Figures 6.23 and 6.24. Figure 6.23 shows a falls in the state of Washington and Figure 6.24 shows the falls below the house Falling Water, designed by Frank Lloyd Wright in Bear Run, Pennsylvania. Constructed free-falling waterfalls can be found at The Fountain of Arethusa and the Terrace of the Hundred Fountains at Villa d'Este, in the central water display in Constitution Plaza in Hartford, Connecticut, at the Auditorium Forecourt in Portland, Oregon, and at Freeway Park in Seattle, Washington.

One variation of free-falling water suitable for urban settings is the water wall. A "water wall" is as the name suggests, a wall of falling water. Usually the water is pumped to the top of the wall whence it is allowed to fall in a continuous sheet down the front of the wall. The result is a spectacular treatment of a vertical plane with both sight and sound stimulus. Examples of water walls can be found at Paley Park in midtown Manhattan, next to the Stan-

FIGURE 6.25

dard Oil Building in Chicago (Figure 6.25), and in Robson Square in Vancouver, British Columbia (Figure 6.26). The water wall in Paley Park provides a dramatic focal point for the minipark as well as a source of sound for shutting out the cacophony of the city.

Obstructed fall. The second type of falling water is obstructed fall, caused by water striking various obstacles or planes while dropping between two elevations, as illustrated in Figure 6.27. These obstacles act as commas or pauses in the continuity of the dropping water. Obstructed falling water is apt to produce more commotion in terms of sight and sound and consequently be more easily noticed than free-falling water. Many interesting theatrical effects can be made by controlling the volume, height of falls, and the surface(s) on which the water falls.

FIGURE 6.26

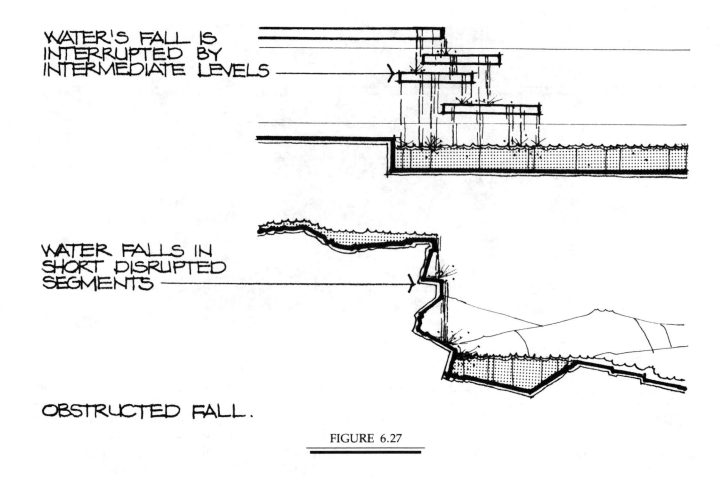

WATER'S FALL IS INTERRUPTED BY INTERMEDIATE LEVELS

WATER FALLS IN SHORT DISRUPTED SEGMENTS

OBSTRUCTED FALL.

FIGURE 6.27

One possible variation is to imitate the water falling in a rocky mountain stream by making it fall onto a large boulder or concrete mass before allowing it to drop to the next lower elevation. An excellent example of this is the water display in Lovejoy Park, Portland, Oregon, designed by Lawrence Halprin. Caution should be exercised to limit the number of interruptions in obstructed fall so as not to negate the feeling that the water is indeed falling.

Sloped fall. The third category of falling water is water dropping along and down a steeply sloped surface, as illustrated in Figure 6.28. This type of falling water is similar to flowing water but occurs on a steeper slope in smaller controlled volumes. For small volumes of water, the visual result is a surface that merely looks wet and glistens in the light. For larger volumes, distinct patterns of moving water result. Again, the material and character of the sloped

FIGURE 6.28

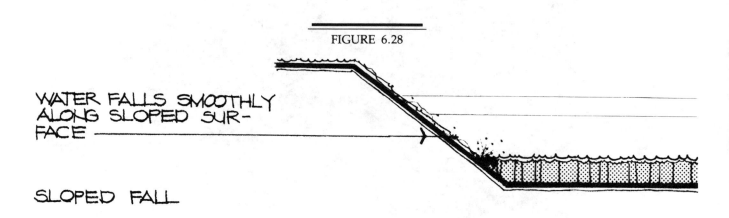

WATER FALLS SMOOTHLY ALONG SLOPED SURFACE

SLOPED FALL

FIGURE 6.29

FIGURE 6.31

FIGURE 6.30

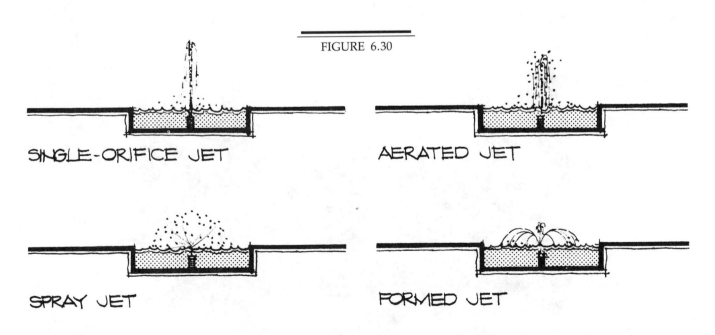

SINGLE-ORIFICE JET

AERATED JET

SPRAY JET

FORMED JET

TYPES OF FOUNTAIN JETS.

FIGURE 6.32

surface significantly impact the behavior of the fall-ing water. The water can be made to fall in clear thin sheets, in scalloped patterns, or in miniature rippled waves, as shown in Figure 6.29. An area of turbu-lence and white water usually occurs at the bottom of the slope where the falling water meets a more static body of water. Sloped fall tends to be more placid and reserved than either free-falling or ob-structed falling water. One example of sloped falling water is found in the central water feature in Copely Square in Boston. Here, water that initially rises in the central water jet falls and strikes the sloped sides of the fountain's pyramidal base. Then the water falls down the sloped surfaces, which are groved, until it reaches the bottom where it is captured and recirculated.

FIGURE 6.33

All these classifications of falling water can be combined, if desired, in a design to provide different effects within a related sequence. They can complement one another to form a diversified sculpture in water. Furthermore, an additional dimension of possibilities occurs when falling water is allowed to freeze during the winter. Unique, one-time formations occur through the whims of nature interacting with water and light.

Jets. The fourth fundamental form by which water can be introduced into exterior spaces is fountain jets. A fountain jet is created by forcing water up into the air through a nozzle in defiance of gravity. Yet all water in a jet must at some point respond to gravity and fall earthward. Therefore a fountain jet simultaneously contrasts and echoes the essence of falling water discussed earlier. Almost all fountain jets are effectively used as focal points in a design composition based on their verticality and interplay with light. The exact amount of attention drawn to any one particular fountain depends on the volume of water and the force of the jet (a factor of pump size). A fountain jet can vary from a simple, unpretentious element to a theatrical display of many jets of all sizes and behaviors. Most fountain jets are located in a quiet, static body of water so that they can be fully appreciated against a neutral setting. There

FIGURE 6.34

FIGURE 6.35

278

FIGURE 6.36

FIGURE 6.37

FIGURE 6.38

FIGURE 6.39

in quiet garden settings or restful outdoor spaces, as in Figure 6.31. Used in combinations of more than one jet, as in Figure 6.32, single-orifice jets may be employed as a more noticeable center of attention in an outdoor space.

Spray. A spray fountain jet is produced by many fine, mistlike streams of water that result from water being forced through a nozzle with many small openings. A spray jet characteristically has a fine texture that is light and airy in appearance. The sound created by this type of jet is a soft "hiss." A spray jet may be used as a design element for its delicate texture or to portray a refined, quiet mood. A spray jet may also be incorporated into an outdoor space as a means of increasing the moisture content of the air and as a natural air-conditioning element.

Aerated. An aerated fountain jet is similar to a single-orifice jet in that the nozzle has one opening. However, the primary difference between the two is that the opening of the nozzle in the aerated jet is much larger, thus producing a turbulent, white water effect. Hence the aerated appearance is a consequence of the forced water mixing with air. An aerated fountain jet is particularly attractive because the white water interacts with sunlight to create a fresh, sparkling appearance, as shown in Figure 6.33. Aerated fountain jets are easily and appropriately used as dominant focal points in the landscape because of their visually compelling nature. Examples of aerated jets used as predominant elements in the outdoor environment include the fountain jet at Point Park in Pittsburgh, in front of the City Hall in Dallas, and at L'Enfant Plaza in Washington, D.C. (Figure 6.34).

Formed. A formed fountain jet is any type of jet that is shaped to furnish a special effect. "Morning glories" or "mushrooms" are two of the more common formed fountain jets. Formed jets appear exact and studied, therefore, requiring special attention in their location. They often have the appearance of a perfectly shaped glass or plastic sculpture placed in the outdoor environment, as shown in Figure 6.35. Formed fountain jets are best used in those spaces where a formal, precise shape is required.

Combination Water Features. All the types and characteristics of water described in this chapter may be used alone in a design or combined with each other to establish effects that can be gained only in a synthesis of various types. One notable example of

are four basic types of fountains characterized by their form and appearance: single orifice, spray, aerated, and formed.[10] These four types are graphically portrayed in Figure 6.30.

Single–orifice. This is the simplest type of fountain jet, with water forced through a single opening nozzle. A single-orifice jet produces a relatively clear stem of water that is generally simple but striking in appearance. The height of a single-orifice jet is apt to be limited to the point where the water stem begins to break apart and fall downward, a factor of both water volume and pressure. The sound produced by a single-orifice jet is typically a distinct dribbling or dripping one made as the falling water of the jet strikes the surrounding water. Individually, single-orifice jets are effectively used as accents

[10]Ibid, p. 483.

FIGURE 6.40

different forms of water used collectively is the Water Organ and associated pools at Villa d'Este, Tivoli, Italy (Figure 6.36). Here flat water, falling water, and fountain jets are used in combination to create a variety of visual effects and sound. For falling water alone, one can see a large central fall with a voluminous mass of white falling water juxtaposed with smaller, lower falls that furnish a light, lacy effect. The fountains include both single-orifice and aerated jets. The result is a sensitive yet exciting composition

playing the contrasts of falling water and rising water against each other.

Another example of varied mixtures of water forms is in Mellon Square in Pittsburgh. Here, fountain jets are incorporated with flat, quiet water as a base and falling water emitting from large dishlike structures (Figure 6.37). An added dimension of dynamics is provided by the periodically changing height and overall appearance of the fountain jets (Figures 6.38 and 6.39). Consequently, the overall ef-

FIGURE 6.41

FIGURE 6.42

Washington, D.C. Here, the aerated fountain jet changes volume and height to produce dramatically varied visual effects (Figures 6.40, 6.41, and 6.42).

No matter what type of water form or combination of water forms are used in an outdoor space, it should be based on the intended character and objectives of the design project. Closely associated with this is the relationship of the water to the climatic character of the region. As one example, water is a helpful and required element in those regions of the world that are hot and arid. Here, water serves as both a physical and psychological cooling agent. On the other hand, extensive use of water is inappropriate in regions that are generally cloudy and/or receive heavy rainfall. Here, water only adds to the perceived dampness and gloom of the environment.

Finally, water should be coordinated with all other elements so that it appears and functions as an integral part of the entire design. Like other design elements, it should not be added on to a design as an afterthought. If used correctly, water can add to the vitality and enjoyment of an outdoor space.

Summary

Water is an extremely varied element whose character and appearance depend on factors external to it. To design with water, one must first study the shape, size, height, and bottom slope of the containing element. Even then, uncontrollable elements such as sun, wind, and temperature can influence the visual quality of a body of water. Visually, water may be used in the outdoor environment as a flat, reflective element to suggest tranquility and contemplation; as a moving, flowing element to provide activity and sound; as falling water to express the forces of gravity, or as vertical fountain jets as accents and exclamation points. Used in any of these capacities, water is a specialty element that adds meaning and a sense of life to outdoor spaces.

fect of the water display alters from moment to moment, giving the viewer numerous combinations of water sounds and displays. Gushing water, white water, water stretched like cellophane, water sculpted like glass, dripping water, and splashing water are some of the assorted sights and sounds created. Water can even vary from moment to moment, as seen in the central fountain at the Hirshhorn Museum in

7

The Design Process

Previous chapters have dealt with the characteristics and potential uses of the basic landscape architectural design elements in the outdoor environment. For the most part, the discussions in those chapters considered the design elements as separate, individual elements. This permitted focusing on each element alone without interference or confusion with the other design elements. Yet the landscape architect rarely designs with landform, plant materials, buildings, pavement, site structures, or water individually. Although the designer must have a thorough understanding of each of these elements, ultimately the true success of an outdoor space depends upon the thoughtful and sensitive combination of all the design elements.

When worked with collectively, all the landscape architectural design elements can reinforce one another to meet the objectives of a project, solve problems, and create outdoor environments of a desired quality. The design elements should be coordinated to accentuate the positive aspects of each while simultaneously negating the weak qualities. To do this, the design elements must be studied in concert with one another while developing a design. They should not be treated in a piecemeal or sequential fashion. The landform of a site, for example, cannot be completely or properly studied without considering how it will affect the integration of buildings, plant material, and pavement. Each of the design elements affects the others.

To effect a suitable integration of the different landscape architectural design elements with one another as well as with the site and the requirements of the client, most landscape architects employ a series of analytical and creative thinking steps referred to as the "design process." The design process helps the landscape architect arrive at a finished site design that collectively utilizes all the design elements to meet the requirements of the project in the most efficient and aesthetically pleasing manner possible.

The design process has a number of other uses including the following: (1) it provides a logical, organized framework for creating a design solution, (2) it helps to insure that the solution that evolves will be appropriately suited to the circumstances of the design (the site, the client's needs, budget, etc.), (3) it aids in determining the best use of the land for the client by studying alternative solutions, and (4) it serves as a basis for explaining and defending the design solution to the client.

The design process, also sometimes termed a "problem-solving process," includes a series of steps that usually (though not necessarily) follow a sequential order. In general terms, these same steps are also used by architects, industrial designers, engineers, and scientists to solve problems. For site designers, the design process typically includes these steps:

1. Project acceptance
2. Research and analysis (including site visit)
   a. Base plan preparation
   b. Site inventory (data collection) and analysis (evaluation)
   c. Client interview
   d. Program development
3. Design
   a. Ideal functional diagram
   b. Site-related functional diagram
   c. Concept plan
   d. Form composition study
   e. Preliminary design
   f. Schematic design
   g. Master plan
   h. Design development
4. Construction drawings
   a. Layout plan
   b. Grading plan
   c. Planting plan
   d. Construction details
5. Implementation
6. Post-construction evaluation
7. Maintenance

These steps of the design process represent an ideal sequence of events. Many of the steps overlap one another and blend together so the neat ordering of the outline is less clear and apparent. Furthermore, some of the steps may parallel one another in time and occur simultaneously. For example, client interview and program development may occur while the designer is visiting the site and conducting a site analysis. Or the form composition phase may take place as an integral part of the preliminary design. At other times, the process is not apt to proceed in a neat sequence of phases in which one step is absolutely completed before the next. In many instances it is necessary to move back and forth between the various phases with information gained at one step feeding back to an earlier step. As an illustration, the extent and type of information sought during the site analysis should directly depend on the character and complexity of concepts prepared in a later phase. Likewise, one may find it necessary to revisit the site or talk to the client again once the design phase itself has been started because some item of information was overlooked the first time or one's memory and impression simply need refreshing. And sometimes it helps to revisit the site after starting the design phase because then the designer can look at the site with experience and greater understanding of what limitations or opportunities are present. In other words, no one step of the design process occurs independently of the others.

Several other points also need to be made. First, the application of the design process may vary from one design situation to the next. Each project represents a unique set of circumstances and, therefore, requires a different method for proceeding through the design process. Similarly, the emphasis placed on each of the individual steps may also change. For example, the site may be so barren or nondescript that the site analysis is meaningless. In other cases, the client may not care what is done and have little or no input in the process. In many situations, the entire process may end with the preliminary design. The need to undertake any of the steps of the design process or the emphasis placed on each can be justified only so long as it contributes to the other phases as well as the overall process. In all cases, the limits of a budget dictate how much time can be spent on the various phases of the design process. So the process may be applied slightly differently each time a design is produced.

It is important for a novice designer to understand that beautiful and practical design solutions do not appear out of thin air like magic. There are no esoteric formulas or secret states of mind that produce good designs effortlessly, and the design process itself is no guaranteed recipe either. The design process is only a framework or outline of various steps. Its success relies upon the designer's observations, experience, knowledge, ability to make proper judgments, and creativity. All these factors must be utilized within the structure of the design process. If any one of them is weak or lacking, the design will suffer no matter how faithfully the designer may have attempted to follow the steps of the design process. The design process requires the landscape architect to be continually thinking about what is occurring and asking the questions, ''Why am I doing this?'' ''What do I hope to accomplish?'' ''Is this necessary?'' ''Is there a more efficient way of doing this task?'' In the final analysis, designs that work well and affect our emotions require a great deal of sensitive observation, analysis, studying, thinking, and restudying as well as inspiration and creativity.

It should be noted here that producing a design involves both rational aspects (inventory, analysis, program development, construction knowledge, etc.) and intuitive aspects (the feel of putting forms and shapes together, aesthetic appreciation, etc.). The design process, then, is a framework of steps, incorporating both rational and intuitive phases that aid the designer to organize work, thoughts, and feelings in an effort to produce the best possible design solution.

Because of the significance of the design process in organizing the designer's procedure, it is essential for the beginning designer to cover each step thoroughly. This is necessary to prevent any factor from being forgotten or any possibility overlooked. Therefore the novice should carefully record and document each step as a reference and as a learning tool, provided time and budget permit. Thus the design process may be somewhat laborious and time-consuming the first few times one proceeds through it. For an experienced designer, some of the steps of the design process can be covered rapidly without extraordinary effort. Having utilized the process a number of times, the designer is apt to proceed through the various phases automatically.

The following sections of this chapter cover each of the steps of the design process in greater detail. Again, we emphasize that these steps represent *an* approach, not *the* approach. The information studied and the procedure of each of the steps should be carefully analyzed and tailored to each new project undertaken.

Project Acceptance

The first step of the design process is to have a project proposal accepted by both the landscape architect and the client. At the first meeting between the two parties, the general needs and requirements of the client are discussed and the landscape architect presents the type and scope of services offered. If the terms of each party at this meeting are agreeable to the other, then the landscape architect prepares for the client a written proposal detailing the scope of services, products, and cost of services to be undertaken. If the client agrees to the proposal, both parties sign the proposal or written contract. It is always advisable, no matter what the size of the project or the scope of the work, to have the agreement in writing to avoid misunderstandings or legal problems at a later date.

Research and Analysis

Once an agreement on the project has been made between client and landscape architect, the landscape architect needs next to obtain a base plan of the site and conduct a site inventory and analysis. A site visit is almost always necessary to accomplish this step. These early steps of the design process are much like those undertaken in any other creative endeavor such as writing a speech or paper or conducting research. One must have a thorough understanding of the background of the project and the conditions that will affect the end product before proceeding to the later phases where new and creative ideas are formulated.

Base Plan Preparation. One of the first items that must be obtained or prepared before any analysis or design proposals can be undertaken is a base plan. Normally, the information required for the base plan (property survey, topography, etc.) should be supplied by the client. If such information is not available, a professional property and topographic survey must be undertaken by on-site survey, aerial photography, or a combination of both. The expense for such a survey should be billed directly to the client.

For small sites such as private residences, the client or home owner may have a scale base plan in the form of a deed description, a plot plan, or a site plan accompanying the house plans. When the client does not have this information, and frequently this is the case, the landscape architect must then visit the site, take field measurements, and prepare a scale base plan. For small sites (1/4 to 5 acres), the most efficient scales for drawing a base plan are 1 in = 10 ft, 1 in = 20 ft, 1/8 in = 1 ft, and 1/16 in = 1 ft. For bigger sites, the scale is larger (1 in = 30 ft, 1 in = 50 ft, 1 in = 100 ft, etc.). The scale chosen will also depend on the amount of detail in the design proposal. For preliminary and schematic design proposals, the scale of the drawings is often larger than for design development drawings. Sheet size is frequently a determinant of scale too. The base plan should show the following existing information:

1. Property line with bearings and distances, if known
2. Topography (contour lines shown as dashed lines with spot grades indicated where necessary)
3. Vegetation (for small-scale sites, it may be necessary to identify the size, caliber, and species of trees)
4. Bodies of water (streams, lakes, ponds, etc.)
5. Buildings, including the following for detail scale plans:
   a. floor plan with all doors and windows
   b. basement windows
   c. down spouts
   d. outside water spigots
   e. outside electrical outlets
   f. air conditioning/heat pump units
   g. exterior lights (both on the building and in the site)
6. Other structures such as walls, fences, electrical and telephone junction boxes, telephone poles, culverts and head walls, fire hydrants, etc.
7. Roads, driveways, parking areas, walks and paths, terraces, etc.
8. On-site and off-site utilities including electric, telephone, gas, water, sanitary sewer, and storm sewer.
9. Immediate off-site conditions such as adjoining roads and streets, nearby buildings, telephone poles, vegetation, bodies of water, etc.
10. Any other elements considered necessary for developing the design.

As shown in Figures 1.4 and 7.1, the base plan should be drawn in a simple and legible graphic style because it (or more probably copies of it) will be used for later steps of the design process. Fancy, elaborate symbols or graphic textures are not appropriate on a base plan. For example, existing trees should be drawn as simple circular outlines, not as complex symbols with branches and foliage. Notes should be kept to a minimum so as not to clutter the sheet or reduce its flexibility for subsequent drawings. Any element that will be removed as part of the design proposal, such as an existing walk, road, building, or tree, should be drawn lightly with dashed lines (if at all) so it will not graphically interfere with the new proposal.

Site Inventory and Analysis. After a base plan has been prepared (or while the site is being surveyed and measured in order to prepare it), the next step is to conduct a site inventory and analysis. There are several objectives for this step. Primarily, the purpose of the site analysis and inventory is for the designer to become as familiar with the site as possible (as if the designer lived or worked there) in order to evaluate and determine the site's character, problems, and potentials. In other words, what are the site's good points and bad points? What should be preserved and enhanced? What should be changed or corrected? How does the site function? What are its limitations? How do you feel and react about the site? In essence, this step of the design process is very much like going to the library to do research when writing a paper or preparing a speech. You cannot do a design or write a paper without knowing the subject or its qualities.

Each design should be specifically tailored to fit and adapt to the conditions of the given site. Therefore the second major purpose of a site analysis and inventory, which is very much a part of the objective stated in the previous paragraph, is to identify those "keys" or "clues" of the site that will indicate how the design proposal can be best suited to the existing site conditions in a manner that takes advantage of the site's positive aspects while simultaneously eliminating or minimizing its negative aspects. Consequently, the site inventory and analysis is undertaken essentially as a tool for the landscape architect to aid in developing the most appropriate solution for the given site. The site inventory and analysis is conducted to a lesser extent for the client, although it does serve as useful information when explaining the logic of the solution to the client. The site analysis can often provide defensible reasons for doing things in subsequent design phases.

There are a number of conditions to record and evaluate during the site inventory and analysis, as indicated in the accompanying outline. For each condition, there should be two distinct phases: (1) inventory: identify and record the condition (i.e., data collection; note what and where it is), and (2) analysis: evaluate or make a judgment about the worth/importance of the condition. Is it good or bad? How will or should it influence the design proposal? Can it be taken advantage of? Will it limit what can be done on the site at a particular point? Recording the site data (inventory) is relatively easy. One needs to be observant and organized in recording the information. A camera is a helpful tool for this procedure because photographs can be used to check the information in the office or simply to refresh one's memory of the site from time to time. Determining the importance of the data or information (analysis) tends to be more difficult. It is, in fact, the step most inexperienced designers tend to skip

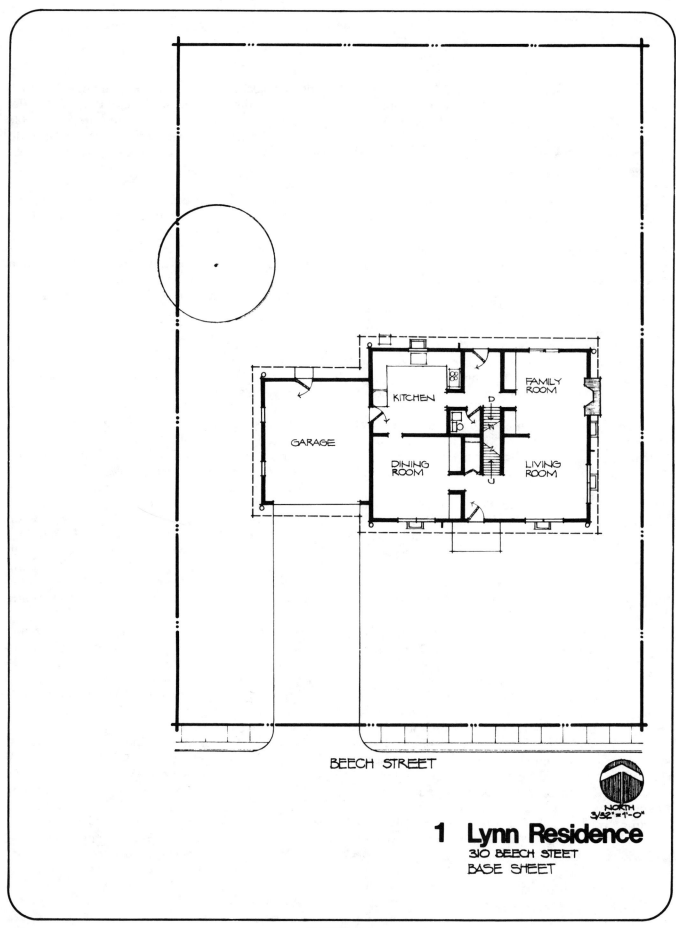

KITCHEN

FAMILY
ROOM

GARAGE

DINING
ROOM

LIVING
ROOM

BEECH STREET

NORTH
3/32"=1'-0"

1 Lynn Residence
310 BEECH STREET
BASE SHEET

FIGURE 7.1

over or cover inadequately. Analysis requires experience in knowing the probable impact of an item on the design proposal and the ability to think ahead about how a solution may respond to the condition. Analysis requires thoughtful judgment and foresight. Written examples indicating the difference in thought and terminology between site inventory and site analysis are given in the following outline.

Inventory	Analysis
A. 40-ft-(12m) high sugar maple good condition 10-ft (3m) canopy, 30-ft (9m) spread bright orange fall color	• should be preserved and used for shade on west side of building • might be used as a "ceiling" over the terrace
B. southwest slope good view toward valley	• view toward valley should be taken advantage of; might be good orientation for lodge • has good exposure to southwest summer breezes; should not be screened • needs shading from hot summer afternoon sun
C. wooded area of beech, maple, and oak	• has a dark, enclosed feeling in summer • should be used only for low-intensity functions • restrict grading and soil compaction in this area
D. building entrance with a double set of doors; walk is 6 ft wide	• good southern orientation; maintain openness for winter sun exposure • entrance area feels tight and congested; should be widened to avoid this problem • need closer vehicular drop-off for ease of access to building entrance
E. OsB Soil Type; clay loam with moderate to slow permeability; pH 5.9	• should be developed only at low density, 2 to 5 units/acre • septic systems should not be located here

In conducting a site inventory and analysis, a number of conditions should be studied. The following outline of various site conditions is an ideal checklist (inventory) of items to consider. Not all conditions will exist on or apply to every site. Others will be common knowledge from working in a given area. Use the outline as appropriate! For each new site, the landscape architect should determine the most relevant conditions to be inventoried and ana-

lyzed. If the condition is of little significance or will not affect the eventual design solution, it should not be included. Don't make your work any more difficult or complex than necessary.

A. Site Location and Context
 1. identify conditions and land uses surrounding the site
   • type and condition of adjoining land uses
   • adjoining street or road(s): how heavily traveled? when?
   • how much noise and headlight glare is generated from street?
 2. identify character of neighborhood
   • style, age, and condition of architecture; height
   • maturity of vegetation
   • feeling and character of neighborhood
   • fabric and "texture" of neighborhood
 3. identify location of significant functions in the community and neighborhood
   • schools
   • police/fire stations
   • churches
   • commercial centers and type of business in each
   • parks and other recreation centers
 4. identify pattern of vehicular circulation in the neighborhood
   • hierarchy of road types, intensity and type of use (i.e., residential, commercial, etc.)
   • note daily or seasonal fluctuations in the intensity of traffic
   • identify primary means for arriving at the site. is there more than one? which one is the most frequently used? when?
   • identify location and schedule of nearby bus routes
 5. identify zoning ordinances and building codes for the neighborhood
   • building types allowed
   • building height and length restrictions
   • setback requirements
   • ROW and road width requirements
   • building permits
   • restrictions on fence and wall locations and height

B. Topography
 1. identify degree of slope at various locations throughout the site (slope analysis)
   • identify restrictions for building on the various slope conditions
   • identify land uses most appropriate for the different slope conditions present on the site

2. identify major landform types and the significance of each
   - convex
   - concave
   - valley
   - ridge
3. identify areas of erosion (too steep) and areas of wet ground (too level)
4. identify grade change between inside (floor elevation) and outside (grade around wall of building) of existing buildings
5. check comfort of walking on different areas of the site (this will also indicate relative steepness)
6. identify elevation changes between top and bottom of all existing steps and retaining walls

C. Hydrology and Drainage
1. identify watersheds and divides between each
   - check to see if water drains away from existing building(s) at all points
   - identify where water flows from building down spouts
2. identify major bodies of surface water
   - check water quality
3. identify seasonal fluctuation of streams and lakes
   - flooding and elevation of high water
   - check for areas of erosion
4. identify wet spots or areas of standing water (when and for what lengths of time)
5. identify subsurface water conditions
   - water table elevation; fluctuation with season
   - aquifers and recharge areas
6. identify drainage onto and away from site
   - does any surface water run onto site from surroundings? if so, how much and when?
   - where does the water go when it leaves this site?

D. Soil
1. identify soil type
   - acidic or alkaline?
   - sandy, clay, or gravel?
   - fertility?
2. identify depth of topsoil layer
3. identify depth to bedrock
4. identify general rate of percolation
5. identify the limitations for building on the various soil types

E. Vegetation
1. identify and locate existing plant material
2. for large-scale sites, identify
   - zones of different plant material types
   - crown density for wooded areas
   - age (maturity) and height of wooded areas
3. for small-scale sites, identify
   - plant species
   - size (height, spread, and canopy height for trees)
   - form
   - color (foliage and flower) and seasonal variation
   - texture
   - any unique features or characteristics
4. for all existing plant material, identify condition, value, and client's opinion (like or dislike?)
5. identify restrictions for developing in or around existing vegetation

F. Microclimate
1. identify plan direction of sun at sunrise and sunset at critical seasons of the year
2. identify height of sun at critical times of day and seasons of the year
3. identify and locate areas that are predominately sunny during critical times of day and seasons of the year
4. identify and locate areas exposed to intense summer afternoon sun
5. identify and locate shadow patterns at critical times of day and seasons of the year
6. identify prevailing wind direction through the year
7. identify and locate areas exposed to or protected from cooling summer breezes
8. identify and locate areas exposed to or protected from cold winter winds
9. identify overall temperature ranges at critical times of day and year
10. identify areas of cool air drainage
11. identify time periods and amounts of heaviest and least precipitation
12. identify depth to frost line

G. Existing Building(s)
1. architectural style
2. overall massing and height
3. identify materials of façade
4. identify location of doors and windows. For doors, identify which are used most frequently and when
5. for small-scale sites or those involving close association with the building, identify
   - location of rooms inside building
     - how used and when?
     - are any of the rooms used more frequently than others?

- location of basement windows (and depth below ground)
- height of bottom and top of windows and doors from ground
- location of down spouts, outside water spigots, outside electrical outlets, outside lights attached to building, electric meter, gas meter, clothes dryer vent, etc.
- location of overhangs and height above ground
- views to the outside from inside the building
  - what is seen?
  - should it be enhanced or screened?

H. Other Existing Structures
  1. location, condition, and materials of walks, terraces, steps, walls, fences, swimming pools, etc.
  2. for three-dimensional elements, identify height above ground

I. Utilities
  1. location, height above ground or depth below ground of water line, gas line, electric line, telephone line, storm sewer, septic tank, and leach field (if present)
     - identify easements associated with utility lines
     - location of telephone and electrical junction boxes
  2. location and height of air conditioner or heat pump
     - check direction of air flow (front? top?)
  3. location of pool equipment and any pipes or lines servicing it
  4. location of lights and electric lines servicing them
  5. location of irrigation system

J. Views
  1. observe and identify what is seen from all sides of the site
     - good; should it be taken advantage of?
     - bad; should it be screened?
     - indifferent
  2. observe and identify views from inside the building looking out (especially from rooms used most frequently)
     - how should these be worked within the design?
  3. observe and identify views from off the site looking on
     - views from different sides of the site
     - views from street
     - where are the best views of the site?
     - where are the worst views of the site?

K. Spaces and Senses
  1. identify the existing "outdoor rooms"
     - where are "walls" (fences, walls, hedges, plant masses, landform slopes, etc.)?
     - where are ceilings (tree canopies, etc.)?
  2. identify the feeling and character of these rooms
     - open, enclosed, cheerful, gloomy, etc
  3. identify and locate unique or disturbing noises
     - traffic noise
     - flowing stream
     - wind moving through pine boughs
  4. identify and locate unique or disturbing smells

L. Site Functions
  1. identify how the site is currently used (what, where, when, and how?)
  2. identify location, time, and frequency for such things as
     - employee arrival and departure
     - office/store hours
     - work/maintenance
     - parking of cars
     - garbage collection
     - service people
  3. identify and locate maintenance problems
  4. identify and locate special areas of wear and tear
     - worn grass edges along walks or driveway
     - worn lawns due to children's play
  5. identify how one arrives at site
     - how do you feel?
     - what do you see?
  6. identify location for dumping snow in winter

An example of a site inventory and site analysis for a residential site is provided in Figures 7.2 and 7.3.

Client Interview. During or after the site inventory and analysis, the designer should obtain detailed information about the client's needs and wishes. One should conduct a client interview, similar to the site analysis, so that the eventual design solution will respond correctly to the desires and needs of the client. A design solution that fails to respond to the client's needs is just as ill-suited as one that does not properly fit the conditions of the site. The best way to obtain the necessary information is to personally discuss thoughts about what is wanted, liked, and disliked, and how the client intends to use the site in the future. To be most useful, all the people who

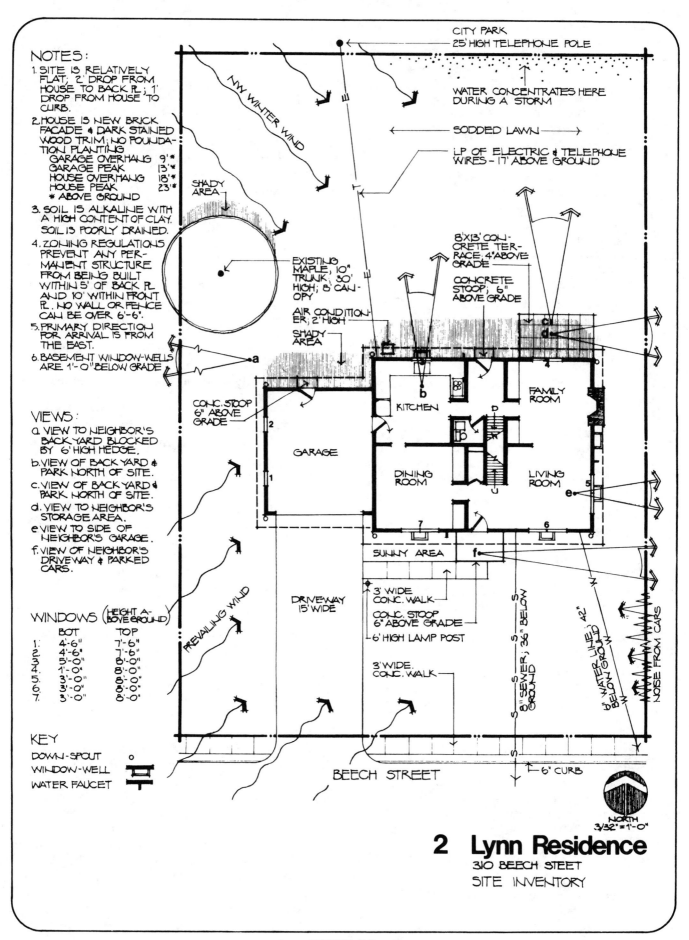

FIGURE 7.2

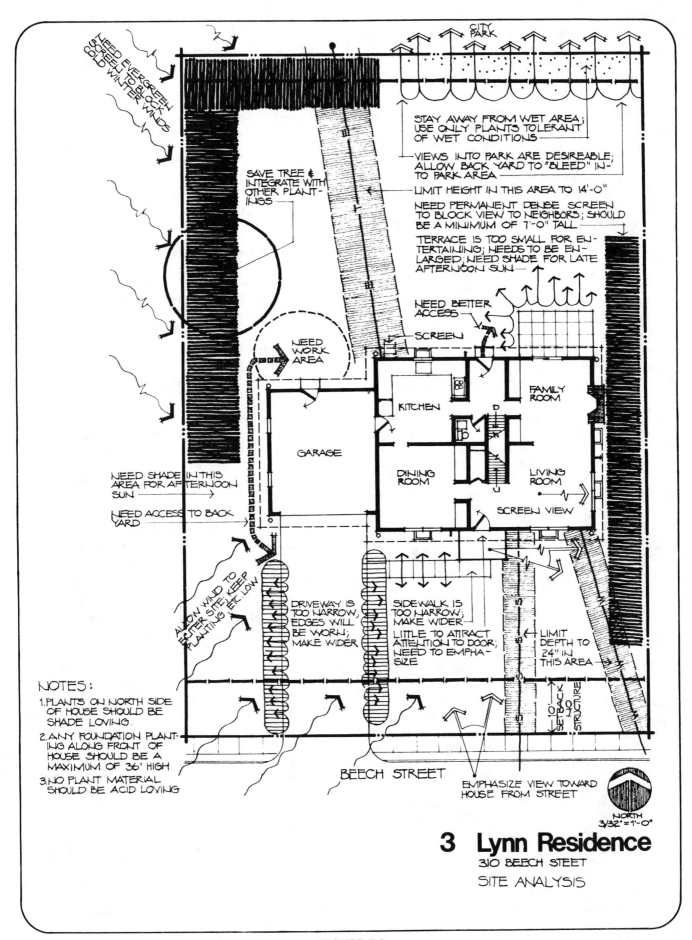

NEED EVERGREEN SCREEN TO BLOCK COLD WINTER WINDS

CITY PARK

SAVE TREE & INTEGRATE WITH OTHER PLANT-INGS

NEED WORK AREA

STAY AWAY FROM WET AREA; USE ONLY PLANTS TOLERANT OF WET CONDITIONS

VIEWS INTO PARK ARE DESIREABLE; ALLOW BACK YARD TO "BLEED" IN-TO PARK AREA

LIMIT HEIGHT IN THIS AREA TO 14'-0"

NEED PERMANENT DENSE SCREEN TO BLOCK VIEW TO NEIGHBORS; SHOULD BE A MINIMUM OF 7'-0" TALL

TERRACE IS TOO SMALL FOR EN-TERTAINING; NEEDS TO BE EN-LARGED; NEED SHADE FOR LATE AFTERNOON SUN

NEED BETTER ACCESS

SCREEN

KITCHEN

FAMILY ROOM

GARAGE

DINING ROOM

LIVING ROOM

SCREEN VIEW

NEED SHADE IN THIS AREA FOR AFTERNOON SUN

NEED ACCESS TO BACK YARD

ALLOW WIND TO ENTER SITE; KEEP PLANTING ETC. LOW

DRIVEWAY IS TOO NARROW; EDGES WILL BE WORN; MAKE WIDER

SIDEWALK IS TOO NARROW; MAKE WIDER

LITTLE TO ATTRACT ATTENTION TO DOOR; NEED TO EMPHA-SIZE

LIMIT DEPTH TO 24" IN THIS AREA

10' SETBACK NO STRUCTURE

NOTES:
1. PLANTS ON NORTH SIDE OF HOUSE SHOULD BE SHADE LOVING.
2. ANY FOUNDATION PLANT-ING ALONG FRONT OF HOUSE SHOULD BE A MAXIMUM OF 36" HIGH
3. NO PLANT MATERIAL SHOULD BE ACID LOVING

BEECH STREET

EMPHASIZE VIEW TOWARD HOUSE FROM STREET

NORTH
3/32"=1'-0"

3 Lynn Residence
310 BEECH STEET
SITE ANALYSIS

FIGURE 7.3

will eventually use and maintain the site should be involved in this phase. In the case of an office building, this might include the owner of the property, a representative group of employees (from top management to secretaries and office boys), and the person or persons who will be responsible for actually taking care of the site. For a residential design, all members of a family should participate in the client interview because they often have different and opposing opinions on what the design should or should not do. If conflicting ideas do occur, then they need to be resolved so the designer will have a clear direction to proceed in. Although it is desirable to sit down face to face with the client, it may in some instances be difficult or impossible to do so. For example, the users of a park or housing project are typically a large group of people who cannot all be personally interviewed or even identified. In this case, the designer may wish to talk to users of existing parks or housing projects that are similar to the one the designer is working on.

The following is a sample outline of items that might be identified and discussed with the client in the context of a residential site design. The list is meant as a general guideline and would of course change with different types of design projects and clients. It is not meant to be all-inclusive or apply to all situations.

A. Family Members
   1. identify family members and their ages, employment, hobbies, interests, activities, habits, etc.
      • how much time is spent on each activity or hobby? how should this affect site design?
      • how much time is spent at home or away from home? inside or outside?
      • identify pets, especially those who might use or be outside
      • identify personal pleasures such as outside cooking, sun bathing, lounging, reading, etc.
   2. identify specific wishes and needs of each family member for the site, and have family members list these in order of priority
B. Entertaining
   1. identify frequency, time (day/night), and numbers of people involved (average and maximum)
   2. identify requirements for outside uses
      • are there any special needs or activities?
C. Recreation
   1. identify types of recreation of family members at home (throwing baseball/football, badminton, volleyball, frisbee, swimming, croquet, etc.)

   2. for each activity, identify which members of the family participate, frequency of activity, time of day or season, and amount of space required
   3. identify special needs of children if present
      • where do they play?
      • what do they like to do?
      • what problems, if any, do they create?
D. Gardening
   1. is gardening enjoyed by the family?
      • if so, how much time is spent gardening? by whom?
      • are there any special gardening likes (vegetables, flowers, herbs, ferns, etc.)?
      • are there any preferences on the location of a garden?
   2. identify favorite plants of family; a ranked list of preferences would be helpful
      • note disliked plants
E. Maintenance
   1. identify how much time is currently spent or would like to be spent in the future on maintenance
      • is all maintenance done by the client?
   2. identify special maintenance problems in the eyes of the client
   3. identify type of maintenance equipment client owns. Will it place limitations on the design?
      • riding lawn mower vs. push lawn mower?
F. Budget
   1. identify how much client is willing to spend and when (only at one time? over a span of several years?)
   2. although the budget must be realistically taken into account, it should not stand in the way of proposing a good design solution. A client can sometimes be persuaded to spend more than originally intended if the result can be shown to have value. Moreover, a design does not have to be installed all at once; it can be spread out over a period of years. Remember, however, that labor and materials will never be cheaper than they are today.

Program Development. A program is a list or outline of all the elements and requirements the design solution must include and satisfy. It serves two purposes: (1) it acts as a summary and synthesis of the site inventory/analysis and client interview, and (2) it functions as a checklist to compare the design proposal against. Under the first purpose, the program does bring the findings of the analysis steps previously conducted into an ordered summary of things that must be accomplished. If the site inventory/analysis and client interview were themselves well organized and recorded, this part of the program might seem redundant. Therefore this aspect of the program can be shortened or even omitted completely. The second purpose of the program can remind the designer of what should be done and included in the solution. While studying a design or already having completed a preliminary proposal, the designer can check back with the program to see if everything that was intended was actually accomplished. Were the correct number of dwelling units included on the site? Are there enough parking spaces? Is there adequate shade on the southwest side of the buildings? Was the terrace made the proper size? Was the view screened from neighbors on the west side? Do the play facilities accommodate the desired activities? Did I solve the drainage problem next to the garage? And so forth. If time and budget allow, the program may also serve as a basis for returning to the client for a quick review of what the design proposal intends to do.

The written program should consist of three related parts: (1) a list of goals and objectives (these may be part of the program or outlined as a separate part of the design process), (2) a list of the elements (spaces or things) to be included in the design, and (3) a list of special requirements the design is to fulfill. The list of elements to be included in the design should identify the element, its size, its material, and any other important characteristic.

The first aspect of the program is a list of goals and objectives. Goals may be defined as general statements of intent. They identify thoughts and ideas that should be accomplished by the design solution. Often the goals set the tone and philosophy of the entire design. Objectives are more specific statements that suggest how the goals might be accomplished. Objectives tend to be more action-oriented. For each goal there should be a subset of objectives that more explicitly outline how the goal is to be accomplished. An example of the subtle difference between goals and objectives is as follows:

Goal. Maintain a clearly identifiable entrance to the plaza

Objectives
1. Create an entrance space that is "public" in scale.
2. Provide a pavement change at entrance that is easily seen and recognized.
3. Allow some controlled views of the plaza from the entrance.
4. Provide a focal point at the entrance that will catch people's attention and cause them to stop.

The other elements of a program are more detailed. To make this more clear, a sample list of the various aspects of a program follows.

Element/Space	Size	Material	Notes
A. Walk to front entrance	5 ft (152cm) wide	Concrete or brick	Should extend along edge of driveway; include low lighting
B. Shade trees on west side of house	50 ft (15m) high, 30 ft (9m) spread at maturity	? (don't know yet)	Be careful of telephone wires
C. Community recreation center	3,000 sq. ft (280 sq.m)	Natural cedar siding	Should be centrally located with views to all areas of the site
D. 3 tennis courts	78 ft (23.78m) × 120 ft (36.59m) each	Asphalt base with aluminum fence	Should be located on 1 to 3 percent slope next to parking
E. Screen on north side of property	5 ft (152cm) high minimum	Wood fence or plant hedge	Must provide year-round protection
F. Front lawn	1,200 sq. ft (110 sq.m) maximum		Keep simple shape for easy maintenance
G. Work area with work bench and storage	about 100 sq. ft (9 sq.m)	Concrete floor	Keep close to garage and garden; protect from sun; screen from terrace
H. Bus stop	about 200 sq. ft (20 sq.m)	Enclosed brick shelter	Should be located on Maple Drive within convenient walking distance to community center
I. Climbing structure	8 ft (2.5m) high maximum	Rough timbers	Place on sand next to balance beam
J. Water feature	about 150 sq. ft (14 sq.m) 5 ft (152cm) high maximum	Concrete	Should act as a focal point to the entrance space

As can be seen from this outline, some early design decisions have already been made. The more thought that can be given at this time, the easier subsequent design steps will be because many decisions will already have been made. However, you will note that some information has been left undefined to allow a choice when more is known about the actual design solution. It should also be understood that some ideas formulated at this point might change in later phases. That is okay and is to be expected. Again, the program helps to clarify thoughts and give direction.

Design

Ideal Functional Diagram. This is the first step of the design phase (i.e., the phase when one actually starts to study design possibilities on paper in graphic form. Note: some designers start this phase with an "ideal diagram" that is even more abstract and general than the ideal functional diagram). It puts into action all the conclusions and proposals that have grown from the previous steps of site inventory/analysis, client interview, and program development. In the design phase, the studies begin with general and loose arrangements of the solution (functional diagram and concept plan) and proceed to very specific and exact considerations (detail design).

The ideal functional diagram is, again, the beginning point of the graphic development of a design. The purpose of an ideal functional diagram is to identify the best and most appropriate relationships that should exist between the major proposed functions and spaces (outlined previously in the program) of the design. The intent of this objective is to gain insight about which functions and elements should be associated with each other and which ones should be separated. At this point, the designer is striving for the absolute functional relationships among the various parts of the design.

The ideal functional diagram is nonsite related. It should deal with the design's functions and spaces as general bubbles or outlines in an abstract graphic manner. There is no pictorial or graphic realism in the solution at this initial design step. The bubbles should be arranged to establish ideal relationships among the functions and spaces. In preparing the ideal functional diagram, the designer might ask the following questions:

1. What functions/spaces should occur next to one another and how close?

2. What functions/spaces should be separated from one another and how far? Should there be barriers or screens established between incompatible functions?
3. How should one move through a space or function? Through the middle or along the sides? Should the movement be direct or meandering?
4. Should the function/space be open or enclosed? Should one be able to see into or out of the space?
5. How should one be able to enter the function/space? Should there be one way or several ways?

The ideal functional diagram can be drawn at any scale on a blank sheet of paper not relating to any condition of the known site. An example of an ideal functional diagram for a residential site is shown in Figure 7.4. It should show the following:

6. The major proposed site functions/spaces as simple bubbles.
7. The relative distance or proximity of the functions/spaces to one another.
8. Type of enclosure for each function/space (i.e., open or enclosed, etc.).
9. Barriers or screens.
10. Significant views into and from the various functions/spaces.
11. Points for entering/exiting the functions/spaces.
12. Interior functions/spaces as well as proposed exterior site functions/spaces.
13. Notes.

Various alternative arrangements of the ideal functional diagram should be studied. The designer should not settle upon the first idea unless the problem is so simple that the solution is obvious.

Site–Related Functional Diagram. The next step of the design phase is to adapt the relationships established in the ideal functional diagram to the known conditions of the given site. The site-related functional diagram should show the same information as the ideal functional diagram along with two additional considerations: (1) the functions/spaces should relate to the actual site conditions including the interior rooms of associated buildings, and (2) the functions/spaces should now be drawn keeping in mind their approximate size and scale. At this step of the process, the designer should be most concerned about (1) the location of the major functions/spaces with respect to the site, and (2) the relationship of the functions/spaces with respect to each other. All functions/spaces should be dealt with as generalized areas, as shown in Figure 7.5.

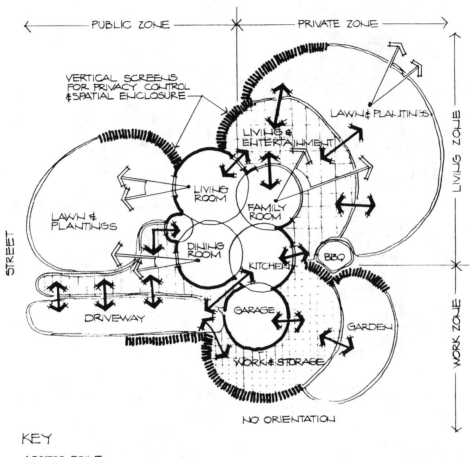

PUBLIC ZONE | PRIVATE ZONE

VERTICAL SCREENS
FOR PRIVACY CONTROL
& SPATIAL ENCLOSURE

LIVING &
ENTERTAINMENT

LAWN & PLANTINGS

LIVING ZONE

STREET

LAWN &
PLANTINGS

LIVING
ROOM

FAMILY
ROOM

DINING
ROOM

KITCHEN

BBQ

WORK ZONE

DRIVEWAY

GARAGE

GARDEN

WORK & STORAGE

NO ORIENTATION

KEY

ACCESS POINT
BETWEEN AREAS/
SPACES

VERTICAL SCREEN

VIEWS WHICH
SHOULD BE EN-
COURAGED & EN-
HANCED

4 Lynn Residence
310 BEECH STREET

IDEAL
FUNCTIONAL DIAGRAM

FIGURE 7.4

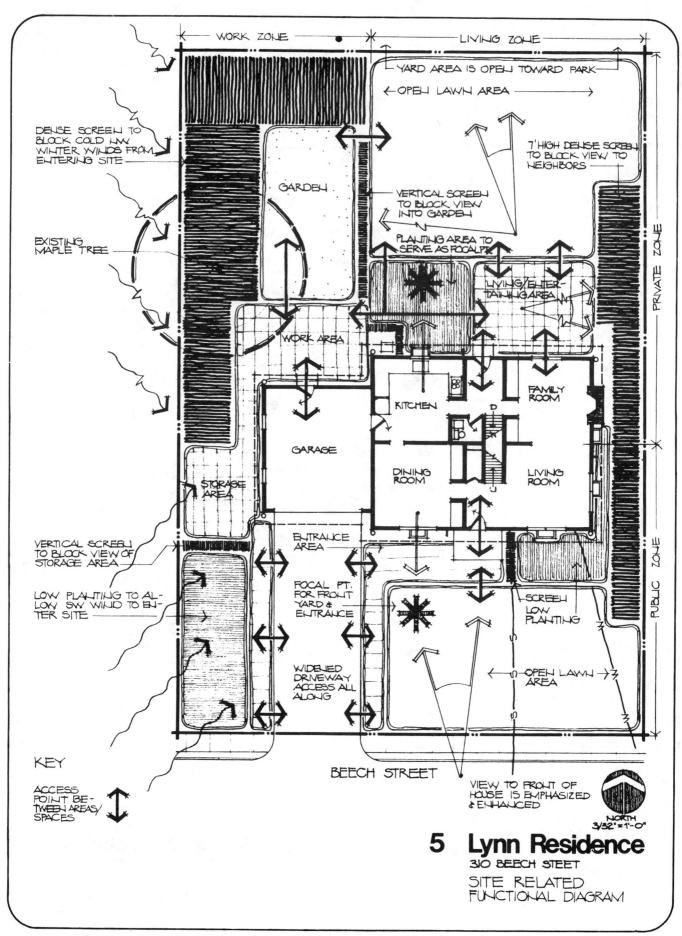

WORK ZONE — LIVING ZONE

YARD AREA IS OPEN TOWARD PARK
← OPEN LAWN AREA →

DENSE SCREEN TO BLOCK COLD NW WINTER WINDS FROM ENTERING SITE

7' HIGH DENSE SCREEN TO BLOCK VIEW TO NEIGHBORS

GARDEN

VERTICAL SCREEN TO BLOCK VIEW INTO GARDEN

EXISTING MAPLE TREE

PLANTING AREA TO SERVE AS FOCAL PT

LIVING/ENTER-TAINING AREA

WORK AREA

PRIVATE ZONE

FAMILY ROOM

KITCHEN

GARAGE

DINING ROOM

LIVING ROOM

STORAGE AREA

VERTICAL SCREEN TO BLOCK VIEW OF STORAGE AREA

ENTRANCE AREA

LOW PLANTING TO ALLOW SW WIND TO ENTER SITE

FOCAL PT. FOR FRONT YARD & ENTRANCE

SCREEN LOW PLANTING

PUBLIC ZONE

WIDENED DRIVEWAY ACCESS ALL ALONG

OPEN LAWN AREA

KEY

ACCESS POINT BETWEEN AREAS/ SPACES

BEECH STREET

VIEW TO FRONT OF HOUSE IS EMPHASIZED & ENHANCED

NORTH
3/32" = 1'-0"

5 Lynn Residence
310 BEECH STEET

SITE RELATED
FUNCTIONAL DIAGRAM

FIGURE 7.5

Because the designer is now taking the site itself into account, the basic relationships established in the ideal functional diagram (nonsite related) are apt to change a little to respond correctly to the site's actual conditions. Such variations should not be feared or prevented if they appropriately correspond to the site. The designer should develop and study the site-related functional diagram as an overlay placed directly on top of a copy of the site analysis. This is desirable to force the designer to keep the site's potentials and limitations in mind as the proposal is studied. And because the site-related functional diagram is now concerned with approximate sizes of the functions/spaces, the overlay technique helps the designer see the size and location of the proposed functions and elements in direct relation to the site conditions. As with the previous step of the process, alternative studies should be made to help ensure the best solution.

Concept Plan. The concept plan is a direct outgrowth and elaboration of the site-related functional diagram. The essential difference between the two is that the concept plan is more detailed in both content and graphic representation. The concept plan takes the generalized areas of the site-related functional diagram and subdivides them into more specific uses and areas. The generalized "entrance area" shown in Figure 7.5, for example, now becomes segregated into bubbles for walk, exterior foyer, and planting of various sizes and types, as illustrated in Figure 7.6. Or the "central meeting space" now becomes detailed into subspaces such as open paved area, sitting, planting areas, and kiosk location. The concept plan should also note major grade changes between levels or high points and low points with spot grades. Again, freehand bubbles and other abstract symbols should be used for the graphic representation of the solution. However, no specific shapes or forms of areas are studied. The concept plan should be developed as an overlay on the site-related functional diagram so that previously developed ideas, locations, and sizes are easily carried forward. It should be noted that some designers combine this step with the previously described site-related functional diagram. The result is often the same though the title of the drawing varies among designers.

To elaborate, a concept plan for a residential site design would show, for example:

1. Property line.
2. House/garage with a bubble outline of the rooms and an indication of door and window locations.
3. Bubble outline of major functions/spaces including the subareas for each
   a. entrance area including subspaces for
      • walk
      • court or exterior foyer
      • sitting area
      • steps
      • potted plants, sculpture, water feature, etc.
   b. terrace/entertaining area including subspaces for
      • lounging/sitting
      • picnic table
      • barbeque
      • deck
      • potted plants, sculpture, water feature, etc.
   c. lawn area including subspaces for specific types of recreation (unless the recreation activity can occur anywhere)
   d. service/work area including subspaces for specific types of work (carpentry, potting plants, etc.) and storage
   e. garden
   f. planting areas subdivided into outline of masses for plants of different type and height (example: 3-to-4 ft-high (91.5cm–122cm) high deciduous shrubs, 7-to-8-ft-high evergreen shrubs). Do not show individual plants. The general location of shade trees and ornamental trees should also be identified.
   g. access walks (example: walk from front yard to backyard or walk to garden).
4. Entrance/exit points into and from each of the above spaces.
5. Walls, fences, barriers, vegetative hedges, plant screens, mounds, etc.
6. Spot grades for major elevational changes.
7. Significant views that are to be either taken advantage of or screened.

Again, all these spaces and elements should be drawn to scale with bubbles and other abstract symbols. Specific shapes or forms should not be studied (this occurs in the next step). The challenge of this step is to be as detailed as possible in thinking about the functional relationships and sizes without becoming overburdened or strangled with the aesthetic considerations of design forms. The more thought that goes into a concept plan, the easier subsequent steps become. Notes on the concept plan should not only identify each space or element but also the desired height and material of each.

Form Composition Study. Until this point in the design phase, the designer has been dealing with rational, practical considerations of function and loca-

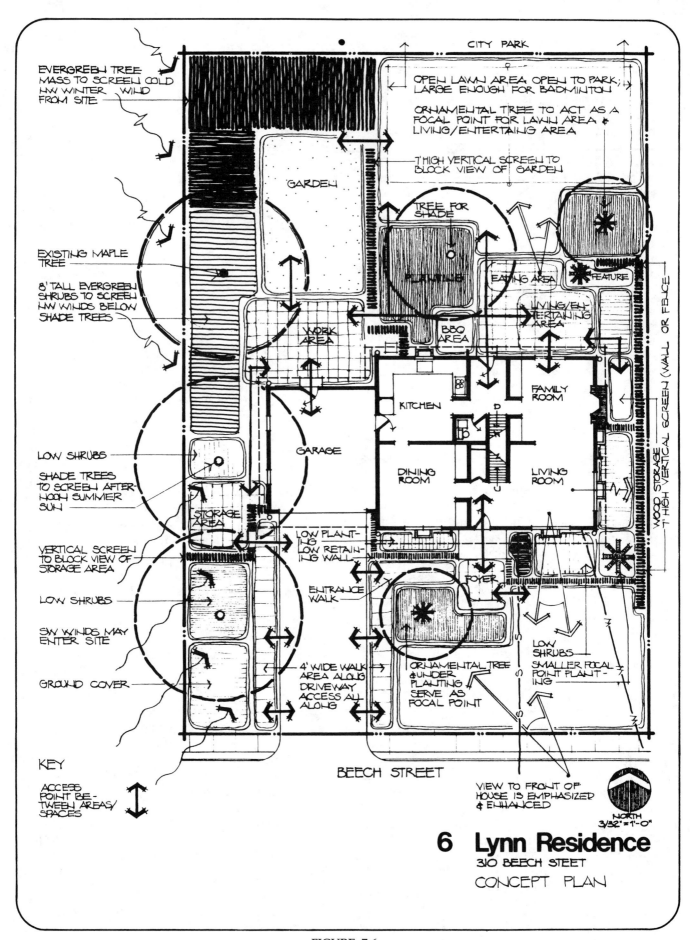

EVERGREEN TREE MASS TO SCREEN COLD NW WINTER WIND FROM SITE

CITY PARK

OPEN LAWN AREA OPEN TO PARK; LARGE ENOUGH FOR BADMINTON

ORNAMENTAL TREE TO ACT AS A FOCAL POINT FOR LAWN AREA & LIVING/ENTERTAINING AREA

7' HIGH VERTICAL SCREEN TO BLOCK VIEW OF GARDEN

GARDEN

TREE FOR SHADE

EXISTING MAPLE TREE

8' TALL EVERGREEN SHRUBS TO SCREEN NW WINDS BELOW SHADE TREES

LAWN

EATING AREA

FEATURE

LIVING/ENTERTAINING AREA

WORK AREA

BBQ AREA

FAMILY ROOM

KITCHEN

LOW SHRUBS

SHADE TREES TO SCREEN AFTERNOON SUMMER SUN

GARAGE

DINING ROOM

LIVING ROOM

VERTICAL SCREEN TO BLOCK VIEW OF STORAGE AREA

STORAGE AREA

WOOD STORAGE
7' HIGH VERTICAL SCREEN (WALL OR FENCE)

LOW PLANTING
LOW RETAINING WALL

LOW SHRUBS

ENTRANCE WALK

FOYER

SW WINDS MAY ENTER SITE

GROUND COVER

4' WIDE WALK AREA ALONG DRIVEWAY ACCESS ALL ALONG

ORNAMENTAL TREE & UNDER PLANTING SERVE AS FOCAL POINT

LOW SHRUBS SMALLER FOCAL POINT PLANTING

KEY

BEECH STREET

ACCESS POINT BETWEEN AREAS/ SPACES

VIEW TO FRONT OF HOUSE IS EMPHASIZED & ENHANCED

NORTH
3/32" = 1'-0"

6 Lynn Residence
310 BEECH STEET
CONCEPT PLAN

FIGURE 7.6

tion. In other words, the designer has been solving the factual problems. Now the attention is turned to the appearance and feel of the design, a more subjective area. Taking a single concept plan, the designer can create a series of solutions all with the same basic functional arrangement, but each with a different theme, character, and set of forms. For a small scale site such as that related to a residence, office building, or urban plaza, the design solution might have a theme of forms that are rectilinear, curvilinear, circular, angular, arc and tangent, or a combination of these. The shapes and forms of a design can be developed in any desired style from the same concept plan. Consequently, one should choose a design theme (i.e., style of forms) that will work and appear best for the situation. The selection of a design theme may be based on the character and size of the site, the location of the site, or the preference of either the client or the designer. The theme establishes order or structure for all the spaces and design elements to fit into. The theme is the framework of the design.

With a basic theme of forms in mind, the designer converts the bubbles and abstract symbols of the concept plan into specific and exact forms. This is done as an overlay on top of the concept plan so that its basic arrangement is retained. While trying to adhere to the functional and spatial arrangement of the concept plan, the designer is also attempting to create a composition of forms that are attractive to the eye. The form-to-form composition should be based on basic principles of design and form composition.

One of the major considerations of this step of the design process is the visual relationship between a building and the surrounding site. In a good design the building and site are unified and appear to be strongly integrated parts of the same theme. The building and site should blend together. To achieve this goal, an initial step in studying the form composition of the design is to extend imaginary lines, sometimes referred to as "lines of force," relating to the edges of the building's walls, doors, and windows outward into the site. Remember that these lines were previously discussed in Chapter 3 for aligning buildings with each other in a cluster (Figures 3.38 and 3.39). These extended lines can serve as guidelines for aligning selected edges and forms in the site design with those of the building itself. For example, the form of an entrance area will appear to be visually related to the adjoining building if certain edges of the entrance are aligned with an edge of a door, window, or wall. This concept is most critical immediately around the building with those planes

and lines that extend to and touch the ground. The idea becomes progressively less important the farther one moves from the building. Furthermore, the extended imaginary "lines of force" should be used only as generators of ideas, not restrictions for creativity. They should be applied only when useful.

As seen in Figure 7.7, the form composition study deals almost entirely with the outline around hard structural elements of the design (pavement areas, walks, pools, planters, etc.) and the lawn areas. It does not deal with plant material in any more detail than the preceding concept plan, nor does it deal with the pattern of materials within the outlines. The form composition study is drawn as a simple, freehand line drawing with all elements and areas drawn to scale. In addition, it often helps to include the lines of force and their construction lines on the form composition study as long as they do not become too confusing. No graphic textures or elaborate symbols are used. As with the previous steps of the design process, a number of alternative studies should be undertaken before selecting the best one.

One last word about the form composition phase is that, as described, it is most applicable to small sites (5 acres/2 hectares or fewer) where the shape of areas and spaces is critical. The form composition phase is less essential for a large site such as a park project or condominium development at the scale of the entire site, though it still might be undertaken as specific areas of the site are dealt with in more detail. Some designers undertake the form composition as an integral part of the development of the preliminary master plan.

Preliminary Master Plan. In the preliminary master plan all elements of the design are put together and studied in association with one another in a realistic, semicomplete graphic manner. All design elements are considered, some for the first time, as interrelated components of a total environment. Within the framework established previously by the concept plan and the form composition study, the preliminary master plan moves ahead to take into account and study the following:

1. The general material of all elements and forms (wood, brick, stone, etc.).
2. Plant materials as masses drawn to approximate mature size. The size, form, color, and texture of the plants are now considered and studied. In this step, plants are described in general terms such as ornamental tree, low evergreen shrub, tall deciduous shrub, and so forth. No plant species are identified.

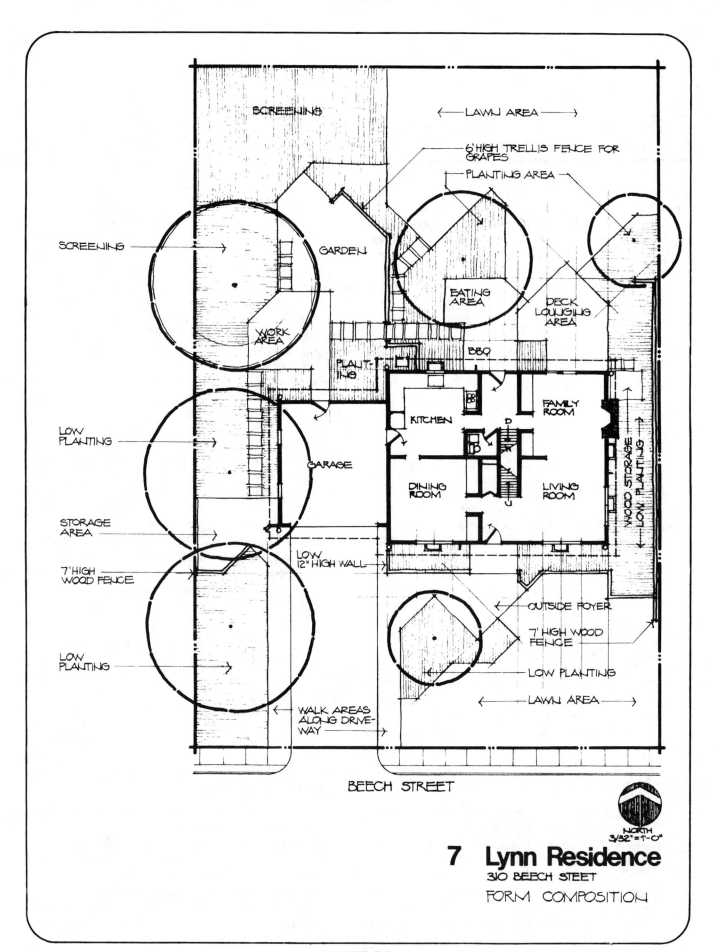

SCREENING

LAWN AREA

6' HIGH TRELLIS FENCE FOR GRAPES

PLANTING AREA

SCREENING

GARDEN

EATING AREA

DECK LOUNGING AREA

WORK AREA

PLANT- ING

BBQ

LOW PLANTING

GARAGE

KITCHEN

FAMILY ROOM

WOOD STORAGE
LOW PLANTING

STORAGE AREA

DINING ROOM

LIVING ROOM

7' HIGH WOOD FENCE

LOW 12" HIGH WALL

LOW PLANTING

OUTSIDE FOYER

7' HIGH WOOD FENCE

LOW PLANTING

WALK AREAS ALONG DRIVE-WAY

LAWN AREA

BEECH STREET

NORTH
3/32" = 1'-0"

7 Lynn Residence
310 BEECH STEET
FORM COMPOSITION

FIGURE 7.7

3. The three-dimensional qualities and effects of the design including the location and height of such elements as tree canopies, awnings, overhead trellises, fences, walls, and earth mounds. In other words, the relative height of all elements of the design to one another should be considered.

4. Sketch grading shown by proposed contours drawn at 2- or 5-ft (1 or 2m) contour intervals depending on scale and complexity of the design layout. Major elevation changes between terraced levels as well as tops of walls and fences might also be noted.

The preliminary master plan evolves best as an overlay on top of the form composition study. A number of studies and reiterations on different layers of tracing paper will most likely be undertaken before concluding with a solution with which the designer feels happy. It is also quite possible that initial ideas developed during the form composition study or concept plan (or earlier) will change during the preliminary master plan because new thoughts have come to mind or the designer feels differently about a particular element or form when it is seen in the context of other elements. Having completed the preliminary master plan, the designer should check it against the program to make sure all intentions were implemented. Next the designer should review the plan with the client for feedback. This may be the first time the client has seen the design, so a few days might be allowed for review. Hopefully, the client will accept the solution and have a few suggestions or requested revisions. The designer then makes the necessary revisions and proceeds to the master plan or even to schematics or design development. This depends on how many changes result from the client's review and how elaborate the design proposal is. In some cases the designer's services to the client may end with the presentation of the preliminary master plan and proceed no further.

The preliminary master plan should be drawn freehand and show all the elements of the design in a semirealistic, illustrative fashion, as in Figure 7.8. Variations in line weight, textures, and values should be used to make the drawing read clearly. The preliminary master plan should show the following:

1. Property line.
2. Existing topography and significant spot grades for design proposal.
3. Adjoining roads/streets (at least to centerline) and other significant elements such as buildings adjacent to the site.

4. Outline or "footprint" of all buildings and structures.
5. All major design elements of the site plan illustrated with their proper graphic texture
   a. driveway, walks, terrace, deck, lawn, etc.
   b. roads and parking.
   c. bridges, shelters, docks, etc.
   d. masses of plant materials (both existing that are to be retained and proposed).
   e. walls, fences, etc.
   f. steps, ramps, curbs.
   g. sketched proposed contours.

In addition to graphically showing the above, the preliminary master plan should also identify the following with notes:

1. Major use areas (examples: lawn, community open space, service area, natural wooded area, amphitheater).
2. Materials of the design elements and forms.
3. Plant materials by general characteristics (size and type; e.g., deciduous, evergreen, broadleaved evergreen).
4. Major level changes by the use of spot grades.
5. Description or justification for special situations.

Master Plan. The master plan, the next step in the design process, is a refinement of the preliminary master plan. After gaining the reactions of the client from the preliminary master plan, the designer may need to revise and restudy certain portions of the proposal. With these changes included, the designer once again draws the site plan in a presentable fashion. One of the primary differences between a preliminary master plan and a master plan, in addition to the necessary design revisions, is the graphic style of each. While the preliminary master plan is drawn in a loose, freehand, yet legible manner, the master plan is typically drawn with more control and refinement, as in Figure 7.9. Rather than drawn entirely freehand, the master plan may have certain parts such as the property line, building outline, and edges of hard structural elements (walls, terrace, walks, decks, etc.) drafted with a triangle and T-square. However, other elements such as plant materials are still drawn freehand. To give the plan a controlled appearance, more time is usually spent drawing the master plan compared with the preliminary master plan.

Because of this additional time required and because the master plan is somewhat redundant, many designers elect to prepare a master plan in a graphic style similar to a preliminary master plan to save

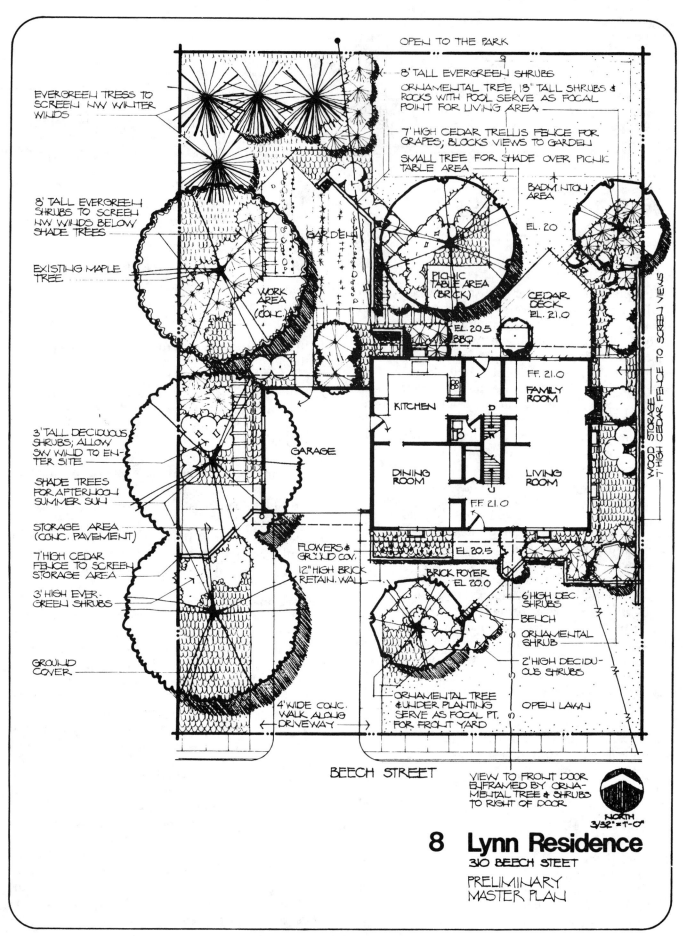

OPEN TO THE PARK

8' TALL EVERGREEN SHRUBS
ORNAMENTAL TREE, 18" TALL SHRUBS & ROCKS WITH POOL SERVE AS FOCAL POINT FOR LIVING AREA

EVERGREEN TREES TO SCREEN NW WINTER WINDS

7' HIGH CEDAR TRELLIS FENCE FOR GRAPES; BLOCKS VIEWS TO GARDEN

SMALL TREE FOR SHADE OVER PICNIC TABLE AREA

BADMINTON AREA

8' TALL EVERGREEN SHRUBS TO SCREEN NW WINDS BELOW SHADE TREES

EL. 20

EXISTING MAPLE TREE

GARDEN

WORK AREA (CONC.)

PICNIC TABLE AREA (BRICK)

CEDAR DECK EL. 21.0

EL. 20.5
BBQ

FF. 21.0

KITCHEN

FAMILY ROOM

3' TALL DECIDUOUS SHRUBS; ALLOW SW WIND TO ENTER SITE

GARAGE

DINING ROOM

LIVING ROOM

SHADE TREES FOR AFTERNOON SUMMER SUN

F.F. 21.0

STORAGE AREA (CONC. PAVEMENT)

7' HIGH CEDAR FENCE TO SCREEN STORAGE AREA

FLOWERS & GROUND COV.

EL. 20.5

12" HIGH BRICK RETAIN. WALL

BRICK FOYER EL 20.0

6' HIGH DEC. SHRUBS

3' HIGH EVERGREEN SHRUBS

BENCH

ORNAMENTAL SHRUB

2' HIGH DECIDUOUS SHRUBS

GROUND COVER

OPEN LAWN

4' WIDE CONC. WALK ALONG DRIVEWAY

ORNAMENTAL TREE & UNDER PLANTING SERVE AS FOCAL PT. FOR FRONT YARD

WOOD STORAGE
7' HIGH CEDAR FENCE TO SCREEN VIEWS

BEECH STREET

VIEW TO FRONT DOOR ENFRAMED BY ORNAMENTAL TREE & SHRUBS TO RIGHT OF DOOR

NORTH
3/32" = 1'-0"

8   Lynn Residence
310 BEECH STEET

PRELIMINARY MASTER PLAN

FIGURE 7.8

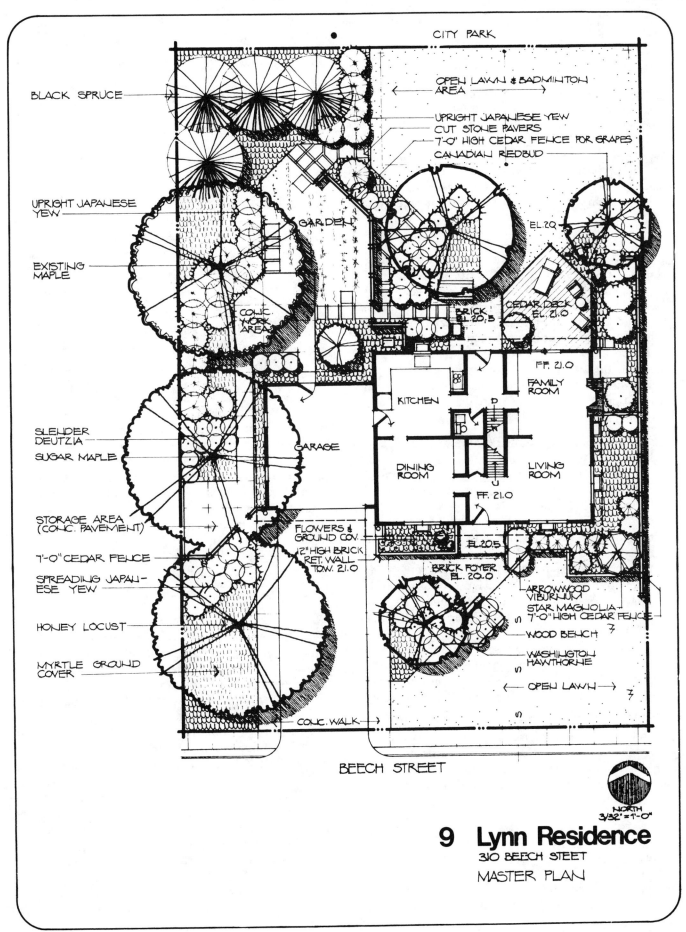

CITY PARK

OPEN LAWN & BADMINTON AREA

BLACK SPRUCE

UPRIGHT JAPANESE YEW
CUT STONE PAVERS
7'-0" HIGH CEDAR FENCE FOR GRAPES
CANADIAN REDBUD

UPRIGHT JAPANESE YEW

EXISTING MAPLE

GARDEN

EL. 20

CONC. WORK AREA

BRICK EL. 20.5

CEDAR DECK EL. 21.0

FF. 21.0

FAMILY ROOM

KITCHEN

SLENDER DEUTZIA

SUGAR MAPLE

GARAGE

DINING ROOM

LIVING ROOM

STORAGE AREA (CONC. PAVEMENT)

FF. 21.0

7'-0" CEDAR FENCE

FLOWERS & GROUND COV.

SPREADING JAPAN- ESE YEW

12" HIGH BRICK RET. WALL TOW. 21.0

EL. 20.5

BRICK FOYER EL. 20.0

HONEY LOCUST

ARROWWOOD VIBURNUM

STAR MAGNOLIA
7'-0" HIGH CEDAR FENCE

MYRTLE GROUND COVER

WOOD BENCH

WASHINGTON HAWTHORNE

OPEN LAWN

CONC. WALK

BEECH STREET

NORTH
3/32" = 1'-0"

9 Lynn Residence
310 BEECH STEET
MASTER PLAN

FIGURE 7.9

both time and money. Some designers stop with the preliminary master plan step as noted previously because the cost to the client does not justify the time to draw a highly ornate "pretty picture." Consequently, budget restraints have a direct impact on what is or is not done at the master plan step. A master plan typically shows the same information as the preliminary master plan with similar labeling as well.

Schematic Design. For some projects the design process continues on to schematic design. For small-scale sites such as residence or a vest-pocket park, master plan and schematic plans are synonymous. However, design projects entailing many acres with multiple land uses utilize schematic design to study the proposal in greater detail. Like the master plan, schematic design concerns itself with the entire site.

Graphically, the schematic plan shows the same information as the master plan with the following additional detail:

1. Building floor plan showing all first-floor rooms, doors, and windows.
2. As appropriate, the plan may show such items as roof overhang (by means of a light, dashed line), down spouts, water spigots, electrical outlets, window wells, air conditioner, etc.
3. Individual plant materials within masses. Plant materials are identified and labeled according to size, form, color, and texture. If the schematic design is the final step in a design proposal (no design development or contract documents are to be undertaken), then species of individual plants may be identified.
4. Grading shown by proposed contours drawn at 2- or 1-ft (1 or .5m) contour intervals. In addition, spot grades should be used to represent major high points and low points as well as the tops of walls and fences.

The schematic plan is drawn in a neat, controlled style. Like the master plan, the schematic plan may combine both drafted and freehand lines for the various elements of the plan, though typically the schematic plan tends to be almost entirely drafted.

Design Development. The final step of the design process is design development. In this step of the process, the designer is most concerned about the detail appearance and integration of materials. For example, design development might study the ac-

tual pavement pattern, the appearance of a wall or fence, the design of an entrance sign, or the detailing of an overhead trellis. This is often accomplished by studying specific areas of a project (site entrance, arrival court, terrace, pool and deck area, etc.) in plans, sections, and elevations at a detailed scale between 1 in = 20 ft and 1/4 in = 1 ft. Design development drawings give both the designer and the client a clear idea of what the project will actually look like in critical areas. While quite specific, design development is primarily concerned with the visual quality of the design, not the technical or construction detailing.

Construction Drawings

Having completed the design phase of the design process, the designer next prepares construction drawings. These typically include such drawings as the layout plan, grading plan, planting plan, and construction details as well as the writing of specifications. All these drawings are prepared as a means of communicating how to construct all elements of the project from overall building location to the size and location of individual bolts in a fence. The contractor(s) use these documents as instructions to build from. At this point in the process, the designer is most concerned with the technical and mechanical issues, though aesthetic concerns cannot be dismissed.

Implementation

Once all the construction drawings have been completed, they are made available for bid. Although procedures differ from one situation to another, the contract is usually awarded to the lowest bidder. After the construction contract has been signed, the contractor then proceeds to build and install the design. The amount of time required may vary from a matter of days to many months. The designer's role at this point is usually one of observation. Although usually not held by contract to supervise officially, the landscape architect may want to watch over the construction phase to make suggestions as necessary. In addition, questions and problems often arise during construction that the designer must answer and solve. It is not unusual in the implementation of a design that unforeseen circumstances require changes in some aspect of the design. The designer must keep abreast of the construction so that these changes can be made as quickly as possible.

Post-Construction Evaluation and Maintenance

The design process does not end once the project has been built. Rather, the designer should observe and analyze the project from time to time to see how well it works and grows with time. Much can be learned after a project is in use. The designer might ask: "Does the design appear and function the way I intended?" "What is good about the project?" "What are the weak points?" "What would I do differently, if anything, the next time?" It is vital the designer learn from the built project so that the positive aspects can be carried forward into similar projects in the future while the negative qualities are corrected the next time around. When the design process is looked at in this light, it is seen as a continuing procedure. What has been done and learned in the past should always be taken into account on current and future design projects.

One last item that is also an ongoing aspect of the design process is maintenance. To be successful, a design must not only work well on paper and be constructed with the utmost care and quality, but it must also be maintained properly throughout its existence. Too often a design that meets the first two criteria suffers owing to poor maintenance. It has been said that the maintenance person is the ultimate designer. There is much truth to this statement because the alignment of a bed line, the size and shape of plant material, the replacement of a defective element, general upkeep, and so forth all tend to be the responsibility of the maintenance person. If the design was originally ill-conceived in terms of maintenance, or if the maintenance person is not sensitive to the designer's intentions, then the project over time will not be of the highest quality. It is important for the designer to consider maintenance from the very beginning of a project and for communication with the maintenance person to occur on a continuing basis.

Summary

As can be interpreted from the preceding sections, the design process is a complex undertaking intended to encourage the best design solution possible for any given situation. The process is a framework of steps and phases that structure, but do not inhibit, the designer's creative thinking in problem solving. The designer should use the design process as a tool that can be modified as needed to aid in solving the particular problem at hand. The design process requires the designer to be as knowledgeable and experienced as possible. Moreover, the design process should be thought of as an ongoing procedure that extends from one project and experience to the next.

Conclusion

As with all art forms and design disciplines, there is a distinct set of media characteristic of the profession of landscape architecture. Landform, plant materials, buildings, pavement, site structures, and water are, in numerous combinations, the primary physical components comprising most works of landscape architecture. They are the media that landscape architects utilize to formulate space and establish experiences that delight the eye as well as the emotions. In a purely artistic sense, the physical design elements of landscape architecture are analogous to the words of a poem or notes of a piece of music. Collectively, they constitute a composition affecting the human physical and emotional senses.

Individually the physical design elements of landscape architecture each have their own unique qualities and roles to fulfill in the outdoor environment. Landform is the base or floor plane of the landscape. It is the one element that supports and unites all the other components of the environment. Landform's configuration affects such diverse factors as the structure of the outdoor environment, land use location, views, drainage, and microclimate in addition to spatial definition and character. Furthermore, landform is a plastic medium in its own right that can be molded to create solids and voids on the ground plane in many possible ways.

Plant materials provide the aspect of life in the landscape. They are living, breathing elements that grow and change with time. Their relatively soft, sometimes irregular shape along with their living green appearance provide a habitable feeling in the outdoor environment. In addition, plant materials fulfill a number of more practical functions such as defining space in all three planes of enclosure, modifying microclimate, cleansing the air, stabilizing soil, and acting as important visual elements based on their size, form, color, and texture.

Buildings, the locus of numerous human activities, are solid volumes in the outdoor environment. Compared with either landform or plant materials, buildings are a relatively hard, firm medium in the landscape. As compositional elements, buildings may be treated as either single objects of individual significance in the environment or located in clusters that define spaces and spatial sequences of numerous possible temperaments. Building masses usually establish fixed, nonpliable spatial limits in the organization of outdoor functions and activities.

Pavement is one of the materials that can be employed on the ground plane. Pavement, in contrast to landform, plant materials, and buildings, is a flat, planar element that can be used as a durable, fixed support of human and vehicular functions of intense or repeated use. Furthermore, pavement may function as both a directional and nondirectional element, accentuate different uses on the ground plane, influence perceived scale, provide unity, and impress spatial character.

Site structures are constructed three-dimensional elements of the outdoor environment directly relating to the ability of people to use the outdoor environment conveniently. Steps, ramps, walls, fences, and seating contribute to the comfort and safety of outdoor spaces as well as to the delineation of humanly scaled outdoor rooms. As a group, site structures are hard elements of an architectural quality used in the landscape to reinforce the spatial and functional organization provided by landform, buildings, and plant material.

Finally, water is a specialty element of the landscape with a strongly compelling quality. Water, similar to plant materials, is a life-giving element that helps to provide a feeling of vitality and animation. As a fluid element, water is a highly varied and flexible medium. It may be utilized as a static element in the outdoor environment to calm the senses of sight and sound or it may be employed as a dynamic element of motion, exciting the eye in addition to providing a sound stimulus. However it is used, water is a unique feature easily attracting people to it.

Besides the individual qualities of the major landscape architectural design media, they possess other distinguishing characteristics when considered collectively. Perhaps one of the most notable aspects of landscape architectural design elements is that they are components of the exterior environment where they are directly subjected to the forces of nature. Unlike the media of certain other design disciplines that must be protected or delicately treated, landform, plant material, buildings, pavement, site structures, and water are all exposed to such factors as sun, wind, precipitation, temperature variations, and erosion. In some circumstances, these forces are mild and insignificant in their influence on the physical design elements of the landscape. In other situations, the natural forces of the exterior environment are so harsh as to be destructive.

The consequence of natural forces is that all the design media of the landscape weather and change over time, if only subtly. A pavement may become worn, a slope may erode slightly, plant materials may grow and die, the coloration of a wall may either fade or darken with age, or the water in a pond may vary in level and quality. The landscape architect must accept these changes and allow them to occur and recognize that nature provides the final touch to a design located in the exterior environment. The challenge for the landscape architect is to be able to properly anticipate and understand the influence of the natural forces so that they enrich the quality of a landscape architectural design with time, not the opposite.

Another distinctive quality of landscape architectural design elements is that they have both utilitarian and aesthetic uses. Landscape architectural design media are typically not used solely as visual elements to attract the eye or stimulate the mind, as the media of painting and sculpture often do. Yes, landform, plant materials, buildings, pavement, site structures, and water often provide beautiful, emotionally moving experiences, but this is most often done while serving the other functions that have been outlined in the previous chapters of this book. The design elements of landscape architecture can be considered as constituting an applied art. The goal of the landscape architect should be to utilize the design media of the profession in a manner that is practical while at the same time visually inspiring. This is not easily accomplished, with errors sometimes made in creating landscape architectural designs that are visually beautiful and delightful while being impractical or very utilitarian yet dull in appearance. A truly successful landscape architectural design imaginatively combines the design media so that the practical aspects coincide and complement the visual aspects.

Perhaps the most noteworthy consideration about landscape architectural design elements is that they should be applied collectively in a design. Much of the focus of this book has been on each of the elements as an individual medium in the outdoor environment. This was done to permit a thorough understanding of the significance and role played by each element in the context of the total environment. But landscape architectural design elements are rarely used by themselves in a design. What is important is not how each element functions or looks by itself but how it is woven into the fabric of the whole design and surrounding environment. In creating a landscape architectural design, the design elements are not the end product. Rather, the design media are the means to an end, or facilitators. Ultimately the design elements are composed to create carefully choreographed outdoor rooms and spatial experiences that deal with all the human senses. Works of landscape architecture should sensitively unite people with the outdoor environment in a symbiotic association making life a beautiful experience worth living.

Index